Turner

Turner

The Extraordinary Life and
Momentous Times of J. M. W. Turner

FRANNY MOYLE

PENGUIN PRESS

NEW YORK

2016

PENGUIN PRESS

An imprint of Penguin Random House LLC
375 Hudson Street
New York, New York 10014
penguin.com

First published in Great Britain by Viking, an imprint of Penguin Random House UK.

ISBN: 9780735220928 (hardcover)
ISBN: 9780735220935 (ebook)

Printed in the United States of America
1   3   5   7   9   10   8   6   4   2

Set in Bembo Book MT Std

*To my darling family, Rosa,
Tommy, Vincent and Richard*

Contents

List of illustrations

Illustration acknowledgements

National Portrait Gallery, London, 1, 17, 45

Tate © London, 2015, 2, 10–11, 15, 18, 22, 25–6, 28, 29, 40–41, 46, 48, 49

The Royal Academy of Arts, London, 3

Indianapolis Museum of Art, 4, 6–8, 14, 24, 31, 35, 39, 47

Royal College of Physicians, London, 5

Bridgeman Art Library, 9, 12–13, 16, 19–21, 27, 30, 33, 36–7, 38, 42, 44, 51

Turner's House Trust, 23

National Maritime Museum Greenwich, London. Greenwich Hospital Collection, 32

The Collection of Nick Tapley, 34

The National Gallery, London, 43

The Collection of Mrs Diana Coker, 50

Turner

1.   Admiral Booth

A wet, wintry day in mid-December 1851. The man from Mrs Foord's frame-makers stood in the rain and knocked on the door of 47 Queen Anne Street in Marylebone, the professional address of the most famous living British artist, J. M. W. Turner RA. Foord's man had work to do there.

'Turner's Den', as it had become known, looked more like the premises of a painter long dead than the workplace of a living legend. The quiet classical frontage, which once sat respectably alongside the street's other examples of Georgian restraint, had been let go. The windows were filthy, their cracked panes patched with paper. The paint on the front door had blistered and the iron palisades were rusty.[1]

A short hag of a woman answered the frame-maker's knock. Her large head was draped with a piece of flannel, striving to conceal a nasty skin affliction. This was Hannah Danby, Turner's long-time housekeeper. She led Foord's man into a square vestibule barely illuminated by the neglected arched windows to either side of the door, which had become caked with dust. The hall was an empty brown space, bereft of ornament.

As he followed Danby upstairs, the gothic adventure continued. The tradesman was led into the top-lit custom-made gallery where Turner's paintings were displayed. The rain was 'flooding in by the skylight', Foord's man would later remember. 'Turner would not pay for plaster – so they had to put paper as well as they could – several pictures damaged.'[2]

Foord's man saw nothing of Turner himself the day he worked in his rain-soaked gallery. This was not unusual. The old painter had become increasingly retiring in his dotage, and over the last twelve months or so had even begun absenting himself from his business engagements at the Royal Academy.

For Hannah Danby, however, it was less her master's absence from

his professional commitments that was of concern. It was his absence
from his *own home* that was causing her considerable anxiety in
December 1851. The seventy-six-year-old Turner had not set foot in
Queen Anne Street since June. This was not entirely out of character
for a man who for the last five years had, clearly, been keeping a
second home, and from whom she was used to receiving instructions
via the postboy. But as Christmas approached, Hannah Danby was
beginning to fret. She did not know exactly *where* her master's second
home was, and she sensed something was wrong. She began to search
for anything that might suggest its location. A letter discovered in a
coat pocket with a Chelsea address was what she needed.

And so on 16 December Hannah Danby sought out a friend, probably Maria Tanner,[3] the woman who assisted her in the care, such as
it was, of Queen Anne Street, and the two of them headed south to
Chelsea. They found themselves on the stinking Cremorne New
Road, a small lane along the Thames that ran from the old wooden
Battersea Bridge to the Cremorne Jetty, where penny fares brought
revellers by steamboat to the Pleasure Gardens of the same name.

Skirting a muddy foreshore, smelling of the open drains that spilled
into the river and peppered with dogs and chickens picking their way
through the flotsam and jetsam of the river, Cremorne New Road
presented a sharp contrast to the grandiose streets of the West End.
Nevertheless, here, facing the timber yards and chemical works of
Battersea, was a row of cottages that made up Davis Place. And at No.
6, between Alexander the boat builder and a couple of beer sellers, she
found a modest yellow brick house, dating from the 1750s.

Despite the seedy location, it was charming enough in its own
way — a three-storey, mid-terrace house, fronted by a low wooden
picket fence and gate that contained a cottage garden, it betrayed the
personal touches of domesticity that accompany a lengthy tenancy. A
wooden lattice porch over the front door housed potted plants and a
caged starling. The property's three front-facing windows all had
lovingly planted window-boxes, and creepers had been allowed to
grow up from one of them and crawl over the uppermost reaches
of the façade. But most significantly, in contrast to the neighbouring houses, No. 6 had been customized, at no little expense, to

accommodate a high-level balcony or viewing platform, which, cut into the roof and contained by wrought-iron rails, offered an artist a bird's-eye view of London's river stretching out below.

But Turner was not on his platform the day Danby called. And though she quickly ascertained from neighbours that a man fitting her master's description was at home, she also discovered from the hushed tones and shaken heads that they believed he was dying. On hearing this news, Hannah could not bring herself to go in. Instead, distraught, she determined to seek the assistance of Turner's cousin and solicitor, Henry Harpur.

Henry Harpur lived in Lambeth. He was seventeen years his cousin's junior. The Harpurs and the Turners were strongly entwined. They shared not just blood, but plenty of family business, not least the final revisions Turner made to his will. They had also travelled together on the Continent. On 17 December he visited Chelsea at Hannah Danby's request.

The interior of the little house in Chelsea was modestly furnished, though its few contents reflected the interests of its occupant. The *Art Journal* and *Illustrated London News* were on the parlour table; the walls were hung with engravings. Here, on the uppermost storey, Harpur found the old painter in a soporific haze, having been spoon-fed for the past few days a diet of milk and brandy. He had lost all ability to talk. The bird-like man, whose intense gaze and beaky nose had once complemented a robust, if short, square frame, was now a mere waif, ebbing away. He was being nursed by plump and homely Sophia Booth, the woman who shared his life at No. 6 Davis Place. She was a widow, more than twenty years the painter's junior.

Harpur grasped the seriousness of Turner's condition immediately and knew that he must begin to prepare the world for the departure of one of its most eminent men. The very next day, 18 December, he wrote to Turner's long-time family friend, the architect Philip Hardwick, warning him that Turner's demise was imminent. Hardwick, now turning sixty, white-haired and balding, was the spitting image of his own father, who had known Turner as a boy. Like the Harpurs, the Hardwicks had shared a long history with the Turners.

A day later another note from Harpur was in Hardwick's hand.

Turner was dead. He had passed away at 10 a.m. on 19 December. Hardwick had been deprived of the opportunity of saying goodbye to a friend who had known him man and boy. But on 19 December Harpur, no longer constrained by his eminent cousin's instructions, furnished Hardwick with the details of the whereabouts of the body. Hardwick alone was afforded this privilege and he went straight away to Davis Place to say his goodbye.

Harpur met Hardwick at the little house in Chelsea. It must have become immediately clear to both men that the circumstances of Turner's death could, if not properly managed, erupt into a national scandal that would eclipse the plaudits for his extraordinary work and compromise his ardent desire to be buried in honour in St Paul's Cathedral. After all, Turner had not only been discovered in an insalubrious location, in an undisclosed second home, he had also been discovered living in what much later would be described as a state of 'moral degradation'.[4] Taken alongside his recent reclusivity, and the state of affairs in Queen Anne Street, this new twist in Turner's story was an unwelcome one. Were it to become public knowledge, it would only add fuel to the persistent theories in circulation that the old painter had lost his mind during the course of the last decade.

These allegations of madness had been prompted by what his public considered the increasingly bizarre and indecipherable paintings Turner had produced across the 1840s, works that critics were not afraid to condemn as utter 'abortions'.[5] For the last decade he had turned out canvases that explored light, and the elements, in unique and highly experimental ways. Ships rocked, whales thrashed, and trains sped through raging storms and whirling mists that were unlike anything that had been presented to the public before. In what often felt like dreamscapes, the sunsets and sunrises he had once been so famed for painting with delicate luminosity had become substantive. His ghostlike characters were no longer bathed in light but swept up by it, in a parallel world of fog and fiery chaos.

Harpur understood only too well that if the true circumstances of Turner's death were to become widely known, it would be all too easy for the public to dismiss his final decade of toil and experiment. How convenient for Turner's critics to be able to confirm that the exquisite painter had indeed departed some ten years previously, leaving just this Chelsea relic to finish his career. A reputation already much dented was on the cusp of being roundly destroyed. Turner's fame was on the point of tipping into infamy.

As Hardwick left Davis Place he took with him a letter he saw that Turner had written to the stockbroker Charles Stokes. Apart from being a close friend, Stokes, a man now well into his sixties, had been both a dedicated collector of Turner's work for many years, and a business associate who oversaw some financial matters for him.

'Dear Stokes,' Turner had written. 'Enclosed is a wish for Mr F Marsh to advance on my account £100. I do not like the debts of Mr Woods – not paid. Have the goodness to do it.' These were almost certainly the last lines the artist wrote.

Now Hardwick scribbled his own postscript. 'Knowing the interest you have taken in all matters connected with Mr Turner,' he wrote, 'I thought you should be informed that we have lost him.'[6] The letter reached Stokes's rooms at 4 Verulam Buildings, Gray's Inn Road, the very next day, 20 December.

As Stokes grieved in Gray's Inn, the news of Turner's death spread further through his closest circle. On 21 December, a stormy Sunday, another black-bordered envelope found its way to Denmark Hill. John James Ruskin returned wet and wind-swept from church to find correspondence from Thomas Griffith, Turner's agent. Griffith explained that he had not wanted Ruskin to discover news of Turner's demise in print.

John James Ruskin was exactly the same age as Charles Stokes. Both had been born in 1785, and were ten years Turner's junior. Like Stokes, Ruskin considered himself a friend of the artist. Ruskin had built a considerable fortune as a wine merchant, and with it he had indulged his son John's passion for Turner's work. John Ruskin junior had adored Turner's painting since he was a boy. As an undergraduate at Oxford he had written a defining defence of the artist's work that had launched his own career as the most pre-eminent art critic of his generation. Thanks to his father's generosity, he now had twenty-five watercolours as well as two oil paintings by the artist – a collection that at this stage still hung in the family home.

From the elder Ruskin's point of view at least, the timing of Turner's passing was somewhat ironic. Just three days earlier he had been bidding at Southgate and Barrett's Christmas sale for a water-colour by Turner, of Carisbrooke Castle, on the Isle of Wight.[7] That evening, the Fleet Street sale-room had been packed to the brim with dealers and collectors. But Ruskin, a man who had not become rich by spending his money freely, had sent his picture framer to bid for him, under express instruction not to pay above fifty guineas for the work, only to see it go to a dealer prepared to pay £80.

On reading Griffith's note John James now sat down solemnly, in front of another of Turner's watercolours that hung at Denmark Hill. It was *The Red Rigi*,[8] painted nearly a decade earlier, a depiction of the mountain that dominates Lake Lucerne in Switzerland, bathed in a fiery red evening glow. And then he picked up his pen to write to his son, who had been in Venice since September:

> I have another loss to announce . . . Mr Turner – I can say no more
> till I go to Norwood and see Griffith who kindly sent me a note
> this forenoon during Church . . . a suitable day for the intelligence –
> the shortest and darkest – wet & tempestuous . . . I thank you for . . .
> a liking for the Red Rigi for the solemnity of that picture has fed &
> soothed me like a dead march all this evening. It is the only picture
> I care for tonight – I earnestly hope you will not let this hurt
> your health – There is no power gone exactly with his Life for his
> power had already departed – & you seemed to be prepared for this
> event.[9]

Once unburdened of its grave intelligence, John James's letter revealed another reaction to news of Turner's death – a commercial one. He had recently put aside £650 for the purpose of enlarging his collection of Turner's work further. Now John James was regretting letting *Carisbrooke Castle* go. But he realized that with the artist's death a huge amount of new work would most likely come on to the market with the sale of his estate. It would be an opportunity that the Ruskins must be prepared for.

'I do not think you need distract your arrangements to acquire any remains,' he suggested. 'There is little chance of Executors bringing anything to sale till . . . May or June – but please tell me all you want. There will be excitement & high prices as in Wilkie's case in the period of his Death which will afterwards give way.'

Over the next few days Ruskin continued to ponder the market ramifications of Turner's death, news of which had not yet broken in the press. Despite the imminence of Christmas, he was impatient to find out more about the disposal of Turner's estate.

On 22 December he wrote to his son again, this time explaining: 'Mr Griffith . . . has gone to a meeting of Executors . . . No one at present knows where he died but they promise to let us know particularly and there will be plenty of time for you to say what you wish.'

Harpur and Hardwick, meanwhile, had been busy making sure that despite the increasing curiosity as to the place of Turner's departure from mortal life, *no one* would find out. They had been swift in removing Turner's body from Chelsea and installing it where Turner *should* have died, in his professional premises at Queen Anne Street. A lavish hearse had arrived in Davis Place along with a large, expensive and heavy coffin, lined with lead and satin. Bemused locals watched as the undertakers, more used to the spacious homes of wealthy clients, could barely get the coffin through the door, and when it failed to go up the narrow stairs, the men were forced to bring the body down to it.

But it was only when the thirsty undertakers had a drink at the King's Arms on Cremorne Wharf that the most astounding revelation about J. M. W. Turner came to light. For the undertakers quickly found out that, as far as the locals were concerned, it was an old sea captain who had died in No. 6, a man they knew affectionately as Admiral Booth. The ruddy-faced, plain-speaking mariner had lived there for a good five years with his 'wife'. The Chelsea boys sometimes called him 'Puggy'.

When appraised of the facts, the locals were just as astonished to discover that Admiral Booth was in fact the celebrated painter J. M. W. Turner as Harpur and his men were to discover Turner had been living under the assumed name of Booth. That the great painter of seascapes who had captured the Battle of Trafalgar, and depicted the *Temeraire* being towed to her final berth, had adopted the fictional persona of an old seadog was a total surprise. As was the detail that he had a 'wife'.

At the executors' meeting in Queen Anne Street on the 22nd, Harpur and Hardwick remained silent. Even while the latter was standing over the coffin with two of the other officials 'looking at the corpse in the Picture Gallery',[10] when his colleagues began speculating that Turner's body had been brought to Queen Anne Street from an unspecified location, Hardwick kept his nerve and his secret.

By 23 December John James Ruskin was able to report much of the executors' meeting to his son. To his enormous pride, he had learned from Griffith that Turner had named Ruskin junior one of his eight executors. The others were the poet Samuel Rogers, the painter George Jones, Philip Hardwick, Harpur of course, the engraver Charles Turner, Griffith, and Turner's friend, another collector, Hugh Munro of Novar.[11]

Most significantly, however, Griffith had ascertained that very few of the vast number of works that remained in Turner's studio would be sold. 'I hear that some pictures go to N Gallery but that very few are to come to sale,' he disclosed.[12]

And it was this last piece of information that informed Ruskin's decision to then and there throw caution to the wind. On 23 December, a date that would usually encourage most people to defer business transactions until plum pudding had been consumed and carols sung, the normally financially cautious John James Ruskin sought out the dealer who had bought *Carisbrooke Castle* and paid one of the highest amounts he had ever set out for a comparable watercolour by Turner. For the work that had just a few days ago not been worth more than fifty guineas to him, John James now laid out one hundred and five. And what is more, he now urged his son to return home.

Ruskin did not stop there. After lunch on Christmas Day, he went to Norwood in Surrey to visit Turner's agent Thomas Griffith in person. When John James arrived he found the poor man in an agitated state, his skin sallow with worry. 'I was very sorry to find Griffith a perfect anatomy,' Ruskin later related, 'very yellow & a most excited state – I never saw him so much so – he said the events of the last few days excited him – sad look of poverty in man.'[13]

For a man who had been at the centre of the nineteenth-century art market for a quarter of a century, it was becoming clear to Griffith that a storm was about to break over it. This was because Turner had not just left a substantial amount of work to the National Gallery, but had also left the majority of his vast fortune to the services of art and his own legacy, his family barely considered.

Griffith assured John James that what just a few days ago had felt like a high price for *Carisbrooke Castle* would in a few weeks feel like a bargain, adding, 'every picture by this will is in an exaggerated state – double in value'.[14] The picture dealers, for the moment assuming in ignorant bliss that they would soon benefit from immense sales, would erupt with fury when news of Turner's will was known. But worse, some executors were already exploiting their privileged position. One dealer, John Clowes Grundy, had already been taken particular advantage of by Hugh Munro of Novar. According to Griffith, Munro had already snapped up a view of the Trossachs in oil by Turner from Grundy at a just 'moderate price', the dealer none the wiser.

It wouldn't just be the art market that would have its say. There were already rumours that some members of Turner's family were furious at their lack of recognition in his will, and were going to challenge it. Griffith could sense a fight, from which the only real beneficiary was going to be the legal profession.

And there was still the nagging issue of *where* Turner had died. This was a question that everyone was still continuing to ask, an answer to which was still tantalizingly unforthcoming. Griffith related that though Turner's body was undeniably now lying in the artist's leaky old studio, 'some would not believe the body was at 47 Q A Street'.[15]

On 26 December, seven days after Turner's death, the rumours that Harpur and Hardwick had tried to suppress began to break. Sir Joshua Reynolds, the first president of the Royal Academy of Arts, had lain in state in that institution before being buried at St Paul's Cathedral, as had other presidents thereafter. Some had felt that Turner, though never a president of the R A, nevertheless merited the same honour. But now John James wrote with horror to his son that

'Turner would have lain in state at the Academy but he died under an assumed name at Chelsea – Gods highest Gifts . . . did end in aberration – say not a word of this'.[16]

Fortunately the emerging figure of Admiral Booth, with his common-law wife, was still beyond the sight lines of journalists. By 27 December obituaries in the press were appearing, without mention of Booth or Chelsea. The *Illustrated London News* praised the considerable accomplishments of the younger version of the painter and presented a circumspect, brief mention of 'obscure, original, and, as some think, unapproachable productions of his later years'. The only small hint of something less salubrious was the mention that 'his personal habits were peculiar, and even penurious' and that 'he was never married, he was not known to have any relatives nearer than cousins; and his wants were limited to the strictest simplicity'.

And so, with disaster averted, Turner did at least get his grand funeral at St Paul's. At noon on 30 December, with London laden with a fog so heavy that its tendrils crept through the great doors of the cathedral and, curling upwards into the dome, hung like a pall over the proceedings below, Turner's coffin, draped in black velvet, was carried up the nave on the shoulders of fellow artists, accompanied by music composed by Croft and Purcell.

An impressive procession accompanied the body to the cathedral. Most of the characters who had played a role in the last act of Turner's story turned out. All in all eleven mourning coaches followed the hearse, their occupants noted by the press. Harpur was the chief mourner, and he was followed by the other executors, with the exception of the very ancient Rogers, whose age precluded his attending. The president of the Royal Academy, Sir Charles Eastlake, whom as a young artist Turner had befriended, led a procession drawn from the artistic community.

But there were some attendees at the funeral who, though innocently noted by the press, spoke further of that secret life that Harpur and Hardwick were keen to keep just that. There was a woman in the funeral party, mis-identified by the press, whose real relationship to Turner would have scandalized them if they had known it. Alongside Turner's housekeeper Hannah Danby, the press wrongly identified another Mrs Danby as the wife of Francis Danby the painter.

In fact the Mrs Danby that the press had erroneously named as a painter's wife was a woman called Mrs Sarah Danby, and she was Hannah's aunt. But far more significantly, *this* Mrs Danby had once shared Turner's life and borne him two illegitimate daughters, one of whom was still alive, though apparently absent from the funeral.[17]

In the great cathedral the service was read by the Dean and chanted by the full choir. Hannah Danby remained close to the coffin at all times. Visibly distraught, according to the press she 'sobbed her responses'.[18] At the conclusion the coffin was deposited in one of the vaults.

But if the 500-strong crowd who assembled outside St Paul's to pay their respects to Joseph Mallord William Turner thought this was the end of his story, they were quite wrong.

For one thing, there were some determined to cause the painter trouble, post mortem. Elhanan Bicknell, a man who had made a great deal of money in the whaling industry, had been a keen patron of Turner's before the two fell out in the 1840s. Someone in Turner's entourage had omitted to invite Bicknell to the pomp and ceremony and as a result he was making trouble. Bicknell 'is angry not being asked to funeral', John James wrote straight afterwards. 'He or others speak openly of his [Turner] having died in a Hovel at Chelsea where he had a Woman.'[19]

Two days after the funeral Sir Charles Eastlake wrote to the near-nonagenarian Samuel Rogers, whose infirmity had so far prevented him from fulfilling any of his duties as one of Turner's executors. Eastlake provided the old man with the details that were finally emerging. It was not just the actual circumstances of Turner's death that were proving a talking point. It was also his will.

'He had been residing at Chelsea for some years, with a widow named Booth or Brooke, and it seems that he was there known only by her name,' Eastlake explained without any of the moral judgement that some of his contemporaries felt the need to apply to these facts.

He had not more than 80,000*l*. in the Funds. The property in dilapidated houses and land is not considered important. On the other hand, there is a vast amount of proof impressions of engravings from his works, sketchbooks, drawings, and unfinished pictures. All the finished pictures are bequeathed to the nation, provided a room be built for them within ten years; if not, they are to continue to be exhibited in his gallery and house till the end of thirty years, and then to be sold for the benefit of the R. Academy. The unfinished pictures and all drawings and sketches are to be sold, together I presume with the engravings. You doubtless know that he has left his Executors (you being one) 20*l*. apiece, but almost all his Executors were his warm admirers, and he intended to honour them by the selection. To his (natural) daughter he has left nothing, to his old housekeeper in Queen Anne St. 150*l*. a year and some bonds; to the Chelsea lady nothing; 60*l*. a year for a professorship of landscape painting in the Academy, and an annual medal for landscape; 50*l*. a year for an annual Academic dinner! The great bequest is for a proposed foundation of almshouses for decayed painters on some land of his at Twickenham; some legal difficulty is expected with regard to this, the question being whether the Statute of Mortmain will interfere with his intentions or not. If it does, the bulk of his property will go to the nearest of kin. Many of the bequests are contingent and depend on the residue after the almshouses are built and endowed. He has left 1000*l*. for a monument to himself.

The bequest of his finished pictures excepted, his will has not given satisfaction; the wisdom even of the almshouses is questioned by many, the Academic dinner is folly; the old housekeeper's legacy alone meets with universal approval. More will come out by degrees, but I send you what I have heard so far.'[20]

The ease with which Eastlake mentioned the lack of legacy to Mrs Danby's daughter is evidence enough that those who had known Turner long enough were well aware of *her* existence, and by default the relationship with Mrs Danby. Eastlake's other observations about the will proved all too prescient, though he was wrong in some of his assertions, for Mrs Booth had in fact been provided for.

By early January 1852 the Chelsea story finally reached the press, though in a comically sanitized and partially fictional form that one suspects reflects Hardwick and Harpur's best efforts to explain the surprising circumstances of Turner's death to a judgemental Victorian public.

A syndicated piece appeared across a range of newspapers. 'Some ten days ago a man who had resided in a squalid lodging, in a squalid part of what at best is squalid Chelsea, was taken seriously ill,' the reports read. 'His name as far as the owner of the house knew anything of this, was Booth . . . Then it was discovered the man – who seemed to shun the world, who spent little and lived upon less, and one who lived not at all in a condition of one who enjoyed means to make friendship with him a thing to be coveted . . . was none other than the semi-deity Mr Ruskin's Turner!'[21]

A week later a follow-up article also appeared nationwide, this time offering a slightly different version of events.

> Mr Turner died in an obscure lodgings in Chelsea . . . he was living under an assumed name. The story is as follows. He loved retirement and entertained a peculiar dislike to having his lodging known . . . he saw board and lodging to his liking, asked the price, found them cheap . . . but the landlady wanted a reference. 'I will buy your house outright my good woman' was the reply somewhat angrily. Then an agreement was struck – met by an exhibition of bank notes and sovereigns . . . an offer which proved satisfactory. The artist's difficulties were not however over. The landlady wanted the lodger's name . . . 'Name, Name' he muttered in his usual gruff manner. 'What is your name?' 'My name is Mrs Brook.' 'Then I am Mr Brook'.[22]

In both versions the sexual commitment to the landlady in question is completely ignored, and as such something of the perceived shame around the arrangement was diminished in favour of a portrayal of eccentricity. It was perhaps the best that those who cared about managing Turner's reputation could do with a press determined to say something about the intrigue.

What moral rope these pantomime versions of events gave Turner in the long run was limited, however. Turner's story continued to unfold, and as it did the memory that the nation held of the painter continued to distort. Gradually a caricature of the artist grew.

Turner's sexual shame came up again in the later 1850s, as his executors worried their way through the piles of material in Queen Anne Street. It was John Ruskin who, though he decided to renounce his official position as executor, took on the onerous but fascinating job of cataloguing all Turner's 30,000-odd works on paper. And it was he who, in the winter of 1857, as part of this endeavour, discovered Turner's erotic drawings. It was a find that the prevailing moral climate in Victorian Britain could not accommodate. Packaging them up and labelling them as work worth keeping for posterity only 'as evidence of the failure of mind', Ruskin went on to claim that he burned the offending material with the assistance of Ralph Wornum, who was the Keeper of the National Gallery.

Despite this claim the package of erotica survived, its existence seeping into the public consciousness.[23] Amid the thousands of works produced by the artist, his erotic drawings made up the merest tiny fraction, far less than one per cent. Nevertheless the presence of the package loomed disproportionately large in the nineteenth century, where sex, shame and apparently mental deterioration were intrinsically linked.

In July 1861, Henry Lennox MP felt moved to mention the 'prurient' work of the artist as part of a select committee meeting in the House of Lords, which was examining the future of the Turner Collection that the artist had bequeathed to the nation.

It must have been with some weariness that Sir Charles Eastlake batted the question away by noting that he had not examined the package in question since it was marked 'not fit for general inspection'. But it was with real outrage that Turner's friend, the seventy-five-year-old artist George Jones, wrote to Lennox to point out that:

> Very few drawings in the enormous collection by Turner can bear the character your Lordship describes as 'prurient' and whether they were executed by him is uncertain, they bear much character of French works with colouring I admit similar to that of the deceased

great artist, and of those the greater part seem to belong to surgery or
natural history.

I was most intimate friend of J. M. W. Turner RA during twenty
five years, and although he was in the habit of shewing me all he did,
I never saw a work of his hand of the character described.[24]

But despite his friends' protests, the myth of Turner as an artist
with dirty secrets grew, as did the myth of Turner the madman, this
thanks to his family who had chosen to challenge his will on these
grounds.

Although the Turners' attempts to have the will declared invalid
on grounds of insanity failed, Turner's cousins launched a second
legal case to have his wish to provide a home for destitute artists
overturned. The litigation lasted three years before, in 1856, Turner's
charitable scheme was scrapped and his relatives received a significant
portion of his estate, including his engraved works, the house and
gallery in Queen Anne Street and his financial investments.

The bequest to the nation became the next battle. Turner had
asked that all his finished *pictures* be left to the nation, to be housed
and shown together as a collection, either in the National Gallery in
custom-built rooms, or shown in rotation in his own gallery in
Queen Anne Street. In nineteenth-century parlance the term *picture*
was more specifically applied than today, and referred to finished oil
paintings, while watercolours were known as *drawings*.

The outcome of the final court case, however, was that not just the
100 finished oils Turner had originally intended, but '*all the pictures,
drawings and sketches by the testators hands without the distinction of finished
or unfinished*'[25] were to be handed over to the nation. This added not
only the vast amount of works on paper Ruskin was working his way
through, but another 182 unfinished oil paintings. Though this far
greater bequest to the nation was arguably a far greater legacy, it flew
in the face of Turner's desire for his specific selection of paintings to
represent his life's work. The vastly increased size of the bequest
would also present problems with storage and display of his work in
the future.

While this saga continued, Turner's friends and admirers strove to redress the legacy of the man himself. Ironically, the attempts to reclaim the real Turner from the semi-fictional caricature of him that the Victorian era began to develop simply added another layer of misrepresentation. Part of the problem was that the voices of Turner's direct contemporaries had grown weak. Most men who had known him man and boy were now dead or very old. In the 1860s it was almost exclusively the voice of John Ruskin that was heard by the wider public.

But John Ruskin, born in 1819, was more than forty years Turner's junior. He had encountered the artist when the latter was in the last two decades of his life and career — a point at which Turner's work was undoubtedly reaching its most controversial. In the 1840s Ruskin's youthful defence of these works, and the power of his passionate prose, was such that it eclipsed other supporters of Turner's work, who were in fact plentiful enough. Ironically Ruskin's loud advocacy of Turner cemented the idea more forcefully than ever before that Turner's work needed defending.

After the revelations about Turner's life in Chelsea, Ruskin once again attempted to save the reputation of the artist he adored. In the 1860s he attempted to contextualize the Victorian perception of his hero as a vulgar, damaged man, by providing an account of his boyhood that would have made Dickens blush for its imaginative and romantic reinterpretation of fact. More than twenty years after *Oliver Twist,* he cast Turner as a slum-based urchin from an underprivileged background in order to mediate the final outcome of his life. This became another caricature that would not be shaken.[26]

By the time Ruskin wrote this fanciful account of Turner as a younger artist, those who had been young alongside Turner were gone. The accounts of Turner's reputation and achievements as they were witnessed and judged by his direct peers had evaporated.

And so time conspired against Turner to create a very particular mythology around him. To the Victorians, Turner was an artist who was reclusive, squalid, seedy and eccentric. He was the gruff, unfriendly genius who had lost his mind and lost his way. He was the rags-to-riches urchin who had overcome adversity to create a body of work that was largely misunderstood and yet had genius at its heart, a genius that it had taken a member of a later generation to spot and nurture.

The changing taste in art in the twentieth century did yet more to skew and distort the story of Turner's life and work. As the national galleries sat on the vast Turner bequest, those works that Turner himself had never considered finished were viewed through the lens of a society for whom impressionism, surrealism, and abstraction had stretched the boundaries of art. Not only could the late works that Turner's own public had failed to appreciate be reclaimed and rediscovered in the twentieth century, but his 'unfinished' work was looked at anew, and hung alongside. Works that the artist himself had never considered complete and had never displayed were suddenly shown on gallery walls. Colour sketches and formative beginnings, work in embryo, were displayed with the same sense of gravitas and importance as those Turner had seen fit for exhibition himself. As such, in the twentieth century, the word 'Turnerian' became associated with a particular aspect of his work that was extremely loose and often almost abstract. Work that was deemed miraculously out of its time.

The Turner myth has proved a distraction from the greater narrative of his seventy-six years on this planet. Looking back at his full life, one can in fact see Turner as not so much a man out of his time, but profoundly the product of it.

In terms of a lifestyle deemed bizarre and morally deviant, one must reconsider the fact that Turner's moral and sexual compass, though perhaps out of step with the apparently sexually suppressed and marriage-minded 1850s, was far from divergent from the standards of the eighteenth century in which he had grown up, when a great many of his peers had lived with women out of wedlock.

Far from being a loner and eccentric, he had been a man who, in his middle years in particular, had led a busy social life. Fascinated by progress, hungry for knowledge, Turner was a man who drank in his own time with an unquenchable thirst.

And in terms of his work, he can be redrawn less as the misunderstood genius, and more as an arch manipulator and central player in the great game of art that evolved across the late eighteenth and nineteenth centuries, a man praised to the hilt by a great many of his contemporaries as someone who set the bar in his profession. It was these contemporaries who recognized his role in the birth of modern art and acknowledged his significance in the creation of the idea of the independent artist. He oversaw the extraction of art from the iron grip of eighteenth-century aristocratic patrons, and he witnessed its reach extend beyond Britain's gentry and into the homes of the wider public. Born before the idea of public art, Turner died leaving his work to the nation. In an era when democracy was being forged, Turner saw the democratization of his métier.

One cannot deny the existence of Admiral Booth of Davis Place. But Turner's life had an epic sweep far beyond his final caricature. For all the wry smiles or raised eyebrows that the comical, smutty figure of Puggy Booth might invite in 1851, and for all the praise that John Ruskin would heap on the misunderstood work of the genius of the 1840s, the tale of J. M. W. Turner that began in 1775 is far greater. If ever there was a story of an artist worth telling properly, from the start, it is Turner's. And to do that one must, inevitably, put aside a life that has often been viewed in reverse, and instead, begin at the beginning. Only then can one begin to understand just who J. M. W. Turner R A really was.

2. The beginning

Even though he died a Victorian, Joseph Mallord William Turner was born very much a Georgian.[1] Baptized in May 1775, his actual birthdate remains unknown, though Turner himself later claimed he shared a birthday with William Shakespeare on 23 April. Whatever the date, he was born at 21 Maiden Lane in London's Covent Garden, the son of a barber and wig-maker.

If anywhere represented the insalubrious side of Georgian life it was Covent Garden, full of whorehouses and taverns, mobs and mollies, and right in the centre of a heaving metropolis that a contemporary described as 'a sink of corruption . . . where the poor wallow in wretchedness, and the rich stink in state'.[2]

But despite these attributes, Covent Garden was also the beating heart of Britain's creative industries. Its tone was set by the proximity of London's two great theatres, Covent Garden and Drury Lane. Being born there, Turner found himself in the right place, at the right time, to take full advantage of emerging professions that centred around that busy Piazza. The talented sons of bricklayers, inn-keepers, clerks and cobblers were fast becoming the artists, architects and actor-managers that defined their age, their studios circling that small patch of London between Drury Lane and the Strand. There was room for the son of a barber to join their ranks. Particularly one with extraordinary drive and determination.

Ambition was woven into the fabric of Turner's ancestors. His mother was from petty-bourgeois stock. Her forebears, the Mallords and Marshalls, were established London folk whose hard graft and commercial success had brought considerable recognition and comforts. Turner's maternal great-grandfather, Joseph Mallord, came from a long line of London tanners and butchers based in the City and had twice been honoured with the title of Master of the Worshipful Company of Butchers. His considerable wealth is evident in the

inventory he made in 1731 of the contents of his ample home in Sugar
Loaf Court, Leadenhall Street. This four- or five-storey home with its
six bedrooms, dressing rooms, parlours, dining room and kitchens
was well stocked with aspirational items. Apart from feather beds,
chests full of linen, several sets of walnut chairs, and two dining tables,
walnut escritoires, quantities of decorative china, japanned cabinets
and mirrors, there were also silk curtains and quilts, tea tables and
services, an extensive collection of plate including two silver teapots,
a dozen teaspoons, tobacco jars, punch ladles and fine dining china.
And there was also art on the walls, including two pictures of flowers,
one picture of a ship, one depiction of the King's Arms, six black and
white prints, eight other pictures, and a painting with shepherds.[3]

Given the sumptuous contents of his well-appointed home, it
comes as little surprise that the will Mallord made a decade later also
noted four houses in New Gravel Lane, Wapping, 'four acres of
marsh land lying at Ripple Side near the Breach in the Parish of Bar-
kin in the County of Essex' and tenements 'near New Chappel upon
the Pyrly Forist in the . . . county of Essex'.[4]

Joseph Mallord's only child, Sarah, Turner's grandmother, married
her cousin William Marshall, who was also in the meat trade. He was
a salesman who acted as a middleman between the farmers bringing
their livestock into town and the London butchers. And Marshall's
commercial acumen was certainly good enough to allow him and
his young wife to set up home in one of London's more affluent areas.

By the 1730s William and Sarah Marshall, Turner's grandparents,
had moved out of a city plagued by 'roll chaises, carriages and
drays in an unending stream' and defined by the 'din and the hum
and clatter of ten thousand of tongues and feet. . .',[5] to the leafier
town of Islington. Established on higher ground to the north of the
metropolis, Islington was a growing spa and retreat for the middle
classes, known for its clean air. Here they rented a reasonably large
house, 5 Church Row, from Henry Harpur, a solicitor. The comfortable property came with a paddock and a carriage, and was not far
from the church of St Mary's, where William was church warden for
a while. Here the Marshalls embarked on a family.[6]

Turner's mother, Mary, was baptized at St Mary's on 13 November

1735, a sister to the Marshalls' two older daughters, Anne and Sarah. The girls' younger brother finally makes an appearance in the church registers five years later and the family delight at the male heir is indicated by the suitably grand name given to the child. It was a name that would provide the template for Mary's own future child: Joseph Mallord William Marshall would have embodied the hopes and dreams of his upwardly mobile family.

From these encouraging beginnings, silence envelops Mary Marshall's progress through her first three decades. Sarah, her elder sister, appears in the registers of St Mary's as making a good, socially advantageous marriage in 1755 to the landlord's son, Henry Harpur II,[7] who had become the local curate in Islington. Her brother Joseph had meanwhile become apprenticed to a City butcher. But news of Mary does not emerge until August 1773 when, nearly twenty years after her sister Sarah was wed, she is finally married to William Turner at St Paul's Church in Covent Garden, in something of a hurry.

In the couple's application for a licence to marry speedily without banns, William records his age as twenty-eight and Mary hers as thirty-four. However, if this is the same Mary that appears in the register of St Mary's Islington in 1735, her actual age would have been around thirty-eight, which by the standards of the day would make her an almost geriatric first-time bride and a decade older than her prospective spouse. Mary must have become something of a lost soul over the course of the 1750s and 1760s. While two of her siblings were making lives for themselves, she was sitting on the shelf. Perhaps the mental illness which would plague Mary's later life had already tarnished her youth.

As a spinster, Mary's life would have become much harder with her parents' deaths. Mary's mother died in 1758 and her father not long after, in 1761. Like so many unmarried women of her generation, from this moment she was entirely dependent on the charity and goodwill of her extended family. Her precarious position was exacerbated by the fact that William Marshall had failed to make a will that might have catered for his single, mentally fragile daughter. As a result, the properties that had passed down the family from Joseph Mallord and John Marshall bypassed the needy Mary and instead landed in the laps of the men of her generation, her brother Joseph and Sarah's husband Henry Harpur. This left Mary and her sister Anne entirely at the mercy of their relatives' generosity.

Fortunately for the girls, there were members of the extended Marshall family capable of accommodating them. After all, the upward mobility of some branches of the Marshall family was continuing apace. Mary's sister Sarah and Henry Harpur were now installed in a vicarage in Tonbridge in Kent. Other branches of the family had done better still. A cousin, Sarah Marshall, had married Jonathan Stiles of Shelford Manor in Nottinghamshire and as such had joined the minor gentry. So when the large comfy house in Islington was let go there were options.

Mary's sister Anne died next, in 1762, and was buried in the cemetery of the Nottinghamshire village of Burton Joyce, close to Shelford Manor. Anne's resting-place indicates her fate in the immediate months after her parents' demise and, unless she went to the Harpurs, it seems likely that Mary may well have also stayed with the Nottinghamshire relatives, until perhaps 1768 when her brother Joseph managed to establish himself in his own butcher's business. At this point it seems likely that she would have joined him. The greatest indication of the kindness that Joseph Mallord William Marshall showed his unlucky and dependent sister is, after all, the name she would give to her own son. Joseph Marshall would prove a man of founding importance in Turner's life and career.

Joseph Marshall had finally finished his butcher's apprenticeship with Francis Baker of Bell Alley and had left the City to set up business in the heart of Brentford, a town to the west of London. It was a place surrounded by market gardens supplying the metropolis, and where goods being transported by river were stored and split up for redistribution. It was also a major stopping point for livestock and other goods coming into town by road. It had a thriving corn market, boasted breweries, potteries and brickworks, and was a place of great opportunity for business-minded entrepreneurs.

It wasn't just the goods that came into Brentford that made it such an interesting commercial proposition. It was the people too. Located on the Great West Road, all major traffic from the West Country into the capital came through Brentford's wide, dusty streets. Stagecoaches arrived every half hour, spilling their contents into the many coaching inns, the largest of which could stable one hundred horses a night.

And so one can see that for an entrepreneur, Marshall could have done worse than set up here, where his butchery skills could furnish a local retail business, but where there was also a huge wholesale opportunity to buy some of the stock being walked into town and sell it on to the contacts he had in the City. Marshall took a lease on a property owned by a wealthy local brewer that sat in the town's market square next to one of Brentford's many inns, the White Horse. It was modest but brilliantly located. And from here he began to build himself a reputation in the town.

Though a tenant in Brentford, Joseph had inherited the property from the Mallord line, and as a freeholder elsewhere was an enfranchised man. In his very first year in residence at Brentford, he was able to vote in one of the most notorious elections of his time, one that encapsulated an emerging democratic movement, and marked the town down as being of particularly radical bent.

The radical MP John Wilkes had been provoking George III. A rake who fathered several illegitimate children, and a member of the notorious Hellfire Club, he was nevertheless the son of a distiller whose sense of the rights of the common man ran deep. Deeply critical of the King in his newspaper the *North Briton*, Wilkes had been arrested in 1763 for sedition and treason and had fled to Paris, leaving behind him a reputation for swagger and bravura that had captured the public's imagination. He had become an embodiment of liberty.

Though Wilkes was sentenced to prison *in absentia*, he returned to Britain in 1768 to seek re-election, and had been greeted with an enthusiasm that took the status quo aback. And in Brentford this enthusiasm was particularly high.

In October 1768 the Middlesex MP George Cooke died and John Wilkes put his man Sergeant John Glynne[8] up for the seat. He stood on a ticket that promoted the right of voters to determine their candidates, rather than Parliament.

Joseph Marshall turned up to the hustings on 8 November to vote for Glynne, as did the majority of Brentford's businessmen, and in doing so he was lucky to escape with his life. The election was hijacked by an armed mob, almost certainly orchestrated by Wilkes's opponent, Sir William Beauchamp Proctor. At least one voting free-holder was bludgeoned to death and many were injured, and only after subsequent re-elections were Glynne and Wilkes confirmed as successful.

Though little more is known about Joseph Marshall in Brentford, his property and political choices suggest something of the man. His modest tenancy was indicative of a man who valued commonsense business above personal comfort or ostentation. His support of Wilkes indicates liberal tendencies and a concern for the rights of working men. These are values that in due course would become absorbed by his famous nephew.

But that famous nephew was not yet a twinkle in his mother's eye. Quite how Mary Marshall met her future husband remains a mys-tery. But it may well have been that while keeping house for her brother in Brentford, Mary fell in love with one of the many travel-lers coming into town. For William Turner was a Devon man who, seeking his fortune, would have come to London along the Great West Road.

William Turner hailed from South Molton, a small market town close to Exmoor. In his own chosen profession he was following in the footsteps of his father, John Turner, who, though he began as a tanner, ended up a wig-maker and barber. William and his four brothers between them tell the tale of the mass exodus from the small rural communities towards the larger urban centres that were devel-oping fast at the outset of the industrial revolution. By the turn of the century not one of them was left in the town in which they had been born. John had moved to Barnstaple, where he became the overseer of the workhouse, and Price had gone to Exeter, where he was a saddler. Jonathan, Joshua and William had all gone east. While the former set up shop as a baker in Bath, Joshua and William headed for the capital.

The love affair between Mary Marshall and William Turner must have come as no small relief to Joseph Marshall. It may well be that he provided the £200 bond, required when marrying without banns, which offered a guarantee to the church that the marriage was legal. This must have seemed a small risk for someone who would otherwise be financially responsible for Mary for the rest of his life.

In marrying William, Mary kissed goodbye to the relatively comfortable life she had pursued in Brentford, Nottinghamshire and Islington and committed herself to living in a highly overbuilt, stifling, noisy and smelly central London, where William determined to set up his barber's shop.

Turner's father had chosen Covent Garden for his business premises with good reason, however. The Garden was just about the best place a barber and wig-maker could be in the whole of London. For that infamous portion of town was not just the hub of the capital's vice and creativity, it was also the centre of style.

A hundred and forty-odd years earlier the wide square Piazza had been designed by Inigo Jones as a place for people of quality. And it had quickly become the nexus of London fashion. It was the place where the dramatist George Etherege had drawn inspiration for his ostentatiously attired Man of Mode Sir Fopling Flutter, where Colley Cibber had spotted Sir Novelty Fashion and John Vanbrugh's Lord Foppington would have mingled seamlessly amid a crowd of similarly clad fashionistas.

The real-life descendants of these icons of high fashion were still promenading around Covent Garden in the 1770s when William and Mary Turner moved there. Known as 'macaronis' because of their exclusive culinary exposure to pasta during their Grand Tours of the Continent, these modish men, inspired by the excesses of Louis XVI's French court, wore powdered, and often coloured, wigs from which long curls cascaded down their backs. Even the politician Charles Fox returned from his own continental excursion with a pigeon-wing hair style tinted blue.

But though the macaronis insisted on strolling under Covent Garden's covered walkways in the 1770s, they no longer lived there. By the 1750s the wealthy gentry had moved west to Mayfair, leaving just their rakish sons to haunt their former homes, which were now converted into glee clubs, coffee houses, gambling parlours and worse.

All the better for the artists who moved in. These glee clubs and coffee houses became the arena of creative debate in the later eighteenth century, and the de facto offices of those involved in it. Henry Angelo, a much fêted fencing master, remembered Covent Garden as the 'residence of a succession of men, renowned for genius, talent, wit, humour and eccentricity above every other spot in the metropolis',[9] adding that 'in the year 1764, no less than ten painters occupied houses or apartments' in the Piazza, including Zoffany, Richard Wilson, Dock the miniaturist, Sir James Thornhill (who had an academy for nude studies there), the scene painter George Lambert, a landscape painter called Pugh, and more.

By the time of Turner's birth this figure was if anything growing, and yet more luminaries of the art world were living close by. Sir Joshua Reynolds, perhaps the most famous artist of his day, was just yards away at Leicester Fields, today known as Leicester Square.

William Turner's shop was in the midst of it all, in Maiden Lane. Running parallel to the Strand, the lane was effectively a cul-de-sac, narrowing to a passage only passable on foot at its eastern-most end. It was muddy and dirty, and that narrow passage far too convenient for a quick sexual transaction, but it was also a vibrant microcosm of Covent Garden as a whole, with its own set of taverns, clubs, craftsmen, bookbinders and booksellers, printsellers and sales rooms, all concentrated along one stretch.

William Turner initially had the ground floor of No. 21, a large building that accommodated at least two other commercial enterprises. Directly below in the basement was the Cider Cellar, a notorious song and supper venue that had a reputation for staying open all night. Here it wasn't just new glees that the Turners would have heard wafting upwards through their floors, but a riot of voices as theatre people, journalists, swells and literary types leant across the long trestle tables to debate the latest politics, religion and stage performances.

Immediately above the Turners was John Moreing's Great Auction Room. This vast space, which transferred ownership during Turner's boyhood, but never lost its connection with art, would have been an Aladdin's cave of delights for a young boy who found himself interested in painting.

Moreing's provides a wonderfully informative entry point into the state of British art in the second half of the eighteenth century, and a fine example of how Covent Garden had become its geographical centre. In the 1760s, 1770s and 1780s the Great Auction Room at 21 Maiden Lane would, crucially, have been one of the few places where people could see art in the flesh.

In the eighteenth century, fine art was far from familiar to the general public. Most people would not have seen an Old Master painting, and neither were they likely to have seen a thing by a living British artist.

You could certainly see prints of Old Masters in the windows of booksellers and engravers. And some enterprising artists would put their own works in shop windows. But from 1775, the year in which Turner was born, another thirty-six years would pass before two enterprising men, the picture dealer Noel Desenfans and the artist Francis Bourgeois, left a collection of work to form the nation's first public picture gallery in Dulwich. And though John Wilkes had proposed as early as 1777 that Parliament buy the great art collection at Houghton Hall to begin a national collection, the British people had to wait until 1824 before its government could be finally persuaded to set up the National Gallery.

There were many collections of paintings in Britain, but these were in the capacious homes and private galleries of the aristocracy, an elite for whom connoisseurship and taste was just another currency used to reinforce their sense of social superiority.

What is more, these aristocratic collections were heavily dominated by sixteenth- and seventeenth-century Renaissance and continental art, which was seen as superior to anything produced on British shores. This preference meant the market for work by living British artists had been marginalized, ever since collecting had first become fashionable under the auspices of Charles I. The aristocracy also had a stranglehold on the few living British artists fortunate enough to work, for they did so on commission, and were entirely dependent on those contacts and recommendations that could get them into the right drawing rooms to show their work.

The cultural elite did not buy from commercial galleries, which were also yet to develop. They bought from agents or dealers, some

of whom were artists themselves. During the course of the seventeenth and eighteenth centuries, however, auctioneers had begun to
play a role in a nascent art market. As aristocratic estates inevitably
broke up or sought cash injections, fine art began to find its way to
auction houses, where it was both exhibited to the public, and sold.

It was not just sixteenth- and seventeenth-century paintings that
found their way into auction rooms. With no developed commercial gallery system, living British artists were beginning to sell their
work via auction houses too. As such, places like Moreing's Great
Auction Room in Maiden Lane provided the people of Covent
Garden with the rare privilege of looking at art, an experience
afforded very few outside central London.

Although John Moreing eventually moved on from the Great
Auction Room, its use as a place to exhibit art continued after him,
this time under the auspices of Mr Burghall who, though also using
the premises for dancing and fencing lessons, as well as a meeting
place for debating societies, continued to allow painters to hire them
for selling exhibitions.[10]

It is hardly surprising that with the concentration of artists and art
events around Covent Garden the first society for artists should also
be founded there. In 1754, just around the corner from Maiden Lane,
in Rawthmell's Coffee House on Henrietta Street, a drawing master
called William Shipley founded a Society for the Encouragement of
Arts, Manufactures, and Commerce. By the end of the 1750s Shipley's vision had crystallized into the Society of Arts.

The formalization of artists into a society reflected more than just
a means of self-representation. To the eighteenth-century mind art
remained a field to be explored, its secrets yet to be tapped, its techniques yet to be refined, and what is more, its laurels to be prised
away from the Continent. The need to make discoveries in art was as
keenly felt as it was in science. The newly created Society of Arts was
the first organization to award generous prizes to contemporary artists and encourage their experimentation with new techniques and
materials.

This kind of incentive for British art was long overdue. For if this
island had ever had the beginnings of its own school of painting, that

is an identifiable national tradition and aesthetic, such as those developed in Italy, France and the Netherlands, the Reformation had put paid to its development. While the rest of Europe enjoyed a Renaissance that in turn developed the great continental artists of the sixteenth and early seventeenth centuries, painters in Britain had been largely classed as craftsmen, responsible for signage and decoration, and regulated in London by the Worshipful Company of Painter-Stainers. While on the Continent schools and academies had been established to train artists, Britain had no such resource.

Only in the eighteenth century did the notion begin to emerge that Britain might catch up. For the first time it became conceivable that a home-grown school of painting might become a source of national pride, and that its members might even compete on a world stage. By 1760 another society had been formed, the Society of Artists, with the aim of mounting an annual exhibition to showcase British contemporary art.

This action marked the tiny beginnings of a breaking away from the monopoly the aristocracy had had over art and its practitioners up to this point. The Society of Artists began using London's auction spaces to exhibit its works. Cock's auction house in Charing Cross became a favoured venue. Meanwhile another rival society, the Free Society of Artists (so called because they did not charge an entrance fee to their exhibitions), used Moreing's.

The pent-up appetite for contemporary work was massive. When the Society of Artists launched its first annual show in 1760, even with an entrance fee, a thousand people a day poured in to have a look.

The potential of the market for British work only served to highlight a huge problem at the heart of British painting. And that was the lack of a prestigious drawing school. In 1714 the *London Tradesman* had put the point baldly: 'The present State of this Art in Britain does not afford a sufficient Education to a Painter. We have but one Academy meanly supported by the private subscription of the Students, in all this great Metropolis.'[11]

The academy referred to was a school set up by the artist Godfrey Kneller, which in its day took sixty paying pupils for figure drawing.

In the 1730s Hogarth had established a drawing school in St Martin's Lane with an attendance fee of 2 guineas a year. Things could only improve.

The painter Joseph Farington witnessed an influx of foreign drawing masters as the century progressed. After one morning spent with 'Mr Malchair the music and drawing master', Farington noted in his diary that the former 'came to England abt the year 1754. He mentioned how much the Arts had advanced in this country, and said that when he first taught music and drawing in London there were only 5 or 6 drawing masters – viz P Sandy – Bonneau – Chatelain – and a few others. Now he said there are hundreds.'[12]

However, by the late 1760s there was still nothing recognized as a national school for the arts until the Society of Artists, under the presidency of the landscape painter Joshua Kirby, set up its own drawing and painting school, again using Moreing's Auction Room as a venue, and this survived until 1773.[13]

In the same year that the Society of Artists launched its school, a number of its foremost members broke away and launched another institution. With this last, British art was finally granted the kind of representation it needed, one that would irrevocably transform the landscape of patronage and education. One that was endorsed and encouraged by a king who believed in the need for an organization that would inform and disseminate taste and enhance Britain's cultural currency on the world stage. This was the Royal Academy of Arts, founded in 1768.

Just a year after its foundation the Academy set up a school that offered its pupils the most comprehensive practical and theoretical training available in the country. This training was free of charge. And significantly for Turner, it was on his doorstep, in the Strand. Those attending the Royal Academy Schools were, if not the sons of painters themselves, the sons of cobblers and bricklayers, butchers and barbers. But unlike their fathers, this new breed of artist could find themselves moving with genuine alacrity into a world of celebrity. For the first time in the history of British art, becoming a painter offered kudos. And that Joseph Mallord William Turner wanted to be a painter from a very early age is without doubt.

3. 'A pleasant good tempered youth, not fond of society'

J. M. W. Turner did not begin his career so styled. As a boy he was known simply as William Turner, his father's namesake. And from the start young William Turner's drive to draw was evident.

Even when he was a very young child his environment was a tantalizing proposition that demanded his attention. He was a compulsive artist straight away, obligated to record, jot down, sketch. This obsessive aspect of his character defined him his entire life. His pockets were never without sketchbooks or small pieces of paper.

The very first recorded witness of this compulsion was a goldsmith called Humphrey Tomkinson, who lived in Maiden Lane in the 1770s. When Turner senior came to coiff Tomkinson at his home, and brought his son with him, the young boy began to draw from the glistening objects that were Tomkinson's stock in trade. It was a pair of silver castors for an ennobled client that Turner finally settled on, carefully copying the coat of arms that Tomkinson had engraved there.[1]

There were many homes and workshops in the area that were going to provide inspiration in this vein for Turner. Even Turner's father's shop would have been a stimulating and colourful place for a young boy. Contemporary depictions of barbers' and wig-makers' shops often feature several clients chatting away with one another in convivial, busy surroundings, where pictures can be seen adorning the walls, and wigs and other paraphernalia hang from stands and hooks. It would have smelt of the ointments, salves and perfumes that William Turner would have rubbed and splashed. The shop window would have been full of colourful painted mannequins sporting his latest perrukes and periwigs. His hair powders, many of them coloured, would have been in use, and his clientele were undoubtedly vivacious men of the world. Actors, artists, print-sellers, architects, and writers would have made up the bulk of his business, and with them went a liberal attitude and lively, intellectual conversation.

Beyond Turner's immediate environment, the visual arts were beginning to play a wider role in late eighteenth-century life, crucial in articulating the cultural reaction to the turbulent political climate of the times.

The British empire was crumbling and threatened. The year after Turner's birth, America declared its independence, drawing Europe and the Americas into world conflict. The French just a few miles across the Channel were the enemy, with only the Royal Navy's prowling ships of the line preventing invasion. It is not surprising that in this time of extended crisis, a profound sense of nationalism grew. And it was London's new breed of painters who seized on this sense of nationalism and fed it.

They responded to the fears of the moment by depicting recent events as part of an heroic narrative to prop up national solidarity. The early Royal Academicians created some of the first truly popular images that were then widely reproduced by Covent Garden's engravers and printers. Benjamin West painted *The Death of General Wolfe*, for example, and the engraver William Woollett (as well as many pirated versions) made sure the image of an heroic general became one of the first visual bestsellers, adorning coffee shops, and probably pinned up in the barbers' shops.

But the scope and realm of London's artists went far beyond paper and board. The nation's favourite artists doubled up as scene painters and transformed stages into forests, cities and faraway lands at a time when the setting and scenario in theatre was as important and impactful as the play and action. At night the city itself could also become the artists' domain, when, at times of celebration, they used entire buildings as their canvases. On 20 February 1779, for example, when Turner would have been not quite four, London was transformed by illuminations celebrating the acquittal of the national naval hero Admiral Keppel from a charge of treason. The city's painters transformed it into a twinkling fantasy as they took their brushes to panes of glass which, once placed in front of lanterns, projected their imagery on a massive metropolitan scale. The flat brick façades of London's Georgian architecture were metamorphosed by projections of fantastical landscapes, mythical cities, magical beasts and heroic figures floating on high.

Turner's parents were not blind to the talent that began to spring up amid this maelstrom of visual and sensory stimulus. Turner's desire to become a painter was encouraged by his family, and the boy's talents were heavily promoted by them. Perhaps his parents also realized that their son did not have the temperament to take on his father's business. Barbers needed to be chatty and friendly, they needed to have some form of social grace and a bucketful of pleasantries to entice and retain their clientele. Turner's father was apparently such a character. According to accounts of him as an older man he 'was ... a head below the average standard [height], spare and muscular, with small blue eyes, parrot nose, projecting chin, fresh complexion, an index of health, which he apparently enjoyed to the full. He was a chatty old fellow, and talked fast; but from speaking through his nose his words had a peculiar transatlantic twang.'[2] In contrast to this talkative man, the few accounts of Turner as a child are of 'a pleasant good tempered youth', who was, however, 'not fond of society' and 'wholly devoted to his drawing'.[3] A young man who was neither 'striking nor was his conversation brilliant'.[4]

But before Turner might become a successful artist, he had to become an adult. And navigating the childhood perils that Georgian sanitation, or lack of it, presented was the first challenge the Turners faced regarding their talented son. London air was a soupy fog of sea coal smoke that suggested the observation from foreigners that Londoners rarely saw the sun. Tuberculosis was rife. As were related diseases such as scrofula, a terribly disfiguring disease related to tuberculosis that saw inner-city children erupt in great growths around their face and neck.

This was brought home all too clearly to the Turner family, who lost at least one, but possibly two children in the 1780s. The parish registers of St Paul's Covent Garden record a Mary Anne being born to William and Mary Turner in 1778, a little sister to their three-year-old son. But a child of the same name is recorded as being buried in 1783. And then a further record from 1786 reveals the burial of yet another Mary Anne Turner, daughter of William and Mary.[5]

The tragedy of certainly one and perhaps two premature deaths must have weighed heavily on the family. If Mary Turner had had some respite from mental health issues around the time of her marriage, her troubles probably returned with the loss of her daughters. The few accounts of her depict a handsome but unhappy woman. The Victorian journalist Walter Thornbury gathered accounts from those who had known her, but was able to make only the briefest description of her, as short, with blue eyes, an aquiline nose and a 'slight fell in the nether lip'. She wore her hair fashionably frizzed, but was 'fierce' with an 'ungovernable temper' who 'led her husband a sad life'.[6]

The illness of the Turners' second daughter, and perhaps the declining condition of Mary herself, prompted drastic action. As William turned ten his parents decided to protect their son from the inner-city smogs and infections, and send him to live away from home. It was an act that would force him to grow up fast, and it is fair to say he did. From the difficulties of his domestic situation rose an intrepid, self-determining, self-sufficient, extremely ambitious, and rather self-centred young man; though one who would also be seen to suffer the psychological scars of being distanced from his family at such a young age.

The Turners had been in the habit of sending their son out of town during the summer holidays for much of his early childhood. Sometimes he went to Mary's sister Sarah Harpur in Tonbridge in Kent. He was also 'in the habit of spending his vacations' in Bristol with John Narraway, a very close friend of William Turner senior.[7] But as William grew older, the Turners decided that holidays from London smog were not enough. Something more permanent was called for, and he was to be schooled elsewhere too.

The ten-year-old Turner may have already been quite unwell when he was dispatched out of town. A sizeable portion of Turner's extant correspondence contains reference by Turner himself to bouts of ill health and his tendency to be affected by the heat. There is some suggestion in some of the medical remedies that he noted down that he may have been asthmatic.

Brentford was the obvious place to send the boy first, to stay with his uncle Joseph Marshall. The latter had no children of his own but he now had a wife called Anne who could provide some motherly attention. Turner's father was doing well enough to pay for Turner to attend a day school there, as well as for his son's board. So Turner set off, probably travelling the eight miles much as he would as a young man, his belongings wrapped in a square of cloth and carried at the end of a stick, just like Dick Whittington.

It may not have been solely Joseph and Anne Marshall's residence there that suggested Brentford as a place to stay. There were other Brentford people with connections to Covent Garden who may have encouraged the Turners to think that the market town was ideal for a budding young artist.

One such was the young architect Thomas Hardwick, who was working on the construction of the new Somerset House on the Strand. The construction of a set of public buildings that would house the Royal Academy of Arts had begun in the year Turner was born. As a very young child he must have smelt the dust, heard the clang of the masons' hammers, and witnessed the chaos as the new classical edifice, designed by William Chambers, slowly rose from its foundations. He would have been four when the western portion was completed and the Royal Academicians found themselves the first occupants of the brand new scheme. There were other societies to house there too, and so building works continued throughout Turner's childhood, until the whole project was finally completed in 1801, when he was in his mid-twenties.

A strong friendship was formed between Turner and the Hardwick family once the young boy settled in Brentford. Turner found himself just a stone's throw from the family home where Thomas Hardwick had been brought up and where his architect father, who shared the same name, still lived. Thomas's son Philip would one day look down on Turner's coffin.

A friendship of similar strength and longevity was forged between Turner and the Trimmer family, who also lived in Brentford in the

1780s. Turner became fast friends with John and Henry Scott Trimmer, the former being the same age as himself and Henry just three years his junior. Members of the extended Trimmer family, who dominated the brewing and brickmaking industries in the town, were Joseph Marshall's landlords. And this might have been enough of a link to effect an introduction between Turner and the Trimmer boys. But as with the Hardwicks, there was also a coincidence of interest and geography that suggested that friendship was inevitable. For the boys' mother, Sarah Trimmer, was none other than the daughter of Joshua Kirby, the one-time president of the Society of Artists. Kirby had trudged down Maiden Lane many times to visit the exhibitions at Moreing's, and what is more, as the Society's authority on perspective, he had also attended the drawing classes held in the very building in which Turner senior would later have his shop.

By the time our Turner knew her, Sarah Trimmer, a landscape painter who had also exhibited at Moreings in her time, was well on the way to becoming one of the foremost educationalists of her generation. Turner may well have attended the Sunday School she opened in Brentford in 1786, as a complement to his studies at John White's Free School in the town, which he attended during the week. But whether he was her pupil or not, it is impossible that he could have escaped her instincts to embrace and inform all the children who came within her orbit. Some of her publications, such as her *Easy Introduction to the Knowledge of Nature*, which encouraged children to look carefully at nature, may well have inspired Turner as he explored the fields and hedgerows in his new semi-rural environment. In Brentford and its environs the inner-city boy encountered nature for the first time, and his peers remembered the delight he took in the trees and birds so evident here, yet marked by their absence in central London.

But above all it must have been the paintings in the Trimmer house that enraptured the young Turner. Joshua Kirby had been close friends with Sir Joshua Reynolds, Thomas Gainsborough and William Hogarth. Gainsborough's handsome portrait of Joshua and his wife Sarah, captured sitting under a brown-leafed tree, their black and white dog by their side,[8] was there, alongside other works by Gainsborough and the Welsh landscape artist Richard Wilson.

Some of the pictures in the Kirby house seem to have had a fundamental and lasting effect on the young Turner. One day he would paint gypsy scenes in the manner of those by Gainsborough that he saw in this house. And he would go in search of the birthplace of the artist Richard Wilson, who brought a classical sensibility to the landscapes he painted of his native Wales, and depicted glowing sunsets over the hills and valleys of his homeland.

The Trimmer house was a hive of cultural activity. Sarah held musical parties that were very popular, and artists who knew her through her father would still come by. The German painter Johan Zoffany, who lived at nearby Chiswick, was one regular visitor. Sarah Trimmer encouraged her children to pick up a pencil or brush. She taught Henry, who had certainly inherited the inclination to draw from his grandfather, and perhaps young Turner joined him in copying some of the Gainsboroughs on the walls.

When Turner died, among his possessions was a copy of Joshua Kirby's *Dr Brook Taylor's Method of Perspective Made Easy*. The book had been given to him by Henry. As a child Turner perhaps leafed through this practical guidebook, which offered the artist the basic rules in how to construct a convincing scene. Its frontispiece by Hogarth is a hilarious Escher-like image of perspective gone all awry, with a fisherman in the foreground dipping his rod into a lake in the mid-distance, and a woman in the mid-ground leaning out of a window to hold a conversation with a man who is ascending a hill in the far distance. The very childish delight in poor perspective that Hogarth takes matches the earnest attempt by Kirby to put in layman's terms the mathematical science behind the discipline of perspective.

That book must have felt like treasure trove for an eager young artist. Within its covers Kirby had laid out the artists' fundamental tools and described the essential science of drawing and painting. What instruments were needed and how to use them; how the eye worked; the principles of reflection and refraction; the theory of shadows; aerial perspective; chiaroscuro; even scene painting. There were architectural and landscape engravings that illustrated the proper application of the techniques Kirby had just unlocked.

The Trimmer household could have done little but encourage further William Turner's compulsion to draw. Henry Trimmer related that Turner regularly defaced the town walls on his way to school, with chalk scribbles of birds. Meanwhile Turner was regularly reprimanded by his Brentford schoolmaster John White for gazing out of the window and sketching rather than listening to his lessons.[9] It seems highly likely that he was probably making childish watercolour studies too.

But early images of Brentford by him, if they still exist, are yet to be discovered. Instead, the earliest known watercolours by the juvenile Turner are from visits he paid to the seaside town of Margate, in Kent, at around the same time.

A love of travel would come to define Turner. He would become a man endlessly on the move, hungry for the experience of new places and the sense of freedom that travelling could provide. But in Turner's youth there was no need to go abroad for a sense of adventure. In the late eighteenth century even a trip to Margate was an exciting and sometimes precarious undertaking, enough to fire the imagination of an inner-city boy. For Turner, his early seaside trips were the beginning of a passion for the sea that would dominate his entire life and career.

In the last quarter of the eighteenth century the coastal town was fast developing as a resort for London's socially aspirant. Contemporary caricatures depict barbers and city aldermen enjoying Margate, renowned for its leisure pursuits and health benefits. One shows a barber who, on his return, unable to control his horse, has seen his curling tongs and powder boxes fall from his pockets and luggage, the implicit message being that disaster will happen if the lower orders try to ape their betters.[10] Meanwhile the caricatures of the Margate Hoy – the low-slung barge that ferried passengers between London and the Kentish town – reveal that the journey itself could be something of an ordeal, with crowded, windy decks dotted with buckets where sea-sick passengers could vomit at will while others held on to their hats and wigs.

But regardless of the discomfort associated with a sea trip that at best took ten hours and could take up to a day and two nights if the winds were less favourable, for those Londoners who had never seen the sea before, nor strayed far from the city, the trip to Margate was a revelation.

The writer Charles Lamb was a direct contemporary of Turner, born in the very same year not that far away from Covent Garden in the Inner Temple. He describes his very first seaside excursion on the Hoy aged fifteen. He talks of a sun-tanned captain, and his story-telling mate who was all too ready to spin sea tales to gullible and 'unseasoned Londoners'. He also mentions the child who had been put aboard in order to benefit from the sea bathing that the Margate infirmary offered as a cure for scrofula.

Sarah Trimmer's diary reveals that she was sending her children to Margate for health reasons right through the 1780s. It may well have been her motivation to move her ailing son John there in 1787 that cemented the Turners' inclination to move their son from Brentford to the seaside as well.

But it was perhaps less the health aspects of the town, and more the fun to be had there, that made the resort a favourite with Turner for the rest of his life. In fact it is a visitor to Margate some thirty years later who puts into words just how impressive Margate could be for those visiting it. A Mrs Pilkington recounted the delight of her son arriving and seeing that 'The tide was up, two packets had just reached the harbour, the parade and pier were crowded with pedestrians; streamers were floating from a number of sailing barges, whilst on the smooth surface of the sea . . . a variety of vessels were discerned as far as the eye could see.'[11]

Margate, though in the 1780s not quite yet the playground for 'the million' it would become in the age of the steamship, was nevertheless on its way. It had indoor seawater baths on the Parade; bathing machines on the beach; a pleasure garden at Dent-de-Lion; a couple of competing theatres and Assembly Rooms where there was card playing, dancing, music, and more. Not surprisingly these activities had salacious aspects and the town was also associated with illicit romantic liaisons. The boy brought up in the country's capital of prostitution, Covent Garden, would have been able to spot the Margate whores who were caricatured prowling the sea front looking for sailors and swells alike.

But in the evening the resort was often bathed in the most exquisite light. It is no small wonder that in later life Turner described the loveliest skies as being over the Isle of Thanet. Mrs Pilkington certainly noted that, sitting on a public bench on the cliffs over the town, she gazed on a horizon 'marked with flames of burnished gold'.[12]

While staying in Margate, Turner attended Thomas Coleman's School in Love Lane. Coleman was an evangelical Methodist who had been inspired by the preaching of John Wesley in London and had moved to Margate in 1767. Although Wesley (seemingly rather unkindly) disassociated himself from Coleman, the latter nevertheless used his schoolroom as a base for his preaching, as well as taking to Margate's streets in Evangelical fashion. But despite his bible-thumping, Coleman developed quite a nonconformist following in the town and, his preaching aside, his school was still going well into the next century. His Methodist emphasis on personal experience as the basis of knowledge chimes with the romantic sensibility that would come to define Turner's work.

What emerges about the adults and places embracing Turner in these formative years is how varied and complex, and seemingly contradictory, his world was. The seeds of those complexities and contradictions that would emerge in his own life and character are all sown here. Here was a boy exposed on the one hand to the evangelism and piety of Coleman, and at the same time the bawdy fun of Margate's entertainments. He saw the hard graft of his no-nonsense uncle and the enterprising spirit of Sarah Trimmer. He saw the products of the creative impulse, from the oil paintings on the Trimmer walls to the buildings that the Hardwicks were overseeing. And always beyond the busy urban life he lived, he glimpsed the adventure of the open sea and the open countryside.

And there were women. Margate was a romantic place. So perhaps it is not surprising that Turner found love there, though initially of the puppy variety. One of his friends at Coleman's school was Edward

White, who would go on to become a builder and surveyor in the town. And it was White's sister Elizabeth who caught Turner's eye. Turner's early biographers provided anecdotal accounts from his contemporaries about the significance that this young girl would have for Turner, and how ultimately what would develop over the years into a proper love affair informed his relationship with women for the rest of his life.

Though resorts like Margate were encouraging an emerging tourist industry, this was the era when the British were substantially a nation of armchair travellers. George III's own enormous collection of maps and views, recording different parts of his country and those governed by other monarchs, identifies him as the perfect embodiment of a taste for vistas that was shared by his subjects.

Initially in the eighteenth century, the walls and showcases of London's dozen or so printsellers had been dominated by imported engravings from the Continent, often featuring works by seventeenth-century French and Italian landscape painters such as Salvator Rosa and Claude Lorrain. But gradually over the course of the century there had been a move among the entrepreneurs of the publishing world to commission engravings of British views from British artists too.

This fascination and fashion for topography grew alongside an equally growing interest in antiquarianism. People were becoming enthusiastic about the 'stuff' of history that littered Britain. From ruined abbeys and standing stones down to old seals and coins, this debris from the past was being re-presented to the British as something of interest and value.

And so the appetite grew for topographical views capturing both the British landscape, and its human history. In their own ways these images served to oil the wheels of nationalism just as much as the heroic depictions of wounded generals and victorious sea battles also being reproduced at the time. For they served to remind the British what lay at stake should their homeland be invaded.

By the time of Turner's childhood the country had become swept up in print mania. If not hung on walls, prints would be bought bound, like early versions of the modern coffee-table book. Collecting prints was a hobby in its own right and drawing rooms also often displayed scrapbooks of engravings. For the majority of people the closest they got to sampling new destinations was by leafing through a book of prints.

The printsellers in Covent Garden used to glue their prints directly on to the glass of their shop windows, to present a gallery of images to the passer-by. That Turner stood in front of these bay windows to soak up the images of Britain's churches and monuments, abbeys and medieval manors, is evidenced in his juvenile views of Margate.

He painted St John's Church in the town. Venturing further afield, he made two watercolours of the ancient church at nearby Minster. One is observed from a distance, where a dusty road can be seen wending towards the village through countryside that Mrs Pilkington described as 'picturesque and beautiful'. The second is a fuller depiction of the church itself, known locally for being a 'most ancient and handsome structure'.[13]

To achieve these watercolours Turner made his own portable painting kit, a leather wallet that would fit nicely into a pocket and in which he kept watercolour tablets. Up until about 1780, painters who wanted to use watercolour had to prepare their own paints, grinding and mixing pigments and then moulding them with gum into portable lumps, often with unsatisfactory results. But by 1782 Messrs Reeves had begun to manufacture prepared watercolour 'cakes', and it was these shop-bought colours that enabled the young Turner to undertake his early views.

But the sea was a challenge too great for Turner at this stage, and his early images are also devoid of the human activity that would become a trademark of his work later on. Figures, though eventually introduced to his work with enthusiasm, were never Turner's strongest point as an artist, and one suspects that in his very earliest artistic attempts, the challenge of capturing his environment was sufficient without the added exertion of peopling it.

The pride that Turner's immediate circle took in his juvenilia, though, was considerable. On seeing his depictions of Margate, Turner's mother gave them to a friend living in Piccadilly, who had been born in Margate. Mary Hunt's husband was a card-maker, and supplied the King himself with brightly coloured playing cards.[14]

Turner's juvenilia was put on sale in his father's shop, displayed close to the door lest anyone miss it.The spirit of the eighteenth century was entrepreneurial. People made their money as best they could, and often had more than one business venture running concurrently and marketed simultaneously. Why could a barber not sell topographical views? He could. And did. For up to three shillings a go.

In addition to views he worked up from his own sketches, Turner copied published work by other living artists to sell in his father's shop. In 1780 the *Oxford Almanack* published a view of Folly Bridge and Bacon's Tower at Oxford, taken from a drawing by Michael Angelo Rooker, one of the greatest topographical artists of the day. Turner carefully copied the work and added a border around it to give it a finished, framed aspect, ready for sale.

The Turners' concern for their son's education continued alongside their pride in his artistic talents. As he entered his teens they recalled him from Margate and put him into one of the most esteemed schools in London, the Revd William Barrow's Academy at No. 8 Soho Square.[15] Despite a notorious murder at the school in the 1780s, when one boy had knifed another over a slice of cake, the Soho Academy was considered one of the best in London and reflects the Turners' aspirations for their son, as well as their own sense of social mobility. It had turned out a number of celebrated men, many with radical inclinations, with whom Turner's career and social connections would later resonate. The political agitator, bon viveur, and one-time Brentfordian John Horne Tooke had attended the school forty years before Turner. Edmund Burke, the philosopher and politician, sent his son Richard there briefly. The painter and caricaturist Thomas Rowlandson, who lived and worked near Turner in St Martin's Lane, was at the school a decade before him. And when Turner himself attended the school in the 1780s, he did so alongside fellow pupil James Boswell, the son of the biographer of the same name, the painter, caricaturist and actor John Bannister, and William Henry Ireland, who infamously wrote *Vortigern* in the guise of William Shakespeare.

In the 1770s the school was known as a multi-disciplinary academy that, under the master, the Revd Cuthbert Barwis, had built an impressive reputation for its theatrical productions, which fed the boards of Covent Garden with a new intake of eager actors each year.

By the time Turner enrolled, Barwis had died and the puritanical educationalist Revd Barrow was in place. He suffered the plays reluctantly, worrying that they cultivated a false sense of the ease of success among boys who might go on to be disappointed by the real challenges of the professional theatre. He viewed the value of drawing lessons with an equal degree of scepticism.

Drawing 'as a part of general education at school . . . may reasonably be doubted,' Barrow would write in 1804. 'To a private gentleman it is unquestionably a very elegant accomplishment . . . But by a student of any other description the very large proportion of his time required for its attainment must be deducted from more necessary and more valuable employment . . . Of the numbers, who engage in the study, few have talents and industry sufficient to attain excellence, and still fewer practice the art when the master has left them.'[16]

The Turners would have had to find £30 a year to send their son to the prestigious Academy, but then, as one contemporary notes, William Turner 'conducted a decent trade' at this time.[17] But despite the celebrity of the school, its limitations in the field of drawing must have been quickly felt by their son. The drawing master presiding during Turner's era was a Mr Palice, whose repertoire, confined to flower painting, would not be able to help Turner's ambitions to become a topographical artist.

Undeterred, Turner continued his own fieldwork. From about 1789 Oxfordshire, after Margate and Brentford, became his next subject of exploration. His uncle Joseph Marshall's wife, Anne, had a sister who lived at Sunningwell, not far from Oxford. She was the housekeeper to the local vicar there, Joseph Benet, and lived in the rectory with her master. The young Turner began to visit.

The views in and around Sunningwell that he made in 1789 make up a significant number of the few known early works by Turner. And by the time he came to make them, his work had undergone an enormous leap.[18]

A sketchbook exists from a trip to Sunningwell. It is among the earliest of a vast collection of sketches left either loose or in bound books that Turner kept in his studio until his dying day. In an era before photography and easy travel, these marks on paper, some just in pencil, others coloured with watercolour and ink, had a far greater and different significance to artists. An artist might never have the opportunity to return to a place. And as such the artist should be able to use the sketches to conjure the image of a place for any future request. Each sketch then became not only preparation for a speculative work, but a precious record of a place for potential future works too. Turner would return to his archive of sketches again and again, often using ones he had made years earlier. And looking at his sketchbooks across years, one gets a sense that he developed a language within them that was designed to evoke his memory of a place.

In what is known as his Oxford Sketchbook, Turner drew views of the church at Sunningwell. There are convincing studies of cows with their bony behinds and soft underbellies, and studies of branches and trees seen from the ground.

The book reveals a young man making daily excursions in search of subjects. A watercolour of Lacy's Court in Abingdon, which was only about a mile as the crow flies from Sunningwell. The great house at Nuneham Courtenay, which was also within walking distance from the Revd Benet's rectory. Elsewhere a watercolour of a distant view of Oxford from the Abingdon Road.[19]

However, the views that Turner selected to work up for sale in his father's shop were of Radley Hall, the grand house nearby. It may well have been the accommodating Revd Benet who secured his access to the grounds, since Benet was related to the Hall's occupants, the Stonhouses.

But it is not just the privileged access that allowed him to spend time in the grounds sketching from several points of view that accounts for a difference in Turner's work. Compared to his earlier works, his drawing already shows signs of significant change. Now Turner takes the hall and views it from an angle, so it offers depth. He frames it within trees no longer solid and clumpy, but tall, elegant and shapely, their branches curling across the paper. The leaves are a combination of russets, greens and browns, indicating perhaps an October or

November visit to the region, while hatching in ink indicates them rustling in a breeze. His foreground, far from being solid or flat, is now a dappled play of light and shade, and the near foreground is broken up with roots and plants. And there is a far distance too, beyond the house. Here the farthest reaches of the grounds are suggested by distant blue trees and woods. What is more, his sketchbook is marked up with squares which indicates that he now understands how to plan his sketch as well as use the grid to transfer it on to larger paper.

Stylistically the work is reminiscent of perhaps the greatest topographical artist of the day, Paul Sandby. There was a good drawing school in the Strand run by Henry Par, where students would have copied Sandby's work. And it may well have been here that Turner received more refined instruction than Mr Palice could offer at the Soho Academy.

Turner had evidently learned much from Sandby. That artist, for example, often had a dark tree in the left of his foreground, casting a dark shadow and throwing the eye towards a brighter mid-distance. And so now too does Turner's depiction of Radley Hall. These trees were not there in real life, and represent the lesson Turner had already learnt that part of the job of the artist is to improve on the actual view as it is reimagined on paper.

But it is by no means solely to Sandby that Turner owes the new confidence and sophistication in his style. Mary and William Turner must have felt that if their son was determined to be an artist, allowing him to get on with his ambition as he turned fourteen was better in the long run than keeping him at school. At this time Turner's name suddenly becomes associated with a whole range of artists and architects. However, his name appears nowhere in the official records of paid apprenticeship. This suggests a canniness at work in the Turner household: never pay unless one had to. William Turner must have brokered some form of deal for his talented son that avoided the scrutiny of the authorities and the tax that was applied to apprenticeship indentures. Despite the 'informal' association between Turner and a range of masters, nevertheless their influence can be seen in his work as it begins to transform.

There was the painter and publisher John Raphael Smith, who

moved his shop and studio to King Street, Covent Garden, just around the time that Turner's schooling in Margate was ending and he returned to Maiden Lane. Smith employed a number of talented boys ad hoc, alongside formal registered apprentices, to colour his engravings, perhaps when publication dates were looming and a large number of works were being printed. He was a generous and enthusiastic man who had a keen eye for up-coming talent, which he was more than happy to exploit. The gifted Thomas Girtin, the same age as Turner and the son of a brush-maker, was also working from time to time at Smith's on an unofficial basis. So it was probably here that Turner first encountered the young man who would become both his friend and his absolute rival. If there was anyone in London who would go on to match Turner's appetite for art and keep pace with his progress as its student, it was Girtin.[20]

Meanwhile the artist Edward Dayes, who would formally apprentice Girtin, had his studio in the very same road and it seems that Smith and Dayes horse-traded assistants. Both artists sometimes worked in miniature, and it may well have been under their tuition that Turner learnt how to use an enlarging glass to deliver astonishing detail.

Another influence was Thomas Hardwick, whose home Turner knew so well in Brentford. The architect took the boy into his studio in the late 1780s when he was working on a new church at Wanstead. His unofficial apprentice dutifully sketched it for him, probably in 1789. The orientation of the building is reminiscent of the same oblique view Turner chose for Radley Hall. And the marking up of the paper into squares is also the same. The finished watercolour that Turner did for Hardwick remained in the Hardwick family for many years, though it has now been lost. But one imagines it too may have enjoyed a framing with curly trees in a suitably Sandby-esque manner.

Hardwick's Brentford associations, along with those of his uncle, who kept his business there until 1797, provided Turner with plenty of opportunity to develop a relationship with the landscape of the rural Thames. Another early sketchbook reveals sketching trips to nearby Isleworth, Syon and Kingston.[21]

It was back in Brentford that Turner took on a fairly substantial paid commission in the last years of the 1780s, specifically colouring engravings. This was a type of paid work that Turner had begun with the engraver John Raphael Smith. It is not surprising that with experience that now boasted positions with Smith, possibly with Dayes, an unofficial apprenticeship with Hardwick and a number of finished watercolours in circulation, Turner's name was suggested to a Brentfordian distiller, called John Lees, who was after someone to colour plates in an important new book he had purchased: Henry Boswell's *Picturesque Views of the Antiquities of England and Wales*.

This impressive book, with some 400 engraved plates featuring views of ancient castles, forts, abbeys and towns, captured for posterity by 'artists of the first eminence', was published on 25 November 1786, and John Lees invested in an un-coloured edition. Professionally coloured plates vastly increased the cost of books such as these, but those keen to keep an eye on the pennies could always colour the plates themselves. It is unknown whether Lees's own handiwork is among that of at least three or four different artists who took on the task with varying degrees of success. The truly appalling work executed in thick daubs of lime green paint towards the end of the book (unless perhaps undertaken at a far later stage by a child descendant of Lees) suggests he may not have been a man with the powers to discriminate between good and poor work. But whether Lees truly appreciated the remarkable quality that young William Turner brought to his table as he coloured some seventy of the plates, nevertheless he paid two pennies for each one he completed.

There are no signatures on the Lees engravings, but by a process of elimination one can work out which are most probably by Turner. They are those encountered earliest in the book, are generally the finest, and have an intensity of workmanship, neatness of execution and delight in detail, along with a close observation of sky and reflection, that suggest a boy who is excited by the world around him, and having learned the basic principles of drawing, is now really turning his attention to colour and effect.

In these plates, it is the way Turner chooses to apply his coloured wash that suggests someone who is beginning to understand how landscape might also offer narrative possibilities, whether it is the time of day, or the changeability of the weather, or the story of the people or animals featured. For, extraordinarily, working with just the monochrome outlines of an engraving, Turner found ways of turning compositions into persuasive, delightful stories.

In the image of Donnington Castle in Berkshire, he has washed the left hand side of the frame with a delicate pink to suggest an evening light. And he has chosen a pale Cotswold gold for the castle, enriching the colour of the tower to suggest that it is glowing under the last rays of the sun.

In the colouring of Edgar's Tower in Worcester, the juvenile Turner has an overriding colour theme of blue and golden yellow. Whereas there are plenty of other plates in the edition where fellow colourists have stuck to just two colours, in this plate the colourist bothers to open up his paintbox for just one pin-prick of a third colour. But in using red just once in the coat of the rider in the foreground he transforms the image and reveals something of the personality of an artist who instinctively now understands how such a small addition can enliven the effect of a work overall. This sparing but transformative use of red as an accent within a wider composition to give the overall picture a piquancy and liveliness would be employed by Turner throughout his career.

His attention to detail highlights Turner's ravenous interest in the world about him. In colouring the plate of Carisbrooke Castle in the Isle of Wight, he has given the cow black patches. A touch that not only displays technical confidence (some of the other colourists can barely keep their brushwork within the lines, let alone break up tiny images to deliver the detail of a piebald hide), but also suggests a boy who had observed the world in all its variety. One senses Turner's hand in similar vein in the depiction of Skipton Castle, where the natural colour of the paper has been used to give a horse a white face.

It is these touches in this otherwise somewhat laborious work that give a clue into the mind of the young budding painter. Compared with the work of the other colourists available in Brentford, whose work in the book is at worst very careless, and at best very careful but formulaic, Turner's already stands out as replete with invention and delight in the moving, shimmering, living world about him.[22]

The content of this book was formative in other ways. For a boy who had been given one view to copy and then another, now he had a stack of images to systematically work through in bulk. As such the commission proposed a series of locations and established a range of subjects to which Turner would return, again and again, until the end of his life. This book laid out the whole of Britain before a boy who had so far barely strayed from London. In effect, it became a blueprint for Turner's future career, and offered a depiction of views that he would one day make his own. His future repertoire is all there: his as yet un-begun oeuvre, from Carisbrooke, Donnington and Dunstanburgh Castles, through Edgar's Tower in Worcester, to Rochester and Shrewsbury and Warkworth. The book, pedestrian by the standards that Turner would one day set, nevertheless already captures a sense that the British landscape can contain its own narrative of historic achievement.

In 1855, after Turner's own historic achievement had been recognized, and he had long made those images of Britain his own, Thomas Carlyle was attempting to raise money to buy an annuity for two aged spinster sisters, the Miss Lowes. The god-daughters of Samuel Johnson, and distant relatives of Carlyle himself, the women were the surviving offspring of a rather unsuccessful painter called Mauritius Lowe who, in the 1780s, had lived in abject poverty in Hedge Lane, Covent Garden. As part of his fundraising push Carlyle revealed, first in letters to friends and finally in a missive to *The Times*, his new discovery that Mauritius Lowe was 'the benevolent Painter by whom Turner, at that time a barber's boy, was first recognised, befriended, and saved to Art'.[23]

The claimed association with Turner may have been a convenient ploy by the couple to tug further at Carlyle's and, by his ability to relay it, the nation's heartstrings. But the tale is worth repeating because, as the 1780s drew to a close, there is a sense that there were quite a few artists, engravers and architects working in Covent Garden who might have been able to make similar claims to Lowe. In addition to those mentioned above, the names of the architects Joseph Bonomi, James Wyatt and William Porden are also associated with the teenage Turner.

But these rival claims over Turner's juvenile years nevertheless offer us insight. They speak of the drive in a boy keen to learn from everyone who would have him, rapidly and avidly absorbing the techniques that would improve his work. They speak of an instinctive and tireless networker, massively self-motivated, undeterrable in his determination.

The spiteful but ultimately tragic Edward Dayes said as much himself. Dayes, like a fair few of his contemporaries trying to make their way in an art world full of challenge and disappointment, committed suicide, but not before making an account of some of his contemporaries. Of Turner, Dayes pointed out that 'he is indebted principally to his own exertions . . . He may be considered as a striking instance of how much may be gained by industry . . . even without the assistance of a master. The way he acquired his professional powers was by borrowing, where he could, a drawing or picture to copy from, or by making a sketch of any one in the Exhibition in the morning, and finishing it at home.'[24]

At the time he passed through their studios and workshops sketching this, colouring that, and having the odd quick lesson, Turner benefited from his association with these architects, engravers and artists. In later years the associations were sought in reverse, and it would be they who wanted the accolade of having nurtured the young genius, no matter how brief the encounter.

For some this brief relationship was genuinely cherished. That the Hardwicks kept their Turners with pride is known by the fact that they lent them long after Turner's death as part of a celebratory exhibition. Lees's colouring book was passed down his family with great care until it was given to the Chiswick Library. The Trimmer family too cherished watercolours and sketches that Turner gave them in a series of affectionate gestures over the years. Even John Raphael Smith eventually received something to commemorate his early liaison with William Turner. Years after the small bright-eyed boy sat colouring his engravings in his King Street workshop, John

Raphael Smith painted a portrait of Walter Fawkes of Farnley Hall in Yorkshire. He depicted Fawkes, who had become a close friend of Turner and an ardent collector of his work, with a portfolio of Turner watercolours lying close by. After the sitting Fawkes gave Smith one of these watercolours, which the latter treasured for what was left of his life.[25]

4.   A bee of the same hive

London had a spring in its step in the early months of 1789. The news of political disarray over the Channel in France was welcomed in the press. Finally, the papers declared, a despotic and dissolute neighbour was putting its house in order. Louis XVI was calling the Estates General to account. He was finally trying to sort out the aristocracy, who rode rough-shod over the rest of the populace.

But at root, the British reaction to France's troubles was driven by a mixture of smugness and relief. As France's king grappled with rioting, looting and striking in response to a tax-exempt aristocracy, and appalling economic strife, the British congratulated themselves that their own system of government seemed by comparison a model of common sense, liberality and fiscal shrewdness. Moreover, at a time when the French king seemed to be sinking into a mire of troubles, the British were sighing with relief that their monarch seemed to be emerging from his own plight.

In February news had begun to filter from Kew Palace that King George III, who had been incarcerated there after suffering a sudden and totally incapacitating physical and mental breakdown the previous November, was on the mend. Daily, *The Times*'s reports of the King's health became more positive, until by March it was clear that the monarch was sufficiently restored that various poems and songs to his regained health could be published. By April there were celebratory illuminations, a grand gala at Windsor in honour of the King's recovery, and it was announced that he would attend the opening of the Royal Academy of Arts' annual exhibition.

When the Royal Family did arrive to view the paintings at the RA, the press noticed that the Queen was particularly impressed with Benjamin West's depiction of King Lear.[1] Given that the version of that play performed in the eighteenth century was Nahum Tate's, featuring a happy ending, this makes some sense of the otherwise unfortunate parallels between Lear and George, and what might have been considered a considerable faux pas by the Academy.

But if the Academy got away with the potential embarrassment of West's Lear, there was plenty more for the newspapers to complain about with regard to that particular institution. There was a prevailing line in the press that the Royal Academy, founded amid such hope and ambition more than twenty years earlier, had failed. The institution was portrayed as a place of backbiting political intrigue, whose Academicians still fell short of delivering art that could match that of their continental rivals.

True to form, on 28 April 1789 *The Times* informed its readers that 'The Rooms at Somerset House opened yesterday, and we must say that this year has not much increased the fame of painting. The walls are covered, it is true, but merit is scarcely to be found.'

The Academy had its apologists. Around the time of the annual exhibition they would circulate their defence of British art, often in the form of a non-official annotated catalogue that was hurriedly put to press as soon as a sight of the year's offering was possible.

In April 1788 one such commentary, *The Bee: a Critique on Paintings at Somerset House,* was doing its best to make sure 'every painter become a BEE of the same hive, working to the same great end – the advancement and perfection of his Art'.[2] With an anonymous Humphry Repton wielding the small furry insect's pen, he declared, 'It is a very bad exhibition.' But then he added, 'This has been a general complaint for some years past; and now, tired of being mere echoes in connoisseurship, some have ventured to declare that "the exhibition this year would be very bad" many days before the pictures were even sent to the Academy.'

Repton's argument is, broadly, that the so-called connoisseurs dominating the discussion of art couldn't tell a good picture if they wanted to. Their judgement was poor and biased towards continental stereotypes. *The Bee* did its best to offer the general public a guide on how to judge a picture for itself, using five criteria: Composition, Drawing, Colouring, Expression and Finishing.

Repton explained that composition was essentially an arrangement of forms, and drawing the manner in which objects are 'imitated with correctness and elegance', and he goes on to explain that colouring is the manner in which the artist gives 'each colour the proper shade and hue which its situation in the piece requires' and that when combined with good composition and drawing 'gives the highest mechanic finish to a picture'. For Repton, 'expression' was quite specifically 'the power of painting which conveys the ideas of characters and passions of the person represented . . . [and which] serves to equally mark the peculiar qualities and properties of every object. By expression in draperies we distinguish silk, linen, cloth . . . in landscapes land from water.' On the matter of finish he is liberal, and lays into his peers. 'In this the judgement of pretended connoisseurs often betrays their ignorance; for when the effect is fully produced the picture is always finished: and it is of little consequence whether the colours be laid on as with a trowel, or smoothed over with the polish of enamel.'

This set of guidelines offers a fascinating insight into just what eighteenth-century expectations about art were. The artist is still seen as essentially there to portray an exterior world. And even if there is the allowance for invention and ingenuity that might arrange and rearrange this world imaginatively for the sake of an elegant and pleasing composition, the notions of inner psychological worlds and emotional expression are not seen as part of the visual artist's repertoire. This remains the domain of the poet. Clearly Repton believed that British artists were fulfilling these expectations of their métier, if only the connoisseurs could put aside their own prejudices and look at the work of their own countrymen objectively.

Against this unhappy background the young J. M. W. Turner held his course, like one of Repton's bees. Despite the brickbats levelled against it, the RA remained the only properly endorsed school for someone who wanted to pursue a career as an artist, and the achievement of having 'RA' after one's name was still a badge that would attract commercial opportunity and open doors. Fortunately for Turner, in the autumn of 1789 he found a sponsor prepared to forward his name to the institution for consideration.

Many vicars seem to have helped Turner's career. If the Revd Benet in Sunningwell had in his small way sponsored his sketching trips to Oxford in the form of board and bed, the next in line was the Revd Robert Nixon from Foots Cray in Kent.

William Turner senior's likeability must have been one of his biggest commercial assets. Revd Nixon was a customer, prepared to forgo his local hairdresser in favour of a trip to London to have his hair cut by William Turner. But Nixon had other reasons to visit London. His brothers were there. James Nixon was a leading miniaturist. His other brother, John Colley Nixon, was a larger-than-life city merchant and bon viveur whose talent stretched not only to amateur theatricals, but to caricature as well as genre and landscape painting.

The artistic talents running in the Nixon family extended to the Reverend too. He was an amateur painter who would eventually become an honorary exhibitor at the RA annual show in the 1790s, but in 1789 his brothers were already showing there.

It is hardly surprising that as the passionate and well-connected art enthusiast Nixon settled down for his regular haircut and saw the level of talent displayed in the topographical views by his barber's son, he offered to help the boy. He introduced Turner and his work to John Francis Rigaud RA.

Corpulent and balding, Rigaud's career as a painter of decorative ceilings and panels, portraits and history subjects was in the ascendant in the late 1780s. And though he was a man whose temper would eventually lose him friends within the Royal Academy, he was warm and generous towards those wishing to try for it. Perhaps it was the artistic talents of two of his own children, Stephen and Elizabeth, who were much the same age as Turner,[3] that made him sensitive to the talents of other youngsters less well placed to secure admission to the Royal Academy Schools.[4]

Rigaud's influence was swift and pertinent. On 11 December 1789 the Keeper of the Academy presented six drawings by prospective students made from plaster casts of classical statuary. All six were approved by the President, Sir Joshua Reynolds, for entry into the Academy's first school, the Plaister Academy, where students drew from casts of antiques and Renaissance sculptors. William Turner was one of the successful candidates.

At fourteen Turner was, like his parents, well below average height. He had inherited his father's beaky nose, and his mother's 'slight fell in the nether lip'. His eyes were blue like his mother's, but darker and intense. He also looked decidedly young for his age. He walked through the doors of Somerset House at the close of 1789, into William Chambers's entrance hall, not just any boy, but one with an ivory ticket in his pocket. These round tokens had the name of the student engraved on one side, and the school to which they were admitted on the other, and allowed the young men to pass freely through the building.

The square lobby contained framed casts of famous statues. A screen of fluted Doric columns announced a winding staircase that floated to the state rooms above. The library was on the first floor, next to which was the Academy of the Antique, or the Plaister Academy, comprising two spacious rooms stacked with plaster casts. Here students worked on figure drawing, either sketching with a board on their laps, or at a low easel. For the first time Turner was a member of an institution that conveyed prestige and privilege. In an instant he had accessed a massive degree of social leverage.

Not that such leverage was reflected in the behaviour of members of the Schools. Though a contemporary depiction of the Plaister Academy by Edward Burney reveals the students sitting in front of casts of ancient statuary, keen and hard at work, there is plenty of evidence that, left to their own devices, these 'classes' could descend into chaos. The pieces of bread the boys used to rub out their work were handy missiles and the Academy's bread bills were far too high as a result.

The students' antics could spill beyond the study rooms too. The artist Benjamin Robert Haydon, who attended a little later than Turner, remembered the schoolboy pranks enjoyed by young men who would later emerge as respectable painters.

'I remember . . . Lascelles Hoppner, Jackson, Wilkie and myself were all making a great row in the hall of the Academy. I was standing with my back to the Academy stairs fighting them with my umbrella. Of a sudden they ran away. I turned round and saw Fuzeli's fiery face behind me. Out I scampered.'[5] The bad behaviour went far beyond the Academy walls. When Stephen Rigaud joined the establishment three years after Turner, his father warned him against some of his colleagues, advising, 'I don't wish you to make the acquaintance with the students at the Academy, and much less lose your time in going to their lodgings, yet amongst the number, there may be found some young men, of promising abilities, and who, having their parents in London, are not entirely let loose to their own will and pleasure . . .'[6]

In taking up his seat on a wooden box before one of the Academy's plaster casts and in placing his drawing board on his knee, Turner was beginning a journey that could often see boys training for up to seven years at the Academy, first working in the Antique or Plaister Academy for a good two to three years, until they graduated to the Life Academy where they could sketch from nude models.

We know the names of some of his companions in the Plaister Academy since the boys signed a register. Alongside Turner's own signature in thick black ink were 'Warburton, Peter Ogier, Alex Scott, Wallis, Thos Hargreaves, Robinson and William Dixon'.[7] But Turner was evidently the class star. Of the year of 1789 only Thomas Hargreaves and William Dixon would go on to have traceable careers as painters, the former becoming a miniaturist and the latter a maritime painter. However, no one in the class had the bravura and audacity to get a watercolour selected for the forthcoming RA exhibition of April 1790. Except for Turner, that is.

No. 644 in the catalogue of the Royal Academy's Exhibition for 1790 was *The Archbishop's Palace, Lambeth* by J. W. Turner.[8] The Exhibition opened on 29 April. Turner had just turned fifteen, and had served only a few months as a student at the RA Schools. His achievement in having a work selected for public exhibition was astonishing. He was the youngest exhibitor since the foundation of the institution, an accolade that would not have been lost on Turner and his growing circle of associates.

The view of the Archbishop's Palace is a different kind of watercolour from the views of stately homes and places of interest that Turner had been capturing during his country walks. This was an urban scene, a wide vista, with an open foreground. And it was a view that reflected his latest influence. That of the one-legged painter Thomas Malton.

Malton, who had had his limb amputated in childhood, and consequently wore a wooden one, was a celebrated topographical artist and stalwart of Academy shows. He had a steady and secure professional reputation, particularly for urban views.

Though the young Turner would have been delighted to have qualified for a place at the Royal Academy Schools, he must have been equally aware that the Academy's focus on figure drawing would not help his skills progress as a topographical artist.

Malton fitted the bill. It may have been Turner's sponsor Francis Rigaud who encouraged Malton to take Turner as his student, since Rigaud sent his own son Stephen to Malton 'for a course of instruction in that Science [perspective] so essential for an Artist to be thoroughly acquainted with'.[9] In later life Turner would gratefully credit Malton as his first master.

Like Joshua Kirby, Malton's father had also written a book on perspective and he had constructed a number of perspectival models for teaching purposes. These teaching aids were brought to life under the guidance of the son in the evening classes he offered in Conduit Street from 1789. Malton provided Turner with the thorough grounding he needed to give his work convincing dimensionality. But Malton did more than just show him how to properly convey space and form, he taught him his own tricks of the trade.

Malton was producing a series of views of London that would ultimately form his publications *A Picturesque Tour through the Cities of London and Westminster*, and he took Turner out on to London's streets to draw alongside him.[10] Malton's views are formulaic in composition. He understood what worked for a viewer and how best to capture London's streets and edifices. In the majority of the London views he fills his foreground with the width of a street which then diminishes quickly away from the eye, favouring one side of the street in a strong diagonal. The triangular precinct in fore- and midground of the paper is now a space that, while at once emphasizing the solidity and drama of the buildings as they recede from the eye, serves as a playground for Londoners. Malton depicts them going about their business, more sparsely than in reality perhaps, but nevertheless adding a sense of both scale and narrative to the work.

Malton's views of Westminster were being quickly bought by the indefatigable collector John Charles Crowle. Another subscriber to the craze for topography, Crowle's personal project was to create an 'extra illustrated' version of views of London otherwise published as *Pennant's London*. Pennant's survey of London was massively expanded by the enthusiastic Crowle, who added his own commentary on engravings and watercolours bought from the leading topographical artists of the day, until he had created something akin to a massive, high-end, scrapbook. Today Crowle's *Pennant* is housed in the British Museum. In the section on Westminster Abbey is a watercolour attributed, in Crowle's original index, to the young Turner. [11]

It is an interior of Westminster Abbey; the view looking up the nave features a vaulted ceiling high above, and large arches to the right in that strong diagonal that Malton so favoured. And, like Malton, Turner has created a group of figures in the foreground, and a trickle of other figures beyond.

But though Turner's work at this period shows its debt to Malton, there is something that differentiates the pupil from the master, something that becomes evident in Turner's exhibited *The Archbishop's Palace, Lambeth*. In fact the generous and encouraging Thomas Hardwick had commissioned an earlier version of this view from Turner. Just as in the version he executed for Hardwick, his exhibited one retained an unconventional aspect of the Palace, seen from the landward side, up Church Street, and consequently featuring the Lambeth public house as well as the ancient Palace. Whether through naivety or consciously provocative, Turner's view, in contrast to Malton's tendency to focus on the universally grand, provides a comment about time, as well as about high life and low life. Such juxtapositions would become common in Turner's work across the next few years, perhaps as the great age of his own country, and the vast difference in the fortunes of its people, really began to dawn on him. But already in this early work, his eye is all-encompassing. He sees a place not just as it is in the here and now, but he senses and seeks out its history. He sees a vast and intricate world with all its social complexities. And already he is trying to convey this vast vision.

Years later, when Hardwick's son reminded him of the view, Turner recalled the most prosaic details of the real place: 'Ha! Yes,' he said, 'up against that inn there was a board stuck up, on which was written "Be sober, Be Vigilant"; and close by were the parish stocks.'[12] This is typical of a man for whom human narrative would also become of paramount importance. Already in his *Archbishop's Palace* Turner's handling of London's residents hints at a fascination with story-telling that goes beyond that of the more experienced Malton. Compared to the figures in Malton's views of London, often kept small to accentuate the scale of the buildings, Turner's Londoners are larger, and give the scene a more human scale. A couple stroll towards the viewer. The fashionable gentleman with his French-style beaver hat and striped waistcoat is busy chatting to the elegant woman on his arm. In a bold move, Turner has this woman gaze straight out, her eyes directed at the viewer, engaging him instantly in the human story unfurling before him. This bold interaction gives the picture vivacity. The humanity, communicated by that gaze, extends to the other little scenes of everyday life that Turner invests in, from the couple in the mid-ground talking to one another through a shop window and the boatmen attending their vessels on the Thames in the distance. It was a brave beginning. But only a hint at what was to come.

Turner's astonishing ambition can be measured by what he shows over the next five years at each of the RA's annual exhibitions. In 1791 he shows two watercolours. A view of the ruined King John's Palace at Eltham, and a depiction of Swakeleys, near Uxbridge, a grand seventeenth-century manor house that was at the time inhabited by another Reverend, Thomas Clarke. Both locations would have been walkable from central London by Georgian standards and are today part of what is considered Greater London.

From now on the number of Turner's exhibited works increased rapidly, and his subject matter reflects a boy travelling further and further from home. In 1792 another two watercolours are exhibited.

This time one subject is Malmesbury Abbey in Wiltshire, the other a view of the Pantheon in London's Oxford Street. In 1793 he increases his number of exhibited works to three, two of which are views of the River Avon. By 1794 he is managing to get five selected, and by now he has been to south Wales and the West Midlands. In 1795 he shows eight, and his repertoire extends from Lincolnshire and Shropshire to Cambridge and Monmouthshire. And by 1796, when he is just turning twenty-one, he shows not only his first oil painting, but a further ten watercolours showing an array of new views of the great cathedrals and church architecture across the Midlands, Wales, Cambridgeshire and the West Country. In that year only two other painters managed to exceed this quantity of work in the RA's most important annual event. Henry de Cort RA – an academician of both Paris's and Antwerp's Academies – showed twelve works, while Turner's master, Thomas Malton, showed thirteen.

This extraordinary achievement by the teenage Turner was made at no little cost. During the summer months, when the Schools were typically on holiday, Turner did what he could to gather more subject matter and expand his repertoire. He understood that at the end of the day, a work on show in the RA's summer exhibition was worth a hundred sketches in a student sketchbook. The boy may have been elevated from his Covent Garden roots, but the Garden never left the boy. Turner understood the concept of a market. And he knew that to survive in one, one had to have something to sell. And to thrive in one, one's goods had to be more desirable than those of the competition.

Though ambition and determination was written through Turner, he did not *look* like a conquering man. He did not even look like a man. In 1791, aged sixteen, as his own self-portrait shows, he was still a very slight boy: small, unspectacular. Puberty hit him late, and he was dismayed at his own immature appearance.

As such Turner, shy, and lacking in physical confidence, kept to himself. He had to be cajoled to join in, being by temperament 'singular and very silent' according to Ann Dart.[13] She had got to know Turner when he stayed with her relatives, the Narraways, in Bristol. He was there several times across the 1780s and 1790s. 'He was in the habit of spending his vacations at the house of my uncle for several years previously to 1791,' Ann Dart explained.[14] His trip there in the summer of 1791 is well documented.

The Narraways were jovial and noisy. They sang songs and entertained one another with homespun plays in the evening. When they saw the talent of their young guest they asked Turner to entertain them by sketching the family, and to make his own self-portrait too. Turner obliged with the latter request only under duress. When pushed he confessed his fear that 'People will say such a little fellow as this can never draw.'[15] And yet he faithfully captured his own prepubescent features, a small chap with shoulder-length hair, gazing out at those who care to study him.

John Narraway and William Turner senior were exceptionally fond of one another. The Narraways, like the Turners, hailed from the West Country. John had been born in Cornwall at Kilkhampton but had moved to Devon, where he and William had almost certainly been childhood friends. But while Turner had gone to London to deal with hair *dressing*, John Narraway had settled in Bristol to deal in hair *removal*. He was a fellmonger, someone who specialized in removing and grading wool from fleeces, as well as stripping unwanted hair and hooves from other animal skins.

The Narraways, like the Marshalls and Trimmers, Hardwicks, Nixons and Benets, became one of the families that the quiet, determined Turner would regularly visit and rely upon over the next years, as he began to weave his way around the country in search of views.

The mail coach had been running between Bristol and London since 1784 at a cost of twenty-eight shillings for those wishing to ride on it. This cost was justified by the provision of an armed security guard who, with his cutlass, blunderbuss and pair of pistols, offered genuine protection against the very real threat of highwaymen. And it flew at a speed unmatched by any other form of transport. Leaving in the evening from the Swan with Two Necks in Lad Lane, Cheapside, or from the Gloucester Coffee House in Piccadilly, it offered a journey to Bristol in around sixteen hours, not least because the guard blew a horn which alerted the gatekeeper to open the toll gates and let the mail fly through. Nevertheless this travel cost was a substantial outlay. And so it is no wonder that Turner made use of all the personal connections he and his family had. By putting a roof over his head and providing his meals they were effectively subsidizing his career.

The Narraways could easily accommodate the small Londoner. Their business was extensive and the house was already full of servants and apprentices. One more mouth to feed was not going to make much difference. But at least Turner didn't turn up empty-handed at the Narraways' door in September 1791. He brought a gift with him, his view of the Archbishop's Palace that he had shown at the RA a year earlier. Perhaps the present was at his father's insistence, a payment in kind for his bed and board.

In the early 1790s Bristol and its environs offered good subjects for Turner's expanding repertoire. This city, that had grown rich on Britain's slave trade, was lively and buzzing. Grand houses built on transatlantic business adorned the surrounding countryside and there were plenty of potential clients, whose vanity might well extend to a commission of a view of their home. This would be a step up from making speculative views to sell in the barber-shop window.

Turner made good use of his time with the Narraways. Dart remembered that: 'he would talk of nothing but his drawings and of the places to which he should go for sketching . . . he seemed . . . desirous of nothing but improvement in his art . . . Sometimes [he would] go out sketching before breakfast . . . and sometimes before and after dinner . . . he was not particular about the time of returning to his meals.'[16]

The sketchbooks that remain from this time confirm Dart's description of the Narraways' lodger. Turner was determined to collect a series of composed views good enough for exhibition and for sale, and was prepared to take no small risk in getting what he wanted.

Some of his excursions were close to home. He drew the Hot Wells, where warm springs bubbled up close to the mouth of the Avon, and where in the eighteenth century a fashionable pump room had been built for people to benefit from the spa water. He walked the Avon gorge and earned the title 'Prince of the Rocks' from the Narraways, who observed him to be 'so fond of sitting among the rocks overhanging the river'.[17] And he explored the shores of the Severn Estuary, finding exquisite viewpoints.

He even ventured out into the estuary at low tide, to Chapel Rocks near Beachley. This tiny island has a ruin of a thirteenth-century chapel once dedicated to St Tecla, though it is frequently cut off by the dangerous tidal waters swirling in from the Atlantic. Turner clearly felt the venture worth the risk, though he noted the seaweed-covered rocks in the foreground of his sketch of the island, as if a reminder that before too long his route home would become submerged again.

Turner sketched the grand houses of the region with their proprietors in mind. He visited Stoke House at Bristol, built by the slave-trading Cann family and inhabited by their descendants the Cann Lippincotts. He captured Blaise Castle, another mansion built on the slave-trading activities of the merchant Thomas Farr, though when Turner came to sketch it, the property was in the hands of an abolitionist banker, John Scandrett Harford. And he drew Cote House, the residence of a merchant seaman, a Captain Fowler.

He took longer excursions in search of abbeys: to Bath, and even to Malmesbury, some thirty miles north, where he must have stayed for a day or two given the number of sketches made in and around the ruins there. In one sketch he takes time to write down a note of the trees he can see near the ruins: ash, willow and apple.

When he returned to the Narraways, he worked up these sketches into finished watercolours. Some were for sale back home, others were to order. Aside from the Bristol homeowners he had persuaded to commission him, the Revd Nixon bought a view of Hot Wells. Turner also left the Narraways with a fairly large number of his finished watercolours, along with 'the portrait, & sketch book & other drawings . . . as slight remembrances'.[18]

In the watercolours he makes of Bristol and its environs, Turner provides narratives and surprises that give his work an exceptional vivacity. He frames his main point of interest in different ways, using trees around the mansions, or if it is a river scene, perhaps the mast of a boat to force the eye into the centre of his drawing. Now his foregrounds are also presented as micro-worlds, where a story is unfolding. Where boats were upturned and out of use in his sketches, in his finished piece he rights them and has them rocking on the water as boatmen struggle to pull them ashore. The empty road to Westbury-on-Trym from which he sketched the fashionable Cote House over a shut gate is transformed in the finished version to reveal an excursion. The gate is in the process of being opened to let a houndsman and his dogs through, a red-coated huntsman — presumably Captain Fowler himself — on horseback behind them. And in his worked-up version of Stoke House, Turner, with some of the warmth and humour that is so often evident in his work, places himself in the mid-ground, his sketch pad on his lap, John Narraway's son of the same name at his side, with Mr Henry Lippincott himself standing over him.

Sometimes he experiments with depth, and double frames. One view of Malmesbury Abbey has the subject of the picture in the far distance, framed between trees and the roof of a picturesque cottage. The cottage itself is framed by trees in the foreground.

But in all instances Turner uses devices that prevent his viewer from moving on. Just when the main subject has been absorbed, a detail elsewhere catches the eye and draws one in again. He grips his audience.

There is a set of sketches Turner made of the Avon valley that has an almost electric vibrancy compared to the others. He climbed the steep sides of the valley at Clifton to a gothic villa known as Cook's Folly, from where there are views of the navigable river as it stretches out towards the sea. Again it was a long and arduous walk. But one that paid dividends. Walking through the parkland at the top of the valley, through oak trees that another visitor twenty years later described as 'an avenue of Primeval oaks planted far enough from each other to stretch out their giant arms on every side to their full extent before they touch',[19] Turner found a view that conveys a sense of grandeur and wonderment beyond anything expressed in his depiction of manor houses and abbeys. The picture is a symphony of lushness, devoid of people. The rich green oak trees frame the winding river below, which in turn stretches out to a hazy blue distance. Far below, ships under sail are making their way out to sea like tiny toy boats.[20]

In these watercolours one senses that Turner is seeing the British countryside for the wonder it is. These are the first sketches he makes where landscape and nothing more is enough to convey a sense of pride and patriotism. The oak trees, which one can practically hear rustling, betray an intense love for nature. A love that, according to Ann Dart, the Narraways and Turners spoke of often. 'The father said he was passionate fond of trees . . . my cousin said that Turner in all his drawings wd always introduce trees.'[21]

But beyond a personal passion, the trees over the Avon hint at a deep English heritage, just as the tiny ships in the distance convey the might of the navy that continued to protect a green and pleasant land, and the mercantile power of a seafaring nation.

Here was a young man discovering the power of Britain at a most crucial time. For the magical appeal that the Continent had held for Britons was vanishing. Paris, once the most fashionable city in Europe and the gateway to a Grand Tour that would take in the wonders of the classical world, was becoming a place of terror and perplexing turmoil where foreigners would travel at their peril. By September 1791, as a boyish Turner sat sketching a serene vista of the River Avon, Britain found itself gazing in astonishment at its near neighbour. In the very year that Turner had gained entry to the R A Schools, his contemporaries across the Channel had found the most disturbing and gruesome subject matter available to them. The painter Anne-Louis Girodet had rushed into the streets twice in July to record the horrors. First to capture the severed head of Bernard de Launay, the governor of the Bastille, thrust on to a pitchfork, on the day the prison was stormed. Later in the same month the Finance Minister Joseph-François Foulon de Doué suffered a similar fate, the mob stuffing hay into the mouth before skewering the head on a pike. His son-in-law, an intendant of Paris, Louis-Bénigne-François Berthier de Sauvigny, not only saw this atrocity as he made his way through Paris in a carriage, but soon after was lynched himself in the Place de Grève, strung up at a lamppost before having his torso cut open, his face sliced off, his heart removed and spiked, and his head severed and mounted above the mob.

No one living in London or the south of England could have been immune to the troubles in France. Regardless of the tales being recounted in newspapers, the docks at Southampton and the streets of London were filling up with French émigrés. The French nobility who had lost everything were turning up as music teachers and journalists, translators and theatrical prompters, their wives forced to take up embroidery, flower painting and portraiture, no longer as a diversion but as a means of survival.

Within two years Britain would become embroiled in a new war with France. Travel to that country would soon be made illegal. Channel crossings would cease completely. The French institutions that the British upper classes had patronized for years shut their doors. British gents could no longer learn their horsemanship and military skills at the Academy in Angers, as the future Duke of Wellington had done in the 1780s. The daughters of generals and dukes could no longer be 'finished' at Pentemont Abbey. And though technically northern Germany, Italy and beyond were still available for touring, they involved lengthy and perilous voyages. Italy, without the gateway of France, would become reachable only via a massively circumventing land trip, or by sea via the Atlantic, and Lisbon or Gibraltar, into the Mediterranean, where North African corsairs and privateers lay in wait for English hostages.

With the Continent so unattainable, it was inevitable that tourism would refocus. British tourists, inspired by views they had seen captured by pioneering, intrepid artists, began to turn their attention to their own land. This would do nothing but fuel further the national appetite for topographical views.

On the back of one of his watercolours of the Avon, there is evidence that Turner considered getting his views engraved.[22] He had had enough exposure to his chosen profession to know that making a watercolour was one thing, but both exposure and money lay in the successful publication of engravings of the original for a wider public. Turner the business entrepreneur was nascent.

This small commercial gesture hints at the macro-transformations occurring in British society. Where art had once been in the almost exclusive control of the connoisseur aristocrat who imported or commissioned work, ventures such as this imagined series of views of the

Avon by the teenage Turner marked a moment when the artist began to challenge a system of specific, individual patronage. Now there was the beginning of public patronage, or, more bluntly, the power of the consumer.

Whether it was time or money that ran out, or just an ambition too far for a young man, Turner's published views of the Avon did not happen. Nevertheless, his field trips around Bristol provided material for show pieces for the next two years. He showed a watercolour of Malmesbury Abbey in 1792 at the RA, and views of the Avon and Hot Wells the following year.

As the enterprising Turner expanded his repertoire of topographical and urban views in the early 1790s, he also grasped the Georgian appetite for depictions of topical events. On 14 January 1792 an event occurred that gripped the public's imagination, and Turner determined to exploit it. In the small hours of that morning a cry of 'Fire!' went up in Oxford Street and the watchmen began frantically whirling their wooden rattles to alert the slumbering city to an imminent crisis. Within minutes the wooden fire engines were in attendance, bolting their leather hoses into the branch pipes and attacking the fire with gusto. The Pantheon theatre was on fire.

From Covent Garden you would have smelt the cinders and perhaps have even seen the flames licking the sky as the theatre went up; one contemporary account claimed that such was the intensity and scale of the blaze, the flames were visible from Salisbury Plain.

Henry Angelo, a fencing master, lived just behind the Pantheon on Great Marlborough Street, and watched the fire all night, along with his neighbours Mr and Mrs Siddons, still 'en chemise'. He wrote about the 'vast column of fire' which 'raged with such irresistible violence, that the firemen . . . thought it prudent to retire . . . No language can describe the awful sublimity of the scene.'[23]

Sublimity was a popular concept. It was the notion that certain aspects of the natural world might prompt a pleasurable or fulfilling terror. The notion of the sublime had been introduced forcefully into cultural debate in the middle of the century, when Edmund Burke wrote his *Philosophical Enquiry into the Origin of our Ideas of the Sublime and Beautiful.* This treatise on Aesthetics basically suggested that Beauty was pleasing and calming, often defined by smoothness, smallness and delicacy. Sublimity was, on the other hand, terrifying, and defined by vastness and magnificence. Sublimity had elements of darkness as well as light, and encompassed the sense that God had created and was forced to battle Satan in an endless power play.

So for the eighteenth-century person, storms, mountains and turbulent seas were all sublimely inspiring and terrifying. So too, as Angelo recorded, was fire.

When Sir Joshua Reynolds became head of the Royal Academy at its foundation he engaged with the discussion of how the sublime applied to art, and how painters might achieve in their work a grandeur and poetry that could overpower the onlooker 'and take such a possession of the whole mind that no room is left for attention to minute criticism'.[24] As a new member of the RA Schools Turner had attended Sir Joshua Reynolds's lecture in 1790 in which he delivered his last 'Discourse' on Art on Michelangelo, and where he praised the sublimity of that artist. He would have been familiar with the concept, and how the more experienced landscape artists of his generation were considering how to bring sublimity to bear on their genre.

But Turner did not even attempt to draw the sublime fire at the heart of London that January night. By the time he managed to square up his paper and draw the ruined, burnt-out building, the fire was gone. As was one of the most astonishing phenomena arising from it – a phenomenon which thousands of Londoners had flocked to see as dawn broke.

Henry Angelo recalls these 'extraordinary phenomena' very vividly, explaining that on the morning of the fire, there was 'one of the severest frosts in memory'. As a result, after the flames were out, 'there were vast clusters of icicles twelve and fifteen feet in length, and as big as branches of trees, hanging from the North Front Parapet, and the very windows through which the flames had raged for hours; these icicles being the frozen stream projected from the pipes of the fire engines'.[25]

Though Angelo's account sounds fanciful, it is important to remember that the era in which Turner lived is now recognized as belonging to the end of an exceptionally cold Little Ice Age that had dominated Europe between 1560 and 1850. Turner would have witnessed the Frost Fairs on the Thames in the winter of 1787 to 1788, and that of the following year, when temperatures sank so low that the river froze and became an additional playground for Londoners. With this in mind, Angelo's account is not as far-fetched as it might seem at first.

Turner must have cursed his misfortune in missing these magnificent icicles. However, he worked up his sketch into a finished watercolour that, for its topicality at least, he knew would attract attention. Drawing after the crowds had dispersed, he re-populated his foreground with Londoners and firemen drawn from his imagination. He added imagined icicles too. But they are inches, not feet, in length and a pale imitation of what Angelo describes. Nevertheless, the picture was selected for show at that summer's Royal Academy exhibition.[26]

Turner found his way back to the Narraways again in 1792 after the Royal Academy Schools broke for their summer holidays. But this time he used their home in Bristol as a stopping point before moving on into south Wales. His way of life at the Narraways reveals a character so dominated by his art that there is little room for anything else. Already Turner was living and breathing his métier. He was possessed by it.

'Turner was not like young people in general,' Ann Dart related. 'He was singular and very silent, seemed exclusively devoted to his drawing, would not go into society, and did not like "plays".'[27]

Turner's mind that summer was full of other things than plays. One gets a sense that the Narraways, for all their generosity and fun, were probably much like his own family, not engaged in the debate about art. With his friend the Revd Nixon, or with any of the artists in whose studios he had worked, he could talk about drawing and painting. And it was his constant enquiry into the subject that surely recommended him to those who went on to help him in his career. But no such conversation was available in the Narraway house. It is unlikely that they would have been able to share his specific excitement in the undertaking he was about to make. For he was about to follow in the footsteps of one of the most influential eighteenth-century thinkers on the subject of art.

Seven years before Turner had been born, an audacious cleric called William Gilpin had published an *Essay on Prints* that had in one fell swoop taken on Burke's thinking about the Beautiful and the Sublime by adding a new type of aesthetic. With landscape painting in mind, Gilpin began to consider 'that kind of beauty which is agreeable in a picture'. In short, Gilpin's 'Picturesque' was a mediator between the definition of Beauty and the Sublime as outlined by Burke, and defined a series of attributes that he felt were pleasing when expressed in landscape painting. Gilpin argued that between soft, classic beauty and grandiose terrifying sublimity lay a third way that could have elements of both. He suggested that what might be sublime or beautiful in nature could easily become lost when translated into painting. And consequently artists should seek to find a way of combining elements of roughness with order, elements of darkness with colour and light, into what was pictorially pleasing. The rustic views that the Dutch Old Masters had made their own were naturally picturesque. Irregular gothic ruins could be picturesque. Rural landscapes combining a variety of textures and topics could be made to be picturesque.

Gilpin explored the principles of this 'picturesque' beauty further when in 1782 he published *Observations on the River Wye and Several Parts of South Wales, etc. Relative Chiefly to Picturesque Beauty*. As he traced the river between Ross-on-Wye and Chepstow, past Goodrich Castle, Coldwell Cliffs, Monmouth and Tintern Abbey, Gilpin pointed out all the picturesque opportunities the region afforded. The Wye became instantly popularized by the publication – popularized, that is, in the sense that culturally informed middle- and upper-class people began to follow in Gilpin's footsteps, and boats were set up to take them to key points that the Reverend highlighted.

Turner could have seen Gilpin's *Essay on Prints* in the Royal Academy library. And though the Academy did not hold a copy of *Observations on the River Wye*, there were plenty of others in Turner's growing circle of benefactors who may have had a copy. With his keen sense of topicality and marketability, Turner realized that the

River Wye, already brought to the public's attention by Gilpin, was ideal subject matter for him. Tracing Gilpin's journey in reverse, he headed out from Bristol, then followed the river from Chepstow, past Tintern, to Monmouth before leaving Gilpin's route and heading north-west past Hay-on-Wye to Devil's Bridge.

Turner's progress as a draughtsman is marked in his drawings of this summer. His attention to, and ability to handle, the finest architectural detail increased considerably, and now his sketches became full of the most intricate gothic details of the abbeys at Tintern, Llanthony and Chepstow. He captured some of the rural, rustic cottages and farms sitting at the foot of hills, enjoying their thatched roofs and smoky chimneys, which seem to typify Gilpin's definition of picturesque. He was more adventurous in his landscapes too. He attempted more complex views, of the rugged terrain of the Black Mountains. And for the first time he attempted real animation in his views of shores and seas. As he sketched he kept the work of a range of established artists in his mind's eye, always measuring his own ability against them.

When he came across events that amused him, for example, he would summon the warm comic work of that painter who had preceded him at the Soho Academy, Thomas Rowlandson. Certainly one seaside scene he conjured suggests the latter's influence.

In an era before good roads and well-furnished jetties, carts would load and unload their burdens directly on to beaches. Flat-bottomed barges could come aground, and boats would rock in the shallows as they were loaded. A series of pencil sketches of carts and boats culminated in a watercolour account of some Welsh folk struggling to get their piglets into a boat in choppy shallows. The cart is axle-deep in the waves, and the occupants battle to hand over wriggling animals to sailors, as the boat lurches violently up and down. One piglet is diving into the grey water, another is grasped by its trotter. One can see how this struggle amused the young artist as he stood and watched.

There was another artist who had been winning huge acclaim in London throughout Turner's childhood. This was the Franco-British artist Philip James de Loutherbourg. The painter's repertoire extended across landscape painting, through history painting and theatrical scene painting to seascapes. At the heart of his work was a sense of drama that captivated his audience. In the late 1780s he had travelled to Wales and produced a series of breathtaking views. In the 1790s he had been producing stormy seascapes for the Royal Academy shows that had clearly excited Turner. Just months before Turner set out on his latest trip, de Loutherbourg's virtuoso painting *Smugglers Landing in a Storm* hung as No. 13 in the Royal Academy show of 1792.

De Loutherbourg enjoyed scenes that went beyond the geographically specific work of topographical artists. He dealt in generics. His works were often entitled 'A Storm', or 'A Fight'. As such he sought to elevate his work into something more timeless and grand. And what is more, he painted his dramas in oil.

Smugglers Landing in a Storm features a boat crashing towards a rocky beach, a ruined castle atop a steep cliff in the near distance. Setting himself a challenge, Turner's sketches of that summer show his attempts to match the far more experienced painter. He challenges himself to depict waves crashing on a rocky Welsh coast and boats struggling in coastal swells, in compositions deeply reminiscent of de Loutherbourg.

Turner had a vast, almost unquenchable thirst for exposure to the work of his contemporaries. And one senses that the more he saw, the greater his desire to become part of the debate about art in general and landscape art in particular.

Fortunately for Turner there was a man in Bedford Square who was at the heart of conversation about landscape painting. Yet more fortunate still was that he would play a crucial role in the next stage of Turner's story, by taking the eager, talented young painter under his wing. This man was Dr Thomas Monro. Not a publisher, nor an engraver . . . but the physician of Bethlem, London's main lunatic asylum.

5.   The most liberal encouragers of watercolour art

Dr Thomas Monro was an exceptional man. He came from a family of eminent physicians who had been at the helm of the Bethlem Royal Hospital since 1728. His grandfather James and father John preceded him in the role of the Physician of the hospital, a role he took on after his father's death in 1791. The Monros also ran private mental asylums in and around London, most notably Brooke House in Hackney, and Northampton House at Smithfield in Clerkenwell.

Monro was a passionate amateur artist. He took drawing lessons from the landscape artist John Laporte, and became a very competent watercolourist. His father, John, had been an enthusiastic collector in the vein of the more typical mid-century connoisseur, with a collection of European engravings and prints. A friend of Hogarth, he had given him access to Bethlem when the latter was conceiving his *Rake's Progress*.

But the son had more modern tastes. He belonged to a new generation of art enthusiast who wanted to see British artists thrive. His own personal penchant was for landscape art and watercolour. Thomas Monro adored Gainsborough and by the early nineteenth century had a large collection of that artist's work, as well as his 'show box', a portable wooden box into which viewers could peer to view painted transparencies, backlit by candles. He also owned works by de Loutherbourg, Richard Wilson and George Morland, as well as Thomas Hearne, Edward Dayes and Michael Angelo Rooker.

Meanwhile his print collection included some of the most popular seventeenth-century masters, including Salvator Rosa, Rembrandt, Claude and the immensely popular sea painter Van de Velde the Younger, as well as the Venetian luminary Canaletto. Monro was quite simply one of 'the most liberal encouragers of watercolour art' according to Henry Angelo, with 'the finest collection of drawings of any collector in the kingdom'.[1]

Monro's passion for art dominated his physical environment. His family recounted how he had a net attached to the roof of his brougham carriage in which he kept drawings and prints to look at as he travelled between appointments. And in a property he bought in later life, he literally papered the walls of his study with prints by British artists.[2]

Not content with the work alone, Monro sought the company of artists. He was close friends with the high-profile amateur landscape painter and Tory Sir George Beaumont, who showed work at the RA. Beaumont's great friend the landscape artist Thomas Hearne was part of the circle too, as were the painters John Hoppner, Henry Edridge, and, to a lesser extent, Joseph Farington. This group were drawn to one another by their shared enthusiasm for the experience of sketching *en plein air* in the countryside, which was as much a leisure pursuit as it was a professional exercise.

This group was heavily involved with the Royal Academy. Beaumont and Hearne were exhibitors; by 1792 Hoppner had been elected an Associate of the institution, and Edridge had trained at the Schools. But Farington's influence at the RA was almost unparalleled. He was 'at the time, intimately associated with every internal or legislative proceeding of the body, over whose movements, for good or evil, he exercised so powerful a control as to procure for him the appellation of "Dictator of the Royal Academy"'.[3]

Thomas Monro had not expected to take over his father's onerous commitment to Bethlem. But when his eldest brother, John, died unexpectedly and his other older brother, James, in service as a sea captain for the Royal East India Company, declared himself not disposed to leave his 778-ton, 26-cannon vessel, Thomas stepped up to the mark.

When his father retired from his duties at Bethlem, Thomas moved into his Bedford Square house in 1791 and began to take over his responsibilities. He was suddenly thrust into a whirlwind of consultations, committees and appointments that left him with less time to visit the studios of his artist friends, or take sketching trips into the country he so loved. A few years later Joseph Farington would note in his diary that Monro's 'professional situation does not allow of his quitting London for several days together. He has not been four days together absent from London in the last 4 years.'[4]

With less time to seek out art, Monro determined to create a kind of club for artists, so that art could come to him. He opened his home on Friday evenings, in the winter, when the RA Schools were in term and artists were generally in town. On these occasions he shared his extensive collection and library in Bedford Square with his artist friends. He also wanted to encourage younger artists to come and learn amid this company, where more experienced artists who already excelled in the landscape genre might supervise them. After all, there was no school for landscape studies. He was even prepared to pay these youngsters. If they came and copied works, not only would Monro feed them an oyster supper but he would pay them half a crown.[5]

The cantankerous Edward Dayes had moved into premises in Francis Street, off Bedford Square, in 1789, and taken on Turner's friend Thomas Girtin as his formal registered apprentice that June. It is likely that it was Dayes who brought Girtin to Monro's attention as an obvious candidate for his patronage.

Girtin may have introduced his friend Turner as another deserving talent for Monro's attentions, though at least one early commentator has suggested that Monro was also a client of William Turner's barber shop in Maiden Lane.[6]

However the introductions were made, Turner and Girtin were the first 'students' that Monro took on. As years went by and his club gained a reputation, others would pass through his doors,[7] but for the time being, these two young men were Monro's project and experiment. Their task was to copy watercolours, in those days referred to as 'drawings'. The works of Hearne, Dayes and Michael Angelo Rooker were put in front of them. Girtin was apparently usually tasked with drawing the outlines, while Turner was tasked with applying ink washes.

That the artists whose work they were copying were also available to teach on occasion was also a significant aspect of Monro's club, and lent it the name among the art world of Monro's 'Academy'. The influence of this small band of artists on Turner should not be underrated. Years later Turner's friend and stockbroker Charles Stokes, who built up an important collection of Turner's work, also acquired watercolours by Dayes and Hearne, with the annotation that the latter was 'Turner's second master' and the former his 'third'.[8] These tributes almost certainly came from Turner himself.

As Turner worked over the next two or three years, assiduously copying the work of his older contemporaries, he was effectively exploring their different interpretations of the 'picturesque'. Turner showed nothing but eager readiness to learn from the technical and compositional quirks of these different artists, and adopted a conscious porosity as he adopted their styles and techniques in his own work. Sometimes he would paint in the muted palette of Dayes. He would simulate the effect of stone masonry in the same manner as Rooker, by working up a scale of tones from dark to light of just two or three base colours.[9] Leafing through Monro's print and drawings collection, the work of Canaletto caught his imagination, and he experimented with the rather nervous drawing style of that artist, where the paper is punctuated with small dashes and dots.

For Turner, each imitation of another artist was a learning process. But it also marked Turner measuring his own ability. It is as if he needed to match the work of his contemporaries and forebears, then better them, as part of his march towards his own success. His work in these early years is an amalgam of influences that testify to his technical prowess. But as such, a unique personal style still eluded him.

It was not all copying chez Monro though. The doctor took his students out on sketching trips. Monro had a love for the readily accessible countryside in Surrey, and would later go on to take a long lease on a property at Fetcham. One of his favourite places to sketch was Box Hill, at the summit of the North Downs, and today the Victoria & Albert Museum holds a watercolour of Box Hill attributed to Turner from this time.[10]

Monro's influence on Turner extended far beyond those Friday evening sessions, and he became a 'material friend'.[11] Monro recommended Turner as a drawing master for his brother James's family, who lived at Monken Hadley in Middlesex.[12] This was the beginning

of a short but fruitful episode in his life, when the five shillings a lesson he got for drawing instruction seemed worth the while. Within
a couple of years he would list just some of his pupils in a sketchbook,
revealing that in Lewisham he had a Mr Jones and a Mr Davis, while
in Barnet there was Mr Burner. Alongside these were Mr Murwith,
Miss Palin, Miss Hawkins and Mr Goold. The kind Revd Nixon
would also eventually become a pupil of his protégé, one of a group
whom Turner taught by correspondence, sending drawings and
instructions out to his pupils by post, and then annotating the results
that came by return.[13]

In 1793, however, Turner was very much in situ to instruct the
James Monros, since he drew the tower of St Mary's Church in that
village, with the family house just visible in the background. It is one
of a series of views of towers, gatehouses and abbeys that he made in
1793 and 1794 during various sketching excursions across England. In
his watercolours of Malvern Abbey, Christ Church Gate at Canterbury, Tom Tower in Oxford, King's College in Cambridge, King
Edgar's Gate, Worcester, and many more, the looming mass of ancient
edifices seems to be his major preoccupation, and a low viewpoint is
adopted to accentuate the imposing splendour of the subject. As such,
the lessons he was learning from Hearne and Dayes are evident, and
his ambition to achieve that grandeur of which Sir Joshua Reynolds
reminded his students begins to appear. As a group the work adds up
to a very particular vision of Britain. The views share a sense of power,
solidity, continuity and heritage. Those who go about their business
in the shadow of these edifices are contented people who, though minute against the towering structures in their midst, are nevertheless in
some form of harmony with their history and country.

In reality Britain was not as calm and balanced as Turner's watercolours suggest. Just when Thomas Monro was creating his own little
society of artists, other clubs and societies were growing up all over
the country in response to the continuing revolution in France. In
fact 1792 saw Britain in a moment of crisis. The French continued to
pour into Britain. Some were aristocrats and royalists, and a huge
number were members of the clergy. But there were fears that some
of those coming to British shores were spies, intent on distributing

subversive literature and spying for a revolutionary army that now had an international agenda. There were rumours of men taking particular interest in the details of British harbours, sketching the ports, making maps. Reports began to be circulated of large orders being made from British arms sellers. It was unclear if these were arms intended to go back across the Channel or in fact equip a revolutionary force at home.

Pro-revolutionary 'Jacobin' societies began to distribute Thomas Paine's *Rights of Man*. Sporadic riots and strikes began to break out. Four key British ports, Great Yarmouth, South Shields, King's Lynn and Ipswich, became totally incapacitated when sailors stopped work. In the north word went around that the pitmen, keelmen and wagonmen were on the point of revolt, impressed and inspired by the new doctrines of Liberté, Egalité, Fraternité coming from France. Similarly, Birmingham was about to ignite.

London was not immune to outbursts of anti-monarchy sentiment. At the Royal Academy's annual dinner, held in the Crown and Anchor on the Strand to celebrate the King's birthday in June 1792, the assembled Academicians had to listen to a rowdy mob throwing stones outside and chanting 'Jacobin' slogans in protest at the King and those saluting him.

Francis Rigaud's son Stephen had joined Turner as a student at the Royal Academy Schools by 1792, and his own memoirs recall the panic and upheaval that seeped into the Academy as members and students alike began to show their allegiances.

'The state of the country during the latter part of this was most alarming,' he wrote, 'seditious and tumultuous meetings were being held in and around the metropolis . . . at this crisis a Public Meeting was called by John Reeves Esq Barrister at the Crown and Anchor tavern in the Strand on 20th November to form a loyal association for the protection of liberty, and property against the Jacobins . . . my father enrolled.'

But for all the Academicians like Rigaud prepared to pledge for the King, there were those at the Academy whose sympathies lay elsewhere. 'I shudder at the recollection of the scenes I there witnessed,' he remembered. 'The peaceable students in the Antique

Academy being continually interrupted in their studies by others of the opposite character, who used to stand up and spout forth torrents of indecent abuse against the King . . . I rose and protested . . . but they shewed their spite by pelting me well with the pieces of bread which were supplied . . . for the purposes of rubbing out the chalk.'[14]

In the autumn of 1792 the Government was forced to issue a proclamation against seditious literature in a bid to stem the tide of 'democratic' material. In December the Prime Minister, William Pitt, was sufficiently concerned that the people were about to take up arms that he took the drastic measure of mobilizing the militia, fortifying the Tower of London and preparing for insurrection.

The popular rising did not happen, however, and when on 21 January 1793 Louis XVI became the most shocking of Madame Guillotine's conquests, a counter-revolutionary movement intensified in England instead, with more 'loyal associations' declaring themselves. After Pitt expelled the French ambassador in response to that country's regicide, the French declared war on Britain. This, along with the deepening terror that saw the guillotine fall with increasing frequency across 1793, dissipated much of the pro-revolutionary zeal and replaced it with numbed horror and pity. Joseph Farington noted: 'The events which are succeeding each other in France and which posterity will consider with Horror & almost doubt of from their atrocity, are received here as the news of the day; so habituated are we, by repetition, to the shocking accounts received, that the natural effect of a first emotion is weakened – the situation of the people at large seems every day to become more desperate.'[15]

Far from engaging with the tragedy unfurling overseas, Turner, driven by his work, simply continued his relentless and intense pursuit of technical brilliance. That he now wanted to be the finest topographical artist of his day was obvious. It was at this time that George Dance junior, a founder member of the RA, an architect who was also an enthusiastic portraitist, made a formal drawing of Turner in profile.

Another of Monro's 'material' contributions to Turner's career might have been the suggestion he enter one of his Surrey sketches for the Society for the Encouragement of Arts, Manufactures and Commerce awards. This society's emphasis was quite different from the august RA. It remained focused on invention, craft, technique, and was quite catholic in its approach. It was this institution that had awarded M. R. Reeves a silver palette in 1781 for inventing the portable moist watercolour paint cakes that Turner benefited from personally.

Like Reeves, Turner did well with the Society. Submitting a drawing of Lodge Farm, Hambleton, Surrey, in the category that awarded a prize for the best 'drawing of a landscape after nature', he found himself awarded the Society's 'Greater Silver Pallet' in the spring of 1793. It was yet another feather in the cap of this rising star.

The house in Bedford Square did not quite suit Monro's ambitions for his homespun academy. In 1793 he bought a new house at No. 8 Adelphi Terrace, off the Strand, one of eleven prestigious homes designed by Robert Adam that looked out over the Thames. The roadway accessing the terrace overhung the river shore and underneath this, at shore level, were premises that also belonged to the grand houses above. Monro was installed there in the early months of 1794.

An added attraction of Adelphi Terrace was that Monro's friend John Henderson lived at No. 4. Henderson, a property developer whose income was derived from rentals in Whitechapel, was a rival to Monro in terms of his passion for art. He too was a landscape painter, though with more enthusiasm than skill, but he had an enquiring mind, a generous disposition and, like Monro, a private collection.

At Adelphi Terrace, with Henderson also a regular, Monro's 'Academy' took off. The artists would come by and occupy the lower portion of the house on Fridays. Monro's wife would take her dinner upstairs, with a degree of despair at the house being overrun by men. The evenings must have been enjoyable. The 'members' of this unofficial society sketched one another at work. There are three pencil sketches of Turner by his comrades, two of which emphasize his rather beaky nose more fully than the other. Unlike his friend Girtin, who is sporting short cropped hair, Turner still wears his hair long and tied back, as per his juvenile portrait.[16]

Aside from the light-hearted portraits of one another, the copying that had begun in Bedford Square continued. Sketches that John Henderson had made in Dover were added to the drawings by Rooker, Dayes and Hearne that Turner and Girtin were invited to copy. But just sometimes the boot was placed on the other foot, and when the young Turner produced particularly good work, it was his mentors who copied from him for a change.[17]

There was also an experimental side to the club. Henderson had used a camera lucida on his trip to Dover, and it is worth considering that this piece of equipment was demonstrated in Adelphi Terrace. Turner would retain a fascination with science and how it might inform art, totally in keeping with the spirit of his age, and it has been suggested that he used a camera lucida himself after a patented version became commercially available in 1807.[18]

But perhaps the most significant exposure Turner had at the Monro Academy was to the work of John Robert Cozens. Cozens was the talented son of a talented father. Alexander Cozens had been the drawing master at Eton and had tutored a young Sir George Beaumont. His son Robert had proved an equally talented painter who had thrived under the patronage of two of the most powerful art lovers of the day, the unfathomably wealthy William Beckford and the controversial but kind Richard Payne Knight. Cozens had travelled with both these patrons on the Continent in the 1770s and 1780s, making a series of breathtaking views of Italy and the Alps.

But by mid-1794 he found himself adrift after making commercial misjudgements, as well as having suffered at the hands of whimsical patrons. The notoriously mercurial Beckford had commissioned much from him in the early 1780s before suddenly breaking off the relationship.

The loss of such a major patron placed Cozens at the whim of an equally mercurial market. Towards the end of the 1780s Cozens had attempted his own publishing enterprise, compiling a series of works under the general title *Delineations of the General Character of Forest Trees*. In early forms of topographical art, the tradition was to depict foliage as a series of zig-zags, and there was much headway still to be made among the watercolour community in the portrayal of this aspect of the natural world. But despite the clear need for this kind of reference material, Cozens's *Trees* was a financial non-starter. In the same year as he published it he auctioned thirty watercolour views of Italy in what feels like an act of financial desperation.

To be in debt was a common state for the eighteenth-century artist. The aristocracy on whom artists relied were appalling at paying for services rendered. Farington's diaries are littered with the complaints of his contemporaries, who delivered commissioned goods only to find them rejected on a whim, or received only to find they were never paid for. Artists had to balance the onerous but necessary task of reminding their patrons of the monies owed them against the risk of annoying their clients. Credit was the currency of privilege.

By 1794 Robert Cozens had suffered a serious mental breakdown. Unlike Beckford, both Beaumont and Payne Knight were concerned about their less fortunate associate, and they turned to Monro on hearing of the painter's affliction. They also rallied the artistic community to raise sufficient funds to pay for Cozens's board and lodging at Monro's private asylum on St John Street in Islington, Northampton House, while Monro agreed to provide his own consultations free of charge.

There is some evidence that the Turners also availed themselves of Monro's professional services at around this time. When Turner stood drawing the church at Monken Hadley he would have been well aware of the small private asylum that the Monros also ran there, and there is some suggestion that Mary Turner may have been treated there for her mental problems.[19] Turner's drawings of another Monro institution, Brooke House in Hackney, have remained in the Monro family, along with the family tradition that Mary Turner was treated there too at some stage in the 1790s.

Monro's transactions with Turner were not entirely selfless. The art-loving doctor would surely have appreciated the sense of obligation and gratitude they instilled in one of London's rising stellar talents. In the case of John Robert Cozens too, Monro made sure that he enjoyed some benefit from his patient.

Most of Cozens's watercolours were in the hands of patrons, and there was practically nothing of his work in public circulation. So Monro used his privileged access to his patient to borrow his sketchbooks and portfolios containing rarely seen views from his continental trips. Cozens, who when in good mental health had been a sombre, silent man, had become a childlike patient, babbling nonsense and eager to please. Monro brought armfuls of the artist's drawings from his trips to Italy and Switzerland back to Adelphi Terrace. The copies that Girtin and Turner would make of these views served to swell Monro's collection of contemporary British art.

Another insight into Turner's precociousness emerges at this point. In relatively recent times Cozens's original drawings have re-emerged and can be compared to the copies made by Turner and Girtin. While the latter is assiduous in his faithfulness to Cozens's outlines, to the point that they could almost have been traced, Turner experiments with the colouring. In these drawings, Cozens uses a very mute, monochromatic wash of grey inks over white paper. Occasionally Turner, rather than being faithful, reverses Cozens's scheme, placing in light what the artist had placed in shade and vice versa, altering the drama of the view.[20]

But the audacious liberty Turner took in copying it belied a growing respect for the work by the now-demented artist. Particularly the finished watercolours that Cozens had executed.

Cozens's views of Italy and Switzerland stand apart from the topographical works of Dayes, Hearne, Rooker and the like. They have a poetic impact, and an emotional charge that must have surged through Turner.

Cozens's work achieved a strong moody presence in a number of ways. Whereas the topographical artists whom Turner had been beholden to emphasized line as much as colour, Cozens's use of line could be minimal, and instead he relied to a greater extent on the colour in his brush to establish form. He created misty atmospheric effects, subduing the impact of buildings that the topographers' line would often accentuate, and instead dissolving form to create something altogether more atmospheric. Cozens's sense of composition was also dramatic. He sought wide vistas, and tended to emphasize either the landmass or, by contrast, the lack of it. So in his depiction of the Roman campagna he captured huge skies hanging over bleak flat lands, while in Switzerland he sought out high mountains sheering into deep valleys. And often in Cozens there is a burst or a glow of light, a bolt of lightning, a milky sun glowing through a break in the clouds, or the glow of a fire and a haze of smoke.

Without knowing it, Monro's oversight of Cozens's mental health would change the course of British art. For in the latter's work, Turner saw a departure in watercolour that would influence him profoundly. He saw an artist not just recording an aspect of the world, but responding to his physical environment and capturing that emotional reaction with the tools of his craft.

Turner had unwittingly done just this in the lush and vibrant views over the Avon gorge he had made three years earlier, where the very intensity of his vertiginous viewpoint and the richness of his colour conveyed his own personal enrapture with the environment encircling him. But in the intervening years, in which he had so relentlessly pursued a quest to learn every aspect of technique that the best contemporary painters had to offer, his own responses to his environment had become secondary to observation, mechanical aptitude, and attempts to work in the style of others.

This point was not lost on the critics. In the spring of 1794 Turner attracted his first press attention. It was yet another milestone, but one that gave the artist a salutary, early warning.

The constructive criticism that accompanied the praise of the young artist had its desired effect. It would not be too long now before the painter we know today began to emerge, if cautiously.

In the meantime, however, the young man still had plenty of things to occupy him. Not least, the opposite sex. The pre-pubescent version of Turner had finally gone. At some time during his late teens he sat down and painted his self-portrait again. This time he used oil paint to mark the moment of importance.[21]

Oil paint was a medium that Turner was destined to master, but this particular portrait reveals a painter in his very first experiments with it. He is able to capture only the most general and broad features of his subject. In terms of that 'expression' that the Bee told his readers to look out for in judging works of art, Turner is lacking. His necktie is neither cottonish nor silky, it is impossible to determine what material his coat is made from, or what material the large round buttons are made of. He struggles with the foreshortening of his hand too, and the colouring of the skin is saccharine. The background is worked from the same green as his coat, the highlights in the hair from the same white as the shirt. The limited palette he was working with perhaps reflects his cautiousness as a novice with the medium. Or are these just a few colours a friend had given him?

Nevertheless, in terms of his person he managed to convey his luxuriant, curled, dark glossy hair, worn long to his shoulder, with a degree of pride. The childish face set amid tiny shoulders that he conveyed so honestly for the Narraways has become more chiselled, the nose grown long and adult, and the shoulders have broadened into the version of the young man that Dance captured in profile in 1792. This is the 'short, sturdy, sailor-like youth' described by his contemporaries.[22]

It could well be a portrait painted to impress a girl. Covent Garden was awash with women whom Turner would have had no need to impress. Such was its reputation as the centre of London's sex trade that one publisher, Mr Harris, brought out an annual booklet with the updated names and addresses of all the prostitutes in the area, offering his own summary of their appeal or otherwise. Turner's father's shop, like most barber shops at the time, almost certainly sold the prophylactics made of either treated linen, animal bladders or intestines that clients used in the dark alleyways around Maiden Lane, or in certain parts of the theatres, eateries and bath-houses.

But there was still a girl in Margate he was keen to impress. Turner had continued to make trips to the seaside resort where Elizabeth White was still resident. His watercolours are testimony. There is one of Dent de Lion, where he captured the solid medieval gateway to a manor in his Sandby-esque manner. The style suggests a visit dating to 1791, the same year in which his dear friend John Trimmer was succumbing to his tuberculosis at the newly inaugurated sea-bathing hospital.[23] This alone would have been an incentive for Turner to visit. But the added inducement would have been Miss White.

Later there was a six-week tour he made in 1793 with a friend called Edward Bell, who would go on to become an engraver. The tour took in much of Kent, as Turner's views of Canterbury are testimony. Bell's recollection of the trip was that it incorporated a trip to Margate too.[24]

It is little wonder that Turner travelled with someone when he could. Travelling remained perilous throughout his younger years. The roads from the Kentish ports into London were notorious for being watched by highwaymen, particularly Gad's Hill near Rochester, where both those on foot and those in coaches were slowed by the steep incline. Towns were not much safer, especially in the era of the press gang. At a moment when France and England were once again at war, travelling with a sketchbook could lead to accusations of espionage. As he returned to London in the summer of 1793, Turner must have reached the Revd Nixon's parsonage at Foots Cray with a degree of relief.

After Nixon's help with his entry into the Academy Schools, quite a friendship had flourished between the vicar and the young man. While he was with Nixon, Turner experimented with oil paint again. He tried to work up a sketch of Rochester Castle in the medium. This, and the experiment with his own self-portrait, tells us something of Turner's new ambitions.

Life in Turner's world was so much about hierarchy. Despite the levelling of society in France, in Britain rank still counted. The art world was no exception. The Royal Academy had an exclusive membership of just forty fully fledged Academicians. A larger number of Associates (ARA) existed, from whose ranks Academicians would be elected on the death of a member. Though new Associates were elected annually, it was still a struggle to get nominated and voted for.

What is more, there was a further hierarchy of media and subject matter operating within the institution. History painting was still perceived to be the most important genre, portrait painting was considered worthy enough, but landscape painting was generally thought of as among the lower orders of art. Watercolourists were less highly regarded than oil painters. And engravers were barely regarded at all. They had been deemed irrelevant to the Academy at its foundation, though by Turner's era there had been an accommodation to allow engravers to become Associates at least.

Turner, naturally ambitious, needed to elevate his status by painting in oils and to not just be seen as a topographical watercolourist. And so he began to experiment with the 'superior' medium. Nixon may have given him some preliminary instructions in how to use it.

But it wasn't just becoming accomplished in oil painting that was on Turner's mind in 1793. He wanted to get into print too. His ambition towards a 'higher' art was not at the expense of the popular work that could provide a ready income and help spread his name.

Since his friend Girtin had already had his work engraved and published in the *New Copper Plate Magazine*, it is not surprising that in the summer of 1793 Turner had also secured interest from the men behind the publication: John Walker, who did most of the engravings, and the publishers, Harrison and Co. Part of the purpose of his Kent expedition had been with this interest in mind. The *Copper Plate* paid two guineas a picture.

Is it a mere coincidence that in the year Turner's first views are reproduced in the *Copper Plate*, so too are two views by his friend and benefactor the Revd Nixon? Or did Turner reveal to Nixon the purpose of his sketching trip and urge him to submit views too? In the following year, 1794, the *Copper Plate* published views of Chepstow and Rochester Castle by Turner, and of Bush Hill Park House in Middlesex and Camden Place in Kent by the Revd Robert Nixon.

However, Turner's work for the *Copper Plate Magazine* is rarely mentioned in the vast academic studies of his work that have been undertaken over the last 150 years. The engraving, by Walker, is of mediocre quality, and as such they are often passed over.

But for the young Turner, seeing his work mass-produced for the first time, the appearance of these prints must have felt like another watershed moment. And, in spite of Walker's limitations as an engraver, the audacious composition that Turner employs in these two views stands out and is testimony to his talent.

His view of Rochester is taken from the river. The castle is not central in the composition but placed to the right in the distance, lit up by faraway sunshine. Boldly, Turner leads his viewer's eyes towards the castle in a diagonal trail from left to right. A fore-grounded tree on the left is his starting point. The tree in turn frames two boats, their rigging slicing across the central foreground but nevertheless directing the eye towards its ultimate subject. His sense of narrative does not escape him. In minute detail he captures the people of Rochester about their business, a couple approaching from the town along a fenced road; two more in the distance, this time heading towards the town perhaps, and the arched bridge that they must cross to it. And in the far left of the view a tiny ship can be spied, under sail, heading off out to sea.

The view of Chepstow is equally precocious. Here he uses the line of the Old Wye Bridge, and the fast-flowing water below it, to direct his viewer's eye to a distant Chepstow, nestling in the left-hand corner of his picture. Again Turner is alive to the story contained within his image. The Old Wye Bridge, which straddled the Wye between Gloucestershire and Monmouthshire, was one of the tallest but also most eccentric bridges in Britain, betraying the long dialogue between England and Wales. It stood forty feet high to accommodate the huge tidal range of the Wye, but history had unfolded in such a manner that Monmouthshire was responsible for the upkeep of half the bridge, and Gloucestershire the other. It says something of Anglo-Welsh relations that the Welsh half of this gigan-tic bridge was supported by huge stone limbs, while the English left their half constructed from spindly ladders of wood. Turner shows just one of the English supports, and uses the solid Welsh footings to march the eye towards Wales. Beneath, the water is frothing, and pooling towards the Welsh bank. Here a beached boat, a horse and cart and a dwelling with smoke trailing towards the left take our eye to its final resting place in the distant town. And then as the eye pulls back he gives us the ruined castle, sitting above the bridge in the mid-distance, somehow untouched by the business of men carrying on below it.

The pattern of Turner's career in print is rather familiar. It mirrors his career as an exhibitor at the Royal Academy summer show: once he has his foot in the door, he opens it wide and strides in. After a modest start with just two engravings of his work commissioned in 1793, in the following year he departs on another tour with commissions for four of Walker's publications. This time, Turner ventures to the Midlands and into north Wales with a mission to make views not just for the *Copper Plate* but also for the *Ladies' Pocket Magazine* and the *Pocket Print Magazine*. Over the next few years the quantity of work he produces for each publication grows.

Turner did what research he could ahead of his trip. The first few pages of the sketchbook he would fill that spring of 1794 comprise lists of suggestions. Written up fairly neatly in ink, they probably represent the transcriptions of notes he had made from interviews with friends and colleagues. 'Warwick,' someone has told him, 'has a castle, bridge, town hall and gothic church.'[25]

Turner's notes sometimes feel verbatim and retain the enthusiasm of the original conversation. At Bridgnorth, for example, there is 'a remarkable Tower on a steep rock' as well as 'an upper and lower town with steps for foot passengers' and 'a bridge with seven arches'. Sometimes the spellings of the places he has been recommended are fuzzy. Is it 'Sutton Colfield' or 'Coldfield'? Turner is not sure and writes both down.[26]

At the end of his tour Turner tots up his achievements. He already has one good view from Peterborough, two from Chepstow, three from Ely, but now he can add in four new views from Matlock, five from Bridgnorth, six from Parkgate and seven from Birmingham.

One of the views the Revd Nixon had submitted to the *Copper Plate* in 1793 was of Bush Hill Park in Middlesex, the residence of William Mellish Esq. One wonders how well Nixon knew Mellish? Did Nixon take a break from his painting and take tea with Mellish? And if so, did they discuss the benefit of the Bank of England's investments? Mellish was after all a director of that institution.

In 1794 the nineteen-year-old Turner opened an account with the Bank and began investing there. The Revd Nixon was a trustee of his account, appointed because Turner was under twenty-one. Whether it was Mellish in the previous year who had been behind the recommendation or not, the fact remains that both Turner and the benevolent Nixon had had a strong sense that the former was about to make a lot of money. They were right. On 4 March 1794, Turner invested £100 in the Bank of England's three per cent consolidated stock. He invested the same amount in March the following year and by 1797 had put away a total of £660 11s. 11d. Turner's career as a professional topographical artist had properly begun.

6. M'lord Turner

On 3 November 1809 Turner walked up the steps of No. 8 Adelphi Terrace. The day had been showery. He probably had his trusty umbrella in one hand as he reached out with the other to pull the bell and announce his arrival. It was a Friday of course. The day that Monro generally opened his home to artists.

Nearly fifteen years after he had first walked into that house, Turner's life had been transformed. He was by this time an extremely rich and celebrated artist. And as he waited that evening at the door he was accompanied by the robust, middle-aged George Capel-Coningsby, the fifth Earl of Essex and owner of Cassiobury Park in Hertfordshire.

Turner and Essex were on extremely familiar terms. The latter, another Georgian with a taste for antiquarian studies and fine art, was building up a collection of Turner's work. Essex also happened to be a very close friend of Thomas Monro. Monro had even given up his country house at Fetcham in Surrey and bought a 'cottage orné' in Bushey, in 1807, on land that bordered Essex's Hertfordshire estate. When the Monros were at their new property in Bushey there was always much traffic between their modest villa and the neighbouring gothic mansion.

Although it was 'Academy' day at Monro's, this time Turner had probably not come to draw.

He had remained a close friend of the Monro family and his visits were as often social as they were practical.[1] So many years after he had been paid for copies and given his supper, he was still a frequent visitor to their homes in both London and Bushey.

Despite the long-continuing friendship, however, Turner had changed dramatically. He was no longer the amenable, if shy, boy whose hard work and enthusiasm had charmed his father's friends. His character had undergone a transformation into something altogether more complex and, frankly, tricky.

On that November evening when Essex and Turner visited Monro there was another guest who had just arrived. Monro had bought a 'house dog', and the family were in the process of finding a name for it. Thomas Monro's son, Edward, notes in his diary that they decided to call their new pet 'Mallord Turner'. It is unlikely Turner was let in on the joke, for it was at his expense. Edward annotates his diary entry further with the revelation 'm'lord'. They weren't really calling the dog *Mallord* Turner at all, they were going to take delight instead in calling out '*M'lord* Turner' as they threw sticks for their dog to fetch, or told it to sit and beg.[2] While at one level this gag may well have been a recognition of the massive social elevation Turner had enjoyed since the family first knew him, it was also clearly an amusing way for the family to vent some of its frustration with their old friend, who had become a little imperious in his manner. Edward also noted that the very next day the family began building a kennel for M'lord Turner. And by 7 November he was installed in it. Put very much in his place.

The Monro family's frustration with Turner is not an isolated case. In the second half of the 1790s there are several accounts of a brusqueness of manner emerging, or a thoughtlessness that offended. He became a challenging and contradictory character who was often seen as taking the generosity and kindness of others for granted. For every description of him as amusing and considerate, there is one of him being dull and ungrateful. For every example of him behaving modestly, there is a tale of his self-importance. For every example of generosity, another of meanness. He is at once intelligent and informed, and uncouth and vulgar. He is sometimes smart and presentable, at other times slovenly. He becomes unpredictable and idiosyncratic.

From the mid-1790s Turner began to play the great game in earnest. The great game, that is, that one had to play to work one's way up through the highly political Royal Academy, and ingratiate oneself with the equally demanding and often mercurial group of important clients who still dominated the patronage of art.

The beginnings of artistic democracy and a free market might have been in place but they were not going to give Turner the career he wanted in the next decade. Making work for the *Copper Plate* and other similar publications for two guineas a view was one thing, but to paint on a greater scale, and to explore wider subjects, he was still largely at the mercy of aristocratic endorsement. He was going to have to make himself amenable to every nobleman prepared to commission him. And to secure those commissions he was not going to take risks.

That Turner began his campaign for professional leverage with redoubtable determination and unmatchable speed is what one had come to expect of the young man. But that he also did so against a background of a series of personal domestic crises perhaps explains the fracture that emerges in his personality in the late 1790s. It would be a fracture that, over time, would only widen.

The first hint of the trouble that was going to be visited upon the Turners of Maiden Lane came when the Bastille fell in Paris. While the revolution in France would prove professionally beneficial to British artists as appetites for British subject matter rose in response, the demise of the French nobility was, by contrast, very bad news for English barbers. From the moment that the severed head of poor Monsieur de Launay was waved over the crowd on a bloody pitchfork, French aristocrats began throwing off their finery, dressing as tradespeople and paying over the odds to red-faced sea captains to suffer the rough Channel crossings in a notoriously stormy and wet summer. Almost overnight the wigs that had been the hallmark of the French court and aspirant bourgeois were out of fashion. In Paris, those who embraced the revolution rather than fled it were reverting to their natural hair, while the city's wig-makers were on the boat with many of their former masters.

The French hairdressers and wig-makers settled in Soho, far too near to Covent Garden for comfort. Driven by desperation, they could undercut the London barbers on price and match, if not better them, in virtuosity. But there was more. As nervousness grew among London's elite with every report that made its way across the Channel, the ostentatiousness of London's privileged inhabitants began to moderate too.

All those macaronis who had gone to Turner's father to have their heads shaved and their elaborate wigs dressed in the French style now began to grow back their own hair and wear it in a neat pony-tail, just like the new Parisians. Modesty became the London mode. It was the beginning of the end of the wig-making business, which would disappear altogether by the turn of the century.

But the final blow to William Turner's diminishing business came in 1795. And it was all down to a series of very cold winters. Since 1765 Britain's wheat harvest had been generally low-yielding, largely due to poor weather. The country had relied on importing grain from the Continent and America. But in 1793, when Britain and France once again went to war, wheat imports were impaired by naval blockades. Then, making matters worse, the winter that began in 1794 was exceptionally cold.

The poor were beginning to starve. In London, parishes tried to raise money to feed the most needy in their community. 'A collection from House to House has been made in the South Division of this Parish and £228-15 has been given,' Joseph Farington recorded in his diary. '762 families have been relieved with Coals, bread and Money . . . a second collection is proposed to be made on acct of the continued severity of the season.'[3]

The wheat that had been sown perished in the ice-ridden, rock-hard soil of Britain. By spring 1795 it was obvious to every cereal farmer that the crops had failed catastrophically. The national concern over the price of flour and bread mounted dramatically. The Prime Minister, William Pitt, acted. Among other things he introduced a hair powder tax. Hair powder was, after all, derived from corn flour.

As the *Gentleman's Magazine and Historical Chronicle* for 1795 reminded its readers, 8 May was the day 'appointed for the commencement of the operation of the act, imposing a duty on persons wearing hair powder'. Should such persons insist on this fashion they were required to buy an annual certificate for every member of their household wearing hair powder, at a cost per certificate of a guinea a year.

William Turner must have read the announcements about the hair powder tax with deep-seated dismay. For even among those clients who had given up wearing powdered wigs, many were continuing to powder and colour their natural hair, and relied on Turner to provide the powder as well as apply it. What is more, barbers did an important trade in the ointments and perfumed oils that one necessarily had to apply to one's hair to make the flour adhere. In one fell swoop the cosmetic side of his business was decimated.

The Turners were now living not at 21 Maiden Lane, but at No. 26. This four-storey building, accessed by a small courtyard, Hand Court, was an ample establishment for a barber, large enough not only to house his business and his household, but to provide Turner with a studio of sorts on the top floor. 'The old barber's shop was on the ground floor, entered by a little dark door on the left side of Hand Court,' Walter Thornbury would reminisce. 'The rooms, low, dark, and small, but square and cosy . . . Turner's bedroom where he generally painted, looked into the lane and was commanded by the opposite windows.'[4]

The idea of sustaining such a property under reduced circumstances must have filled Turner's father with dread. The fact that his wife's sanity was far from secure could only have added to the family's worries. To make matters worse, other tragedies were unfurling that must have only brought home the precariousness of existence in the eighteenth century.

William Turner senior had been great friends with a composer and musician called John Danby who lived close by at No. 26 Henrietta Street. Covent Garden was full of music. The theatres apart, the area was full of glee clubs and, the precursors to music halls, taverns that featured song and supper.

The music scene was rather similar to that for painters. Success depended on patronage, which came almost exclusively from the upper echelons of society. Danby manoeuvred himself from being a sometime singer filling the chorus with his brother Charles at the Drury Lane theatre to becoming a member of the Royal Society of Musicians and publishing his own work. An able organist, he secured a position at the Spanish Chapel in Manchester Square, where his contributions, over and above playing the organ, extended to composing masses there. When in 1787 Danby had become a professional member of the Noblemen and Gentlemen's Catch Club, his career took off and he saw subscriptions to his books of glees extend beyond his usual clientele of musicians and actors, to noblemen.

Buoyed by his success, Danby married a girl called Sarah Goose in 1788. A farmer's daughter, Sarah was lively and talented, and worked as an actress and singer. Such occupations placed her very much in Covent Garden's demi-monde, where there was a fine line for women between being paid as a performer and being paid for sex. Many actresses were also high-class prostitutes. And though this may not have been the case with Sarah, in marrying an upwardly mobile composer she was leaving such associations behind.

But in 1794 John and Sarah Danby's lives took a very sudden turn for the worse. Though still only in his thirties, Danby became very ill, bedridden and unable to work. The fortunes of the Danby family, who now had two girls, went into rapid decline. As with poor Cozens, the community rallied round. By April 1795 Danby had been unable to move from his bed for seven months. A Benefit Concert was held for the family on 10 April at Willis's rooms and was supported by those who knew them.

With dark shadows cast across the lives of his family and friends, the compulsion that drove Turner to paint hardened into something closer to insularity. Turner's own career was marching forwards. He reduced his exposure to domestic life to its most basic function, the environment in which he slept, or ate, otherwise keeping it distinct from the professional life that so engrossed him.

After his bravura show of five watercolours at the 1794 exhibition, consequent press attention, and his copious commissions from publishers, Turner followed up with another confident showing at the 1795 Royal Academy exhibition. This year he had eight works accepted, showing his supremely confident handling of gothic architecture in a range of views of porches, entrances, transepts and choirs that played to the conventions of the topographical genre. The press were impressed.

What he did not show at the Royal Academy were a range of watercolours also derived from his tour of 1794 that reveal how far he was prepared to experiment with an emotive and dramatic response to scenery, very much inspired by the work of John Robert Cozens.

A windmill silhouetted on a dark bluff, a vast empty sky behind it, and a blue hazy plain beyond; a depiction of Valle Crucis Abbey in Denbighshire caught in the midst of a dramatic, horizontal composition, where the darkened abbey in the foreground contrasts with a huge, misty, melancholic sky, into which distant hills seem to just dreamily melt. Or a view of the nearby village of Llangollen and its church nestling beneath a white enveloping firmament.

But even if he was unsure about this more romantic, charged work that he was beginning to produce, his more conventional output was attracting a new kind of patron. Turner was about to enter a society of privileged patronage. It was in 1795 that Turner first met George Capel-Coningsby, then Viscount Malden, probably through Thomas Monro. Malden commissioned Turner to make views of his property Hampton Court in Herefordshire. This was the type of vanity commission typical among the aristocracy, who wanted to be reminded of the scale and magnificence of their estates. These commissions were an important beginning.

Meanwhile the popular end of Turner's output was still growing apace. In addition to the publishers of the *Copper Plate*, the entrepreneurial engraver John Landseer had him eyed for a project to publish a series of views of the Isle of Wight, an increasingly popular destination for tourists.

Once Turner had launched his latest work at the 1795 RA exhibition, he began making preparations for a trip to satisfy his new clients. He headed yet again to the Narraways. From here he journeyed into Wales on a planned route that would see him follow the coast west to Cardiff and then all the way to St David's before returning cross-country to Carmarthen, then along the Tywi valley to Llandovery, on to Brecon and Abergavenny, and finally crossing back into England to Hereford.

Turner's proposed itinerary, still largely untrodden by the urban British, was in great demand by armchair travellers. Up until the 1770s Wales had been seen as a monstrous place with no aesthetic value for early explorers like Daniel Defoe and Celia Fiennes. But by 1795 the country was beginning to be explored more widely, even if there were no maps and few roads to assist those intrepid enough to venture there. The more accounts of this ancient land that made their way into the public domain, the more the public wanted to hear. In 1795 publishers were crying out for views of the country as an interest in it began to really take hold of the English imagination. The *Gentleman's Magazine* was witnessing so many descriptions of Wales that it was printing compilations of them 'by the most admired writers'.[5]

The paucity of made-up roads and stagecoaches compared to the rest of the country would almost certainly have suggested that travelling by horse or pony was going to be best for Turner, and he probably borrowed a horse from John Narraway in Bristol.[6] As Turner left the comforts of the Narraways' home behind, he must have known the dangers he faced travelling cross-country in 1795. Art came at no small risk to health and personal safety, and that year in particular was a dangerous one. The severe weather of the winter had carried on into the spring. June 1795 was one of the coldest on record. Even in the normally warm West Country, on the nights of 21 and 22 June the temperatures sank so low that thousands of newly shorn sheep perished in the parish of Wincanton in Somerset. Those travelling would not want to be caught out by misjudging distances, or worse, failing to find an inn or house that would take them in overnight. That Turner may well have been forced to overnight *en plein air* is suggested perhaps by notes on Wales he wrote for fellow watercolourist William Delamotte some years later. Drawing a map of a proposed route, Turner marked certain towns with dots. 'Let Dr Jackson or others know well that where the dot is mark there are those places without a hotel,' he warned.[7] One senses this caution derived from bitter experience!

Some of the earliest drawings Turner makes in the smaller of two leatherbound sketchbooks he took with him on this tour reveal just how empty Wales felt at this time to the solitary traveller. One, a sketch on the 'road', such as it was, from Cardiff to Cowbridge, features that village in the far distance with just two lonesome figures making their way along a muddy track in the mid-distance, one on horseback. Turner once again exploits a composition that accentuates horizontals. The sky is wide and empty, hanging over a similarly wide and empty Vale of Glamorgan. The slightly elevated angle of the drawing suggests that it may well have been made while Turner was sitting on a horse or pony. It is equally possible that the figures he inserts in the mid-ground are in fact imaginative projections of himself and perhaps a companion or a guide he had acquired along the way.[8]

A little further into the sketchbook he depicts another similarly bleak and moody view, with a charcoal black/brown foreground – perhaps depicting the burned and ash-ridden remnants of a late spring bracken burn – against another wide sky and distant blue hills. There is some form of man-made structure huddling in the mid-ground, dwarfed by the scale of the landscape all around it. Perhaps a ruined cottage or an isolated kiln? It is not clear. There is no fine drawing here. Just broad washes of colour that speak of how daunting the world can feel.[9]

Though this tour was made with a particular commission for Viscount Malden in mind, Turner's sketchbooks reveal that he was primarily driven by a personal agenda. Sure enough there are the sketches of Hampton Court for his new patron. And there are also the topographical sketches that are now typical of the material Turner would routinely gather, including views of Llandaff Cathedral, of Newport Castle, of Wells Gate and Langhame Castle.

But there are other recurring themes among the sketches that suggest Turner was beginning to explore other genres that went beyond topography. He was trying to expand his repertoire, and he was seeking drama, almost certainly with the determination to submit an oil painting for the next Royal Academy show.

He makes an exceptionally large number of drawings of water-mills during this extended tour of south Wales. At that time mills were so much more familiar as part of the landscape – he sought them out along his way, at Aberdulais, Carew Castle, Nolton Haven and Llanddowror.

Turner had just exhibited a view of Marford Mill in Denbighshire at the Royal Academy. Perhaps it is the typically picturesque attributes of this subject matter that attracted Turner in the first place: the combination of dilapidation and age as expressed by the rustic mill house with its moss-covered roof; the equally ancient wooden

water-wheel, the rush of water pouring off its lower treads contrasting with the stiller reflective waters of a stream in the foreground.

But why was he returning to the subject with such vigour? He
may have been contemplating a series of views of mills for reproduction. Mills, mines, quarries and kilns were as much on the early
tourist routes as stately homes, gothic ruins and beautiful vistas, and
apparently as delightful to a new kind of traveller who found pride in
the nation's manufacturing and engineering achievements. As one
traveller to the north in the 1780s reminded his readers when he came
to write up observations of his tour, 'To have been at Newcastle . . .
without seeing a coal pit would have been a sin of the most unpar-
donable nature.'[10]

But a very early and rudimentary experimental sketch in oil of a
mill found in Turner's studio after his death also suggests that mills
were something he felt might be appropriate for his first major work on
canvas. And this consideration would have been strengthened by the
sale of Sir Joshua Reynolds's collection of paintings earlier that year.

Sir Joshua Reynolds, the first President of the Royal Academy of
Arts, had died in 1792 in his home in Leicester Fields, today's Leicester Square. Britain's ambition to become internationally recognized
as a home of great art and artists had been embodied in Reynolds,
and despite the brickbats that he and the Academy had suffered,
nevertheless in his death he was marked as a hero. His friend Edmund
Burke, who had philosophized on beauty and the sublime, was at his
side as he passed away. Burke reminded the nation in his eulogy to
the painter that 'Sir Joshua Reynolds was on very many accounts one
of the most memorable men of his Time. He was the first Englishman
who added the praise of the elegant Arts to the other Glories of his
Country.'[11]

An unprecedented amount of pomp was conjured to celebrate his
life. The students at the Royal Academy processed before his coffin,
which lay in state in Somerset House, and then took part in the grand
procession that accompanied it to its resting place in St Paul's
Cathedral.

On 5 March 1792 Turner walked alongside his friends from the
plaster and life schools to participate in this momentous event. Ahead

of them, and ahead of the coffin, were two city marshals, the Lord Mayor, two sheriffs, and twelve mourners on horseback. After the hearse were forty-two mourning coaches. Then came the entire membership of the RA, ahead of forty-six carriages belonging to noblemen and gentlemen, all with liveried servants.

The impact of this ceremony on Turner should not be underestimated. For a boy with extraordinary determination, talent and drive, it would do nothing but reinforce how further these qualities might take him with the endorsement of the Academy and its aristocratic sponsors. Being part of that procession served as a 'stimulus to young artists to see a tribute paid to departed genius, and to witness the high social position by which its efforts had been rewarded.'[12]

It was little wonder that, as Reynolds became a legend, the sale of his huge collection of art three years later would also be considered an event of national importance. In 1795 Mr Christie announced a four-day sale, spread across two locations in Pall Mall, featuring over 400 lots, which would begin on Thursday 11 March and go on until Sunday evening. This would be a crucial opportunity for Turner to see original works by some of the greatest painters of all time before they were absorbed into other private collections.

Within a world-class collection featuring works by Raphael, Michelangelo and Leonardo da Vinci, Reynolds had important French School landscapes by Nicolas and Gaspard Poussin, and a number of Dutch and Flemish works by painters of the Golden era such as the sea painter Van de Velde the Younger, and Van der Cabel, as well as the landscape artist Jacob Van Ruisdael. These were of course all oil paintings.

Ruisdael was a master of watermills, windmills, and rocky wooded landscapes featuring rushing rivers and bubbling streams. His skies were grey and brooding, his foliage lush and dark, and his foregrounds often brown and foreboding. His work was dynamic, the gushing water of a river heading straight out of the frame towards the viewer. Although not capturing the mountains and storms that would be considered sublime subjects, he nevertheless found drama in lowland rural scenery. One of his pictures in the Reynolds sale was *Grainfields*, a moody view of a road extending towards a distant windmill, silhouetted against a vast cloudy sky. Turner's sketchbooks, full of mills and gushing streams, suggest that he had Ruisdael's work very much in his mind.

But Ruisdael was not the only painter Turner was thinking about in the summer of 1795. At the Reynolds sale there had been two sea storms by Van de Velde the Younger. As Turner travelled further west, seascapes began to feature heavily in his sketchbooks, indicating that he was also influenced by the work of this artist.

The seventeenth-century Van de Velde was enjoying a revival in popularity. In 1793 a publication, *The Beauties of the Dutch School*, had suggested he was 'the most eminent Sea-Painter that did, or perhaps ever will exist'. Given that influential collectors like Thomas Monro owned Van de Velde paintings, Turner had had occasion to discuss and study his work in some detail.[13]

Much later in his life Turner would look at a print of a Van de Velde depicting a ship facing into the wind in a stormy sea, and relate to a friend that 'This made me a painter.'[14]

As he approached the Welsh coast in 1795, Turner began exploring whether a sea piece would better suit the public mood rather than a watermill. He worked up small coloured sketches of waves crashing over rocks at St David's Head, another of waves crashing against a shore and a boat listing heavily just offshore. He walked to the furthest-most part of the Pembrokeshire peninsula, and trudged the mile of Marloes Sands to paint the curling surf smashing below the great mass of rock, which at high tide becomes a tiny rocky island, and is known to the locals as Gateholm Stack.

But it wasn't until he visited the Isle of Wight later in the summer that he found the dramatic coastal scenery that would finally provide the inspiration for the first oil painting he would show at the RA.

Three years earlier a tourist called Charles Tomkins had made a trip to the Isle of Wight, an account of which he would publish in 1796. Its proximity in words to what Turner offers us in images in his sketchbook gives a sense of the established ritual for visitors to the island that, like Wales, was being reassessed for the drama of its geography.

Turner, like Tomkins, took a stagecoach, along the Great West

Road through Surrey and into Hampshire. He would have passed through Basingstoke and then on to Winchester. Here Turner's sketchbooks reveal him busily at work, capturing the City Mill, the West Gate and Winchester Cross. While Tomkins continued south, Turner made a diversion west to Salisbury.

Turner had shown a number of watercolours of cathedrals at that summer's RA show, including views of Lincoln and Peterborough. It may well have been these exquisite depictions of gothic intricacy that encouraged Sir Richard Colt Hoare to invite Turner to his country seat, Stourhead, west of Salisbury.[15]

Colt Hoare was yet another passionate antiquary, who had come into vast sums of money and a large estate at Stourhead in Wiltshire in the 1780s. After the premature death of his wife he had given up the family banking business, and spent his huge fortune touring the Continent and writing on Italian painting. But when the political unrest on the Continent forced him to return to Britain he redirected his wealth towards antiquarian pursuits.

A brief stay at Stourhead en route to the Isle of Wight would prove deeply significant for Turner. The vast gardens with their lake, grottos and temples were an essay in classicism that had attracted national attention when they were first opened by Colt Hoare's grandfather in the 1740s. It was also Colt Hoare's collection of fine art, which included works by Rembrandt and the eighteenth-century Italian Piranesi, that made an impact. The former's *Landscape with the Rest on the Flight into Egypt*, which depicts the Holy Family illuminated by firelight in an otherwise dark and ominous canvas, made an immediate and lasting impression on Turner.

Turner rejoined his route not only with new inspiration, but with another aristocratic patron in hand. As he passed through Salisbury he sketched the city's North Gate, leading into the cathedral close, and the cathedral itself. Over the next decade Turner would paint *seventeen* views of Salisbury for Colt Hoare. The initial fruits of what would become such a significant series went on show at the very next Academy exhibition in 1796. In his *Gateway to the Close*, Turner combined depictions of the great cathedral steeple rising over the picturesque North Gate in a single composition that belies what can be seen in reality. But in compositional terms the combination works, and for a client the compression of Salisbury's gothic glories on a single page not only intensifies the pleasure to be derived from the watercolour, but represents good value for money.[16]

With his Salisbury views in hand, Turner travelled on to Southampton. Like Tomkins, he made sure he saw Netley Abbey, close to the city. He may well have taken a boat into Southampton Water, as Tomkins did, tying up three miles out of town at Abbey Fort. Here visitors began an adventure, making their way on a country path, through fields, meadows and then woods, until the Abbey finally revealed itself, 'situated in a dell, surrounded with various trees, which greatly relieve the building, and add much to its antiquated splendour'.[17]

The whole experience of 'discovering' ruins such as Netley was part of their appeal. On the day Turner trekked along these rural paths, so did another party of tourists whom he sketched. The Abbey was on land belonging to Cranbury Park, owned by Nathaniel Dance R A, a founder member of the Academy and the elder brother of George Dance, who had drawn Turner in profile in 1792. Dance was probably not in residence at the time of Turner's visit, as Turner's sketchbooks make no suggestion of any further exploration of the house or grounds. However, there are separate sheet drawings and watercolours of Cranbury Park and its views over Southampton, along with drawings of Netley Abbey, and the Isle of Wight, that were discovered loose in Turner's studio after his death. These drawings were not by Turner, but by Edward Dayes. After Dr Thomas Monro's death, his vast collection of work was put up for sale in 1833, and Turner bought a great number of works of sentimental, as well as proper commercial, value. The drawings by Dayes that he picked up at this sale were probably ones he had studied in Monro's 'Academy' in the weeks before heading off on his own tour. That he also studied views of the Isle of Wight by de Loutherbourg is suggested by yet another set of drawings that Turner bought at Monro's sale, made by that artist who toured the island in 1794.

This kind of meticulous preparation seems typical of Turner, a man at this stage so aware of his contemporaries and his need to match, or better, their achievements. As he headed to these locations he did so fully in the knowledge of the approach other artists had already taken to them.

Turner took a packet from Southampton to West Cowes, the place where most tourists stayed since it offered two inns for short stays and lodging-houses for those who were holidaying for longer.

This small island summarized Britain's face to the wider world. It looked out to France, towards Spain, Portugal and ultimately the Americas, and had a strategic position in naval history. Its castles were heavily fortified against the many past attempts to take the island by the French and Spanish. And now in the latest moment of conflict, the island was bustling with activity. Formerly the docking point for ships from the American colonies bringing rice and grain, these once busy ports and quays had been put to new uses after America's declaration of independence. Now they were concerned with providing supplies for the war with France.

The waters around the island were notoriously perilous. As he crossed the Solent, Tomkins noted the masts of a collier ship, visible above the waters, that had sunk near Brambles sandbank. This was just one of many ships that regularly got caught in the changeable weather around the island and were either blown on to rocks or caught in shallows.

If artists were subject to people's suspicions on the mainland, the situation was yet more intense on an island that had often been considered a point of initial conquest by Britain's enemies. Henry Angelo gives a vivid account of his friend the artist John Alexander Gresse, who just a couple of years before Turner's trip, while sketching, was mistaken for a French spy and pelted with rocks by local fisherfolk.

Despite these challenges to drawing on the island, Turner completed an itinerary that saw him make the sketches he needed for Landseer as well as explore the steep cliffs and rocky coves for himself. The level of detail that he could dedicate to intricate gothic façades he now applied to cliffs, rocks, boats and the trappings of coastal life like crab pots and nets.

It is crucial to understand the intensity of Turner's observation on this, and indeed all the sketching trips he made across the summers of the 1790s. Turner had spent years looking at the sky, the effect of wind on clouds, the types of weather, the shape of the countryside, the form of trees, the play of light at different times of day and under different meteorological conditions. Now he looked at the sea, studying the waves as they broke under different conditions. He noted the rock and sway of vessels and the swell of water. He had trained his eye to observe and capture the tiniest detail. His vision had become encyclopedic. That he was able to imaginatively extend his observation into a feeling for the way the world behaved, for the essential science that governed it, is undoubted. That his eye was more encompassing than that of any of his contemporaries was becoming more evident daily.

The result of this final trip was a consolidation of his thoughts. The sea won out over watermills. His first exhibited oil was *Fishermen at Sea*, shown in 1796 at the RA summer exhibition. It was a major statement from the young artist, and betrayed an accomplishment in the 'superior' medium of oil paint that surprised his peers. This was not a topographical view. This was a proper painting. A generic scene intended to convey ideas that ranged beyond a literal capture of a view, yet delivered with breathtaking naturalism. The finish that Turner achieved bedazzled the critics, and today might be considered almost photographic. Not only does it reveal how fast Turner could now master a new medium once his mind was set, but it also serves as a reminder to anyone viewing his late works that if he declined to finish a work to a high degree, it was not for want of technique.

Fishermen at Sea is a night scene. The silhouette of a series of rocks, reminiscent of the Isle of Wight's famous Needles,[18] march out to sea off a steep coast. The silver moon is momentarily visible in a break in the clouds, revealing the dark green waves below, through which fishing boats are battling to get out into the open.

The painting pulls together every element of Turner's career to this point. It is a scene full of theatre as he gives us a sudden fleeting glimpse of the fishermen in their struggle against the vast powers of the ocean. He summons de Loutherbourg's violent waves. And he draws on the Rembrandt at Stourhead as he wraps the dark figures of the fishermen around the warm glow of the flame of their lantern, and then a wider enveloping gloom around a moment of brilliant moonlight.

He draws on a decade of observation to convincingly depict the natural world. The foam of the waves almost sprays off the canvas. One can feel the temperature of the glassy green sea, the chill off the water, and smell the salt.

And his story-telling has now come into its own. His ability to sense the appetite of the market is second to none. Without painting a British battleship, he has nevertheless conveyed the determination of a nation never to give up, to struggle on, and to appear fearless against the odds. Yet this nationalistic pride is mediated by a genuine sense of the human condition. It is an image that combines bravery with dread.

The picture was a commercial and critical triumph for Turner, and was bought immediately for £10 by a General Stewart.[19] This, plus the monies from his teaching, commissions from Essex and Colt Hoare among others, along with his growing orders from engravers such as Landseer and Walker, placed Turner, as he turned twenty-one, in the most beneficial financial position he had ever enjoyed. His astonishing graft and sheer fortitude had paid off in so many ways.

7. 'W Turner called'

'W Turner called on me.' So wrote Joseph Farington on Wednesday, 24 October 1798. It was not the first time he would write this phrase, and it was by no means the last.

Farington was a regular diarist. Over the previous four weeks, his entries had been much taken up with politics, at both national and Royal Academy levels. While he noted the goings-on in the wider world out of general interest, and with an eye to opportunity, he lived and breathed the politics of the great art institution of which he was a dedicated member. His supremacy in dealing with RA politics, and the importance for other members to have the support of this lynchpin of Academy life, could not be underestimated. That Turner grasped this is clear.

Amid his previous entries covering September and October, in which he had noted Admiral Nelson's victory over the French fleet at Bequires and the subsequent celebratory illuminations, there were numerous references to the fact that in the coming November the members of the RA would go to the ballot to elect a new Associate.

In light of the forthcoming opportunity it is fascinating to see how the young Turner, who had been described as being awkward in company as a boy, had grown suddenly so very social, and in particular towards a man who he knew could make or break his attempts to gain acceptance into the Academy.

'It is unquestionable,' Turner's contemporary Martin Archer Shee confessed, 'that by his [Farington's] great personal influence over many of his brother academicians . . . he possessed a degree of weight in the deliberative councils of the body, far beyond what any other member could hope to exert or obtain.'[1]

'W Turner called' on Farington initially on 26 September 1798. This is not the first mention of Turner in Farington's diary per se – in fact he had been charting the young man's rise for a couple of years, but this was the first recorded time that the young man presented himself at the elder Academician's door. One gets a sense that Turner had suddenly engaged as a strategic player in Academy politics.

Turner's new-found sociability began after yet another tour of Wales. Even Farington, who had undertaken many tours himself, was impressed that 'he has been in South & North Wales this Summer – *alone* and on Horseback – out 7 weeks – much rain but better for effects'.[2] Turner's courageous solo tour in the name of Art could only recommend him further to a man who already felt he deserved recognition.

Farington took the opportunity of Turner's call to mention the forthcoming election of Associates, and he informed him that he would get his vote. Turner had prepared himself for this endorsement and, already an excellent strategist, reacted in just the right way. 'He expressed himself modestly for my good opinion,' Farington recorded. Significantly though, Farington did not detect surprise.

Academy politics relied on political allegiances, and there was a sequence of social calls and endorsements that potential Associates needed to follow to secure votes. Turner's friends would have advised him to drop by at Farington's house and Farington would have been waiting for the call. If Turner was to be elected in November 1798 it would present a challenge to the Academy rules, which set the youngest age limit for Associates at twenty-five. Turner was only twenty-three. Farington must have pointed out that Turner needed to campaign in the coming weeks as best he could.

Turner did not disappoint. A month later his hand was on the door-knocker once again. On the evening of 24 October Farington's entry in his diary gives a sense of the confidence he has in his man. Once again, Turner's visit followed a trip, this time to 'Lincolnshire at Lord Yarborough's', where he has been making 'drawings of his Mausoleum [designed by Wyatt]'. But despite this distraction, Turner informed Farington that he had secured 'promises of votes from Bacon – Nollekens – Bourgeois – Gilpin – Stothard &c', and Farington in return reassured him that he therefore saw 'no necessity for any further application – I thought his chance so certain that I wd wait the event, which He said He would do'.

But Turner was risk averse. And so he did what he could to really secure Farington. By 1798 Turner's work was already fetching good prices. The gift of a drawing, that is a watercolour, was a very generous one. The gift of a picture, an oil painting, for which Turner could now command in the region of £16, was even more substantial. So Turner invited Farington round to the studio he had made for himself in his father's house in Maiden Lane to look through his sketchbooks and offered him whatever he wanted, either a watercolour or an oil, painted to order.

'He requested me to fix upon any subject which I preferred in his books, and begs to make a drawing or picture of it for me,' Farington confided to his diary, adding that 'on his pressing it I said I would take another opportunity of looking over his books and avail myself to his offer'.[3]

And so, as winter descended on London in 1798, Turner waited to see what Farington would choose, hopeful that he would soon be able to write ARA after his signature. If he did, he would be the youngest painter ever in the history of that institution to be able to do so. And he would be able to benefit from the not inconsiderable advantages that membership of this exclusive club could offer.

The Royal Academy offered its Academicians and Associates significant financial benefits over other working artists, at a time of general severe economic recession. The continuing war on the Continent was crippling painters and engravers along with everyone else. Farington's diary is littered with news that testifies to the casualties of the squeeze. The publishers Valentine and Rupert Green had gone bankrupt; the printseller John Boydell had put his latest project, *A History of the River Thames*, on hold; the painter Francis Wheatley had been arrested for debts; even Benjamin West, the King's darling, who had taken over the presidency of the Academy in 1792, had seen his overall income fall by 25 per cent, and his earnings from prints decimated.

The last quarter of the eighteenth century had seen London overtake Paris as the main centre for the international export of engravings. But now, with blockades on continental trade imposed by the war with France, the lucrative export market for British work had collapsed.

1. *Self-Portrait, c.* 1790. This little self-portrait of Turner was given by the artist to the Narraways in Bristol. John Narraway's niece Ann Dart then sold it to John Ruskin, who gave it to Mrs Booth.

2. *Radley Hall from the South East*, 1789. This view shows the influence of contemporary topographical artists such as Paul Sandby, who often used the curling branches of trees to frame his subject.

3. Edward Burney, *The Antique School at New Somerset House,* 1780. Drawing from plaster casts of antique statuary was one of the first disciplines entrants to the Royal Academy Schools were required to master. The Antique School, or Plaister Academy, as it was known, was often unruly, with students hurling at each other the bread intended for rubbing out.

4. *A View of the Archbishop's Palace, Lambeth,* exhibited 1790. This painting marked Turner's professional debut when it was shown at the RA's annual exhibition in April 1790, just as the artist turned fifteen.

5. Henry Monro the Elder,
Dr Thomas Monro, c. 1810.

6. Henry Edridge, *Young Turner,*
1794–7. The camaraderie of Monro's
Academy is reflected in a handful
of pencil sketches of its 'students'.

7. J. M. W. Turner and Thomas Girtin, after John R. Cozens, *South Gate of Sargans,* 1794–7. The atmospheric work of John Robert Cozens had a profound influence on Turner, who copied this image from an album that belonged to Richard Payne Knight and was loaned to Monro.

8. *Beech Trees,* 1795. Ann Dart remembered that Turner was very fond of trees, and these beech trees may have been drawn at Norbury Park in Surrey as part of a trip while staying at Dr Monro's cottage at nearby Fetcham.

9. *South View of Salisbury Cathedral from the Cloisters,* 1802. Turner's virtuosity in depicting intricate gothic architecture is matched here by his originality in the choice of an archway in the cloister to frame the view. He takes considerable liberty in his depiction of scale.

10. *Gateholme Stack*, 1795. Though in his earliest depictions of Margate Turner avoided the challenge of depicting the sea, by the mid-1790s his ability to capture water in motion was as great as his ability to represent the other elements.

11. *Fishermen at Sea*, 1796. His first exhibited oil painting, *Fishermen at Sea* marked the level of Turner's ambition. The rapidity with which he mastered the new medium is also evidence of his astonishing technical ability.

12. Sir Thomas Lawrence, *A Portrait of Joseph Farington*, 1795. Farington was both a landscape painter and a friend of Monro; his approval and support were eagerly sought by Turner.

13. George Romney, *William Beckford*, 1782. Beckford, described as the richest commoner in England, extended exceptional patronage to British artists as he pursued his eccentric dream to make Fonthill Abbey a palace of art.

14. *The Fifth Plague of Egypt*, 1800. The painting makes reference to Beckford's own experience of a storm in Padua, and may also make oblique reference to Napoleon's recent campaign in Egypt.

15. *Nude Swiss Girl and Companion on a Bed*, 1802. Some consider that the second, darker figure in the bed is a man rather than another woman and may be an example of Turner putting himself into his drawing.

16. *The Festival upon the Opening of the Vintage of Mâcon*, exhibited 1803. There is no evidence that Turner attended such a ceremony, but by giving this typically Claudian scene a French setting he gave it contemporary relevance, reflecting the renewal of interest in French life during the brief peace.

17. Engraving by John Wright after John Hoppner, *Sir George Howland Beaumont, 7th Bt.* Beaumont was a passionate advocate of the landscape genre. With fixed views on what constituted good art, however, he would become Turner's most ardent critic, and would succeed in significantly undermining Turner's career and his marketability.

18. *The Drawing Room of 45 Grosvenor Place*, 1819. Turner made a point of recording an exhibition of his watercolours held by his great friend and patron Walter Fawkes at his London home. The show revealed the scope and brilliance of Turner's work in that medium.

But for members of the RA at least, there were exemptions from the punishing income taxes that William Pitt had introduced to help pay for the expensive conflict with France. Thanks to the powerful lobbying of that institution, in 1797 Pitt had added a clause to his income tax bill in favour of Academicians and Associates of the Royal Academy. Academicians and Associates had an exemption from a full tax on servants, while their homes would benefit from the same tax allowances afforded shops.

This exemption was something Turner could benefit from. He had revealed to Farington that he was desperate to move out of his cramped rooms in Maiden Lane, admitting that though 'by continuing to reside at his Father's, he benefited him and his mother . . . He thought He might derive advantages from placing himself in a more respectable situation.'[4]

Farington underestimated just how much money Turner was managing to earn. Assuming a degree of youthful impecunity, he suggested Turner 'continue in his present situation till he had laid aside a few hundred pounds'. In fact, by October 1798 Turner had £950 invested in the Bank of England, and was in a very good position to move to a new house.

Turner's meteoric rise and healthy financial position had not come without sacrifice. Stephen Rigaud relates an amusing story from this time that reveals the combination of ceaseless graft and Spartan lifestyle that lay at the heart of Turner's success and mounting wealth. Turner was staying with the Revd Nixon in Kent when the young Rigaud joined them for a sketching weekend. Rigaud was acutely aware that on the Sunday, when he and Nixon attended church, Turner remained 'shut up in his little study . . . diligently painting in Water colours'. The next day the party went on a lengthy walk to sketch. But when they stopped for lunch, Turner's frugality amazed them. 'Some chops and steaks were soon set before us which we ate with the keen relish of appetite, and our worthy friend the Clergyman . . . proposed we should call for some wine . . . but Turner, though he could take his glass very cheerfully at his friend's house, now hung his head, saying – "No. I can't stand that" . . . so we did without wine.' Rigaud was particular to point out that 'at that time he was the richest man of the three; Mr Nixon having then but a very small Curacy, and I having little more than the pocket money allowed me by my father'.[5]

There was more. Turner had garnered new acquaintances and contacts within artistic circles, but he had done so at the expense of the friendship of some of his earliest benefactors. He had also turned against the possibility of marriage, and had sidelined family life, in favour of making his work his sole *raison d'être*.

This hardening of his professional resolve goes back to the year in which he came of age. It was the year in which he had had his first oil painting so well received. But 1796, which should have been the *annus mirabilis* when he turned twenty-one, instead became a year in which Turner was thrown into personal turmoil. He had some form of breakdown. The cause of this crisis was his girl in Margate.

After the annual RA exhibition in the summer of 1796, Turner headed to the resort he so loved to propose to Elizabeth White, only to discover she had become engaged to a local man.

Turner had pushed himself to his limits for the past five years. His output had been prodigious. His toil, non-stop. His earnings impressive for someone of his age and profession. Since he was nineteen he had been investing annually what a curate, civil servant or shopkeeper might earn in a year. Yet when he turned up in Margate with his accolades and investments, his astonishing achievements did not score highly enough for a woman who had become betrothed to a builder called Richard Wiles.[6]

And so instead of setting out once again on tour in the summer of 1796, Turner vanished. It is the only summer in his entire career in which he failed to work. The very few sketches that exist suggest he retreated to the Kent and Sussex coast, where he sat on beaches and sketched the shore life around him, and took refuge in dark parish churches, making accomplished accounts of the daily lives of a community. Something had broken in Turner. The tone of his sketches is newly contemplative.[7]

His sketchbook does reveal that some of that summer was spent in Brighton, a place where one could go to disappear and drown sorrows. The artist George Morland drowned many sorrows at that seaside town when he was hiding from his numerous creditors and it is very tempting to place Morland and Turner alongside one another here, though evidence that they knew each other is only circumstantial.

But circumstantial though it may be, there is something particularly Morlandish about the few sketches, and particularly the subject matter that Turner engaged with, in this lost summer in Sussex. Morland, older than Turner by a good decade, was a painter who could have made a fortune, had he been a half-decent businessman rather than a womanizing pleasure-seeker who put gin and chaos before good sense. His speciality was rural life: pigs and horses, milkmaids and cottages, cattle and farmyards, and sometimes coastal scenes with wreckers or fishermen, or woods with gypsies sitting around campfires.

Turner would have encountered Morland's scenes of rural life in his youth when he was working for John Raphael Smith, because Smith had bought a series of Morland's paintings to form what he called the Morland Gallery, and had made a considerable living off engravings based on it. He might also have caught sight of the painter in Margate, where in the mid-1780s he was being promoted by a 'lady of fortune' called Mrs Hill, and was living in the very street in which Thomas Coleman had his school. While Mrs Hill promoted Morland as a portrait painter, the latter enjoyed the amusements the town had on offer. He also enjoyed Mrs Hill's maid, a diversion which ultimately spelt the end of his patronage.

It was a similar array of distractions that attracted Morland to Brighton over a decade later. For Turner, perhaps wanting to forget a woman, the resort must have also been appealing – not least because it was framed by rocky cliffs from which he could contemplate the world.

Certainly when Turner went to Brighton he didn't do much work. His ambition vanished. His sketchbooks, far from being full of those topographical views of ruined abbeys and local landmarks, simply feature snapshots of seaside life: boats, families on the beach, a study of spotted pigs, a loose, instantaneous colour sketch of moonlight on the water. But little else.

At least one person relates something of Turner's personal pain around this time. In about 1792 Turner had forged a friendship with the landscape painter and drawing master William Frederick Wells, who became yet another of those welcoming folk who would routinely throw their doors open for the complicated but talented Mr Turner. Wells had a town house in Mount Street, where in the 1790s Turner would spend 'three or four evenings in the week' at the fireside, 'sketching or drawing by the light of an Argand Lamp'.

Wells had a daughter, Clara, five years junior to Turner, who became a lifelong friend and who interpreted the difficult and contradictory character with a high level of sensitivity and affection. He was to her, by her own account, 'an elder brother', who was 'a firm and affectionate friend to the end of his life, his feelings were seldom seen on the surface, but they were deep and enduring. No one could have imagined under that rather rough and cold exterior, how very strong were the affections which lay hidden beneath.'

In Clara's accounts one senses the ongoing struggle the Turner family faced with Mary Turner's declining mental health. It must have handicapped William Turner senior's business as much as it made domestic life painful for both him and his son. Clara described how Turner was exhausted by it: 'In early life my father's house was his second home, a haven of rest from many domestic trials, too sacred to touch upon.' She adds, 'Oh! what a different man would Turner have been if all the good and kindly feelings of his great mind had been called into action; but they lay dormant, and were known to so very few. He was by nature suspicious, and no tender hand had wiped away early prejudices . . .'[8]

Suspicion is an interesting attribute to ascribe to Turner's character. It necessarily stems from disappointment, betrayal or exploitation. The first of these sentiments might apply to a mother who had failed him because of her mental frailty, the second from Miss White's choice of husband. In terms of the third sentiment, it is worth noting that at around this time Turner began to measure his monetary value as a painter quite closely. He was becoming attuned to the fact that the patronage he necessarily had to foster was not always as generous as it should be. Artists could easily be undervalued by an aristocracy which monopolized the market. Meanwhile the engravers and publishers he worked for were more than capable of making money off the back of other people's talent.

A case in point was John Raphael Smith's exploitation of George Morland's talent, as well as that of the Anglo-Swiss artist Henry Fuseli. The artist and journalist Benjamin Robert Haydon noted bitterly in his diary that Fuseli, whose 'Nightmare was decidedly popular all over Europe', was paid by Smith '£30 for the Picture and the Engraver cleared 600 by the print!'[9]

The most famous of all the speculative publishers of the day was John Boydell, who had launched his Shakespeare Gallery in May 1789. He commissioned the greatest painters of the day to produce Shakespearian pictures, which he exhibited and subsequently engraved for a mass market. Though Boydell bought his painters out for fairly hefty sums, there were still plenty of observers who portrayed him as exploiting not just the talent of his fellow artists, but the Bard himself. The caricaturist James Gillray was quick to depict Boydell with two large money bags under each arm, entitled *Shakespeare Sacrificed or the Offering to Avarice*.

Later in life Turner's friend the painter George Jones remembered of Turner that 'the hands extended to him sought to profit by his talents at the smallest expense possible; he encountered the extortion of his time and work, but discovered that he was unjustly used to fill the purses of others rather than his own. He became suspicious and so sensitive that he at length dreaded the motive of all by whom he was approached on business.'[10]

Lord Elgin, the ambassador to the Ottoman empire, was a spectacular example of the worst kind of aristocratic attitude towards artists. In 1799 Turner, his friend and rival Girtin, and other artists were interviewed by Lord Elgin for the position of artist to accompany him on a tour of Greece, as part of his ambition to record the monuments there. Girtin was the first young artist to be called for interview. He was made to wait two hours before the Lord deigned to see him and offer him a salary of £30 per year – about half what a gentleman's valet might expect annually. Elgin also suggested that Girtin's duties would include helping Lady Elgin in the decoration of

her firescreens and other domestic enterprises. After Girtin declined
the offer, Robert and Richard Smirke, both reputable artists, were
offered similarly unpalatable terms. So was William Daniell. In the
end Turner was interviewed. The Lord was now aware that he needed
to improve his terms, so the work in relation to his wife's hobbies was
modified to drawing lessons. But for the salary he was offering, Elgin
expected to own all the work Turner produced during the course of
the appointment. At this point in his career Turner could secure 40
guineas for a single watercolour, so he proposed a sum of £400 to buy
out his productivity for a twelve-month period. But even though this
seems a reasonable request, it far outstripped the value Elgin was prepared to put on the young man and his talents.

Turner's collapse in 1796 did more than threaten his personal wellbeing. It compromised his work. Turner must have vowed that never
again would he allow his own susceptibility to emotional hurt to
impact on his career. And so he made a simple choice. He chose his
Art as the sole purpose of his life. Domestic life was no longer allowed
to impinge on what from now on would define him. He would no
longer invest in affection that might be rejected. Marriage was no
longer a viable option. If there was anything Turner was going to be
married to, it was painting, at the expense of everything else.

As for those who might abuse Turner commercially, this must
have strengthened further his resolve to attain a status that would
provide a degree of protection. Becoming an Associate of the RA,
and ultimately an Academician, would place him on an elevated
social level that commanded not only a significant degree of respect
in society, but also provided a floor for the price of his work.

So Turner emerged as a tougher man at the end of 1796. Shyness
became aloofness. His compulsion to draw solidified into a mission-
ary zeal for his painting. Work, status, progress and painting were his
sole focus. Those who did not share his profession or his enthusiasms
were relegated in his priorities.

Across the next couple of years the victims of this new, apparently
sometimes heartless and rather more self-important Turner emerge.
It is not just the Monro family who note M'lord Turner emerging
from the eager boy they once knew. John Narraway witnessed a

noticeable change in the young man's character. His complaint is particularly vivid. For not only does Narraway protest that Turner fails to correspond with the family despite their continuing hospitality, he also cites one instance in the summer of 1798 when he lent Turner a horse, saddle and cloak for one of his trips into Wales which Turner neither returned nor paid for. As a result the self-portrait of this unofficial 'family member' was relegated to the hallway. No longer welcome in the drawing room.

Up until and including 1796, Turner's watercolours had been priced modestly at around three guineas each. From 1797 onwards he was on a mission to increase the value of his work. And astonishingly he achieved a twelvefold increase in prices across just three years.

The modest price he had charged early on in his career had helped fuel Turner's popularity. Alongside his high-profile, aristocratic patrons, the affordability of his work attracted a diverse assembly of keen followers.

Dr Monro was one. He began to acquire some of Turner's work executed outside the auspices of his own Academy. In 1794 he bought a view of St Anselm's chapel, at Canterbury Cathedral. The names of other clients appear in lists that Turner sometimes made in his sketchbooks. In one of his south Wales sketchbooks, alongside the orders for Sir Richard Colt Hoare, Viscount Malden and the engraver Landseer, are the names of other interested parties: a Dr Matthews, a Mr Lambirt (*sic*), a Mr Laurie, as well as Mr Mitchell and Mr Kershaw. Similarly in a notebook dating from 1797 we see the name of Mr Munden alongside Mr Lascelles. Another fan was a Mr William Blake of Portland Place, who employed Turner as a drawing instructor as well as commissioning work from him. It is little wonder that Turner would remark to Joseph Farington in 1798 that he had 'had more commissions at present than he could execute & got more money than He expended'.[11]

Mr Munden is traceable. And his interest in the young artist provides a glimpse into Turner's relationships with his clients at this point. No matter how gruff and remote the young Mr Turner might be to immediate friends and family, when it came to clients, Turner was clubbable, and jolly.

Joseph Shepherd Munden was a successful actor who had lived in

Frith Street in Soho, two doors down from his friend John Bannister, another actor, who had been a direct contemporary of Turner's at the Soho Academy. The fun-loving Munden's memoirs are a wonderfully evocative account of life in artistic circles in the 1790s.

Munden's house in Frith Street burned down at the end of 1794, thanks to a drunken neighbour who, having celebrated the acquittal of a group of radicals, Thomas Hardy, John Horne Tooke and John Thelwall, who had been charged with sedition and high treason, 'took the precaution of placing the candle under the bed . . . [and] soon became sensible to the inconvenience of such a practice'.[12]

The newly homeless actor took a small 'cottage of gentility', Croft Lodge, in Kentish Town, which at that time was still a rural outpost to the north of London. The property was small and unassuming, 'for it has no apartment underground. A little vault beneath the dining room served for a cellar; and the master of the house, when he had guests, was obliged to raise the carpet and descend a step ladder to fetch a fresh bottle.' Despite these inconveniences, some of the most wonderful talent of the day came to visit Munden in his leafy hideaway, including the popular poet and musician Thomas Moore and that old reprobate George Morland. 'Here Moore sang and Morland was accustomed to sit for hours with his favourite gin bottle before him, and sketch cattle from life.'[13]

Turner and Girtin were part of Munden's circle too. '*Wells Cathedral* by Turner and *Durham Castle* by Girtin' were both acquired by Munden through 'an intimacy with the artists and ready admittance to their studios' which 'enabled him to obtain these drawings at modest prices'.[14]

The mention of Turner's studio is intriguing. There is no question that he was still living and working in his cramped room at 26 Maiden Lane. The implication then is that Turner had adapted some of the rooms in the premises into a modest studio-cum-showroom where he could receive clients to present them with sketches, as well as store finished works. Farington visited these rooms, which he referred to as 'apartments'.[15]

The significance of Turner's showroom should not be underestimated. It marks an important shift in how he was beginning to present himself. He saw himself as not just an artist, who could be called upon by patrons to fulfil their desires. He was also an independent dealer. A businessman in fact. This was not unusual. All good professional artists in the eighteenth century were by nature businessmen of varying degrees of success. But it marks a point Turner has reached in his life at which he no longer considers himself a student, but a successful artist. And it is significant that he begins acting like a businessman in 1797, when in November of that year he registers himself as a 'dealer in pictures and drawings' with a fire insurance company, assessing the contents of his 'stock' at £300.[16]

The mention of Mr Lascelles in one of Turner's sketchbooks refers to Edward Lascelles junior, the son of the newly titled Lord Harewood. Harewood had inherited an estate of that name in Yorkshire when his cousin Edwin Lascelles died in 1795. With a vast house near Leeds as well as an impressive townhouse in London, the Harewood inheritance also brought a fortune which Joseph Farington noted with deep interest as being at least £50,000 a year.

Harewood was already a modest connoisseur of art before his windfall, and had become particularly friendly with the portrait artist John Hoppner. From the number of times Joseph Farington's diary records dinners at and visits to Hoppner's house only to discover Turner there, there is good evidence that Turner and Hoppner were on very friendly terms indeed and socialized together regularly. And so it may well have been Hoppner who suggested that Harewood's son, Edward Lascelles, might want to consider spending some of *his* new-found fortune on Turner.[17]

It was fortunate for Lascelles that his introduction to Turner came just as his family's spending power swelled, because now Turner began to boldly raise his prices. In 1796 Lascelles agreed to buy a watercolour of Westminster Abbey that Turner showed in the Academy exhibition of that year for the artist's then going rate of three guineas. In 1797, however, when Lascelles commissioned Turner to draw views of the family estate in Yorkshire, the latter asked ten guineas per watercolour from his new client, and got it.

The bravura of Turner's demand comes into focus when one realizes that 1797 was the year of a great financial crash in Britain, in which those aristocrats and merchant princes who did not lose their shirts at the very least lost their confidence. In February that year reserves in the Bank of England had become so low that Pitt had been forced to suspend specie payments at the Bank of England. People's value on paper was no longer secured. Meanwhile in America, a land speculation bubble burst, one in which many of the country's former colonists had invested. In addition, Pitt was introducing income taxes.

Turner's contemporary Martin Archer Shee described the panic which spread through town. 'In the midst of the London season, and in the very noontide of parliamentary activity, the gay and busy world of fashion was suddenly arrested,' he observed. 'Family after family, of the high aristocracy, under the influence of some ill-defined dread of disastrous consequences to themselves or their possessions, deserted their metropolitan residence, and with all the speed which heavy travelling carriages and over-worked post horses would admit, rushed down to their country seat, there to await, in the dignified retirement of their ancestral halls . . . the shock of that great political and social catastrophe . . . to dream of aught connected with art . . . at such a crisis, would have been, in their estimation, to emulate the recklessness, if not the depravity of him who "fiddled while Rome was burning"'.[18]

Lascelles's preparedness to pay a premium for art while the City crashed not only consolidated Turner's threefold increase in his asking prices, but instigated a trip to Yorkshire that would provide him with the inspiration for his next set of oil paintings. As he had done before with his watercolours, and with his commissions for engravings, once Turner entered a market, he expanded into it rapidly, and then quickly innovated.

Having shown *Fishermen at Sea* in 1796, and two oils featuring similar watery subject matter in the following year,[19] in 1798 he would double his output to show four oils at the RA and, what is more, offer a brand new subject matter that he had not tackled before in any medium: the north.

Since *Fishermen at Sea*, Turner had been searching for the right subject matter with which to consolidate his credentials as a painter in oils. One tiny sketchbook, no bigger than the palm of a hand, is testimony to his turning these new possibilities over in his mind. Called the 'Wilson sketchbook' because Turner noted on its spine that it contained '84 Studies for Pictures, Copies of Wilson', once again one sees his mind at work.

Richard Wilson was a Welsh landscape painter, a generation older than Turner, and had died in 1782. He had travelled extensively on the Continent, where he had absorbed the style of Claude Lorrain, painting light-filled classical landscapes. But on his return to Britain he had begun to view his own Welsh landscape through a classical lens. This elevation of the British landscape into something grander was what Turner was now keen to explore. But above all it was Wilson's tendency to imbue his canvases with the deep golden yellow glow of setting or rising suns that really captured Turner's imagination.

Turner had seen these light-filled canvases by Wilson as a boy in the Trimmer house in Brentford. He now moved in circles where Wilson's work was well represented. Thomas Monro and Sir George Beaumont owned paintings by Wilson, as did the President of the Royal Academy, Benjamin West. Joseph Farington, who had been a pupil of Wilson's, lent his paintings by Wilson to students on a regular basis. Turner mined his connections with these men and others and copied Wilson's Italianate landscapes into his sketchbook: *The Temple of Clitumnus*, *The Bridge of Augustus at Rimini*, and the imposing spectacle of a *Convent on a Rock*.

But rather than making oil sketches of Wilson's paintings, he copied them in watercolour, in a move that would ultimately have a profound effect on his own work. It was probably just lateral thinking that suggested to Turner that he should adapt traditional watercolour techniques to get something closer to an 'oil' effect. Whereas watercolourists apply their watery paint on to white paper, which can be left unpainted or to show through the transparent wash in varying degrees, in the Wilson sketchbook Turner paints his paper with a reddish-brown base colour, the same colour that was traditionally used as a ground for oil painting. This innovation creates something new in watercolour painting. In effect it reverses the process, forcing the artist to work from dark to light, rather than light to dark. Turner also thickens the consistency of his water-based paint to give it 'body'. For his paint to show over the dark ground, he adds chalk, and in doing so makes an opaque 'gouache'.

His work instantly feels more substantial. The mass of buildings, rocks and trees is conveyed with new vigour. There is a robustness and depth that he has not exploited before. The contrast of the palette is greater, with dark browns, blacks and greys placed against bright oranges, yellows and whites. Rather than the delicate and complex scale of tones Turner had spent years mastering, one now gets bold juxtaposition of dark black and bright white, deep red and rich yellow. Suddenly night scenes are in his grasp like never before. And interiors can benefit from the deep chiaroscuro contrasts. Above all, he explores the dramatic potential of light in a totally new manner, fascinated by how it can momentarily define mass, and life.

In this minute sketchbook he captures a deep red sunset breaking through dark grey storm clouds; he frames a russet sky hanging over London, through the black silhouettes of trees; he reveals jet black water as the sun casts a final ray on it; he shows us sailing vessels illuminated by moonlight. And he then explores how light defines interiors. He depicts a dark industrial interior with workers lit up by the light emanating from a kiln; and, with astonishing detail, he goes into dark churches and picks out the shafts of light piercing through stained glass windows.

This sketchbook marked the first moment that Turner declared his true individuality as a painter, because in the years to come it would be this technical cross-referencing between oil paint and watercolour that would encourage him to achieve new effects and convey a vision that would become uniquely his own. In this tiny book one gets the sense of that intense enquiry and captivation with the power of light and its dramatic relationship to mass that would come to define his work in the future. And it was in search of this new kind of material that Turner headed north in the summer of 1797.

Of course Turner also had to fulfil his profitable commissions for Edward Lascelles and his other clients. Lascelles had requested four views of the magnificent Harewood House, and two views of the ruined Harewood Castle, which stood within his estate. But some of the views he made would form the basis of future sales too. A view of Lindisfarne for Joseph Shepherd Munden.[20] And views of Harewood and Norham Castle in Northumberland for William Blake. So Turner mapped out a tour that took him north through Derbyshire, a county he had already explored to a degree, but then into the unknown territories of Yorkshire, north-east into County Durham, to Newcastle and then further north to Northumberland, before heading west into Cumbria and the Lakes, and then returning to Yorkshire for a stay at Harewood.

There were many in Turner's circle who knew the north well. Dayes had travelled and drawn there extensively. And Girtin had made a tour there the year before, and so Turner would have been well equipped with recommendations. And he may well have taken some other equipment unrelated to his art on what was going to be a very major excursion: a whistle and a fishing rod.

In his later life, fishing became a passion of Turner's. And the fact that ballads and glees are jotted down from time to time in his sketchbooks suggests that alongside the solitary and contemplative sport of fishing, Turner would also turn out a song or a tune, not least when it might make the great number of miles he covered pass more swiftly.

These diversions aside, however, his sketchbooks reflect how, on this tour, his professional agenda had changed. Although he dutifully makes the customary pencil sketches of cathedrals, abbeys and other places of historic interest, he is far more selective in what he works up in colour. This newly sparing use of his portable watercolour palette marks a clear distinction in the purpose of the sketches. Those executed in pencil are largely done to enlarge his personal collection of 'views', and are intended to be filed in his studio for future reference – an investment that proved sound, given there is plenty of evidence that Turner continued to refer to these sketches throughout the rest of his career.

When he does apply colour, he reveals what he wants to explore for exhibition. Almost without exception, he is exploring drama and light.

So having made fairly cursory records of Wingfield Manor in Derbyshire, a church at Dronfield, Rotherham Bridge, Conisbrough,

Doncaster, Pontefract and Wakefield, he suddenly pauses at Kirkstall Abbey in Yorkshire to make fuller studies. Kirkstall fired
Turner's imagination, offering him the opportunity to explore further the interior light he had begun to develop in the Wilson
sketchbooks. He made eleven sketches here, the most extensive
series of views he had done on the trip to this point. Significantly,
this ruined abbey was also one several of Turner's contemporaries,
including Girtin and Dayes, had already drawn, and he would want
to be able to produce his own version out of his innate sense of
competition.[21]

Most of the sketches of Kirkstall are just pencil, but one of the dark
undercroft has just a few brushmarks of paint. The ruined abbey provided convenient stabling for some of the local animals, and Turner
discovered a small group of cows sheltering there. In his sketch of the
undercroft he takes just three colours, a red-brown, a yellow-green
and a blue. With the red-brown he just touches the three cows. With
the green and blue he gives the slightest hint of the landscape glimpsed
through an arch that gives on to rural Yorkshire. It is a brilliant personal aide-memoire. For in the finished watercolour, the undercroft
is largely dark, and just a shaft of light from an opening out of sight
reveals the warm rich colours of the cows' hides.

Fountains Abbey, near Ripon in north Yorkshire, was the next
stop on Turner's tour to really catch his eye. This was another hugely
popular site. What had once been the largest Cistercian monastery in
medieval England had been reduced to ruins and, since earlier in the
century, had been incorporated into a vast romantic water garden
created by the Aislabie family, who had accrued enormous wealth as
part of the South Sea Bubble. When Turner got there it was already a
point of pilgrimage for tourists, had become dubbed the Wonder
of the North, and had been depicted by a number of artists. He
sought out a particularly unusual view, working up a colour sketch
of a section of the ruined dormitory and transept that bridged a
stream, creating a particularly haunting silhouette against the evening light.

After three or four weeks on the road Turner arrived at Durham,
and from this point on the bleak landscape of the far north captivates

him. This was a new kind of landscape for Turner. He was instantly gripped by the bleakness of Tynemouth, where he detailed a huge mass of jutting cliff and the silhouette of a ruined priory on its crest.

At Bothal in Northumberland there is a suggestion that he accompanied another traveller for safety and companionship. He sketched two figures on a bridge, one playing a tin whistle, in the same way that in the Wales sketchbooks one senses that his lonesome figures are projections of himself in his new-found surroundings.

But it is unlikely that a travelling companion would be prepared to go to the lengths that Turner was, to capture his subjects in extremis. At Dunstanburgh in Northumberland, the great looming castle sits atop a bleak basalt outcrop. It delivered the mood of resolution and solitude that Turner saw hinted at Tynemouth.

However, Norham Castle, on the banks of the River Tweed in Northumberland, became the star of Turner's northern odyssey. This ancient border castle had once protected the English from endless assaults by the Scots, in a place that had been called the most dangerous and adventurous part of England. At Norham Turner became transfixed by the luminosity of the place.

Whether he walked the six miles from Berwick in darkness or bivouacked on site, that Turner was almost blinded by the sunrise as he sketched the ancient stronghold with the sun rising behind is suggested by the brevity of the drawings he made.[22] That the experience triggered a new level of ambition in him is suggested by a series of experiments he did on his return to London.

Back in Maiden Lane, Turner worked up two different colour trials for a finished watercolour for Blake. He painted a different wash of colour on the back of each trial. Was Turner, enraptured by the luminous dawn he had experienced at Norham, considering making a series of back-lit paintings as some form of novelty? This may sound bizarre, but experimentation went hand in hand with art at this time. Georgian theatres used back-lit landscapes, and Turner must have been aware of the theatrical practice of painting different canvas backings to influence the degree of luminosity projecting forward into the theatre. But there were other instances of back-lit art in the eighteenth century too. During those illuminations that served to celebrate momentous events, while larger images were projected on to buildings, households would often display smaller images in their windows, back-lit with candles. Thomas Gainsborough had also experimented with back-lighting, with his special 'show box' for people to peer into.[23] So passionate was Thomas Monro about Gainsborough's candle-lit show box that he had acquired this novelty from the artist's daughter, and often delighted his friends with what he called the 'Gainsborough Show'.[24] The device showed back-lit landscapes viewed through a magnifying lens. Turner must have peered into it on several occasions, and he would have witnessed the enhanced atmospheric effect provided.

If Turner was considering some form of back-lit novelty, it was entirely in the spirit of the age of invention and experiment. Thomas Girtin had already taken a plunge with his own brave adventure.

In the early 1790s a Scottish painter, Robert Barker, who had already had success with a panoramic view of Edinburgh in that city, set up the first panorama in London. This was a giant 270-degree view of the City, drawn from the top of Albion Mills on the south bank of the River Thames, close to Blackfriars Bridge. Londoners flocked to this spectacle, and such was the success of the show that Barker opened a permanent panorama in Leicester Square the following year. He then enlisted the assistance of his own son Henry, a pupil at the Royal Academy with Turner, as well as that of Girtin in the production of a view of the Grand Fleet at Spithead for his new permanent venue. By 1797 Girtin had embarked on his own massively ambitious project to go further than Barker and make a 360-degree panorama of London. Entitled his *Eidometropolis*, it would be made from drawings, probably using some form of camera obscura, taken from the roof of the British Plate Glass Manufacturing Company, for a spectacle that would, by the time of its completion, take up 1,944 square feet of canvas.

Girtin and Turner were becoming the darlings of London society. After Thomas Monro had paired them, others had followed. Edward Lascelles had invited Girtin to draw Harewood, as well as Turner. Julia Bennet, a society heiress who would go on to become Lady Gordon, determined to take drawing lessons from both young men.

Turner had a particular way of working with his pupils, as Julia Bennet's surviving works suggest. Turner furnished her with his own works to copy and colour, and would then sit next to her taking her through the process of his craft, guiding her hand. 'First with Mr Turner 1797' is written on the back of a watercolour of Cowes Castle they made together. Another, of Llangollen Bridge, is inscribed: 'Julia Bennet with Mr Turner, May 1797'.

Turner got on well with women. Perhaps in the company of the opposite sex his bristling sense of competition and silent determination slipped in favour of something altogether softer and more generous.

The extremely talented amateur painter the Duchess of Sutherland, a woman who was dominating social circles in London after having fled Paris in the Revolution, was another woman who enjoyed Turner's company. She may well have been his student, like Julia Bennet. And like Bennet and Lascelles she clearly enjoyed encouraging the rivalry between Turner and Girtin.

'Hoppner told me Mr Lascelles as well as Lady Sutherland are disposed to set up Girtin against Turner,' Farington revealed to his diary in February 1799 – 'who they say effects his purpose by industry – the former more genius – Turner finishes too much.'[25]

Despite Girtin's progress in his own personal business ventures, Turner ultimately discarded his project to show back-lit paintings. He made a conventional watercolour of Norham instead. That term is used cautiously, for *Norham Castle on the Tweed, Summer's Morn* was still technically very innovative. Turner infused the painting with the colour of the early morning sunshine by using a yellow ground, which he revealed either by stopping out, or simply by leaving it unpainted. This rich yellow ground may have been suggested by the experiments he had done using a coloured ground in the Wilson sketchbook. The painting positively glowed.[26]

The potential effect of painting on the *back* of his watercolour was, however, something that Turner continued to exploit with an ingenuity that astounded his contemporaries.

'Turner was endless in his artistic resources,' the painter John Call-cott Horsley reminisced.

One time I studied almost daily one of his finest water-colours, called *'The Snowdon Range'*, which was a marvel from end to end, so exqui-sitely beautiful in itself and perfect in its executive power. The theme was the combination of the last rays of the setting sun and a moon-rise. There was one passage that I feasted upon again and again. It was the tender warmth of the light clouds encircling the moon, and I tried all kinds of glasses to see if I could learn how it was done, but failed to satisfy myself. Just at that time the drawing began 'to buckle' from its mount, and I discussed many times with its owner . . . Sir Seymour Haden . . . what measures should be taken respecting this unpleasing development. At that time we had in London a supremely able mounter of drawings of the name of Hogarth, whose advice it was determined to ask.

We showed the drawing to him, and he said it must be taken off the old mount and remounted. Haden said, 'But how do you get it off?' And I shall not forget the horror of his look when Hogarth answered, 'Well, sir, we must put it in a bath.' However, after much persuasion, Haden agreed to trust the drawing to his care. To his great alarm he received a note very shortly, begging him to call with-out delay. He did so, and rushed into Hogarth's shop exclaiming, 'What is it, what is it! Have you spoilt the drawing.' 'No, no, sir, we have got it off beautifully, but having so often heard Mr. Horsley speak of the rosy tint round the moon, I thought you would be inter-ested to know that I have discovered how it was obtained!' He produced the drawing, and turned it on its face. There was a revela-tion! A circle of orange vermilion had been plastered on the back with an ivory palette knife where he wanted the effect, and then worked sufficiently far through the pores of the previously wetted paper to give the show of colour, while retaining the smooth surface without a trace of workmanship on the right side.[27]

The lessons Turner learnt with his first expression of Norham Castle were transformative. Many years later he returned to Norham with the publisher Robert Cadell, and on arriving at the castle removed his hat and gave the castle a bow. Explaining the gesture, Turner recalled that 'I made a drawing or painting of Norham several years since. It took, and from that day to this I have had as much to do as my hands could execute.'[28]

When *Norham Castle on the Tweed, Summer's Morn* was exhibited at the RA, it was not just the compelling luminosity of Turner's watercolour that caught his public's imagination. In his depiction of Norham, Turner also managed to capture something of the grandeur and nostalgia that Richard Wilson and Claude Lorrain brought to their subjects. Without being overtly classical, he nevertheless had found a composition combining a magnificent ruin with a pastoral scene that spoke to that school and moved his work beyond the topographical or picturesque, into something altogether more aspirational.

The critics were effusive in their praise. The watercolour was 'a work upon which we could rivet our eyes for hours and not experience satiety . . . Every repeated view of it discovers new perfections. The light and shade are so skillfully managed and the perspective inimitably just, that every division of the picture at once strikes the eyes and seems rather nature in miniature than a transcript.'[29]

But above all it was the fact that Turner had produced a picture of such ambition and power in watercolour that astounded his peers.

'It has the force and harmony of an oil painting,' another critic wrote. 'It is charmingly finished and the effect is both bold and natural. In short, we think it is the best landscape in the present Exhibition.'[30]

Mr Blake was thrilled. He had commissioned the piece for an agreed eight guineas, and now it was the toast of the show. Turner then displayed that wily commercial sense that would give him his reputation of being sometimes just too difficult to deal with. John Pye, an engraver, later recalled that Blake 'was loud in his expressions of pleasure at having become the proprietor of so beautiful a work. "But" said Turner "I have been offered 12 guineas for it". Mr Blake having objected to paying for it more than the sum agreed upon, and also to preventing Turner being the recipient of the larger sum, the work never came into Mr Blake's possession.'[31]

It wasn't just Norham that seemed to be breaking new ground for

Turner in 1798. The whole group of works he showed that year, when taken altogether, reveal a marked shift in his work.

Instead of the topographical views he had been producing to such applause for the last few years, now he delivered a series of ambitious, dramatic landscapes. And it was the fact that he delivered these dramatic landscapes in both oil and watercolour that his contemporaries found so impressive.

Alongside Norham Castle, Turner's other submissions in watercolour included a dramatic depiction of Holy Island, and a haunting view of the transept of Fountains Abbey which, in the vein of Norham, Turner chose to depict in silhouette, this time against a setting sun.

The compositions he produced in oil offer similar theatre. He delivered a windswept and solitary Dunstanburgh Castle, as well as dramatic studies of the Lake District, which he had encountered for the first time in his tour of the north. He painted Lake Buttermere in Cumberland in the midst of a storm, a rainbow breaking through a dark shower of pelting rain, the contrast between the bright rainbow and the grey rain greatly accentuated in the finished work when compared with the sketch.

There is another attribute that Turner bestows on both his watercolours and oils in the 1798 show that marks a departure, and that is a sense of time and event. For the first time in his exhibited work, he provides a sense of narrative in the titles of his paintings. The group of works tell the stories of different transient moments, and in their focus on these moments, they necessarily offer an experiential element. The viewer is not just invited to see a depiction of a place, but encouraged to respond to the sensation of morning or evening, of a squall or shower. Winesdale is shown in the morning, so are the Coniston Fells. Dunstanburgh is seen at sunrise after a squally night. Norham is a summer morn, and Fountains Abbey is evening. Buttermere is in the midst of a shower.

All these aspects of his work for this exhibition suggest his concerted attempts to deliver works that engaged with the continuing debate about what might constitute 'sublime' art, and they really reveal for the first time Turner as an artist who is not just technically brilliant, and innovative, but also operating at a consciously intellectual level.

Burke had suggested that 'The passion caused by the great and sublime in nature, when those causes operate most powerfully, is astonishment; and astonishment is that state of the soul, in which all its motions are suspended, with some degree of horror . . . Astonishment, as I have said, is the effect of the sublime in its highest degree; the inferior effects are admiration, reverence, and respect.'[32]

Sure enough, with this group of pictures Turner went out of his way to astonish his viewers. Crucially, it is not as if Turner depicts the sublime by remove. It is not as if he is transcribing nature, and inviting us to imagine the sublime effect of the real thing. Rather, by encouraging a sense of moment, of experience, he is inviting a genuine reaction to the painting itself. For Turner it is not just nature that can evoke reaction, but Art as well.

As if to make this point all the more emphatically, Turner did something no other landscape artist had done before at an RA show. He added lines of poetry to five out of his ten submissions.

In January 1798 the Academy's professor of painting, James Barry, had given a lecture on the relationship between painting, sculpture and poetry. Barry argued that all things being equal, a painter had to work harder, and needed greater genius to conjure images and evoke emotions that a poet need merely suggest.

Barry's lecture was followed within a few days by a change in regulation governing the submission of pictures to the forthcoming RA show for 1798. The Academy decreed that 'every artist may give in writing such descriptions of his Performance, as he thinks proper for insertion in the catalogue; but it is expected that such descriptions shall be confined to as few Words as are absolutely necessary'.[33]

No other landscape painter took advantage of this opportunity except for Turner. As if he wished to make Barry's point for him. Just as he had consciously thrown down the glove to his elders in the past by delivering works that, in their homage to Dayes or Rooker or Van de Velde, also revealed Turner's innate rivalry with the original, in 1798 he took on Milton, and another immensely popular poet of the day, the author of 'Rule, Britannia', James Thomson.

Against Norham Castle, he included lines from Thomson's *Seasons*:

> But yonder comes the powerful King of Day,
> Rejoicing in the East: The lessening cloud,
> The Kindling azure, and the mountain's brow
> Illumin'd – his near approach betoken glad.

Turner must have felt that his election as an Associate that November was a fait accompli. He had gathered a number of supporters, and had resorted to all the encouragements within his gift. It was not just Farington who had been promised a watercolour. Hoppner too had been invited to Maiden Lane to look through his sketchbooks, and had alighted upon a view of Durham. One assumes that there were other members of the RA also eagerly awaiting their Turner watercolours that winter.

But Turner was to be disappointed. On the morning of Monday 5 November he found himself knocking on Farington's door in a small panic. He had heard that Arthur William Devis, a portrait and landscape painter, had managed to capture the imagination of the Academy and had secured 'great interest'. The other name on people's lips was the sculptor John Rossi, whom Turner admitted he would be prepared to lose to. But his sense of his own worth meant that he 'shd not like the other to be preferred'.[34]

Farington felt that Turner's concerns about Devis were unfounded, and that 'he had a better chance than Rossi . . .' But the master of Academy politics had for once got it wrong. Turner was not elected and Rossi was. It was another blow for Turner. The second in as many years.

8.   Gothick

In December 1797 a theatrical phenomenon packed the Drury Lane Theatre. The stage had been transformed into a great medieval gothic hall. And for the first time since Hamlet's father had spoken to his son on the imagined battlements of Elsinore, a spectre appeared before a startled audience.

The ghost in question was one Evelina, who haunted a medieval Welsh castle. Her first appearance on the stage that winter marked the beginning of a hit run for Monk Lewis's drama *The Castle Spectre,* which would make the play, and its starring spirit, one of the most reviewed, most performed and most talked-about events of the end of the eighteenth century.

Evelina herself was part of the zeitgeist of the 1790s. That Turner had spent much of his career already drawing the kind of medieval castle that the fictional Evelina haunted is a reminder of the extent to which his work was also part of that gothic moment that arose in the late eighteenth century. But as his life and career tipped into the first years of the nineteenth century, it was his own personal story that was to take a decidedly *more* gothic tone. Suddenly illicit sex would feature in his life. He would come into the intimate circle of one of the most profoundly dark and controversial men of his day. His poor mother would find herself incarcerated in a lunatic asylum, death would make its hand felt, and Turner himself would explore more deeply the realms of his personal imagination and individuality.

Turner may well have gone to see *The Castle Spectre* with the woman with whom he had become romantically, or at least sexually, entangled. This was Sarah Danby, that family friend whose husband John had had the misfortune to fall ill in an era where cures were few and far between.

John Danby died in pitiful circumstances. On 16 May 1798 his friends rallied again to raise some more money for their colleague.

That evening they were all assembled in Willis's rooms, in King Street, St James's, to listen to a concert for his benefit. As the *True Briton* newspaper reported three days later, 'the concert was attended by a respectable number of the Composer's friends; and the Performers, Vocal and Instrumental, benevolently gave their assistance to a Brother – Professor of so much merit . . .' But no one in the audience that night could have expected the terrible twist in Danby's tale. As the *True Briton* could not resist but relay, 'at half past eleven [about the time the concert closed] Mr. Danby died!'

Danby at least spared his friends the sight of his final moment. He was in his own bed at 46 Upper John Street, Fitzroy Square. His premature death at just forty-one left Sarah Danby and three small daughters terribly exposed, as the *True Briton* also pointed out: 'To the sons and daughters of harmony and humanity we need only add, that he has left a Widow and three small Children; and that he was for years in a very infirm state, we fear they are totally unprovided for.' What the paper did not reveal was that despite the parlous condition of her husband's health, Sarah Danby was also two months pregnant at the time of his death.

One gets a sense that William Turner senior was a man of enormous warmth and kindness. The great number of his clients, friends and extended family who went out of their way to forward the career of his son offers some reflection of this. And the kindnesses and assistance he encouraged his family to extend to Sarah Danby in the weeks and months after John's death must have been the catalyst for his son's attachment to the distressed widow, who was somewhere between ten and fifteen years older than him. But then, given Turner's disappointments in Margate, his father's failing business and his mother's failing health, it is easy to see how the embrace of an older, motherly figure might appeal.

From Sarah's point of view, she must have seen in her new young companion the shadow of her own, once ambitious and successful, former husband, and the opportunity for social leverage and financial security that went with it.

It was not just the Turners who concerned themselves with Sarah Danby's wellbeing. Just days after John's death, Sarah herself posted

an advertisement reminding the readers of *The Times* of the precariousness of her position, and begging leave to 'to solicit their Patronage and
Support on a future Occasion, being advised by her most particular
Friends to have a CONCERT in the course of the ensuing Winter, for
the Benefit of Herself and Three Infants'.[1] Ten months later Sarah
Danby had moved east to Cumberland Street, New Road, near Lisson
Green. From here she once again fell on the mercy of the public, inviting it to subscribe to an edition of *Danby's Posthumous Glees*, which was
now for the benefit of herself and her enlarged family of *four* children.

One of the co-authors and publishers of the *Posthumous Glees* was
Sarah's brother-in-law, Roche Jaubert. Jaubert's father, of the same
name, was a painter, broker and auctioneer who had died in 1778. His
son was working at Christie's auction house at the end of the 1790s.
The Jauberts had become close to the Danbys, and Roche junior and
John Danby had become firm friends. It was probably Jaubert's entrepreneurial mind behind the various benefit concerts that had kept his
friend's finances afloat during his final years.

The close friendship between the Danbys and the Turners encompassed the Jauberts too. Within a couple of years of John Danby's
death, Turner and Jaubert had taken premises together, and Jaubert
was probably a business partner of sorts in Turner's picture-dealing
business.[2] After Turner's death, the remnants of what would prove a
short-lived foray into dealing in Old Masters were evident in a number of indifferent paintings still in his possession: a couple of Dutch
School pictures in the manner of Van de Velde the Younger; a couple
of Italian School classical landscapes and a handful of drawings by
Herman Saftleven and Cornelius Simonz van de Schalke.

Jaubert and Turner were benefiting from the increased prosperity
in the picture-dealing business that came with the dissolution of the
French aristocracy, as well as the French invasion of the Low Countries and Italy. Art was a portable form of wealth that those escaping
the guillotine or fleeing invading forces brought with them to
London. The city was suddenly full of sixteenth- and seventeenth-
century continental work of varying quality. Perhaps nothing made
this point more clearly to the nation at the close of 1798 than the
exhibition of the extraordinary Orleans Collection, formerly the

property of the Duc d'Orléans, who had met his fate in Paris in the terror of 1793.

The Duc's vast assemblage of world-class French and Italian Old Masters, including works by Leonardo da Vinci, Titian, Raphael and Michelangelo, had been bought by a syndicate of British aristocrats – the Duke of Bridgewater, his nephew Earl Gower and the Earl of Carlisle – who had put it on show in Pall Mall and the Strand for seven months. The paying public who visited the show had never seen such a quantity or range of classical works, and its impact on public taste and enthusiasm should not be underestimated. It is no coincidence that Turner worked up his first attempts at a truly classical subject in the year of that show – a painting of *Aeneas and the Sibyl*, based on a drawing that Sir Richard Colt Hoare had made during his Italian tours in the 1780s of Lake Avernus.

The Romans believed that this legendary lake, situated in southern Italy, was the entrance to Hades. Richard Wilson had painted it in the 1760s, and though he populates his canvas with eighteenth-century folk, the tombs and ruins scattered around the lake's shore are a reminder of its Roman, mythological associations. Turner's view offers a similar show of tombs and ruins; however, he also depicts a scene from Virgil's *Aeneid* unfurling amid them, in which Aeneas seeks advice from the Sibyl on how to enter the underworld. Whether his view conflates time and deliberately presents an eighteenth-century view with ruins and an imagined past, or whether he suggests that even in the ancient past ruins were present at the site, is unclear.

It is interesting that after years working with members of the fledgling British School, and having made British views so much his forte, Turner should feel a need to turn towards the continental Old Masters. But if anything is evidenced by his career to date, it is his need to absorb the work and influence of other artists before moving on to make his own definitive, original contribution. Just a few years earlier it was Michael Angelo Rooker and John Raphael Smith against whom he was measuring himself. Now it was those original masters after whom they had been named.

The heightened sense that Turner had at the end of his career, that his work was part of a great history of art stretching back to the Renaissance, must have also originated around this time. Heritage was a popular topic of conversation. Some, notably picture dealer Noel Desenfans and Benjamin West, were of the firm belief that the Orleans Collection, rather than being broken up and sold, should be bought for the benefit of the British nation and its nascent school. While Desenfans published a pamphlet in favour of the foundation of a National Gallery that could extend the British Museum Galleries, West was hoping to purchase the collection to create a gallery associated with the Royal Academy.

Turner's new-found classicism was well timed. It served to heighten his increasing profile. The sums he was able to command for his work were increasing exponentially. His celebrity was confirmed when he caught the attention of one of the most extraordinary men of his day, William Beckford, a man who, despite a scandalous past, would prove one of the greatest art patrons of the moment.

Beckford was a character that gothic fiction could scarcely have invented. Born in 1760, he was the son of the Wilkesite lord mayor of London of the same name, a man who had built an enormous fortune on slave-dependent sugar plantations in Jamaica. Beckford senior used his vast wealth to spoil his son and indulge the boy's natural inclination for music and art. Beckford junior had counted not just Alexander Cozens and Sir William Chambers, but also the nine-year-old Wolfgang Amadeus Mozart among his entourage of tutors. The premature death of his father made Beckford junior a millionaire when he was just ten. By the time he was a teenager his dedication to art was complete.

But art was not Beckford's sole indulgence. He had also courted considerable controversy in the late 1770s and early 1780s, when he had become notorious for a sexual orientation that ranged through a full 360 degrees.

But it was his infatuation with the youthful William 'Kitty' Courtenay, who would become the Earl of Devon, that turned into a national scandal. In an attempt to deflect matters Beckford made a marriage of convenience to Lady Margaret Gordon, of whom he eventually grew very fond indeed. But the marriage was not enough to eclipse his notoriety. After Beckford and a pregnant Margaret visited 'Kitty' Courtenay at his family seat, Powderham Castle, in 1784, a new set of outrageous stories were circulated about the two men, and this time the rumours hit the press. There was nothing left for Beckford to do but flee.

Beckford took his wife off to what one contemporary noted as a melancholy castle next to a lake in Switzerland, and hid away until Margaret died in childbirth in 1786.[3] After a spell in Paris – where during the height of the Revolution he worked in disguise as a bookseller's assistant to avoid arrest – he moved to Portugal. In exile Beckford completed one of the earliest gothic novels, *Vathek*, as well as meditations on art and his travels.

But by the late 1790s the extraordinary Beckford was attempting a return to English society with a new project in hand. He began the construction of a huge gothic edifice, Fonthill Abbey, on his Wiltshire estate, which he intended to make a gothic temple to British art. This was proposed as a supplementary building to the grand stately home of Fonthill Splendens that his father had built. The abbey would hold his library and art collection, it would be a place of entertainment in the summer months, but ultimately would serve as a tomb, for at its heart Beckford planned a huge mausoleum or 'revelation chamber' in which he intended to be buried. The architecture would be on an unparalleled scale, and the interiors of unequalled magnificence. And he had also begun harnessing the services of the best of British artists to his cause.

News of this bizarre project sent ripples of excitement through the artistic community. Beckford had employed the Royal Academician James Wyatt to design his great scheme, and building began in 1796. Wyatt was one of the most fashionable and sought-after architects of the day. He was also one of the most controversial. While his work for the King at Windsor contributed to his appeal, his restoration work on the country's medieval cathedrals shocked many of his contemporaries. His classical inclinations had led him to tidy up the gothic excesses of the past with drastic interventions in the historic fabric of Britain. His work at Salisbury Cathedral, for example, saw the removal of the bell tower (which had already been partly demolished), the demolition of two porches and the two medieval chantry chapels at the east of the building, and a radical programme of simplifications to the interior. But despite his tendency to clean up the work of the original gothic architects, Wyatt embraced the neo-gothic project for Beckford with verve, and must have seen it as an opportunity to reveal how he could rival his predecessors.

By the close of 1798 Beckford had approached a number of eminent painters to contribute works for it, including Benjamin West. Farington committed to his diary the specific details of Beckford's plan, as related to him by the architect himself.

> Wyatt told me that Mr Beckford's gallery which is to lead to the Revelation Chamber, in the Abbey now building, is to be 125 feet long and 12 feet wide. It is to be wainscotted with ebony and in compartments are to be Historical pictures by English artists. Tresham was introduced to Beckford to propose to him to purchase some of Lord Cawdor's works of Art. Tresham is to paint four pictures for one of the compartments. The largest of them 4 feet 3 inches wide. The revelation chamber is to have walls five feet thick in which are to be recesses to admit coffins. Beckford's . . . opposite the door . . . the floor is to be jasper . . . West is to paint all the pictures for this room.[4]

Wyatt's and Beckford's scheme had in fact been fluid since its inception, and they had been discussing different outcomes for it. They needed a painter able to realize on paper an image of what they were considering in their plans, and significantly they turned to Turner. It is testament to the extent that the young artist was impressing his peers with the virtuosity of his watercolours, and specifically his ability to convincingly depict the most intricate architecture, that Wyatt enlisted him to work up a series of prospective views of how a finished building might appear.

The two travelled to Fonthill, where Turner sat amid the chaos of Beckford's building site and imagined a scheme that incorporated a 145ft tower.[5] Over the next couple of years Turner continued to showcase the wildest imaginings of the millionaire and his architect with watercolours at the annual RA show. By 1798 Turner's *Fonthill from the North West* envisaged a 300ft tower that was intended to rival Salisbury Cathedral.[6]

Meanwhile, any squeamishness about Beckford's colourful past was evaporating as the prospect of the considerable fees he was prepared to pay became evident. Farington, a man who loved to confide sums, noted that West alone was benefiting to the tune of £3,000 from Beckford's patronage. It was perhaps no small wonder then, that when Beckford embarked on another artistic conquest, London's art world embraced him as fully as they possibly could.

By 1797 the revolutionary forces in France had given way to the indomitable personality of Napoleon Bonaparte. He was now pursuing his own crusade to unite Europe under an imperial banner. When his forces marched on Rome in 1797, there was panic among the nobility of that city. One nobleman, Prince Altieri, had done what he could to liquidate his assets. Two of the highlights of his wonderful art collection were *The Landing of Aeneas* and *The Father of Psyche Sacrificing at the Temple of Apollo* by Claude Lorrain, and he allowed two English artists living in Rome to alleviate him of these burdens. The purchase was, however, illegal,[7] and so Robert Fagan and Charles Grignion smuggled the canvases out of the besieged city in the back of a cart. Moving ahead of the French army that was sweeping across Italy, the artists found their way to Palermo, where Nelson's fleet was anchored. When the artists revealed their booty to the Rear-Admiral he immediately arranged an escort for the small ship that would bring the canvases to Britain.

By the spring of 1799 they had found their way to London, along with a number of other pieces from the collection. Though the rumours circulating in London were that the Claudes had been disposed of for just £500, by the time they had made their way across a war-torn Europe and exchanged hands, Beckford finally secured them for the astonishing sum of 7,000 guineas. It was a small amount for a man whose annual income alone, assets apart, was £155,000. It was also a tiny price for someone hoping that art might prove his passport back into London society. By May the Altieri Claudes were on show in Beckford's London residence in Grosvenor Square.

Access to the collections held in London's great private residences was a privilege reserved for the select. One man in London, a dealer called William Seguier, had carved out a role for himself oiling the wheels of access to these treasure troves. But the status of being an Academician opened doors too, and when Benjamin West was supplied with a number of tickets to see the Altieri Claudes at Beckford's town house, Turner was one of a gaggle of eager artists whom he invited to visit with him on 8 May 1799. Farington recalled that 'Hamond, Smirke, Daniell, Rooker, Garvey, Duppa, Kearsley, Bonomi, Mary Smirke and Edwards' all joined Turner in rushing through the doors of the grand house.[8]

The effect of the Claudes on Turner was immense. After all, he had been thinking about Britain's own version of Claude, Richard Wilson, so much of late. The command of luminous light in the latter's work had become a focus of obsession for Turner. It was Wilson, and by default Claude, whom he had had in mind when painting *Norham Castle*, with its sublime luminosity, and when executing his *Aeneas* with its deep yellow sky hanging over a grey-green lake. But viewing these paintings by Claude first-hand represented a moment of climax. Turner's admiration for the works of Richard Wilson was a mere rehearsal for seeing the original master of landscape.

Claude's *Landing of Aeneas* depicts the founder of Rome about to disembark upstream on the River Tiber. His ship is framed between the rounded, wooded banks on the right and to the left tall trees and buildings that rise high above the river. Aeneas stands on the prow of the ship holding out an olive branch to King Evander. The two men frame the misty blue river slinking away into a distant low horizon, over which hangs a vast sky. The *Father of Psyche* depicts a father praying that his daughter will find a good marriage. Again strong vertical features to the right and left of frame, classical temples to the left and tall trees to the right, serve to focus the eye on a diminishing landscape in the centre of the composition. An arched bridge and river give way to a wooded plain and only in the far misty distance is a mountain range suggested in a pale grey haze.

Farington related that 'Turner said He was both pleased and unhappy' viewing these two marvellous works that 'seemed to be beyond the power of imitation'.

Turner recognized an artist who shared a similar fascination with the power of light, and the profound tone it could give to a subject. It was not just the luminosity of Claude's classical landscape that enraptured Turner and his peers, but also the sense of vastness, of time, and of a humankind dwarfed by the greater scope and power of nature. The artists huddled around the works, and analysed what made them so powerful. The general consensus was that some of their potency was achieved by Claude drawing his viewer's eye always to the centre of the canvas, which offered the most distant view. Benjamin West observed 'that the eye always settled upon the distance & the centre of the picture – as the eye naturally does in viewing the scenes of nature', adding 'how carefully Claude had avoided sharp and decided forms in the distance, gradually defining the parts as he came nearer to the foreground'.[9]

So enraptured were London's painters that they could not keep away. The next day the doorbell at 22 Grosvenor Square continued to ring and another procession of art lovers made their way into Beckford's town house. This time they were in no hurry to leave. The paintings had become the centre of a major social and intellectual conference. Joseph Farington arrived for his second sight of the works at eleven in the morning with Lord Walpole in tow. He stayed till five in the afternoon, as did Lord Leicester, Lord Bathhurst, Sir George Beaumont, and the writer Samuel Rogers. As for the painters, the list had lengthened. Now there was Benjamin West, Richard Duppa, John Downman, Thomas Hearne, William Daniell, John Yenn, John Opie, William Byrne, Giuseppe Marchi, Robert Smirke, Francis Bourgeois, Michael Angelo Rooker, Thomas Girtin, William Hamilton, John Constable, and of course Turner, all unable to drag themselves away.

To what extent did those artists visiting William Beckford's London home that May go with the aim of catching the eye of Edward Foxhall, Beckford's agent? Beckford was still out of England as much as he was in it, and he relied on Foxhall's advice. Many of those assembled in front of the Altieri Claudes must have also been hoping that they might be approached to contribute to the ambitious Fonthill project.

Turner's call did not take long to come. After all, he had already made the acquaintance of Beckford and he must have impressed. By 26 May he had received a communication from Beckford in Portugal, inviting him to visit Fonthill later in the year – a commission was certain, it was just the nature of the commission that was to be arranged.

Turner was a man who kept luck on his side. The interest of Beckford, once described as the richest commoner in the country, coincided with another increase in Turner's prices, thanks to the sudden attentions of *another* very rich art lover, who unexpectedly made an exceptionally generous offer for a watercolour of Caernarvon Castle.

In his *Caernarvon Castle*, which he had shown at that year's RA exhibition, Turner attempted many of the same effects as he had in *Norham Castle*. And just as in the view of Norham Castle these effects were – whether consciously or not – Claudian. Just like Claude, Turner has made the central focus of his work a distant hazy sun, in this instance setting behind a moody, foreboding castle. Its golden rays are reflected on the river over which the ancient medieval structure presides. The silhouette of a boat is also caught centre stage in the gloaming.

Turner's transgressive use of oil and watercolour, and determination to challenge the conventions of the day, are developed further in this work, for which he made a preparatory sketch in oil before developing it in a finished watercolour.

The man who bought *Caernarvon Castle* instantly grasped the picture's innate relationship to Claude. He also saw immediately that it would serve as a pendant to a Claude he had in his own personal collection. This man was John Julius Angerstein, a businessman and founder member of Lloyds of London who, just like Beckford, was able to spend huge sums on art, because he had had vast interests in the slave trade.

Angerstein was bowled over by the work. He offered Turner forty guineas for it without even asking the young painter his price. This was significantly more than the ten guineas Turner was achieving for other watercolours and the £21 he had secured from Sir Henry

Mildmay for the oil sea piece he had exhibited at the RA in 1797. It was a twelve-fold and more increase from the three guineas he had been charging just three years earlier.

It is hardly surprising that Angerstein later invited the young artist to see *Seaport with the Embarkation of St Ursula* by Claude Lorrain, which hung in his own picture gallery. Turner's *Caernarvon Castle* is remarkably close to the composition of Claude's painting. In the latter's imaginary seaport, imposing buildings frame the setting sun in the same manner as Turner's Welsh castle, and in both pictures the masts and sails of ships are rendered in silhouette against the sunset.

Turner was taken aback. On seeing the work he burst into tears. When Angerstein, somewhat confounded by Turner's awkward distress, asked him the cause, Turner explained it was 'Because I shall never be able to paint anything like that picture'.[10] He was clearly unaware that he already had.

Meanwhile the details of Beckford's invitation had arrived. Turner was to head to the Fonthill estate in August. He was in exceptional company; the other artists to whom a similar invitation had been extended were the President of the RA, Benjamin West, and Henry Tresham, who had negotiated the purchase of the Altieri Claudes on Beckford's behalf. Turner had been asked to execute seven watercolour views of Beckford's Fonthill Abbey. And thanks to Angerstein's enthusiasm for *Caernarvon Castle*, Turner secured £35 per watercolour. What is more, Beckford would be at Fonthill during the stay.

When Turner arrived at Fonthill, its building was in full flow. The speed and scale of the work were exceptional. Turner sat and sketched the workmen whom Beckford was employing around the clock in night and day shifts. In another sketch he captured the vast brown scar on the hill on which the building was positioned, created by the small forest of trees that Beckford had felled for the work.

As for Beckford himself, he was rarely seen. The group of artists ate their meals with Williams, Beckford's steward, rather than being entertained by the patron himself, who spent much of his time engaged in supervising the work on the house as well as riding in his extensive grounds.

Despite Beckford's purchase of the Claudes, at the point when

Turner returned to Fonthill its master was losing his battle to regain social acceptability and was already showing the signs of a man who preferred his own company. Beckford was beginning to see his abbey as less a summer pleasure house with which to impress guests, and more a fortress against the wider world.

What time Turner did get with Beckford, however, was sufficient to impress on him the profoundly dark tone of his patron's mind, and his romantic response to travel. Beckford had roamed across Italy with John Robert Cozens nearly twenty years earlier, long before the latter had succumbed to mental illness. Thanks to Dr Monro, Turner had a detailed knowledge of Cozens's work and of that very trip – after all, he had copied the sketches from it over and over at Adelphi Terrace. He and Beckford must have discussed this tour and its wonders. Through the lens of Beckford's deeply romantic sensibilities, Turner's desire to see the Continent, its great classical cities and ancient gothic cathedrals, must have been heightened. Among Beckford's vast art collection was a watercolour that Cozens had made after a particularly impressive thunderstorm that had hit while they were at Padua. The picture depicts the cupola of Padua's domed church of Saint Anthony being illuminated by a great flash of lightning, while strong grey diagonal slashes indicate the torrential rain battering the city. The composition is typical of Cozens, with strong horizontals and a vast sky hanging over the city, which is full centre of the picture.

Beckford's letters recall the event: 'It happened to be a festival and high mass was celebrated at the great Church of St Anthony in all its splendor. The ceremony was about half over when such a peal of thunder reverberated through the vaults and cupolas, as I expected would have shaken them to their foundations. The principal dome seemed invested with a sheet of fire; and the effect of terror produced upon the majority of the congregation, by this sudden lighting up of the most gloomy recesses of the edifice, was so violent that they rushed out in the wildest confusion.'[11]

Beckford's imagination had already aligned Padua with more exotic biblical locations. Its Moorish architecture suggested the ancient Holy Land, and Beckford had observed that 'Padua crowns the landscape, with its towers and cupolas rising from a continued Grove; and from the drawings I have seen, I should conjecture that Damascus presents somewhat of a similar appearance.'[12]

The idea of a new commission was hatched. A vision of a storm over Ancient Egypt, such as the Old Testament God had visited upon the rulers of that land. Such a commission would break new ground for Turner and would mark a step on from the lyrical *Aeneas* he had already executed. It would also extend Turner's output beyond its humble origins in the landscape genre towards history painting, a discipline that was considered the most prestigious.

It must have seemed to those around him that despite the fact he had not yet even reached his twenty-fifth birthday, Turner's election as an Associate of the RA was now surely inevitable. Farington was adamant that if he submitted his name once more, he would not be disappointed at the next round of elections. Turner, however, did not dare make any such assumption.

He had not ceased his personal campaign to forward his case and improve his chances. In November 1798, on the day after the Academy had elected Rossi over him, Turner went back to Farington's parlour, making sure that doors would remain open to him. Yet again he showed himself the supreme strategist and duly 'acknowledged his obligation to the members of the Academy for his support He had recd and said he had no title to so much'.[13]

He continued to hover on the doorsteps of Academicians over the course of the next twelve months, making himself visible at Academy events, and working up watercolours for those who expressed their intention to support him in the next year's elections. After Farington and Hoppner, there is a record that Thomas Lawrence and Robert Smirke also benefited from gifts of watercolours.

On 4 June each year, the members of the Academy were in the habit of holding a large dinner party in honour of the King's birthday at the Crown and Anchor tavern in the Strand. And on that date in 1799 Turner attended the event as a 'visitor'.

The Crown and Anchor was no ordinary tavern, but an elegant establishment in the Strand that, four storeys high, stretched a full city block and presented itself like a grand classical town house, with an understated Georgian frontage, decorated with classical pilasters. In addition to a large dining room on the ground floor, it had a great assembly room on the first floor capable of seating two thousand people. It was a location for lectures, and housed celebrations and meetings held by important institutions like the Royal Society and the Royal Society of Musicians as well as the Royal Academy. What is certain is that, unlike most 'taverns', those attending the Crown enjoyed an elevated status, and this was important to Turner.

As 1799 progressed, Turner became more and more desperate to leave his cramped apartments in Maiden Lane. He began visiting properties that became available. Although he initially considered buying a lease on a property, he took the advice of colleagues and decided to rent. After considering lodgings in George Street, Hanover Square in early October 1799, he finally settled on others in Harley Street which were his for around £55 per annum.

It was now just days away from the RA elections and Turner found himself in a state of anxiety. He had been very busy indeed. A constant round of social calls and networking had become part of a life already dedicated to unceasing work and endless travel. He had commissions for *sixty* watercolours waiting to be executed, and was dashing up and down the country in search of views. Since August, when he had been in Wiltshire for Beckford, he had also been through Lancashire for a new publishing project, the Revd T. D. Whitaker's *History of the Parish of Whalley*.

The trip north to Lancashire is worth a brief mention, because during its course Turner met a number of northern men who would prove fundamental in his future life and career. The Revd Whitaker had been introduced to Turner by an admirer of his work, Thomas Edwards, a bookseller based in Halifax, whose family had a London book business in Pall Mall.[14] It was the wider recommendation of the Edwards family that had secured Turner's commission from both Whitaker and his collaborator in the project, the collector Charles Townley. But while Turner was based in Whitaker's comfortable family home, the Tudor Holme Hall, in the village of Cliviger, near Burnley, Edwards almost certainly effected introduction to his other contacts in the region. There was Thomas Lister Parker, who lived at

Browsholme Hall, who would become a very close friend of the
painter in due course.[15] There was also Walter Fawkes of Farnley Hall
in Yorkshire, for whose library Edwards had bound many a book in
his time. Two years earlier, when he had made drawings for Fawkes's
near neighbour and political rival Edward Lascelles, Turner had
passed within spitting distance of the Farnley Hall estate, with its
views over Wharfedale and the impressive ridge known as the Chevin.
Now he met Fawkes himself, and in doing so began one of the most
important commercial relationships and friendships of his life.

But whereas Parker and Fawkes would become part of the fabric of
Turner's life, his relationship with Whitaker and Townley was less
easy. Turner became subject to one of the prevailing prejudices of the
time, that artists were only there as craftsmen, subservient to the
superior opinions of patrons. It was an attitude Turner had encountered many times before, but one which as his reputation rose he
found harder to negotiate.

Writing on 8 February 1800 to a friend, Dr Whitaker recounted:

> I have just had a ludicrous dispute to settle between Mr. Townley
> (Charles Townley, Esq., of Townley), myself, and Turner the drafts-
> man [sic]. Mr. Townley, it seems, has found out an old and very bad
> painting of Gawthorpe, at Mr. Shuttleworth's house in London, as it
> stood in the last century, with all its contemporary accompaniments
> of clipped yews, parterres, etc. This he insisted would be more char-
> acteristic than Turner's own sketch, which he desired him to lay aside
> and copy the other. Turner, abhorring the landscape and contemning
> the execution of it, refused to comply, and wrote me very tragically
> on the subject. Next arrived a letter from Mr. Townley recommend-
> ing it to me to allow Turner to take his own way, but while he wrote,
> his mind (which is not unfrequent) veered about, and he concluded
> with desiring me to urge Turner to the performance of his requisition
> as from myself. I have, however, attempted something of a com-
> promise, which I fear will not succeed, as Turner has all the irritability
> of youthful genius.[16]

After Lancashire and the north, Turner returned home via Liverpool and a journey through north Wales that included a visit to his

hero Richard Wilson's birthplace in Penegoes. En route he had ventured to the newly fashionable village of Beddgelert, in Snowdonia,
where he noted that seven artists had already preceded him that
season.

His sketchbook from this trip shows how the mountains and
valleys of Snowdonia inspired him. He was using watercolour as if
it were oil again, no longer making outlines in ink, but using a
loaded brush to create form with strong broad sweeps of colour. One
exceptional watercolour sketch is of Beddgelert church in the moonlight, the ancient stone building just visible in the dark, dwarfed by
black mountains rising up over an equally black river . . . just the
white moon making its mark in the sky, its beams reflected in the
water. It is the most profound exploration of darkness to date in his
sketchbooks.

Every now and then one spies Turner's vulnerability to depression,
or pressure, and his need to escape. Certainly in the October of 1799,
after his extensive travels around the country, and in face of the forthcoming elections at the RA, he bolted. He sat and drew beech trees
in Kent, probably with his friend William Frederick Wells, who had
developed a liking for the village of Knockholt, where he would
soon buy a cottage.

But by the start of November, he could ignore the imminent elections no longer. Turner's nervousness had been heightened in
September when he had heard that the Academy would be voting for
only *one* Associate, and he began a round of calls to lobby various
members on this matter. Turner had also heard that a number of the
Academicians were backing the election of Samuel Woodforde rather
than him. Woodforde was one of those who, though schooled like
Turner at the Academy Schools, had benefited from some training in
Italy. Turner may well have felt disadvantaged in this respect.

Voting day was 4 November. Turner confined himself to his studio. He had done what he could to persuade members and improve
his chances. It is tempting to see Francis Rigaud's intervention at
the commencement of the voting session as a direct response to
Turner's lobbying. For as the members met to commence the vote,
Rigaud, who after all had first introduced Turner to the Academy,

proposed that the resolution to appoint just one Associate should be rescinded. But Rigaud's motion was overruled by West. And the voting proceeded.

There were to be two ballots. In the first the members were clear in their preference for Turner. He drew ten ballots, with Woodforde, whose rivalry had so concerned him, receiving just one. Devis, who had been his opponent in the previous year, got just two votes, along with George Garrard, an animal painter and sculptor. Turner held his strong lead across the second ballot and was duly elected.

A group of Turner supporters crossed the Strand and made their way to the cramped apartments in Maiden Lane to break the news. It was an immensely jolly occasion. Joseph Farington, Robert Smirke, Thomas Daniell, William Hamilton, Sawrey Gilpin, John Hoppner and Thomas Lawrence held a celebratory supper party until one in the morning. It is not recorded whether they squeezed into Turner's small apartments or repaired to a local tavern. The Bedford Head in Southampton Street was Turner's regular bolt-hole at this time. Wherever they celebrated, this group of men represented a 'bottle circle' that Turner would enjoy many times in the forthcoming years. These were his friends.

Just over a fortnight later, on 22 November, Turner returned to the Crown and Anchor to dine, not as a guest of the Academy members, but as an Associate. He went as a new member of the Academy Club – a dining club held by members of the RA on Fridays between November and April. It was normally a fairly intimate affair, where the more sociable and convivial members of the institution paid their five shillings and enjoyed each other's company. Joseph Farington was in the habit of drawing the seating plans after each meeting, recording who sat next to whom and who attended, and sometimes noting snippets of the conversation. The first time Turner attended, the party was just eighteen strong, with John Hoppner, Joseph Farington, Robert Smirke and Thomas Daniell present from the friendly group who had celebrated his election. James Nixon, the Revd Robert's brother, was there too, along with Henry Tresham, who had been with Turner at Fonthill, and Martin Archer Shee, who was a contemporary of his from the Royal Academy

Schools. All in all Turner was surrounded by a friendly and familiar band of brothers.

It is no wonder, then, that on Friday 6 December, Turner was there again, making full use of the camaraderie that membership of this most exclusive of arts clubs could offer. By the time he made this second appearance, however, Turner was already a very different man.

9. Charitable relief

Two major events had occurred in the two weeks between 22 November and 6 December 1799. First, Turner had moved his studio into new apartments in fashionable Harley Street. But second, Mary Turner had been admitted to St Luke's Hospital – one of just two public mental asylums in the capital.

The incarceration of Mary Turner in a public asylum at a time when her son had enough money in the bank to pay for private care has been a moment in Turner's story that has often perplexed those writing about him. The further assumption that the Turners did not even accompany Mary to the hospital to see her taken in, based on the fact that the names given in Mary Turner's admission papers do not include those of either her husband or her son, has only compounded the puzzle, along with a general sense that the family's behaviour in her regard was unnecessarily callous.

Given the extremely negative press Mary Turner's admission has brought Turner, it is worth spending some time trying to understand the real complexion of the affair.

It *is* true that even if his father was suffering a downturn in business, Turner himself had investments of at least £950 in November 1798, which might have paid for private care. And it is also true that if one looks back over the history of the Turner family to this point, there is little evidence that they enjoyed spending money. On the contrary, the family seems to have been governed by the ethos that one should not pay for something if one does not have to. In the same manner that Turner never had an official paid-for apprenticeship like most of his contemporaries, a similar fiscal logic seems to have been applied to Mary's healthcare. If they could find her good care without having to pay for it – then why pay?

In fact St Luke's had a favourable reputation and was a place that was very hard indeed to secure admission to. It had just a couple of hundred places and yet took patients from the Home Counties and as far away as Cambridgeshire, as well as all areas of London. Further-more, though it did take people classed as parish poor, it had been set up specifically to serve working- and middle-class families of 'no small means', acknowledging in the letters of its foundation that the costs of private asylums could become so onerous that relatives 'through the heavy expence attending the support of one object of this sort have themselves become the object of charitable relief'.[1] This forward-thinking approach to wider social welfare, along with a reputation for an enlightened approach to the treatment of its patients, had made the institution both popular and oversubscribed. It was probably only through the kind of dogged and determined effort that had accelerated his election to the Academy that Turner secured his mother's care there. Getting her into St Luke's would have been considered something of an achievement and Turner would have leveraged all his connections to do so.

Indeed, Turner was very well connected in terms of those able to influence admissions to St Luke's. George Dance R A was the offi-cial surveyor of the hospital and as such a man who could be very helpful indeed. Dance had done Joseph Farington a favour two years earlier, when he had assisted in the admission of a relative of his called Molly.

Dance had introduced Farington to the institution's master, Thomas Dunston. Despite the fact that 'I was . . . told that the Hospital was now . . . full,' Farington reported, 'Mr Dunston, the Keeper, to oblige Dance, hinted to Dr Simmons that one place was vacant – on which I was informed that Molly might be brought next Friday for examination.'[2]

The aforementioned Dr Simmons was another man whom Turner had plenty of opportunity to canvass directly. Simmons was regularly in artistic company, often cited in the company of painters at dinner or tea with the publisher Joseph Johnson; there is one specific account of Turner and Simmons attending the opening of Henry Fuseli's Milton gallery.[3]

The paperwork and protocol of admission was straightforward, as outlined in the hospital rule book. Potential patients needed to be recommended by a governor in the first instance. Upon this recommendation a petition had to be submitted which family members were required to sign. The patient would then be examined, and, if considered suitable for admission, two bondholders were required to submit their signatures at least four days in advance of the patient's actual admittance.

Turner sought out a governor called Isaac Serra to recommend his mother. Serra was a major philanthropist who was on the board of a great many charitable institutions. He also happened to be a member of the Society for the Encouragement of Arts, Manufactures and Commerce, which had awarded Turner his 'silver pallet'. The petition, which either Turner or his father would have had to sign, was then submitted on 22 November, the day that Turner attended the Academy Club.[4]

Next there was the task of appointing bondsmen. The treatment for curable patients was free of charge. As such, bondsmen were not underwriting the cost of the patient, but rather guaranteeing the patient's removal from St Luke's within seven days if so requested by the hospital. The role was more a formality of paperwork, and there is even some evidence that the hospital had a number of philanthropists on standby who were prepared to act as bondsmen without even knowing the patients they were vouching for. This would be for patients coming from outer London and the Home Counties, because bondsmen were required to be resident in one of the London parishes that came within what was known as the Bills of Mortality.[5] Technically, however, these underwriters faced a fine of £100 if the bond was broken and as such they were subjected to a degree of scrutiny by the hospital council.

Turner with his new rooms in Harley Street could not qualify as a bondsman, since Marylebone lay outside the Bills of Mortality. The increasingly parlous state of his father's business would probably have ruled out his ability to find the £100 in cash that was technically the forfeit for failure to remove the patient. So the Turners called on friends to stand their bond. One was a very close friend indeed, a perruke-maker from Air Street called Richard Twemlow. The closeness of William Turner senior and the latter is evidenced by the fact that

Twemlow made Turner an executor of his will and left him five pounds. The other bondholder was a Mr Wicksteed from Cecil Street in the Strand. But the names of Twemlow and Wicksteed, recorded in the hospital clerk's handwriting in both the Patients' Book and the Admissions register, do not imply that the Turners were *not* present when Mary was finally placed in the hospital's care on 29 November.

The Christmas of 1799 marked a significant domestic change for the Turners. While William senior was suddenly alone in his shop, his son was benefiting from the luxury of space at 64 Harley Street. However, it had come with some drawbacks. The property he was renting was owned by a Revd Hardcastle, who, not long after Turner had taken his rooms, gave up his own to another painter, John Thomas Serres. It was a peculiar arrangement that saw Serres have access to the Reverend's parlour and a room on the second floor up until 4 p.m. each day, at which point they reverted to Hardcastle. Serres, a marine painter, had been living in Liverpool, but had recently returned to London with a commission from the First Secretary of the Board of Admiralty, to work up views of the Port of Brest.

It says something of Turner's fretful nature, and his anxiety about his work, that he confided to Farington that he was worried about being disturbed. It was not just the bustle of naval officers and other clients to and from Serres's rooms that was almost certainly on his mind, but also the likelihood that Mrs Serres would also be calling round. Having just managed the difficult behaviour of one woman, his mother, he now had to face Olivia Serres.

Olivia Serres was a woman with some talent as an artist who had taken lessons from John before marrying him. She was attractive, wildly ambitious, extremely extravagant and terribly unfaithful. She spent Serres's money without qualm and, from the moment he married her, he began to be chased by creditors, and thanks to her ended up on the King's Bench on more than one occasion. Though Serres managed to separate from her, he could only watch in horror when, a few years later, she went on to make the bizarre public claim that she was in fact the illegitimate daughter of Prince Henry, Duke of Cumberland, and began styling herself as Princess Olive of Cumberland.

If his father's own experience had not been enough to alert Turner
to the potential downside of married life, the Serres household provided another proximate reminder. It is hardly surprising, then, that
as far as Turner's own relationship with Sarah Danby went, he was
moving cautiously to say the least. He was in no hurry to take on any
responsibility for the widow and her children.

Fortunately for Turner, Sarah had secured a widow's pension from
the Royal Society of Musicians of £31 10s. a year for herself, plus a
further 15 shillings a month for each of her four daughters. This was
apparently enough. And perhaps Turner considered it something of a
blessing that the conditions of this charity stated that she might not
receive more than £10 a year income from any other source.[6]

The Society's rules also stated firmly that should Sarah indulge in
'illicit intercourse, her allowance shall immediately cease and she
shall for ever be excluded all claim on this society'. This meant that,
without matrimony foreseeable, her and Turner's relationship necessarily had to be kept secret. This requirement for clandestine
behaviour set the tone for Turner's relationship with women during
the course of his life. What began as a necessity quickly became a
preference for him.[7]

While in the cramped conditions of Maiden Lane Turner had been
limited as to the size of picture he could physically produce, with
Harley Street came the opportunity to work on a new scale. And he
had of course his commission from Beckford for a biblical scene.
Turner's self-awareness and bravura were such that he knew that the
first history painting from a newly elected Associate of the Royal
Academy needed to be an event. And so he began to work in oil on a
canvas that was six feet long and four feet high. This would inevitably make an impression.

The subject that Turner painted was *The Fifth Plague of Egypt*. Evidently drawing its inspiration from Cozens's *Storm over Padua*, and
from Piranesi's *Pyramid of Cestius*, which he had seen at Stourhead, the
darkness and drama of the work were clearly designed with the client
in mind. A brilliant burst of lightning in the centre of the frame
illuminates an otherwise dark and turbulent night, momentarily
highlighting one of the great Pyramids and the ancient town

surrounding it. In the foreground are a broken tree and the strewn bodies of a dead horse and two men.

Unlike *Fishermen at Sea*, that first oil painting Turner showed at the Academy which was so praised for the high level of finish, in *The Fifth Plague*[8] he displays a much looser approach to his materials. The canvas is almost visible beneath some of the brushstrokes, and the broad handling of the oil paint suggests a new boldness and confidence in the young artist. It marks the beginning of an approach to his work that would provide ammunition for his detractors in years to come, who would hold up a lack of finish as one of the artist's major flaws.[9]

Despite its biblical reference, those viewing the work in 1800 would have considered it in the light of Napoleon's thwarted campaign into Egypt, which had dominated British newspapers for the last two years. The reference to plague was all the more relevant, since only weeks before the painting went on show, correspondence between French generals had fallen into British hands revealing that the French had lost a third of their Egyptian army to disease. Napoleon was both a new plague on Egypt and had, like the evil rulers of the past, had a plague visited upon him for his tyranny.

Beckford paid 150 guineas for *The Fifth Plague of Egypt*, setting a new market high for Turner's work. Turner had judged his client well. Despite Beckford's antagonism to so much of society, he was a supreme fan of Nelson, whom he knew through his old friend the diplomat and collector Sir William Hamilton. Hamilton and Beckford shared many of the same enthusiasms, and both combined a deep love of art with bohemian sensibilities. During the building of Fonthill, Beckford had been planning for a visit from Hamilton and his wife Emma, and their constant companion Horatio Nelson. This was a ménage à trois. Nelson and Emma Hamilton were lovers. The group travelled as a threesome and would eventually live together as such, a fact accommodated by the nation on account of Nelson's supreme heroism.

Turner's painting would have been in place in Fonthill when, on 20 December 1800, the Hamilton party arrived to spend three days there. Beckford arranged a welcoming band to play 'Rule, Britannia' when they arrived at Fonthill Splendens. The last day of the house party culminated in a trip to the abbey for a banquet. Here, in the great 50-foot saloon, Beckford arranged for a huge dining table to be loaded with an enormous line of silver. After supper the party were shown some of the wonders of the incomplete building. They went up a stone staircase that was lit by torches held by hooded figures, and into a room hung in yellow damask. From here they visited the library and then moved on into the half-finished St Michael's gallery, the roof of which was fan-vaulted in plaster in imitation of Henry VII's chapel in Westminster. Later the party returned to the yellow drawing room where the embonpoint of Emma Hamilton entertained the guests with a series of silent tableaux, striking 'attitudes' from tales of Greek and Roman mythology.[10]

Beckford had invited both Benjamin West and James Wyatt to the house party, and though there is no documentation to support the idea, it is nevertheless just possible that Turner was there too, given his proximity to Beckford at this time. If so, the effect of meeting the naval hero cannot be underestimated. Turner was fiercely engaged in his nation's prestige, reputation and place in world affairs. His fascination in the naval prowess of Britain is evident across his career.

Just a year earlier, in 1799, Turner had made his first bold foray into painting naval warfare. He had exhibited a scene from Nelson's victory over Bonaparte's fleet in the Mediterranean, *The Battle of the Nile*. The painting is lost, but its lengthy title suggests how Turner had sought to achieve a highly dramatic rendition of the moment '*at 10 o'clock when the L'Orient blew up*', depicted from the heart of the action, '*from the Station of the Gun Boats between the Battery and Castle of Aboukir*'.

Perhaps it was this vision of the British Rear-Admiral's supremacy over his rival, François-Paul Brueys d'Aigalliers, that suggested Turner as one of the contributing artists to a major monument to British naval victory – the Hieronauticon or Trident.

This huge scheme was the brainchild of one Major John Cartwright, a man of astonishing vim and gusto. Cartwright wanted to build a temple to the British navy and designed a column, nicknamed the Trident. It was to be a super structure, a huge tower incorporating a chapel and banqueting room, coffee rooms, a royal apartment, viewing terraces – even a ladies' rest room. The whole edifice was to be adorned with nautical imagery, 'five nautic orders of architecture, personifications of eight of the winds', and a 'personification of the Genius of Britain'.

In 1800 Cartwright began to 'bring forward his ideas on the subject of a temple of naval celebration'. Joseph Gandy, the architect and watercolourist who otherwise worked for the eminent architect John Soane, was to realize the project on paper for Cartwright and work on elevations of the scheme. The painters William Hamilton RA and Thomas Stothard RA supplied schemes for ornamental decoration and friezes, while Turner was invited to provide watercolours of sea fights, intended ultimately to become low-relief images for the base of the column.[11]

Leafing through one of the sketchbooks he used at this period to plan pictures, one gets a sense of the degree to which naval themes were on Turner's mind. In his Studies for Pictures Sketchbook,[12] a book assembled from blue paper on which Turner sketches in black ink and chalk, he endlessly notes ships under sail and men of war, their sails dark, imposing and billowing in silhouette.

But when the scheme was presented in a major exhibition at Christie's in Pall Mall, in 1801, Turner's contributions were not on show.[13] The clue to his failure to deliver his proposed sea battles lies perhaps within the catalogue itself, where almost every item described carries the signature of Cartwright himself as the imaginative originator (J.C. inven), in advance of the artist's signature and role (J. Gandy delin).[14] As his niece later pointed out, 'though Major Cartwright had never studied drawing . . . natural taste . . . enabled him to give correct and beautiful outlines from which more experienced artists completed the coloured drawings'.

Hamilton, Stothard and Gandy may well have accepted this approach, but it did not sit well with Turner's trajectory as an artist. Particularly at a moment when he was flexing his imaginative muscle. As for Cartwright, the ambitious project was never realized, his personal frustration and dismay eventually culminating in a great bonfire on to which all the preparatory work was flung.

For a man who had for so long tied his work to observation, *The Fifth Plague* and depictions of sea battles fought far away marked a moment when Turner was employing his creativity in an entirely new manner. There is a different sense of adventure and patriotism in the work he undertook and the result is a surprising range of output.

A series of watercolours he executed based on battles in the Anglo-Mysore wars suggest that he may have been planning to contribute to some form of public panorama. The wars were perpetrated by the East India Company in the southern Indian kingdom of Mysore. Though they had been going on for the last three decades of the eighteenth century, 1799 marked a decisive victory for the British at the Battle of Seringapatam. It was another beat on a patriotic drum, and in the same way that Nelson's victories warranted paintings and projected columns, so too did British triumphs elsewhere. In 1800 Turner prepared a series of views of the siege of the fortress of Seringapatam. These may have been prepared in association with his friend Robert Ker Porter, who went on to launch a very successful panorama based on the siege that year, or perhaps as preparatory sketches for a competing project with one of London's other impresarios.[15]

The fact that much of Georgian visual culture was presented in the form of series had a profound effect on Turner's approach to subject matter. Panoramas were structured around series of views, magazines such as the *Copper Plate* or *Itinerant* also offered series of views, even Lady Hamilton offered a series of poses. This sense of repetition and comparison was at the heart of Georgian sensibilities and would become fundamental to Turner. He took the idea of series into a new dimension, because he began to make series that would not only be presented simultaneously, such as five views of Fonthill[16] that were hung at the Academy show in 1800, but as something he worked on through time. He would return to the same theme, the same location, the same idea again and again from this moment on.

The series of watercolours of Fonthill were the largest watercolours Turner had exhibited. At around 27 by 39 inches they were a third larger than anything he had shown to date. Perhaps it was their scale that encouraged the hanging committee for that year's RA show to place the series, not together in one room as Turner would have hoped, but to spread them around the various spaces the exhibition occupied. This was a frustration that Turner was as yet too junior to hope to address. It was a reminder that even when one had achieved the status of Associate of the Royal Academy there remained further heights to be scaled within that institution. Artistic freedom was a privilege reserved for the few artists at the very pinnacle of the Academy who could wield their power to see their work hung where they wanted.

The Fonthill watercolours were nevertheless picked out favourably by the press. In its section on 'Drawings' (watercolours) the *St James's Chronicle* opined that 'Among which those of W Turner take a lead . . . All views of the Gothic Abbey of Fonthill'.

But even amid this praise there was a note of surprise. The *Chronicle* suggested that 'there should have been some point taken wherein the building was decidedly the principal object. In all views it is most distant. The scenery is however most grand and is well chosen for such an edifice. In finishing these drawings Mr Turner has introduced much of that sober breadth of effect in which he excels.'[17]

It is true. The abbey, though apparently the subject of each study, is remote in all the watercolours. This may well have been a ploy to disguise the fact that as Turner was sketching the abbey in 1799 it remained incomplete.[18] To detract from the unfinished building Turner focuses instead on the wider landscape and also the time of day. To each of the five watercolours of Fonthill that Turner showed, he ascribed a moment, be it morning, noon, or sunset. The approach was useful, not least when Wyatt's vertiginous tower was brought down in a gale while Turner's watercolours were on show, a warning of things to come that Beckford and his architect would have done well to heed.[19]

The effect is a bold reversal of traditional estate views. Instead of a study of a grand property, Turner produced a comment on time, landscape and man's relatively minute place in a vast world. The power of the aristocrat is minimized in these works, along with his ambitious folly. What emerges instead is something new. Despite the origin of their commission, these views of Fonthill reflect the view of the artist, not that of his patron, despite the coin the latter laid down for it.

Beckford's response to the series of watercolours is interesting. Though he dutifully paid for the works Turner showed at the RA, he would sell three of them within a decade, explaining, 'The scenery there is certainly beautiful but Turner took such liberties with it that he entirely destroyed the portraiture, the locality of the spot. That was the reason I parted with it.'[20]

Turner painted another self-portrait at this time. It is not by the same person who painted the miniature for John Narraway or a clumsy oil. While these others were painted by a young man still insecure in his abilities and his personal attributes, the self-portrait Turner painted next tells us something quite different.

No longer in the slightly coy three-quarter pose of his earlier self-images, Turner depicts himself face on. His gaze is firm and confident. His features are finely chiselled, adult and masculine. He is well dressed, a white scarf around his neck, and a white silk waistcoat. He no longer has the need of the flamboyant frilled shirt or striped waistcoat that once served as distractions from his lack of other physical attributes. Despite a lack of pretence in his clothing, his hair is powdered at a time when the practice was no longer fashionable among younger men. Girtin wore his hair short, Napoleonic, and unpowdered, for example. But then Girtin was not part of the Royal Academy, most of whom did wear their hair powdered as a mark of their status. Perhaps the powder was a gesture of solidarity towards his father's trade in the stuff, but more likely it was Turner's way of showing he was part of that institution now, an Associate alongside the greatest artists of his day. And very much their equal.[21]

10.   Politics

Christmas 1800 was a jolly affair for the British Royal Family. The very first Christmas tree had arrived in Britain at the behest of George III's German wife, Queen Charlotte. She arranged for a yew tree to be erected in the Queen's Lodge in Windsor on 25 December and children had been invited to decorate it with toys and candles.

The Royal Family must have counted their blessings as they stood around this novel festive decoration and looked back over the previous year. For George had survived another attempt on his life. Just seven months earlier, when he attended a play at the Drury Lane Theatre, a lunatic called James Hadfield had fired a pistol, missing the monarch's head by just fourteen inches. The King was however blissfully free of his own bouts of madness and things were looking up on the political front too. George would get a new title in the New Year. He was to become King of the United Kingdom, Great Britain and Ireland, after Pitt had secured an act of Union with the latter.

There could have been no such joy in the Turner household. On 5 December 1800 Mary Turner was discharged uncured from St Luke's, the best efforts of that institution having failed. Her family and bondholders removed her on the very last day possible before a penalty was due.

There is a heavy dose of irony in the fact that the conception of Turner's first daughter, Evelina, coincided with the release of his mother from St Luke's. But with Mary's discharge his family was surely thrown into a storm of anxiety. Turner was once again forced to use every contact he could in an attempt to find a solution for the problem. And now he turned to Dr Thomas Monro.

According to the eighteenth-century practices of St Luke's and the hospital Dr Monro supervised, the Bethlem Royal Hospital in Moorfields, once patients had been deemed incurable they could only be admitted to an incurable ward. These wards were, however, even more oversubscribed than the curable ones, and what is more, they had stricter admissions policies. For a start, incurable patients could not be admitted direct to the incurable ward, but had to be transferred from the curable ward of the same hospital. But because of the oversubscription such a transfer was far from certain. Most patients could expect to wait for *years* before being transferred into the incurable ward and, short of going to the workhouse, had to be looked after by their family or sent to whatever private institution might take them in the meantime. With St Luke's incurable ward full, this was the new fate that awaited Mary Turner.

Just after Christmas, however, she was admitted to Bethlem, her status mysteriously transformed from the 'incurable' label St Luke's had bestowed to 'curable'. Richard Twemlow stood bond again, alongside a new underwriter, Robert Brown, an upholsterer in Covent Garden. The petition is recorded in Bethlem's paperwork, and it is revealed that Turner's uncle Joshua Turner was the proposing relative. Joshua lived a stone's throw from the hospital in Grasshopper Court, off Finsbury Square. It was this convenience that probably dictated his signature, which again had to be submitted in advance of the patient's admission.

But the hand of Turner can be felt throughout all this. For he must have pressed Monro to ease his mother's admittance – to the extent that the doctor changed St Luke's diagnosis of the patient in order to accommodate the hospital rules.

Despite the terrible reputation Bethlem had had earlier in the century, by now the hospital was seen by many as a good place to be. Not long after Mary Turner was admitted the evangelical preacher John Newton, author of the hymn 'Amazing Grace', saw Bethlem as an appropriate place for his niece Elizabeth Catlett, and visited her there every day before she was discharged cured a year later.

Sarah Danby's pregnancy must have become evident not long after Mary Turner's admission there. But it did not alter Turner's views on his relationship with her. Marriage was apparently not something he would entertain, and he was far from alone in this approach. What fifty years later Victorians would condemn as immoral, Georgian London accepted.

In the midst of the eighteenth century a meagre one per cent of births were illegitimate. By 1800, however, 25 per cent of all Britons being born were illegitimate, an unprecedented number.[1] The eighteenth century was an era when the British commitment to matrimony dissolved, and it remains an era whose liberal attitudes to sexual practice have never since been duplicated. The public condemnation of extramarital sex vanished, the tolerance of adultery, non-conventional living arrangements and common-law spouses was not exceptional. The kind of arrangement that Turner had with Sarah Danby was extremely familiar, and in no way necessarily indicates any poor behaviour on Turner's part – at least in the eyes of his contemporaries.

The key thing for Sarah, however, was to conceal the event from the Royal Society of Musicians, lest her widow's pension be stopped. At some point in the first half of 1801 she moved out of town to Guestling, close to Hastings in Sussex, remote and out of sight. There is no direct indication that Turner paid for a cottage or similar to house Sarah and her family, but it is in 1801 that for the first time he begins to dig into his investments in the Bank of England, removing £50 in March and a further £200 in April.

Of course this money could have been used for other things, including the beginnings of his own collection of paintings. Turner's enlarged wallet gave him the opportunity to purchase some of the work of other artists he admired. It is no surprise that one of the first artists he sought to own was Richard Wilson, buying two paintings around this time. After that topographical artist that he had copied so frequently as a younger artist, Michael Angelo Rooker, died in March, Turner acquired a dozen of his sketches at the sale of his drawings and effects in May.

Meanwhile his own output in 1801 reflected a consolidation of everything to date. His work was varied and embraced all the genres and media he had made his own. Perhaps because of the advocacy of Joseph Farington, who was an important contributor, he was one of the artists approached for the latest high-profile series of views of Britain, a 'Magna Britannia', to be written by the brothers Samuel and the Revd Daniel Lysons and to be engraved by William Byrne.

For Turner the commission was one that could be accomplished with relative ease. The subjects were local by his standards, in Berkshire and Buckinghamshire. Views of Eton College and Abingdon allowed him to indulge his love of sailing a boat down the Thames, and sketch from the water or the riverbank. Other locations such as High Wycombe from the Marlow Road, Donnington Castle and New-bury were short jaunts from London.

Otherwise he prepared a series of works for the R A's annual show that was representative of his past successes. With Beckford in mind, he followed up his *Fifth Plague* with another biblical oil painting that highlighted destructive natural forces, *The Army of the Medes Destroyed in the Desert by a Whirlwind – Foretold by Jeremiah*.

The watercolours he exhibited revealed his continuing desire to add extra narrative to a scene. So he presented *London: Autumnal Morning*, *Pembroke Castle, South Wales: Thunder Storm Approaching*, and *St Donat's Castle, South Wales, Summer Evening*.

But his triumph of that year was an oil painting called *Dutch Boats in a Gale: Fishermen Endeavouring to Put Their Fish on Board*. It had been commissioned by the Duke of Bridgewater, the canal builder who had been part of the consortium to buy the Orleans Collection. It was specifically intended as a pendant to hang alongside a painting he owned by the seventeenth-century sea painter Van de Velde, still considered by many the best sea painter that had ever been, and the artist that Turner had had in his sights when he launched his career in oils with *Fishermen at Sea*.

Bridgewater paid more than anyone yet for the privilege of a Turner oil, £250. If the judgement of Turner's peers is anything to go by, it was money well spent. Audaciously, Turner produced a work that was the symmetrical partner to the Van de Velde. Whereas the Old Master had a Dutch boat in a stormy sea, its sails leaning to the left, Turner's had the same with sails leaning to the right. While the seventeenth-century work had dark storm clouds in the right of frame, Turner's had them in the left. But Turner did two things to provide a greater sense of drama to his work. He made it bigger than its precedent. And he set his listing boat in a sea far angrier that Van de Velde's. The boat is in a trough of foaming white spume that not only gives the canvas a dynamic centre, but also leads the eye to the listing ship and its billowing sail.

When his contemporaries saw the painting, it was less Van de Velde and more that other great Dutch painter, Rembrandt, that came to mind. Then, the Old Master's *Christ in the Storm on the Sea of Galilee* was often held up as the epitome of sea painting.[2]

'Fuseli spoke in the highest manner of Turner's picture of *Dutch Boats in a Gale* in the Exhibition as being the best picture there, quite Rembrantish,' Farington told his diary that April.[3] Even Sir George Beaumont, who would become one of Turner's greatest detractors, thought highly of it. And the president of the Academy, Benjamin West, felt that Turner had managed to express 'what Rembrandt thought of but could not do &c'. Even John Constable, with whom a rivalry was already established, was forced to concede it was good.

But the patronage of Turner by Bridgewater and the other wealthy men whom the painter now counted as his clients was noticeable for another reason in 1801. Because, while Turner's career moved from strength to strength, his contemporaries were struggling.

Martin Archer Shee, Turner's contemporary at the RA Schools, noted that Bridgewater's commission of Turner was an unusual occurrence in a market that was otherwise soft, to say the least, for living British painters.

The mixture of envy and pride that Shee expresses towards Turner was typical of a growing attitude towards him from his peers. He was succeeding where others were stalling. And Turner's strange mixture of hard work, strategic sycophancy and keen business sense was working with infuriating efficiency. Shee was vociferous in his despair at the state of the market otherwise. 'All patriotic interest in the cultivation of British Genius appears to be at an end,' he noted gloomily, adding that 'those who should be the patrons of artists have ceased to be even their employers'.[4] Ironically Shee blamed men like Bridgewater for what he considered a marked lack of support for living British artists. After all, Bridgewater had been one of the consortium who brought the vast Orleans Collection to London, consolidating the appeal of the Old Masters for those with money to spend. 'The

disorders of the continent . . . occasioned such an inundation of foreign art to be poured upon us, as at once swept away all his hopes of
encouragement from a patron.'

Shee cursed the new breed of picture dealers benefiting from the
glut of foreign work. It is ironic too, then, that Turner was also making sure he had a hand in this emerging market, with his partner
Roche Jaubert. Turner was someone determined to succeed in life
whatever. He was delivering art across all the genres bar portraiture,
he had a considerable hand in the market for prints, and he was dealing in works other than his own.

The Royal Academy Catalogue for 1801 lists a new address for
Turner. No longer at Harley Street, his address is now 75 Norton
Street, Portland Row. Norton Street was just a few blocks east of
Harley Street, and Turner had moved into a new set of rooms which
he took in conjunction with Roche Jaubert. A Charles Danby is noted
as the lodger, and this was almost certainly the actor/musician brother
of John Danby. Turner's father also joined his son at these new premises. The barber's shop in Maiden Lane had finally collapsed and in a
reversal of tradition what might have been Turner and Sons became
Turner and Father. William senior, still a relatively young man in his
fifties, gave up the profession he had pursued to become his son's
assistant.

Norton Street was part of an area around Great Portland Street
that had become associated with the arts. There were marble yards on
the Euston Road that supplied sculptors, and the area in general had
become associated with picture dealers and music sellers. It was an
appropriate place to try to get Turner and Jaubert's picture-dealing
business off the ground.

Neither this new commercial venture, nor the swelling belly of
Sarah Danby, prevented Turner making one of his usual summer
tours, however, his furthest yet, a trip to Scotland. His own father
was also heading out of town, travelling with his brother Joshua to
Bath to see their mother, who would die the following year. One
senses that Mary Turner's incarceration in Bethlem, for all its sad-
nesses, had provided her husband with a freedom he had not enjoyed
for some time.

Turner went to Scotland with a captain from the East India Company called William Smith, who lived at No. 113 Gower Street, just a few doors down from Captain James Monro (Dr Thomas's brother, also a captain for the East India Company). Just about every family in Britain had a relative either in the Royal Navy or with the East India Company, such was the country's dependence on its sea strength, and so, were it not for the alter ego that Turner adopted in later life, one might not read too much into the fact that his travelling companion was a seafarer. But Turner *did* become Admiral Booth, and so it is irresistible to imagine the two fellow travellers bound by their shared interest in the sea, with Turner keen to hear all he could about long sea voyages and faraway lands. Living with the marine painter Serres as he had been, his detailed knowledge of the specifics of ships was growing. Serres's studio would have been filled with scale models of ships for reference, and Turner owned a number too.[5]

The summer of 1801 was particularly hot. Heat and humidity can aggravate asthma, and the fact that Turner felt 'weak and languid' adds some evidence to the theory that he may have suffered from this condition. On the evening of 19 June he called on Farington, who was providing him with suggestions for his Scottish trip, and his friend was sufficiently worried by what Turner described as heat-induced 'imbecility' that he suggested Turner postpone his tour for a few days. But Turner did not delay. Travel was his greatest joy, and he had new lands to conquer. He informed Farington he would be away for three months. Farington took this to mean he would be in Scotland for that duration.

Turner was travelling with paper he had prepared specially, with a brownish wash of ink and tobacco water. However, on this trip he did something totally different – he barely picked up a paintbrush, but instead just drew in pencil.

Two years later Dorothy Wordsworth and her poet brother would make a similar trip into Scotland, and her descriptions of the experience give a sense of how foreign this land felt to eighteenth-century English travellers. 'On going to a new country I seem to myself to waken up,' Dorothy noted, 'and afterwards it surprises me to remember how much alive I have been to the distinctions of dress, household arrangements etc.'[6]

Dorothy noted the first 'scotch bonnet' she saw, the women and men in 'grey plaid'[7] and the girls on Sunday with their stockings and shoes tied in bundles as they walked barefoot to church. The architecture and people were so different that she and her brother were 'reminded ten times of France . . . for once of England'.[8]

Just like Dorothy Wordsworth, Turner was so struck by the difference of Scotland that he dedicated a small sketchbook to capturing its figures and their national dress. He carefully detailed the different plaids he saw both men and women wrapped in, capturing the grey and green tartans. He noted the barefoot women with their white caps and shawls, carrying pails. He jotted down a group of men in scotch bonnets, and another group walking alongside their horse and cart.

But Turner's main focus was on the difference in the landscape he saw about him. He took a trip that went from York, through Berwick, past Norham Castle once more, and up to Edinburgh. Perhaps it was here that Turner and Captain Smith parted company, as Turner headed west to Glasgow, then via Luss and Arrochar to Loch Tay, Blair Athol and Dunblane, and from here through Stirling and Lanark to the famous Falls of Clyde. He left at the crack of dawn with his tobacco-stained paper and pencil to capture the wide vistas that Scotland offered.

It is not just the predominance of his use of pencil that is so profoundly different about the work made during this trip. It is also the manner of Turner's drawing. Detail is banished. He is obsessed with general form and simple outline instead. His pages of sketches often amount to little more than a line here, a circle or a hatching there. People become mere dots and slashes, trees indicated by the slightest squiggle. For once he seems to be looking at the most general aspect of this new landscape around him: Dumbarton Rock, the great mass that looms above the castle of the same name in the Clyde, becomes a handful of lines indicating the great bulk, the trees in the foreground whisks or lollipops of pencil, the boats simple crosses indicating masts, and the people little stick men. In the very few instances when his paintbrush is employed, it is with a new and devastating simplicity. Ben Lomond in twilight is realized with a slash of brown across the horizontal, a slash of slate grey and then the mass of the mountain realized in near solid black, the evening sky suggested by a diagonal of watery violet. This is visual note-taking at its most concise.

When he returned home he conceded to Farington that Scotland was 'a more picturesque country to study in than Wales. The lines of the mountains are finer, and the rocks of larger masses.'[9] And indeed line and mass does seem to have been the focus of his note-taking.

His pencil sketches represent another premeditated experiment. Using just the brown of the paper, Turner captures mountains and valleys with just lead pencil, hatching with different degrees of intensity to represent the crumples in a mountainside, or moderating the swirl of his drawing for different textures of foliage and flora. Only now and then does he resort to lifting areas of his picture with white or grey body colour, sometimes highlighting the stone of a man-made bridge as it marches across the wilderness. These are drawings with a focus on technical dexterity.

Turner had so much work in hand at this stage of his career that his clients could wait a while for their commissions. But as he was returning south through the Lake District after his Scottish tour, the debt he owed to his friend and colleague Joseph Farington was finally acknowledged and paid. Farington had supported him from the beginning of his campaign to become an Associate of the Royal Academy; his door was always open to Turner and his advice readily given. Now, perhaps aware that Farington was setting off on his own tour of Scotland along the same route he had advised Turner to take, Turner made sure he travelled home via Derwentwater in the Lakes, returning to a spot he had sketched before, the Falls of Lodore. It was this subject that Farington had chosen when Turner offered to make him a watercolour, and now he finally completed it.

But there was also another incentive to deliver Farington's watercolour. On 28 June, just days after Turner had set off for Scotland, the Royal Academician Francis Wheatley had died. The news must have caught up with Turner. The death of an Academician inevitably meant the election of a replacement, and the acutely ambitious

Turner must have returned to London with his next campaign for self-promotion in mind.

Whether Turner had misled Farington, or the latter had misinterpreted what Turner said, the fact is that Turner was out of London for three months but only six weeks of that was spent in Scotland. With his first child due in September, the rest of his planned absence from London included some time with Sarah and the newborn baby at Guestling. On 19 September Evelina Turner was baptized at the church there, as the daughter of William and Sarah Turner.

When the couple returned with their new baby to Norton Street they found London in a state of excitement. On 2 October news had broken that peace with France was finally on the cards. This had been made possible thanks to a recent change of government. William Pitt the Younger had always pursued a hard line towards Napoleon and his ambitious campaign to spread revolutionary principles beyond France. Pitt's successful negotiation of a union with Ireland had, however, backfired. While Pitt saw the union as an opportunity for the King to support Catholic emancipation in Ireland, the King saw otherwise and the friction with the monarch forced the former's resignation in February 1801. Pitt's replacement, Henry Addington, immediately opened talks with the French, and within weeks the years of resistance to the French that Pitt had so staunchly pursued were undone.

A war-weary country erupted into celebrations. People were sick of costly food, high income tax and the loss of loved ones. That night there were spontaneous illuminations, and as joyous rioters roamed the city, those unwise enough not to illuminate their homes had their windows smashed. Mail coaches spread the good tidings with the headline 'Peace With France' chalked on their doors, their coach drivers wearing celebration ribbons tied to their clothing. As the word spread across the country, bonfires were lit, cannons fired and bells rung.

For some of those around Turner, the commercial opportunities continental travel presented were too tempting to resist. The once familiar capital of fashion and taste, isolated during revolution and subsequent wars, was a place that in just a decade had become utterly foreign to those on the other side of the Channel. The desire to know what had become of Paris and its people was intense.

Artists had been thinking for a while how they might creep into the city undiscovered to capture information about it – only a few months before this momentous political breakthrough, Robert Smirke had considered disguising himself as an American to see if he could access the city, before having second thoughts. But now one artist packed his bags and went. It was Turner's friend and rival Thomas Girtin.

Though all that had been achieved in October 1801 was a preliminary agreement, and though a fully ratified peace treaty was yet to be drafted and signed, by mid-October the French authorities were sanctioning British visitors. Girtin immediately took advantage of this. His plan was to make a panorama of the city and he was in Paris by November.

Girtin's ambition and drive was exceptional, but it was spurred on by the prospect of destitution. The construction of his proposed London panorama was dragging him into a spiral of debt. Days before he took off for Paris he had attempted to auction it off rather than face the cost of mounting it. He offered the venture as a going concern for someone else to complete, at Messrs Greenwood and Co., auctioneers in Leicester Square.[10]

The first British ship docking at a French port in nine years did so at Boulogne on 23 October with 160 released French prisoners on board.[11] Girtin's ship was in its wake. He arrived in Paris on 7 November ahead of any other artists, almost at the same moment as Lord Cornwallis, the man the Prime Minister had appointed to negotiate the fuller peace treaty.

Turner did not follow Girtin. Despite his huge passion for travel and adventure, he resisted the temptation of seeing the wonders of the Continent straight away. Though some might speculate that it was the newborn Evelina that kept him in Norton Street, it is far more likely it was another event that persuaded him to remain in town for the time being.

Francis Wheatley's death in June 1801 was followed three months later by the demise of the architect William Tyler RA in September. And then in early December William Hamilton RA, who had just a year earlier indulged Cartwright's Trident, also passed away. Suddenly three places were available for new Academicians to be elected. Turner could not afford to be away at this crucial moment. Despite having only just been elected an Associate, full membership was suddenly within his grasp. This was a crucial career opportunity that Turner weighed above any other commercial prospect.

There was also the issue of his mother's mental illness. Because as Christmas 1801 approached, so did the anniversary of Mary Turner's arrival at Bethlem hospital. Patients were only allowed a year on the curable ward, and then they had to be discharged. The hospital records give no details of her specific affliction, but the fact that Mary was discharged 'uncured' on Boxing Day 1801 reveals that Monro had made no more progress with her mental health than his colleagues at St Luke's. Turner once again pulled all the strings that he could. Within a week – the very minimum time it would have taken to process the relevant paperwork – Mary was readmitted into Bethlem's 'incurable' ward. The influence of Monro is felt in the fact that she was not forced to wait for the privilege of a place. She jumped the queue.

Meanwhile the RA was due to elect its new members in February 1802. Turner was not the only man who sought election. John Soane the architect saw himself as a candidate. So too did the sculptor John Rossi. The architect Joseph Bonomi had also put his name into the ring, as had the history painter Henry Thomson. All the candidates were senior to Turner, some considerably. The fact that the badge of Academician was one worn for life meant that a great many men had themselves become quite senior in the process of waiting for those who had founded the RA in the 1760s to grow old and die. Joseph Bonomi was in his sixties. John Soane was nearly fifty. Rossi was in his late thirties. In light of these candidates the applications of Thomson, who was only in his late twenties, and Turner, who was just twenty-six, could have been seen as precocious.

But it is clear from Farington's diary that Turner's age did not exclude him. By now, his talents had clearly identified him as one of the most ambitious, inventive, technically brilliant and popular artists of his time. He had also established himself as a history painter as well as the master of landscape art. The men that constituted the Royal Academy were well aware that as they entered the nineteenth century, this young man could only rise further to be the star of the new millennium. Farington was in no doubt he must be elected.

With three members to be elected, but five candidates, it was crucial that supporters aligned their voting to provide a clear favourite and not to split the ballot. Turner began campaigning ardently. He had plenty of men on his side: George Dance, Thomas Lawrence, Richard Westall, Ozias Humphry, Joseph Wilton, John Flaxman, Philip de Loutherbourg, John Russell, James Wyatt, John Francis Rigaud, William Beechey, Francis Bourgeois, John Singleton Copley, Henry Tresham, Johan Zoffany, Robert Smirke, Edmund Garvey, Thomas Daniell and Richard Cosway. But, given there were three votes, this group of advocates had to vote for the candidates in the right order. Farington began to organize the group, conveying the imperative that they should all vote in the same order: for Turner in the first round, then Soane and last Rossi. Anyone voting out of this order would weaken the power of the group. Ever the tactician, Turner teamed up with his fellow candidate Rossi and together they began to visit Academicians to drive this message home.

The lobbying and tactical discussion went on late into the night before the election. And then, at seven o'clock on 10 February 1802, the Royal Academy held its general meeting, with Benjamin West presiding. As the ballots commenced, Farington's tactics paid off. First his group put all their votes behind Turner. Turner drew twenty votes, the second largest draw being for Bonomi, with fourteen votes. In the second ballot the group put its shoulder behind Soane, who secured twenty-three votes, with Bonomi coming second with eleven votes. And in the last vote they swung to Rossi. The three new Academicians were duly elected.

'The business of the Academy was over about ¼ past 10 o clock . . .' a weary Farington disclosed to his diary. 'I left the Academy with Dance & Lawrence & Westall and went to Soane's who we found in his bedroom. At eleven I got home, Smirke, Garvey & Daniell who had called on Turner & Rossi came to me and staid till one o clock.'[12]

At the age of twenty-six Turner had reached a professional status that some men three times his age were still trying to achieve. It was a remarkable achievement, and it was transformative. At this moment William Turner vanished. The 'Picture of London' guidebook for 1802 referred to the artist as 'Mr J. M. W. Turner R A'. His work was to be found at 'Norton Street, Portland Road', and lest anyone were in doubt he was noted as a 'painter of the very first order, and his pictures are marked with a spirit, and distinguished by a manner that is peculiar to himself'.

11. Adventure

Art was an adventure in the eighteenth century. Discovery and re-discovery were part of its proposition. Finding a new painting technique or rediscovering a forgotten one was as much part of the art debate as the ongoing conversation about beauty and the sublime, or the dialogue about the supremacy of certain genres of art over others.

But adventure necessarily suggests jeopardy. And in 1796 the Royal Academy had suffered an embarrassing scandal. A number of the most eminent Academicians – including the president, Benjamin West – had succumbed to a fraud.

Eighteenth-century painters were fascinated by the colour effects the Renaissance Venetian painters had achieved. The works of Titian and Tintoretto were to them the supreme example of a technical prowess that they could not match. It was this obsession with the Venetians that allowed several members of the Royal Academy to be duped by a man called Thomas Provis, who was 'Sweeper to St James's Chapel', and his daughter Anne, an aspiring painter. Anne Provis claimed she had discovered a sixteenth-century manuscript that revealed the material and techniques necessary to achieve the luminous effects of the Venetians. This 'process' the Provises made available for a ten-guinea fee.

Astonishingly, some of the most famous painters in Britain were taken in, paid their dues and began working up paintings in the new manner. Many paintings went on show in the 1797 RA annual exhib-ition using the 'Venetian technique', with Benjamin West's *Cicero Discovering the Tomb of Archimedes* the most prominent.

Such was the poverty of the response to the exhibition that the Provises were unmasked, and by November 1797 the caricaturist James Gillray was enjoying satirizing all the eminent painters who had fallen for the ploy.

But the quest for luminous effects continued despite the scandal.

Luminosity, such as that perceived in the work of the Venetian masters, was a grail that Turner's contemporaries continued to seek.

And Turner was no exception. Just a few days after his election as an RA, Farington found Turner in his studio using a canvas prepared by Sebastiano Grandi. Grandi was a colourman trading out of Long Acre, Covent Garden. Unlike the Provises, he did not rely on tales of discovered manuscripts for his claim to having discovered something of a Venetian process. He had used trial and error, had published the results of his experiments and had been awarded a silver medal by the Society of Arts for his efforts.

There was no lack of toil in Grandi's preparations. He boiled sheep's trotters in water, then ground them to a powder. He then made a paste of wheat flour to which he added the bone ash. This 'bone paste' was applied as a first coat to his canvases. A second and third coat of the same were then added, and each layer was sanded back when dry. Finally this ground was finished with a thin coat of linseed oil. This, Grandi claimed, provided the basis for 'the peculiar harmony, brightness, and durability' of the work of Titian, Veronese and other Venetian masters. For the moment Turner swore by him.

Once Turner took delivery of his canvas from Grandi, it was 'pumissed by himself', according to Farington. 'When finished it requires 3 or 4 times going over with mastic varnish to make the colour bear out – He uses no oil but linseed oil – by this process He thinks he gets air and avoids any horny appearance.'[1]

But whatever magic Grandi could work, nothing could beat studying the work of the Old Masters in the original. Since 1793, when the Louvre Palace had been converted into a museum by France's revolutionary usurpers, it boasted the greatest collection of art anywhere in the world. And exceptionally it was owned by the French people. Since its foundation, Napoleon's conquests had added a further five thousand works of art to those that the people had already taken from the French aristocracy and the Church. And for the past decade French artists had had this treasure trove pretty much to themselves.

As 1802 progressed, an increasing desire grew among Britain's artists to join Thomas Girtin in the French capital. Once the Academy elections were out of the way in February, with the peace Treaty of Amiens signed in March, and the annual RA show over by the end of June, they began to make their preparations to spend the summer months abroad and view the Old Masters that had been beyond their reach for so long.

The sudden press of artists crossing the Channel in July and August to see the wonders of the Louvre was unlike anything that had occurred before. They were part of an even wider group of British cultural elite who were driven by pent-up curiosity to see, not just the Louvre, but everything else the French capital might offer, including the magnetic Napoleon Bonaparte.

'I am ten times more overwhelmed than before by demand for passports,' complained the French emissary in London, Louis-Guillaume Otto. 'There is not one man of leisure here who does not wish to see Paris and above all the First Consul . . . Soon Parliament will be obliged to impose a tax on those who are absent so as to avoid the de-population of some of the best quarters of Westminster.'[2]

The British and French merchant seamen prepared for the traffic. Their governments relaxed the legislation that had prevented postal packets from taking passengers. Meanwhile private ships offered their services as ferries.

Those crossing were a mixed group. The vast majority were the gentry. But there were also politicians (eighty members of parliament, including Charles James Fox, much to the disgust of the monarch), writers, businessmen, soldiers and just the plain curious. Some people were merely on a day trip, keen just to 'see France and judge of the French by a few hours ramble round Calais'.[3]

In the high summer over ninety boats a month were crossing, a huge number by the standards of the day. The hotels filled fast. The most generous assessment of the number of British in Paris at any one time was in September, when at least one chronicler supposed twelve thousand people were there.[4]

The revolution had failed to destroy the Parisian fascination with fashion. The British were dumbstruck by the shockingly sheer, high-waisted muslin gowns that the women were wearing in that particularly hot summer. They were naked underneath. They were known as the Merveilleuses, and their eccentrically dressed male counterparts, sometimes sporting earrings, large cravats, wide trousers and bicorne hats, were dubbed Les Incroyables.

These people flung their doors wide open. Dinner parties were organized, salons opened, balls arranged. Even Napoleon held an audience for the most eminent of the British visitors. The season was one of intense gaiety and socializing, as old friendships were rekindled and new ones ignited.

Turner's friends joined the inquisitive, merry throng, most of them leaving in September. Farington names them: West, Opie, Flaxman, Fuseli, Smirke, Shee, Hoppner, Phillips, Daniell and Cosway. Farington went too. This group was clearly at the Academy's most social and adventurous axis. And arguably at its most Jacobinical.

The art world's fascination for Napoleon was intense. He was a figure who mesmerized, and in an era where the popular living hero had been developed as a subject for artists, Bonaparte was too tantalizing to resist. The group that crossed the Channel that summer became swept up in not just francomania, but Napoleomania. John Opie and his wife Amelia sat in the boulevards and sang the revolutionary song 'Fall, Tyrants, Fall'. Thomas Phillips, a portrait painter, managed to get an audience with the Empress Josephine that enabled him to paint a portrait of her conquering spouse. Maria Cosway, wife of the miniaturist Richard Cosway, began a project to copy paintings in the Louvre for a series of etchings for the British public.

The Parisians reciprocated the enthusiasm of the British. Madame Récamier, the French salon hostess, visited London in early 1802 as part of the new entente cordiale and, having made new connections in the city, now opened the doors of her home at No. 7 Rue Mont Blanc to the visiting artists of the RA. Her home was a study in neo-classicism that Robert Smirke in particular moved fast to record in watercolour.

Turner's behaviour that summer, however, marks him out for the distinct and single-minded character he was, when compared to his colleagues. For while his peers followed one another to Paris and its pleasures like eager sheep, he made other plans. He was determined to make the focus of his first visit to the Continent not the Paris that everyone else wanted to see, but rather a place that no one was much interested in at all. The Alps.

The audacity of this proposition was considerable. Against the background of mania for Paris, Turner stands as an exception. His instincts were different from those of his peers. Yes, he would visit the French capital, but he would arrive in his own time, via his own route.

Turner's plan was an extensive tour that would take in the Alps via a route through Paris, Lyons and Grenoble to Geneva, Chamonix, Mont Blanc and then further east to the Val d'Aosta, zig-zagging between France, modern-day Switzerland and Italy. Only on completing this adventure would Turner join his colleagues from the Academy in Paris.

The Alps had enjoyed a similar reputation to the mountainous territories of Wales and Scotland across the previous century. Seen early in the eighteenth century as barbaric and monstrous, after the midpoint of the century the mountains turned from devilish to sublime, and became the subject of many a romantic comment.

The perception of the people of Switzerland, a country inextricably bound with the idea of the Alps, had also enjoyed considerable change in the course of the century. The British re-conceived those formerly considered uncultured as a group of independent thinkers who between them had created a cradle of democracy, with the legendary tale of William Tell at its heart.

But unlike Wales and Scotland, which had enjoyed increased exposure to tourism in the last quarter of the eighteenth century, the continental wars in the wake of the French revolution had stemmed the growth of tourism to Switzerland and the Alps, and interest in the place had dwindled. In fact Switzerland had ceased to exist and had been incorporated into Napoleon's empire as the Helvetic Republic in 1798. The country was dangerous and depressed, and a battleground for France to wage its campaigns against Austria and Imperial Russia. Any chance for early Alpinists or enthusiastic tourists to continue their exploration of its sublime mountains was out of the question.

So if Turner's intrepid travels into Wales and Scotland were considered brave by the standards of the day, a trip to the treacherous Alps was far, far riskier and more adventurous. Only a few hundred British people had ventured to explore the Alps in the second half of the eighteenth century, and that included only a handful of artists. Turner's trip was nothing short of pioneering.

Significantly, two of those who had ventured there before the country became beyond bounds were William Beckford and John Robert Cozens, and there can be little doubt that the accounts of the former and sketches of the latter, to which Turner had had privileged access, inspired him to go and see Europe's great backbone for himself.

Three patrons put up the funds for Turner to make what was going to be a costly, high-risk trip. Though Turner could have afforded to pay for it himself, as we know, the Turners as a family could see little point in paying for something that could be obtained gratis or at another's expense. Lord Yarborough was one member of the funding consortium, and his name features in the paperwork associated with Turner's passport for the trip. Another backer was the Earl of Darlington, and the third remains a mystery, though both Walter Fawkes, of Farnley Hall, whom Turner had first encountered while staying with Dr Whitaker at Cliviger in 1799, and Sir John Boyd of Danson House in Bexley are candidates.[5] Fawkes had visited Switzerland himself in his youth, and so an interest in that country was well established, and Boyd would go on to acquire two Alpine views from Turner.

The other person who may have contributed to Turner's costs was his travelling companion for the trip, Newbey Lowson, from Witton Hall, Witton-le-Wear, near Durham.[6] His presence on the tour was part of Darlington's terms. Lowson was a wealthy young man, with not inconsiderable mining interests and an appetite for travel which included an ambition to see the Alps. He was an amateur artist too. He and Turner certainly seemed compatible, with a shared enthusiasm for landscape, the outdoors and adventure. They were matched in idiosyncrasies too. Lowson would be described later as 'a curious fellow this',[7] which is exactly the kind of description that Turner also attracted.

Lowson and Turner had their bags packed by 14 July, when Turner called on Farington to say his goodbyes. By this time Turner was in the habit of investing in beautifully, solidly bound sketchbooks, with strong brass clips that reflected the importance he placed on his sketches and their need to survive any conditions that journeys might deliver. As he left London on the evening coach he had his largeish Fonthill sketchbook packed, which still had some spare sheets of paper to be used, a portfolio of loose leaves, and a couple of books small enough to fit in his coat pocket. This was enough until he reached Paris, where he could buy more art supplies.

On a good day the crossing between Dover and Calais could be very brisk, though notoriously choppy. The packed vessels were soon awash with the inevitable outcome of seasick travellers. Turner reached in his pocket for his sketchbook almost as soon as his crossing had begun, heading up on deck and opening the book, not at its first page, but at a random point mid-book – starting in the middle appears to be an occasional practice suggested by the order of other sketchbooks. On the rocking deck he sketched Dover Castle in the distance and a small fishing vessel, its full sail bobbing through robust waves. On the day Turner travelled, the winds were particularly strong. As if transfixed by the experience of being out at sea, he noted page after page of waves. Turner was no stranger to the sea. But compared to the short hop he had made to the Isle of Wight, and the packet he took to Margate, this journey across the Channel must have felt newly exciting. After all, he was for the very first time in his life leaving Britain.

The problem in travelling to France was less the crossing, and more the arrival. Calais harbour is shallow, and depending on the tides, the packets arriving from England could anchor for several hours waiting for a tide that would carry them the very final leg of their journey. This is exactly what happened to a lady travelling a short time after Turner who 'left Dover at about twelve o clock Tuesday morning and in less than two hours arrived in sight of the harbour of Calais' but was 'not able to land until eleven at night for on account of the deficiency of water'.[8]

While the anonymous lady was forced to wait nine hours to set foot on French soil, and only did so after walking across a number of other docked boats to reach the over-subscribed quayside, Turner had no such patience. Instead he clambered aboard a small boat that took some passengers ashore in advance. It was a decision that nearly cost him his tour. With the pier inaccessible at low tide, the little boat instead ploughed through terrible weather to land directly on the beach, taking on water from the heavy breakers as it did so. On his return to London later in the year Turner drew on his memories of this moment and made a drawing in his studio that noted 'our land-ing at Calais nearly swampt'.[9]

Though soaked with sea water, Turner's delight at arriving in France was celebrated in an explosion of drawings he seems to have made instantly in his small pocket sketchbook. Page after page is filled with accounts of the experience of arrival and his immediate impressions of France. Sketching quickly with just cursory lines, he notes the rough sea he has just encountered. Fishing boats off shore. A closer note of fishing boats and the red berets worn by the French fishermen, the pier crowded with people and fishing vessels out to sea, a study of figures clambering on to the pier. The Hôtel de Ville, the walls around the town, a street scene with coaches and travellers, a sunset, Calais church and clock tower.

There was a fair amount of bureaucracy to suffer on arrival. Trav-ellers were met and directed towards 'a miserable place resembling a barn, near the pier', where their 'names were written in a book', and their luggage checked. This was the custom house. The police office had then to be visited, where passports were signed. All these public buildings were noticeable for the motto they displayed: 'Liberté Egalité Fraternité'. All the time the newcomers were hassled by wait-ers and porters to choose lodgings.[10]

The strength of the impression that both his landing at Calais and the excitement of being on foreign soil had on Turner is suggested further by the fact that on his return to London later in the year he developed two major oil paintings from these initial sketches. *Calais Pier, with French Poissards Preparing for Sea: an English Packet Arriving* and *Fishing Boats Entering Calais Harbour*. Both paintings apply the fas-cination with peril at sea that Turner and his patrons admired in the works of the Dutch Old Masters to bear upon something topical, popular and of the moment. They are heroic paintings with non-heroic, human subject matter.

Turner's decision to select these subjects drawn from contemporary life in Calais reflects the importance he placed on what he thought would prove popular and resonant with his public admirers. The packet to Calais was a shared experience in 1802, particularly among the type of people likely to be in the market for art.

British travellers claimed to see instantly the effects of the prolonged war on the heavily fortified town, its buildings untended and damaged and many of the inhabitants suffering in obvious poverty. There was a notable difference in the attitude of the liberated French, which Joseph Farington found too presumptuous for his sense of social propriety. '[At the inn] we had occasion to speak to Ducro, the Master of the Inn who . . . of his own accord took a chair and drew it to the table and became one of our bottle circle. I shd not decide from a single instance, but it has been observed that where the distinctions of rank are most positive and where one part of a community, are in most subjection, to those above them personal freedom is often allowed in a great degree. He that can be crushed at the will of a power may be permitted to approach very near. In England the case seems to be otherwise. Rights being equal, and the laws effective, manners alone can preserve that subordination which is allowed to be necessary . . .'[11]

In the inns the food was a revelation, though. Our lady traveller was astonished by the quantity of food offered. 'To each person was placed a bottle of wine and a decanter of water, and a piece of bread,' she recounted. 'The first course consisted of soups, the second of roast and boiled, the third of made dishes, and the fourth of vegetables, which are never eaten with the meat. We had afterwards an elegant dessert.'[12]

The French wines were not to Turner's taste, however. For a man who, according to his friend Cyrus Redding, preferred 'vulgar porter' or the dark beer popular in London taverns, they were 'too acid for his constitution being bilious'. This must have made the exorbitant prices the French were charging the British tourists all the more frustrating for him. Two shillings and sixpence per person per meal was two or three times the price of a London meal.[13]

Fortunately for Turner, he didn't have to count the pennies. Newbey Lowson took it upon himself to be paymaster and account-ant. He kept a small book in which details of the expenses incurred were duly noted.

The next disappointment for the traveller in France was the coun-try's diligence coaches. Huge in size and with only two small windows, they dismayed many of the travellers, who had hoped to see something of the country as they travelled between Calais and Paris. It may well have been this form of travel that not only accounts for the paucity of Turner's sketches en route to Paris, but also contrib-uted to Turner and Lowson's decision to lay out 32 guineas in Paris and buy their own light cabriolet carriage, an open two-seater in which they would have received some cover from the weather but which would also have given them full views of the country, and a personal servant-guide-driver that would afford them greater flexibility.

The road between the ports and the capital had been rapidly improved since 1 October as part of a major campaign by the First Consul, and even if the journey lacked a decent view it would have been relatively swift and comfortable. If Turner and Lowson had been well advised they would have booked accommodation in advance in Paris, which was massively oversubscribed. The Hôtel des Étrangers in the Rue Vivienne was favoured by many artist travel-lers, and may well have been where they based themselves for about a week to prepare for the next leg of their journey. The Rue Vivienne was just a stone's throw from the Louvre, and also Paris's bohemian quarter centred around the Rue Coq St-Honoré, where, like Covent Garden and the Strand, the capital's publishers, printsellers, stationers and colourmen were centred, and where the city's artists met at the Café des Arts. Certainly Turner patronized the shop of a Monsieur Coiffeur there, where he bought another set of sketchbooks.

Shortly after his arrival in Paris, Turner made for the Louvre. Like other artists, the draw was too great to resist. Napoleon, as part of his campaign to impress his former enemy, had granted foreigners and artists exceptional access to the Louvre, allowing them entry even on days when the French public were denied, and to galleries that were otherwise locked. According to one smitten British visitor who had attended one of the First Consul's fabled monthly audiences, which he held in the Salle des Ambassadeurs in his Palais des Tuileries, Bonaparte had declared to him his ambition for a cultural marriage between Britain and France in this new era of entente.

The very vastness of the Louvre was overwhelming for those who went there. Turner, a man of few and rarely effusive words, later recalled it was 'no small wonder'.[14] But his contemporary Martin Archer Shee put better into words the impact the museum had on the British artists visiting it. 'Description has fallen short of the splendor, the extent, and the merit of this great national museum,' Shee said. 'We have in England a few scattered stars of art; but here there is a constellation, a perfect galaxy, in which the eye is lost.'[15]

And there is a sense from his sketchbooks that Turner, also overwhelmed, was unclear how best to respond to this galaxy of work. He and Lowson had guides to find, carriages to buy, supplies to acquire and passports to secure (for those wishing to leave Paris needed further paperwork). Viewing the Louvre collection alone would have taken days. One senses his struggle in how to approach the material before him given the paucity of time available. The order of his sketchbooks suggests that he sketched just one painting and made written observations on two others. When time ran out he was forced to leave his studies until his return to Paris later on.

But what little he did do in the Louvre gives an important indication of his priorities and his agenda. First he made a point of looking at that great Venetian painter Titian, and his painting of *The Entombment of Christ*. The quest for Venetian colouring still a grail yet to be won, he observed that 'the Flesh is produced by the under colours or ground like Indian Red and Aspaltum. The second colour cold with shadows slightly indicated, the still colours the two mastic tints are like Correggio's Jerome.'[16] He makes similar though much shorter notes about Correggio's *St Jerome*.

But most telling is the sketch that Turner makes during this initial experience of the Louvre. In his brand new French sketchbook he copied Pier Francesco Mola's *Vision of St Bruno*. Of all the wonders before him it might seem an odd choice for a visual note. Mola was far from the most eminent painter in the Louvre. So why would his image of St Bruno, lying beneath two trees and looking up towards heaven, be the one which Turner determined to carry with him on his journey?

St Bruno is the saint most associated with the Alps, a medieval man who had sought retreat there in the mountains around Grenoble and the Grande Chartreuse. And importantly, the story of Bruno was a passion of William Beckford. In his own travel writings about the Chartreuse, Beckford had romanticized the saint's spiritual experiences of the region, recounting how he had 'thought of the days of St Bruno. I eagerly contemplated every rock that formerly might have met his eyes . . . Every pine, beneath which, perhaps the saint had reposed himself.'[17]

It seems possible that Beckford would have shared his enthusiasm for this particular saint with Turner, showing him the rare book on the life of St Bruno which he held in his library and a number of etchings of the saint in his collection. Were Beckford and Turner discussing a depiction of the Alpine saint? Beckford also owned a depiction of Mary Magdalen in the desert by Mola and may have been considering a pendant by Turner to hang alongside it.

Turner's sensibility to Beckford's relationship with the Alps is suggested further by a watercolour he made on his return, *St Hughes Denouncing Vengeance on the Shepherd of Cormayer, in the Valley of d'Aoust*.[18] St Hugh was a twelfth-century monk who had trained in the Grande Chartreuse monastery before becoming prior of the Charterhouse at Witham and ultimately Bishop of Lincoln. Beckford's father had bought the ruined monastery at Witham, a personal connection with the region and its history that Beckford was keenly aware of during his own trip to the region in the 1780s.[19]

With Beckford's enthusiasm for the Alps and his sketch of St Bruno in hand, Turner and Lowson set off from Paris around 26 July and headed south towards their goal, the first sight of the Alps at Grenoble. Anticipating the sublime mountains towards which they were headed, the great stretch of France that lay between Paris and Lyons was initially disappointing for Turner. Farington noted him dismissing 'The country to Lyons' as 'very bad'.[20] This may of course have been an observation on the economic state of the place, and the condition of the roads, as much as his frustration at the lack of any sublime surroundings. Though Napoleon had very recently pursued a frantic schedule of road repairs between Calais and Paris in anticipation of an influx of tourists, the roads heading south had not been subjected to a similar level of maintenance, and the largely agricultural lands would have borne testimony to the years of poverty and famine France had suffered.

But the slight sketches Turner made en route reinforce the notion that he found little to interest him in the France Profonde, and that instead his priority was to press south as fast as he could. To this end he and Lowson chose a route as the crow flies, moving from small town to small town, rather than the less direct but more popular route taken by other tourists and diligences through the larger centres of Troyes and Dijon. Only when the travellers were forced to change horses or overnight did Turner take his sketchbook from his pocket to note his whereabouts. With a barely engaged hand he notes a view from a hill near Fontainebleau, the cathedral of St Étienne at Sens, Auxerre viewed from its ramparts, Avalon from the Saulieu Road, framed by the tall trees that Corot would later make his own. The great wine-making region of France around Mâcon, with hillsides lined with vineyards, found little favour with the artist.

Turner's agenda in what he chose to sketch reflected his sense of what was marketable to his clients, and specifically those funding his tour. He had carved out a reputation as a man who, when not painting seascapes to match Van de Velde, could equal Claude with his neo-classical vistas, and could deliver brooding gothicism in his views of ancient monuments and sublime mountains and valleys. Turner was looking for something specific in this journey through France, and only now and then did he find it.

When he did find something that might be of use to his proven repertoire, his pencil was used with sudden detail and vigour. On what is now the little-used D road between Saulieu and Autun, the

cabriolet was halted at the thirteenth-century chateau at Chissey-
en-Morvan. It was an unexpected surprise that made sufficient
impression on Turner that he quickly executed a handful of different
views of the place. After all, it possessed all the qualities of gothic, its
deep history betrayed by its fortified walls, its fairytale roof, its old
bridge. At Autun it is the Romanesque architecture that is worth capturing with a degree of detail rarely indulged elsewhere in the
sketchbook. But then the ancient first-century Porte d'Arroux could
well inform a classical piece. And the same could be said of the Romanesque church that Turner also vigorously detailed in the environs of
Lyons. Then, between Autun and Châlons, Turner executed his first
view of Mont Blanc. He was lucky. To see the great mountain from the
Saône valley is rare. You must have an exceptionally clear morning.

Lyons must have initially felt more promising, and the pair scheduled a three-day stop in the ancient city. Like many other visitors to
the city before and since, Turner was prompted to compare it with
Edinburgh. There is some similarity in the two cities' narrow cob-
bled streets. But Turner had to concede that though the 'buildings of
Lyons are better than those of Edinburgh, there is nothing so good as
Edinburgh castle'.[21]

However, despite an initial flurry of enthusiasm that prompted
Turner to take out a large sheet of paper from his travelling portfolio
to make a detailed, virtuoso view of the city and its cathedral from
the Quai des Célestins, he soon became discouraged. In the end he
drew hardly anything there, complaining that the place was 'not settled enough' to allow him to draw.

Compared to the welcome and vivacity of Paris, the tone in Lyons
was of suffering and suspicion. It was still considered a hotbed of Royalist sentiment more than a decade after the revolution, and was
consequently full of spies. Artists would have been viewed with dis-
trust, and tourists were set upon and hassled by a populace hardened
to poverty. Consequently it was even more expensive than the capital,
with Turner complaining it was 'very dear, eight livres for a bed'.[22]

One British traveller had visited just a fortnight before Turner and
confirmed the prevailing gloom of the place. 'Of all the Towns I have
seen this has suffered most,' wrote Edward Stanley.[23] 'All the

Chateaux and Villas in its most beautiful Environs are shut up. The fine Square of St. Louis le Grand, then Belle Cour, now Place Buonaparte, is knocked to pieces; the fine Statue is broken and removed, and nothing left that could remind you of what it was.'

The continuing reign of the guillotine was all too evident right outside the window of his hotel.

> I have been witness to a scene which, of course, my curiosity as a Traveller would not let me pass over, but which I hope not to see Again – an Execution on the Guillotine . . . I saw the dreadful Instrument in the Place de Ferreant, and on inquiry found that five men were to be beheaded in the morning and two in the evening . . . They were brought to the Scaffold from the Prison, tied each with his arms behind him and again to each other . . . Of all situations in the world, I can conceive of none half so terrible as that of the last Prisoner. He saw his companions ascend one after another, heard each fatal blow, and saw each Body thrown aside to make room for him. I shall never forget his countenance when he stretched out his neck on the fatal board. He shut his eyes on looking down where the heads of his companions had fallen, and instantly his face turned from ghastly paleness to a deep red, and the wire was touched and he was no more . . . Those who have daily seen 200 suffer without the least ceremony or trial get hardened to the sight.

Turner's relief at putting Lyons behind him and continuing southeast to Grenoble is palpable in his sketching. For as he approached the latter, the Alps finally came into view, and with their increasing proximity, Turner's enthusiasm for his environs increased. Now he turned to a sketchbook he had been saving for more detailed and engaged studies. It is larger in size and has brownish-coloured pages. Taking up the technique he began to explore in Scotland, he sets colour aside in favour of pencil, worked up further with white body colour and black chalk. The depictions of Grenoble and its environs are confident and detailed, and enthusiastic; their completeness suggesting them as studies for pictures.

And for the first time one gets a sense of the extremes of climate in which he was now working. He captures the baking hot sun as it glares down on the country before him, colouring both the sky and land in white gouache in a view of the road to Grenoble. In another view of Grenoble, from the banks of the River Isère, the scorched buildings and their bright reflections in the water are highlighted against an otherwise grey background. But as the month of August breaks, so do the thunderstorms that often accompany the high temperatures of the south. This for Turner was a good thing. As he would later tell Farington, 'The weather was very fine: He saw very fine Thunder Storms among the Mountains.'[24] And of course when he could, he drew them. One sketch in which he invests particular detail is a great thunderstorm raging over the Chartreuse region beyond Grenoble, with sleeting rain and forked lightning bearing down on the small town of St Laurent-du-Pont.[25]

A pilgrimage up the Chartreuse's Gorges du Guiers de Mort to the monastery of St Bruno, which lies to the north of Grenoble, was imperative for Turner and Lowson. They left the cabriolet at Grenoble and proceeded on foot and horseback. Here, Turner's sketching intensifies. He cannot stop himself, he is so stimulated. There are steep cliffs, villages dwarfed by looming rock, and crashing waterfalls. Already what Turner was seeing in France surpassed what he had experienced in Wales and Scotland, as he would later explain to Farington. For him the gorges of the Chartreuse offered rocky 'fragments and precipices' that were 'very romantic and strikingly grand'. 'The country on the whole surpasses Wales; and Scotland too,' Turner would relate, adding that only 'Ben [Nevis?] may vie with it'.[26]

The progress Turner and Lowson made through the Chartreuse gorges is charted in Turner's depictions of its narrow winding road, cut straight into the rock, and the bridges they crossed over swollen and gushing streams. In one sketch a horse is depicted waiting patiently while Turner executes his view. In another the guide walks one horse on slowly. Turner returned from the Alps exhausted, admitting to Farington that he resorted to walking often. As such he and Lowson would not have looked out of place among the many pilgrims whom Turner also captured making their way on foot through the gorges, sometimes stopping at roadside shrines, but ultimately heading for the monastery of the Grande Chartreuse, founded by St Bruno. Of course, in their own way Turner and Lowson were pilgrims too.

With the rugged land of Beckford's saint at last witnessed and duly recorded, the next major stop was Geneva, with its shimmering lake. Back in their cabriolet they headed north once again, following the valley of the Isère initially. On arrival at Geneva Turner found the combination of mountain and lake that he had first witnessed properly in Britain's own Lake District magnified.

But the comforts of a town that had long been on the route of the Grand Tour and was well equipped for tourists were short-lived. Pressing on, Lowson and Turner were next headed towards Mont Blanc, the highest peak in the Alps and in western Europe, a place where few ventured at all. Their plan was to circumvent the mountain from Chamonix to the east of the mountain, to Martigny, which lay to the west. This was something that could only be done by foot and mule. It would be a lengthy and gruelling hike. So while their guide took the cabriolet on to their end destination, they headed south-east along the valley of the Arve, probably by diligence, to the village of Chamonix, which nestled at the foot of the great mountain range, and from where they would begin their explorations.[27]

Turner was tackling the Alps in an era before the mountain guide movement and when the accounts of only one or two earlier explorers were available as rudimentary guidebooks. His trip, though coming nearly twenty years after the first ascent of Mont Blanc, predates the beginning of true tourism to the Chamonix region by as many years. It was genuinely adventurous, difficult and potentially dangerous. But in making it Turner would see wonders that he and most British men had never seen before: glaciers.

Turner and Lowson began by walking through the Chamonix valley to see the very end of the great Mer de Glace glacier that descends the north of the mountain. In their day its huge ice boulders extended all the way to the hamlet of Bois, and from here one could make a perilous scramble up the Montenvers to see the full glory of the glacier from higher in its path.

Turner now took out the largest sketchbook he had with him, so far barely used. Its scale reflected the even greater importance he invested in the experience of Mont Blanc. This was unquestionably transformative. Now out came his watercolour paints. He was not satisfied to remain within the monochrome palette he had used in the Chartreuse, nor just to make loose colour notes. Instead he made a series of watercolours worked up to an exceptional degree. He captured the broken jagged pine trees on the slopes of Montenvers, with the great white bulk of Mont Blanc rising up behind it, and grey rolling clouds embracing it; he stood at the source of the Arveyron river as it burst forth from the cold mountain, above it the huge Mer de Glace glacier, slinking spikily down the northern slopes of Mont Blanc. He walked above the glacier to Blair's hut, a small wooden bothy constructed in 1779 by an Englishman called Charles Blair, from which the glacier could be viewed. But Turner reversed the experience Blair intended, climbing down and clambering over the razor-sharp whips of ice which he then placed in the foreground, the hut silhouetted above, against the sky, tiny amid a sea of ice, pine trees and rock. Turner was attempting to accentuate the scale of nature against the smallness of man's efforts.

Elated by the wonders of Chamonix, Turner and Lowson next planned to move southwards around the mountain, where they could see the Glacier de Bossons descend close to the village of Courmayeur. They would then work their way along the Val d'Aosta, which flanks Mont Blanc's southern aspect, and then travel along the Great St Bernard Pass before heading north once more to Martigny.

The trek south was slow and arduous. The twelve miles between Chamonix and Courmayeur took two to three days to accomplish.[28] The pair had to tackle the steep and sharply zig-zagging path over the Col de Voza. Then over another hill, the Col de Bionnassay, before descending into the village of Les Contamines, where they would have had to spend the night. In 1811 John Murray published a guidebook noting that there was a 'tolerable inn' in this village,[29] though it is unclear if that existed nine years earlier. Just as he was no stranger to long and arduous walks, Turner was no stranger to basic accommodation, but even he admitted to Farington that in the mountains he 'often experienced bad living & lodgings'.[30] One gets some sense of the remote farming community the two Englishmen found themselves in that night, in a sombre watercolour Turner made in the low light of dawn the following morning. Just four basic chalets frame the village's as yet unfinished, spireless, church. A group of people mull gloomily: farmers and shepherds who, like Turner, woke with the light. The only note of optimism in a picture that stands out in his sketchbook for its flatness against the intense images of inspiring mountain scenery is the cold white light of dawn blasting over the ridge of Mont Blanc above.

From Les Contamines it was another gruelling day's scramble over the Col du Bonhomme before the next possible place to stop, Les Chapieux. The Murray guidebook relates how treacherous the path was. The travellers passed through the village of Nant Bourant and then began to climb towards chalets where, assuming the shepherds who occupied them in the summer months were amenable, they could rest and have a drink of milk. The scenery in this stretch of the hike is exceptional: 'huge masses of glaciers extend down the crues on the south-western flank of Mont Blanc; but immediately above the chalets is the vast glacier of Trelaulai. This, and the black rocks which support it on one side of the valley and the precipices and debris over which there is a pass to the valley of Haut Luce on the other, almost enclose these chalets in a deep basin.' And yet Turner does not relate it in his sketchbooks. It may well have been that he barely saw it but was instead walking almost blind through mist and cloud, another frequent Alpine experience.[31] If so, perhaps he was spared the vertiginous view from the path that continued above the chalets and terrified the traveller who took it in clear conditions, for, as Murray recounts, he 'looks down from his mule, and sees his foot overhanging the slope beyond'.

Rising to 8,000 feet, the path then follows the Col de Bonhomme, before descending to Chapieux, where there are 'chalets fitted up in a rude way', and where Turner and his companion probably spent their next night. On the third day another huge climb awaited them across the Col de la Seigne. By the time the pair descended from this into the Val d'Aosta, they must have been totally exhausted.

Arriving in the Val d'Aosta, Turner's sense of his proximity to Italy is indicated by the Italianate tone and composition his work adopts, which differs strongly from the highly original work made in the mountains. Since boyhood he had been studying the Italianate views compiled by those artists who had been lucky enough to undertake continental tours, and now he sees the scenery through their lens.

The views of the Val d'Aosta were valuable. This was a region that was not part of the Grand Tour and consequently had been overlooked by most artists who concentrated on the campagna around Rome and the coastlands around Naples.

But it was not long before this gentle landscape had to be put to one side as Turner and Lowson headed for the Great Pass of St Bernard. From Aosta it is twenty-five miles of steep ascent to the St Bernard Pass, and with this began a section of the journey coloured by 'road and accommodations' that were 'very bad' according to Turner. But while Turner and Lowson made this exhausting climb, they must have been aware of the extensive history beneath their feet. The famous pass had served as a vital route across the Alps between Switzerland and Italy since the Bronze Age. But most recently it had been Napoleon who, just two years earlier, had led his troops from the so-called Republic of Helvetica into Italy to engage the Austrians. The event had been immortalized in the great painting of *Napoleon at the Saint Bernard Pass* by France's most celebrated artist, Jacques-Louis David, and Turner would have seen this heroic and triumphant work, which had been widely reproduced by the time he visited Napoleonic Paris. He must have been all too aware as he reached the Hospice of St Bernard, which sat at the highest point of the pass, that man's frail mortality measured little against the vast timelessness of the natural world.

12.   A little reptile

Turner was not a painter who spent much time depicting sex. But neither was he coy about it when he did. Despite the apparent prurience of those who had to deal with evidence of his sexual appetites at the time of his death, the society in which Turner had been brought up was one in which sex was the most visible it had been in British culture, ever, and where the importance placed on matrimony had sunk to an all-time low. This was a time when the mistresses of monarchs and members of the aristocracy were public figures, often depicted by the greatest artists of the day, without moral judgement. There were celebrity whores too, whose exploits were much publicized and again whose portraits attracted a huge amount of public fascination. Neither was erotica the underground industry it became later in the nineteenth century. Leading artists such as Thomas Rowlandson produced erotic prints. Political satirists often employed the most explicit sexual imagery. Many artists joined the ranks of those who chose to live with women outside matrimony, and those who did marry their lovers often pursued other relationships by mutual consent.

Throughout Turner's sketchbooks, alongside the academic studies of female nudes, are from time to time graphic, arguably pornographic, scribbles. That Turner felt the desire to record or imagine moments of intercourse, oral sex and foreplay is evidence of both his own sex drive, and also his compulsion to draw anything and everything. For although his sketchbooks on the whole represent his professional work, one cannot deny that the birds, cats, bonnets, boats and bosoms that also crop up are simply part of the life of a man who *had* to draw the world around him regardless.

By far the most dedicated study that Turner made of the joy of sex was carried out in Berne, in Switzerland. After the exhausting and exhilarating Alps, Turner worked his way along the eastern and northern shores of Lake Geneva to Lausanne, and then headed north-east towards the comfortable city of Berne. By the time he reached it, he had almost finished his sketchbooks and was in need of new supplies, so he bought three brand new ones. It was on the very first page of one of these that Turner recorded the other key transaction he made while in the city.

In a scene that conveys nothing but warmth and happiness, Turner depicts two naked women in bed, one dark and the other fair, their arms wrapped around one another. They are bathed in warm red light, presumably from the sun shining through the red curtains that indicated the trade of the house in which they were found. A chink of morning sunshine is breaking through a gap in the curtains to reveal the face and breasts of one of the women, the white crumpled sheets beneath her, and a pile of discarded clothes on the floor.

The image is complete and worked up in colour to a considerable degree. Turner takes time to show the striped ticking of the mattress on which they lie and the bolster under their heads. He lovingly colours three large-brimmed, flat straw hats, suggesting yet another participant in the sexual revelry who has perhaps left the party. He delicately outlines the women's shoes, with low heels and buckles, lying on the floor, their red corsets and blue-grey skirts.

In this scene of dozy post-coital muddle, it is remarkably easy to imagine Turner himself, in his shirt or wrapped in a sheet, who, up with the dawn as ever, has slipped out of the warm over-crowded bed to sit and sketch, his compulsion to draw as strong as ever.

It is hardly surprising that a man brought up in London's red light district was no stranger to paying for sex. But there is a non-judgemental warmth in the illustration that also betrays Turner's physical love of women and his delight in their company. His portrayal of these uncomplicated women is palpably joyful. There is a sense of his appreciation of their independence and lack of demands on him.

There is the possibility that this image is worked up to a relatively finished degree not just for the personal pleasure of completion, but because Turner made up the watercolour with a client in mind. Highly finished erotic watercolours that exist elsewhere – notably from the hand of the Swiss-born Academician Henry Fuseli, whose works are far more graphic and detailed than Turner's — serve to remind us that not only was Turner far from exceptional in making erotic work, but it may well have been done for a private market. But quite who Turner's client might have been remains a mystery.

Whatever the motivation for the watercolour of the Swiss prostitutes, it conveys a terrific sense of liberty and freedom in its relaxed, languid tone. Liberty and freedom were qualities inherent in the idea of Switzerland as the fount of democracy. And it is worth considering whether the sexual freedoms he enjoyed in Berne became somehow emblematic of a wider theme of freedom explored by Turner in his imagery of Switzerland.

Certainly the sketch is on the introductory page of a book that became known as the 'Swiss Figures' book and is dedicated to capturing the ordinary working folk of the region, defined by their national dress. These people are depicted with obvious sympathy. He describes their hats and aprons, and captures them at work and at their leisure. He observes boatmen with wide-brimmed boaters, and female peasants balancing bundles on their heads. He watches them as they gather around a plough and notices the striped culottes and red waistcoats of the men at work in the fields.

These and the other sketches Turner undertook on that tour were made in the expectation that his views of Switzerland and the Swiss would be noticeable, not just for their response to the exceptional scenery, but also for their symbolism. And it may well be that they were also a response to a set of commissions already discussed with Walter Fawkes, who would buy several studies based on these sketches when Turner returned, and would continue to purchase Swiss views over the course of the next decade.

The muddied cabriolet finally returned the travel-weary Lowson and Turner to Paris at the end of September 1802.[1] The bustling capital of France, with its urban riches, its ridiculous emphasis on fashion, and its complex social etiquette, could not have been more different from the remote hillsides and rural valleys. After the cool air of the high mountains and deep gorges, the couple were suddenly thrown into a heat that many were describing as intolerable.

In returning to Paris, Turner was once again also thrown back into that complex political world of taste, patronage and professional ascendancy that he had been so artfully negotiating for the last few years of his life. The city was awash with members of the Royal Academy and Britain's cultural elite.

Once rested, Turner slipped into the frantic cultural exchange between British and French artists that was in full flow. French artists had studios within the Louvre and the Academicians were busy visiting their contemporaries at work. Turner went with Farington and Fuseli to the studio of Jean-Guillaume Moitte, a sculptor working like so many French painters of the revolutionary period in a strongly neo-classical style. Although Farington notes that the visit was on Benjamin West's recommendation, it was almost certainly William Beckford's enthusiasm for Moitte that ultimately informed it. Beckford had been in Paris since May and was patronizing the sculptor.

Just across from Moitte's studio was that of another neo-classical sculptor, Antoine-Denis Chaudet, and Turner, Farington and Fuseli dutifully looked in here too, before going to find 'Madame Julia', a young Irishwoman who was studying under Jacques-Louis David. The implication is that the trio met Julia in David's own studio, where they were able to view the portrait that the painter had made of Julia's uncle, the wealthy Irish merchant Cooper Penrose. Madame Julia then took the group to see the portrait of Napoleon in the St Bernard Pass, which must have encouraged some unrecorded comment from Turner, who had after all just been there. After this the group headed out to meet the artist Pierre-Narcisse Guérin and see his highly acclaimed *The Return of Marcus Sextus*.

Turner, who had resisted sketching in the studios of Chaudet, Moitte and even David, finally took out his sketchbook to make a quick copy of Guérin's *Sextus*. Generally, the austere classical work that the French artists were producing failed to impress the British painters, even if patrons like Beckford and Penrose were otherwise persuaded. Martin Archer Shee rushed over to the Farington/Fuseli group to rubbish David's *Sabine Women*, and even Turner, having viewed 'the French exhibition' with Farington, conceded to him that he found the French work 'very low – all made up of Art'.[2] Turner's meaning is not entirely clear, but one surmises from this comment that his objection was that the work was stylized at the expense of 'truth' and thus verged on the artificial. Typical of Turner, however, was his determination to say something positive about fellow artists, and consequently he noted his approval of 'Madame Gerards little pictures' which he considered 'very ingenius'.

Turner's appreciation of Marguerite Gérard is intriguing. It suggests an interest in domestic genre pieces that stands in rather strong contrast to the sublime landscape and seascape pictures on which he had built his recent fame.

Gérard specialized in interior scenes featuring women at their daily duties, in their boudoir, and often with their children. They are beautifully realized, carefully observed and quietly intellectual. And they are intimate without being overly sentimental.

One of her pictures on show in the Louvre in 1802 was *La Nourrice* (the wet nurse), which depicted a young mother in fashionable attire sitting next to a peasant wet nurse breast-feeding the former's child. The wit in the work derives from the careful composition of the child on the nurse's lap, and the arrangement of her own costume in such a way that it is reminiscent of the Renaissance depictions of the Madonna and Child. With this reference Gérard turns a domestic scene from contemporary France into a deeply spiritual contemplation on the cycle and meaning of life, suggesting a fundamental holiness in the nurturing and mothering aspects of women.

Turner's interest in Gérard's work, like the image of the prostitutes in Berne, gives us a rare insight into this side of his personality, and reveals that his capacity for deep emotion was not just reserved for the natural landscape.

La Nourrice must have been one of the prompts behind a very unusual project that he would embark upon on his return to London: the depiction of *The Holy Family*. The oblique reference to that work lies in his depiction of a baby Jesus being adored by his parents, where Mary has just finished feeding her child, the bodice of her dress still undone.

Turner had never yet in his career produced a solely figurative painting. But now, despite having just been in the most spectacular landscape he had ever seen, and while preparing to present that to the wider world, he formulated the idea that he should also paint a traditional figurative piece, in which there was barely any landscape depiction at all.

It is a typical instinct from a man who throughout his entire career had always been driven to measure himself against other artists, and it is clear evidence that despite his recent appointment as an Academician, Turner's ambitions were still very much in the ascendant. Having seen the greatest collection of Old Master works in the world, and in particular the works of Titian, which were the focus of all his compatriots' study, he determined to see if he could match, if not exceed them.

And so, in between the rounds of artists' studios and necessary visits to secure the relevant paperwork for a return home, Turner began the process of drawing and analysing Old Master works in the Louvre. Naturally, he studied sea paintings and landscapes, taking a particular interest in Ruisdael's depiction of *A Storm off the Dutch Coast* and his pastoral landscape *Le Coup de Soleil*. He took care to note elements of Nicolas Poussin's mythological and biblical depictions of a *Landscape with Diogenes*, *The Jews Gathering Manna in the Desert*, and *The Deluge*. But crucially, Turner also made extensive notes on the work of Titian, and that master's ability to provide psychological narratives within his figurative work. He considered *Titian and His Mistress*, Titian's *St Peter Martyr*, his *Entombment of the Dead Christ*, his *Christ Crowned with Thorns* and his *Pastoral Concert*.

These notes and sketches Turner makes give us a vital insight into his intellect and personality at this point in time. If the shy, awkward boy, the selfish and focused teenager, the determined bachelor and the uncouth sea captain (yet to emerge) suggest something other than a man of supreme intelligence and profound feelings, then Turner's Louvre notebooks set the record straight once and for all. He was informed, well read, intelligent, intellectual, thoughtful and of course passionate.

His passion is revealed in a line he jots about Titian's 'mistress', whose 'Bosom' he considers 'a piece of nature in her happiest moments'. The sense of his intelligence comes through his criticism of the works in front of him. He assesses the use of light and shade in them, judging Poussin has the 'grandest system'. He observes how Titian handles colour; he reveals his own personal interest in how to achieve sublimity and emotional response to work, and he displays his reading on art.

A sense of the inner workings of his mind is provided in his account of Nicolas Poussin's *Deluge*, in which Turner's lack of humility towards the Old Master is also revelatory of his own confidence: 'The lines are defective as to the conception of a swamp'd world and the fountains of the deep being broken up,' Turner writes.

> The boat in the waterfall is ill judged and misapplied for the figures are placed at the wrong end to give the idea of falling. The other boat makes a parallel with the base of the picture and the woman giving the Child is unworthy the mind of Poussin. She is as unconcerned as is the man floating with a small piece of board no current or effluvium although a waterfall is introduced to fill up the interstices of the Earth. Artificially, not tearing and desolating but falling placidly in another pool. Whatever might have been said of the picture by Rousseau never can efface its absurdity as to forms and the introduction of the figures but the color is sublime.[3]

The lack of temerity that Turner felt as he stood in front of Titian and Poussin travelled with him back to London. As 1802 drew to a close, he sloughed off the skin of that younger William Turner who had recognized the need to curry favour among the Academicians before his election as RA. The emergent J. M. W. Turner was, by contrast, emboldened, as Joseph Farington was about to find out. And as usual Turner was moving with unprecedented speed and ambition; though only a newly elected Academician, he was determined to make his impression on the Royal Academy as quickly and as profoundly as he could.

At first he pressed Farington with his desire to be made a 'visitor', that is a tutor in the Schools who looked over the work of pupils. 'Turner was very urgent to be a visitor,' Farington noted in December 1802.[4] Though Farington discouraged this, Turner instead got himself elected in early 1803 to the RA's council, an executive committee responsible for managing the Academy's affairs, on which members sat for two years.

The appointment flung Turner into not only the politics but the social rituals of the Academy's executive, an aspect of Academy life that he clearly relished. Council members buzzed around Somerset House. They chatted over dinner at the Academy or dashed to meet one another at Holyland's Coffee House on the Strand, which operated as an informal office for the institution. Farington's diaries note Turner dining or taking tea regularly with him and other RAs . . . always in sight, busy and busying himself with the Academy's affairs. Even more than before, this appointment enabled Turner to be a man living his life in public. Breakfasting, lunching and dining with colleagues. Sarah Danby must have been a particularly independent mother to his daughter, since there is little sense of much time for anything beyond his work and the RA.

But unlike his networking prior to his appointment as an RA, Turner no longer saw a need to strategically inveigle himself with power brokers. Far from it. He now saw himself as *one of the power brokers*, and sought only to wield his influence in the cause of what he considered to be *right*.

However, the internal politics of the Royal Academy were such that the taste of life as an Academician quickly turned bitter. The debate raging within the walls of Somerset House reflected in microcosm the more general question of monarch versus the people that was being played out on the world stage. And if there is any clue to Turner's wider political leanings, it is his behaviour at the Academy, where his sympathies lay with the rights of the ordinary man, and the consensus of the majority, which suggest the influence of his Wilkesite Uncle Marshall from Brentford.

A schism was growing within the RA between those members of more democratic leaning – led by Farington – and a group who saw themselves as Royalists, and became known as the Court party. The Academy's president, Benjamin West, was seen as part of the former party, and his trip to France in 1802 had done little to redress this view.

Turner now stepped into a growing row between the two political poles in the institution that centred around the role of its council. The membership of this executive committee changed each year, with four members standing down annually and four new ones elected. The council had to seek approval for its decisions and suggestions from the general membership of the RA at general assemblies. But in 1799 Henry Tresham RA challenged the power of the general assembly to approve council business, suggesting the council should rule with autonomy. To this end he enlisted the support of the King, who agreed with Tresham's position, and in doing so put Tresham at loggerheads with West.

In 1803 Turner found himself on a council that was evenly split between those who sympathized with West and those favouring the Court party and the King.

On 4 March 1803 he faced his first taste of a bitter and confrontational war. The council from the previous year had commissioned a sub-committee to look into issues of finance regarding the Academy, and its members were due to present recommendations to the council. Suddenly the four Court party members of the council – James Wyatt, John Singleton Copley, Francis Bourgeois and John Yenn – refused to hear the findings of the committee stating that the council could not be dictated to, and yet again referred the matter to the King.

Turner – along with the three other councillors – voted to censure the four rebels. But this was far from the end of the matter. In the following month Benjamin West found himself at the centre of an emerging scandal of his own, when claims were published in the press that he had broken Academy rules by submitting a painting for that year's annual exhibition that he had already shown. It was firmly believed that one of the censured four had leaked the story to the press, and so now council members were asked to sign a declaration that they had not generated the story. Turner and others duly signed such a declaration, but 'the four' did not attend the meeting at which the signatures were invited. After further attempts by the Court party to determine a purely independent council, West called to suspend the Court party members of the council, who had now become five thanks to the defection of the architect John Soane. The

King stepped in to reinstate the men, though their tenure by this time was nearly up, and the fact that four new council members were due for election saw them removed by procedure at the end of the year, with Wyatt, Copley and Yenn all leaving, along with the democratical Ozias Humphry, to be replaced by Philip de Loutherbourg, Robert Smirke, Farington and George Dance.

The battles continued outside the council, however. The next opportunity for conflict came when prizes were due to be awarded for architectural drawings. When there seemed to be consensus that no candidate was of sufficient calibre to be awarded a gold medal, the architect John Soane attempted to overrule this decision. Once again voting was split along factional lines, with Turner, Thomas Lawrence, James Northcote, John Opie and Farington among others voting against Soane. Soane was furious, as was Bourgeois, who ran into Turner and confronted him. Bourgeois suggested that one should vote in support of those who 'were most conversant in those respective studies' (in this instance, Soane). Turner was both precocious and witty enough to suggest to his elder that it would be good if Bourgeois might also follow the lead of those better suited to judge when painting or figure drawing (Bourgeois's specialities) were being considered. At which Bourgeois accused Turner of being a 'little reptile'. Turner's astonishingly bold and amusing riposte was that Bourgeois was a 'great reptile – with ill manners'.[5]

For some the sheer nerve for a young and newly elected Academician to stand up to a senior member of the establishment amounted to pomposity, and this was a label applied to Turner from time to time. As early as February 1803, just a month after his election to the council, Turner's fellow council member Ozias Humphry had grumbled to Farington about 'the arrogant manners of a new member of Council & of the Academy . . . no respect to persons or circumstances'.[6] But pomposity was a badge applicable to many members of the institution . . . and Turner seemed equally sensitive to lack of respect afforded him. Egalité, Fraternité and Liberté were qualities he admired, more so perhaps since his recent trip to post-revolutionary France.

When the position of a new Keeper of the Academy was to be

voted for in February the following year, Farington was annoyed to discover that when he went to canvas Turner's vote for Robert Smirke, the young man would not be drawn. 'He sd. He had declined to say How He shd. Vote. I replied that I only wished to express to him my sentiments that I might have nothing to blame myself for as having been omitted – He spoke of the rudeness of Richards.'[7]

Turner's lack of compliance came as a shock to Farington, who had done so much in rallying support for Turner. The issue of Turner's arrogance came to a head in May 1804 when he and Farington clashed. It was another council meeting. Farington had arrived earlier than Turner and withdrawn from the meeting room momentarily to have a private discussion with Smirke and Bourgeois.

The three council members had stepped into the model academy to discuss the latest scandal that was rocking the Academy. This time rude verses had been circulated at the Academy dinner about the eminent patron Thomas Hope. The verses were now the talk of London. Hope was wounded both by the satirical work at his expense, and by the failure of the Academy to invite him to their dinner. The incident had erupted into a scandal that was engrossing the whole institution and was being discussed at every moment. And it was inevitably on the agenda for discussion at the council meeting.

When Farington, Bourgeois and Smirke returned they discovered Turner had joined the council meeting and was occupying a chair that Farington was in the habit of occupying. 'He had taken MY CHAIR,' Farington scribbled furiously in his diary that night, '& began instantly with a very angry countenance to call us to acct. for having left the Council., on which moved by his presumption I replied to Him sharply & told him of the impropriety of addressing us in such a manner, to which He answered in such a way, that I added HIS Conduct as to behavior had been cause of Complaint to the whole Academy.'[8]

Turner's outburst is evidence enough of his extreme frustration with the petty nonsense that was beginning to drown the proper business of the Academy. But Turner could not afford to fall out with the Academy, nor did he want to. His lifelong dedication to it reveals the importance he saw in it as an institution that still could embody the ambition of British art and artists. Nevertheless, as he joined its disordered ranks it was evident the R A presented him with challenges that he found difficult to navigate without losing his temper.

As Farington gave his dressing-down to Turner that May, he was doing so to a man who had already branched out on his own and set up his own gallery, under his own name. This move was not purely an expression of his discontent with the back-biting Academy. Though the acidic climate within the walls of Somerset House must have made the enterprise easier for him to embark upon, Turner was largely motivated by a spirit of enterprise. As his ambition marched forward he would let nothing come in his way.

While living in Norton Street, Turner had gradually been securing the full occupation of his former address at 64 Harley Street. He took over the garden and outbuildings in 1802 and acquired the sole tenancy in 1803. This enabled him to build at the back of the property a room which extended over the garden, which would serve as his own gallery.

By the spring of 1804 the gallery on the corner of Harley Street and Queen Anne Street was ready to open. Unlike Fuseli's Milton Gallery or Boydell's Shakespeare Gallery, both set up as the titles indicate to celebrate illustrations of these poets' work, Turner's Gallery relied on the fame of no one but himself.

Turner must have decided that he wanted to have his own gallery from the moment he returned from France – if not before. A number of artists and entrepreneurs had been exploring the idea of commercial galleries in different forms. After all, as Henry Fuseli had noted in a letter to his friend William Roscoe, 'There are, says Mr West, but two ways of working successfully, that is lastingly, in this country, for an artist – the one is, to paint for the King; the other to mediate a scheme of your own I am determined to lay, hatch and crack an egg for myself too.'[9]

With prototypes like the Morland Gallery, Shakespeare Gallery, Macklin's Poets' Gallery and Henry Fuseli's more recent Milton Gallery already in mind, Turner would have returned from his travels to see his former co-tenant in Harley Street, John Thomas Serres, also

form part of a consortium setting up the British School, a gallery selling the work of British artists intended to rival the Royal Academy's
annual selling exhibition. The model of a selling gallery where he
could showcase work and also launch a publishing aspect to his output – whereby clients could subscribe to buy engravings of the work
exhibited – seemed a sensible commercial step. It expanded exposure
of his work beyond the annual RA show and casual calls to his studio. It was a step that also, significantly, spoke of an artist determined
not to be wholly at the beck and call of patrons. This was a statement
that suggested those who might want to invest in Turner should go
to him.

But there were risks in artistic enterprise. Artists were more often
debtors than they were successful businessmen. The Shakespeare
Gallery had ultimately failed, as had the others. The risk in cracking
one's own egg was considerable, and it was not just a financial risk.
The stress artists bore had all too often proved fatal.

The latest casualty had been Turner's friend and rival Thomas
Girtin. He had died sitting at his easel in his painting room
on 9 November 1802, just days after Turner returned from Paris.
Girtin had worked tirelessly, spending some five months in Paris
with a view to publishing *Twenty Views* of the city, before returning
to launch his panorama of London – which had not been picked up at
Greenwood's auction as he had hoped.

But the damp conditions of the French city the previous autumn
and his tireless graft took its toll. He did not live to see the fruits of
either enterprise. Asthma, TB, consumption or an 'ossification of the
heart' have all been conditions blamed for his demise. But stress and
disappointment must also have contributed. Though Girtin had
miraculously found the means to finally finish and open his London
panorama at Spring Gardens in September 1802, he could not fail to
have been heartbroken by the simultaneous launch of a *Panorama of
Paris and its Environs* by the painter James de Maria in the Haymarket.
Girtin's drawings for his own Parisian enterprise were all that he
could show by way of competition. He had been first across the
Channel, and yet had somehow missed the boat.

If there is some doubt about the cause, the fact of his death was certain enough, and in the same way that Sarah Danby had had John Danby's glees published posthumously, Girtin's young widow and infant son saw his London panorama and subsequent published views of Paris turn into vehicles to raise charity for their future welfare.

Turner walked behind Girtin's coffin and saw his old friend laid to rest in St Paul's Covent Garden. Such was the destitution of his friend at the time of his demise, there had to be a collection for a headstone. There was no doubt in Turner's mind that had Girtin been able to pursue his career to its full extent, he would have been laid to rest in the *other* St Paul's, alongside Sir Joshua Reynolds. All his life Turner believed that Girtin was the one living artist who could match if not better his own work.

The graveyard of St Paul's Covent Garden would enjoy another significant addition to its ranks soon enough. Just days before his gallery opened, Turner's mother also died, on 15 April 1804. Quite how her physical condition had so rapidly declined in Bethlem is unrecorded, as is the cause of her death. Turner's response is also frustratingly lost. Some early biographers claim that he had not seen her since her incarceration. There is no extant documentation from the hospital archives to help us. The only suggestion that this might just be true, though, comes in the form of family documentation. In July 1804 Mary Turner's brother, Joseph Marshall, made his will, or remade it. The childless butcher, now retired to Sunningwell, left his entire estate to his second wife, Mary Marshall, for the duration of her life. His nephew William is not mentioned, a fact that seems surprising under normal circumstances, but may well reflect the extreme disappointment Joseph felt in his namesake, three months after the demise of Mary Turner. Turner would go on in his later life to erect a simple plaque to his mother's and father's memory in St Paul's Covent Garden, a gesture that perhaps suggests a degree of remorse on the part of the son.

What we do know about Turner in the days leading up to his mother's death in April 1804 is that he was busy fulfilling his Academy duties, as well as writing inviting people to attend his new gallery. He was playing both Academician and independent businessman with considerable gusto. His new elevated status also put him in the way of the commentary about art that went on at the highest levels.

The Royal Academy was a nest of animated vipers when it came to the selection and position of pictures for the annual exhibition. Farington provides a record of the mischievous comments, wranglings and quarrels that bubbled up at this time of year. Though no one was exempt from the back-biting and condemnations that began to be liberally traded between brother Academicians, new divides were emerging. It was not just the Royalist versus the Democratical at the RA, but the traditionalists versus the 'moderns'.

Turner was fast becoming the focus of growing criticism from members of the landscape-painting old guard, embodied by the amateur landscape painter and self-professed connoisseur of the genre, Sir George Beaumont. A certain amount of jealousy at the young man's supreme success was probably behind what would become a campaign of hatred over the next few years.

At the beginning of April, Beaumont held a dinner to warm up Farington, who was on the hanging committee. At it, West was criticized for dealing 'lavish and immoderate praise upon modern works'. The modern works in question were those by Turner, whom Beaumont laid into, claiming his Van de Velde pendant painted for the Duke of Bridgewater had a sea 'like pease soup'. Henry Edridge, who had once looked over Turner's shoulder at Monro's club, joined in the assassination citing Thomas Hearne, another former tutor, who complained that the sea in Turner's *Calais Pier* 'appeared like batter'. With the insults well under way, Beaumont and Edridge agreed with one another that it was not just his seas, but that 'Turner never painted a good sky'.[10]

Turner himself became infected by the vituperative and dismissive criticisms of submitted work being bandied around by Academicians. Most accounts of Turner recall a man generally reluctant to criticize his colleagues. 'He was well aware of his prominence among the Artists of his day but liberal in his praise of talent among them,' one acquaintance would later recall.[11]

However, this generous attitude to his peers was less on show in 1804. 'Turner spoke of the inferiority of Shee's portraits of Woemen when compared with those He has painted of men . . . Of Clarke he said that His art might be considered as "a weed" it bore no resemblance of anything in nature or Art. Woodforde, he said, was incapable of rising to a height . . . He remarked on the extraordinary incorrectness in the details of West's figures . . .'[12]

Turner was also disappointed in the positioning of the works he was showing, but interestingly the anger and remonstration he was able to display was not brought to bear on this occasion. In fact he did not even raise a complaint. 'He told Smirke that He did not much like the situation of His Picture that was on the door side of the lower end of the room, but he did not seem to mind it much.'

Turner did not 'mind it much' because unlike the other exhibitors his reputation no longer hung on this one moment in the arts calendar. In a clearly tactical move he chose to display just three works at the RA that year, a selection that reflected the areas in which his talent was roundly established. He showed a seascape, a classical landscape painted in oils, and a topographical watercolour. Despite this ostensibly conservative offering, each work carried that element of invention that Turner felt crucial in art, and that his audience had come to expect. *Boats Carrying out Anchors and Cables to Dutch Men of War, in 1665* was a piece that merged sea and history painting, a re-imagining of an event in the past that once again invited comparison with Dutch Old Masters. *Narcissus and Echo* was a classical landscape that may have been suggested by Poussin's handling of the same subject Turner would have seen in the Louvre; meanwhile his *Edinburgh from Caulton-Hill* took the same viewpoint as Robert Barker's first panorama of that city, but instead of the rigorous naturalism of the panorama, he viewed the city through the imaginative lens of Claude Lorrain, complete with golden sunlight and misty atmosphere.

In their own different ways each of these paintings displayed the increasing emphasis Turner was placing on his imaginative faculties, harnessing his supreme skills of observation to a personal agenda that chose to rearrange nature, and look back to imagined pasts through an emotive filter: exploring different elements of the sublime.

Crucially, however, Turner reserved all his highly original, adventurous Swiss subjects for his new gallery, where he had the freedom to show what he wanted, in a position of his choosing, on his own terms.

It might have been this tactic that encouraged the RA president, Benjamin West, to observe that Turner's work submitted to the RA show was second-rate. But Turner clearly did not think so. In fact the artist was sufficiently proud of his contributions to the RA that year that he was keen to secure an invitation for Sir Watkin Williams-Wynn to the famous Academy dinner, where potential patrons were lavishly wined and dined. Wynn had been the patron of Turner's hero the Welsh painter Richard Wilson and had begun to commission watercolours from Turner, including a small view of Dolbadarn Castle and larger ones of Tintern Abbey and Brinkburn Priory.

At 2 p.m. on 27 April the Academicians were afforded an exclusive, private view of the exhibition. They were each allowed one guest, and the list that Farington made in 1804 reveals that almost to a man the Academicians brought a family member. This was an event for wives to be admitted into the world of their husbands' affairs. The exception was the presence of Sir George Beaumont. While a friend and occasional honorary exhibitor, Beaumont could not, as an amateur artist, be a member of the Academy. However, he had pursued his contacts to obtain an invitation for himself and his wife, a request which Farington and Dance had accommodated, with Martin Archer Shee taking Farington's guest instead. Turner had no wife, of course. He could, however, have invited Mrs John Danby. But instead he chose Col. Humphrey Sibthorpe, a Leicester-based politician and colonel of the South Lincolnshire Militia who became a minor patron of Turner, buying a couple of watercolours during the course of his life.

Sibthorpe, like Wynn, was one of the many clients that Turner wanted to impress with what he had on show at the RA and at his Harley Street gallery. Both men would have been given invitations to attend both shows, and asked to bring friends. That April, these invitations were lavishly extended by Turner, with his usual energy and determination. He had cards delivered to members of the Academy, while also orchestrating a mail drop to established and potential clients. Remnants of this campaign are extant. A note to Ozias Humphry indicates that the elder Academician's displeasure with Turner's manners had not eroded their relationship, and the younger man was still keen for the latter's approval. Meanwhile a response to Turner from Lord Auckland, whom Turner may well have encountered at the Royal Academy dinner in 1803, thanks Turner and hopes 'in the course of a very few days to gratify Himself and His Family by a visit to Mr Turner's Gallery'.[13]

Turner must have seen a good footfall through his new gallery; after all, his clients were growing in number. In 1803, when Turner showed the work from his Swiss trip at the Royal Academy, new patrons joined the ranks of his existing collectors. Though his depiction of *Calais Pier* and his *Holy Family* failed to sell – the former perhaps because of the renewed hostilities with the French, with Britain declaring war again in May that year, and the latter almost certainly because of a particularly hostile response from critics who felt, with some justification, that the genius of landscape had taken a step too far in his attempt to match the great figurative painters – Turner's other oil paintings all found good homes. Lord Yarborough took Turner's depiction of the *Festival Upon the Opening of the Vintage of Mâcon*,[14] for a splendid sum of 300 guineas, this only achieved in a bidding war between him and Sir John Leicester. Meanwhile a depiction of the *Château de St Michael at Bonneville* was bought by Samuel Dobrée.[15]

Like so many of Turner's new clients, this Hackney-based merchant, with riches built on slave money, had begun a dedicated collection of British art. It was at least Dobrée's second purchase from Turner, since he had also acquired *Fishermen upon a Lee-Shore, in Squally Weather*,[16] which Turner had exhibited at the RA in 1802. It would not be the last.

Turner had meanwhile compiled a special presentation book full of sample views of Switzerland to show to clients. It was an effective marketing tool. Walter Fawkes quickly asked for a view of *Bonneville, Savoy* to be worked up in oil, while Sir John Boyd of Danson Hill, who had perhaps helped fund Turner's trip, asked for oil paintings of the deeply dramatic *Pass of St Gotthard* and the *Devil's Bridge, St Gotthard.*

The only obvious disappointment seems to have been that Beckford did not bite, buying neither one of Turner's exhibited Swiss works, nor choosing anything from his selection of presentation sketches. Despite his vast fortune and resource, even the great Beckford was not immune to economics, and issues with his plantations combined with spiralling building costs saw him selling more than he acquired in 1802. He held a major house sale, and also disposed of his Dry Sugar Work estate in Jamaica to a speculator called Stephen Drew.

In 1804 Turner recalled some of his old works for his gallery opening. He asked Samuel Dobrée, for example, to lend him the view of the *Château de St Michael at Bonneville.* We know about the Dobrée contribution only because Turner's voice bursts through in 1804. It is the year in which his surviving correspondence properly begins. The snippets of communication with Dobrée give us a glimpse of the complicated Turner: generous, eager to please, but also determined to be valued.

Turner returned the Bonneville picture in July 1804, and in the same delivery he included the latest major oil that the enthusiastic Dobrée had bought from him. This was his *Boats Carrying out Anchors and Cables to Dutch Men of War, in 1665*, which he had just shown at the Royal Academy exhibition.

The price on the latter was not quite settled, it seems, but Turner's delight at Dobrée's growing patronage is indicated in two generous gestures: '. . . may I ask once more am I to put out the cloud in the Picture of Bonneville?'[17] Turner asks in one letter, implying that his client was not quite content with the composition of the sky. And then, in another letter, Turner reveals, 'You will find that I have sent you *all* & have added the small picture of Margate which you appeared to like – your acceptance of it, and allow it always to remain in your Eye as a small remembrance of respect will be very pleasant to me, and although it accompanies the "*Boats going out with cables*" consider it not as its make-weight.'[18]

The gift was a wonderful piece of psychological manipulation on Turner's part. With such generosity it would be hard for Dobrée not to pay the price Turner was asking for the main painting. But Turner's generosity was not always tactical. Long after Samuel Dobrée's death his family sold a painting by Paul Sandby of a cricket match that had also been a gift from Turner . . . Dobrée, like a number of Turner's clients, had become a friend.

Another man who would mature into a close friend despite their apparent political differences at the Academy was the architect John Soane. Soane had attended the opening of Turner's gallery, where his wife Eliza had bought watercolours of the *Refectory of Kirkstall Abbey, Yorkshire*, painted some years earlier, as well as *St Hughes Denouncing Vengeance on the Shepherd of Cormayer, in the Valley of d'Aoust*, which Turner had shown at the R A in the previous year, and now showed again under his own roof.[19] From this point on Turner and Soane became close, often walking to Soane's Ealing retreat, Pitshanger Manor, where they might enjoy a spot of fishing. And just as he had done with Dobrée, when Turner sent Soane his pictures, he included an unexpected gift: 'the print enclosed is from a Private Plate of Lord Yarborough's of "*The Mausoleum*" which Wyatt built for him in Lincolnshire, if it is any way interesting unto you, your acceptance will make me happy.'[20]

Walter Fawkes and his friend Thomas Lister Parker also showed their support, the former buying three watercolours – *The passage of Mount St Gothard, taken from the centre of the Teufels Broch (Devil's Bridge)*, *The Great Fall of the Riechenbach in the valley of Hasle* and *Mont Blanc from Fort Roch, in the Val D'Aosta,* and the latter asking for a view of the Bowland.

Sir George Beaumont visited the gallery out of curiosity. He was astonished at the quantity of work Turner was showing, and the distinctive sense of light in so many of his paintings. Naturally his report was derogatory. 'Sir George has been to Turner's Exhibition,' Farington noted. 'He said Turner should not have shown so many pictures together – He remarked on the strong skies & parts not corresponding with them.'[21]

It was only in making his own showroom that Turner's contemporaries were suddenly able to fully take on board the exceptional quantity, quality and *range* of Turner's fast expanding oeuvre. Such a display was at once a wonder for potential patrons, and a source of aggravation for those who could not compete with his precocious talent and prodigious output.

But while he was proving the darling of the emergent new patrons of British art, Turner's domestic situation remained chaotic. He was now at the centre of a business and social enterprise that included his father, Roche Jaubert and Sarah Danby and her daughters. The rooms in Norton Street, where apparently Sarah's brother-in-law also had an interest, were not sufficient and it is understandable that Turner once again found himself looking for space where he could work in peace.

After the RA Keeper Joseph Wilton's death, Turner had briefly made use of his vacant apartments, but as the summer of 1804 passed, he knew that this facility would not be available much longer. The Academy had been waiting for the King to approve Robert Smirke as Wilton's replacement. The delay was down to the fact that the King had succumbed to his recurrent mental illness again, and had been unable to deal with Academy business. But eventually a decision was handed down from the Palace revealing that the King had rejected Smirke's appointment. According to the gossip circulating around the Academy, William Beechey had been unable to resist communicating to the King that Smirke had noted, on the execution of the French royal family, 'That the Guillotine might be well employed upon some more crowned heads.'[22]

The news was a blow to Smirke supporters, of which Turner was one. And it raised yet again the extent to which the Academy and its business remained enthralled to the monarch's whim. This constant political issue was felt yet again when, in December 1804, there was a concerted attempt by the Court party to elect the architect James Wyatt as President of the RA in place of Benjamin West. In the end only seven members voted for Wyatt, and West was reappointed despite his apparent democratic leanings. But three votes in the ballot had been submitted blank and Farington for one felt that one of these votes had been Turner's. After all, Wyatt had been an important influence on his career and had introduced him to some of his most important clients, including William Beckford.

Shortly after this, another general meeting was held to vote again for another Keeper. Farington had put his considerable political heft behind a campaign for Fuseli, who won the day, against Rigaud – another member who had assisted Turner in his youth. This time Turner did not vote. Perhaps he would have submitted another blank paper and felt therefore there was little point in his attending the event. The young man who had begun so full of the importance and propriety of Academy practice had become disillusioned and weary.

The disenchantment with the internal politics of the R A that was planted in 1804 would continue to grow through Turner's life. It was the beginning of a complex relationship with an institution he at once admired and was profoundly proud to be a part of, yet in which he saw so many failings, and which caused him personal agonies.

In addition, the criticism of his work that began to take hold with the audacious opening of his own gallery would never, from this moment on, abate. These voices of dissent would haunt Turner for the rest of his life.

13.   Reimagined pasts

Despite its name, the Thatched House Tavern was in fact a large, elegant building in St James's which boasted a huge assembly room used by many of London's most prestigious clubs.

On 11 April 1805, Turner made his way to a meeting at this landmark venue. His fellow painter Paul Sandby Munn was also heading for the same place. Inevitably, the painters knew each other. Munn had also been taken under Dr Monro's wing, and he had been a friend of Thomas Girtin.

Munn, a watercolourist, was a member of the new Society of Painters in Water Colour, which Turner's great friend William Frederick Wells had been instrumental in founding the previous November. This society was yet another expression of dissatisfaction with the Royal Academy, and the wider system of established patronage in British art, which valued oil painting over and above watercolour. The rising popularity of watercolour paintings among the British public had done nothing to improve the treatment of the medium, which was often shown in the least favourable positions at the RA.

Despite Turner's own efforts to align his oils and watercolours as works of equal worth, many of the painters working in this medium felt under-represented and undervalued. So Wells had formed the society with a view that members would exhibit together. The title of the organization, not remotely contentious to us, was intentionally precocious in the early nineteenth century. Watercolour was not referred to as 'painting' but as 'drawing', and watercolour paintings were normally called 'drawings', terms adopted to diminish the perceived value of the finished work. That the watercolour artists had called themselves a society of painters was in itself a statement of protest.

The Society was planning to stage its first show later in the month, and though Turner's membership of the Academy prevented him from exhibiting with another society, he doubtless followed its fortunes with a considerable degree of interest and sympathy. The show would prove a resounding success, with 12,000 people paying to see the work of its members over a period of seven weeks.

Turner, meanwhile, was planning his own form of protest. For the first time in his short but packed career he had decided not to submit a single painting to that year's RA show. Instead he would exhibit works only at his own gallery.

The new work he was planning to show in the coming May included oil paintings harking back to that dramatic biblical work *The Fifth Plague of Egypt*, painted for William Beckford six years earlier. These were black pieces, drawn from the most gothic part of Turner's soul, their catastrophic themes selected to display his ultimate virtuosity in his ability to invoke shock and awe.

The Deluge was a darkly dramatic response to the failings that he had noted in Nicolas Poussin's version of the same subject in the Louvre. Three years earlier he had criticized Poussin's *Deluge* for its poor drowning souls, who seemed 'unconcerned' in a flood devoid of 'current or effluvium'. And he had slated that artist for a waterfall that rather than 'tearing and desolating' fell far too 'placidly'.

There was plenty of current, effluvium, tearing and desolation in Turner's piece. His figures are shown drenched and limp, their clothes torn from them, as they attempt to find something to cling on to amid huge swamping waves. Above them, an unrelenting sky delivers sheets of rain, hammering down in great diagonal slashes from the thunderclouds above. The figures in his *Destruction of Sodom* are similarly distraught amid a storm of lightning, fire and brimstone.

Both paintings are compositionally chaotic. Each presents strong clashing diagonals. In the *Deluge* a hovering tsunami slices the canvas one way, while windswept trees bend in an opposing direction. Meanwhile the residents of Sodom cling to a slope that contrasts with the outline of the ruined buildings behind. As if to confuse the viewer, Turner immerses the action in gloom, forcing those looking at it to strain to see, as if the soot from the brimstone and fog from the storm has clouded the viewer's vision.

Another major oil that he was preparing was *The Shipwreck*. It was in many ways a follow-up painting to his very first *Fishermen at Sea*, and the *Calais* sea paintings he had shown with mixed results in 1803. But Turner increased the drama in his latest piece to an unprecedented degree. His sea in *The Shipwreck* is more white and furious than before; the angry spume in which the little boats are hopelessly tossed reaches right to the edge of the canvas, as if about to break beyond the frame and drench the onlooker. And the poor sailors in *The Shipwreck* do not even have moonlight to aid them; the sky here is unrelentingly black, they are dwarfed amid the dark and engulfing forces of nature. In fact, the source of illumination of their perilous situation is not specified by Turner. In this respect, the painting defies naturalism. We see the desperate, flailing sailors as if by magic. They are imaginative projections, yet on a sea conjured from Turner's acute observation of waves and drawn from years of relentless sketching. If *Fishermen at Sea* had indicated hope for the men brave enough to venture out into open water, in 1805 the waves that Turner summoned were beyond the navigational skills of the greatest sailor of the day.

It is tempting to see the biblical paintings as specifically targeting Beckford's purse, which was still remaining tightly shut. The oblique reference to Poussin in the biblical works may have also been made with the hope that the extremely wealthy Sir Watkin Williams-Wynn, who owned Poussin's *Landscape with a Snake*, might finally venture to buy an oil from Turner. Having worked to acquire him a ticket to the RA dinner the previous year, he remained in Turner's sights.

But if Turner was not sure that April whether Beckford or Williams-Wynn could be brought to the table, he had at least already secured the sale of *The Shipwreck*, to a friend of Williams-Wynn's, Sir John Leicester.

Sir John was part of the group of northern collectors who were becoming increasingly admiring of Turner's work. A good friend of Walter Fawkes and the godson of Fawkes's close friend Thomas Lister Parker, he was also on intimate terms with that other Turner patron, Sir Richard Colt Hoare. This group of patrons, inspired by their mutual enthusiasm for British art, would over time become a formidable, if informal, collective determined to support a new 'British school' of artists and establish an alternative model for collections, which were traditionally founded on the works of the Old Masters and continental artists.

Sir John Leicester had bought his first Turner in 1792, a watercolour of a storm,[1] but in the spring of 1805, encouraged not only by Turner's now acknowledged celebrity but also by the shared enthusiasm for the artist among his circle, he was in the market for a bigger work. It was not his first attempt to secure a major oil by Turner. Sir John had already gone head to head in a bidding battle for Turner's *Festival Upon the Opening of the Vintage of Mâcon* a couple of years earlier. He had chanced an offer of 250 guineas, which Turner rightly assessed was a little low. A year later he had increased his offer to 300 guineas – a price that his guardian and adviser in matters of art, Lister Parker, had put out for a Richard Wilson at the time. Turner had, however, held out for 400 guineas. This would have been a breakthrough price for him had he achieved it. But he didn't. Sir John walked away at 300 and in the end, sensing this was where the market lay, Turner sold the *Mâcon* to Lord Yarborough for that amount.

The Shipwreck would catch Sir John's eye, and 315 guineas was a price both sides could agree. The purchase was part of a truly ambitious scheme: Sir John wanted to build a gallery to contemporary British art at his Mayfair residence, 24 Hill Street. It would be the only gallery of its kind in London, and it would be open to the public one day a week. The other great private galleries in town in the hands of London's wealthy and aristocratic were founded on Old Master collections, even if, as in the case of the Duke of Bridgewater, they encompassed some contemporary work.

Between 1805 and 1818 ten major Turner works would pass through Sir John's hands, culminating in his final purchase of *Sun Rising Through Vapour* in 1818. This last Turner had first shown at the R A in 1807, and its sale over a decade later is testimony to the painter's stubbornness in waiting to secure what he considered the right price for a work, rather than sell it sooner for less. Leicester would spend over £2,000 on Turner's work and in doing so would endorse Turner as the central figure of contemporary British art and the heart of a new home-grown school.

However, there was another major initiative under way in London that April of 1805 that proposed a different future for British art. Sir George Beaumont was making good progress with his plans for the British Institution for Promoting the Fine Arts in the United Kingdom. Beaumont and a handful of other traditional collectors, including John Julius Angerstein and William Seguier, intended it as a society for patrons rather than artists per se, with a view to holding alternating exhibitions of Old Masters and British artists, reinforcing the pre-eminence of the former and hoping to guide the work of the latter.

The institution would be formally founded in June 1805 in the very place Turner and Munn were now fast approaching, the Thatched House Tavern, and would shortly take over the premises of Boydell's now defunct Shakespeare Gallery in Pall Mall.

But on that April evening, the business to which Munn and Turner were attending was far removed from art. In fact, they were both about to sign up to a business venture which, while promising to line their own pockets, would deliver cruelty and suffering to their fellow man.

As they passed Alexander Rowland's hairdressing shop, which flanked the entrance to the Thatched House at street level, Turner may well have felt a twinge of regret. Rowland had succeeded where his own father had failed. He had managed to persevere in an industry under pressure, not least by his ingenuity in developing a macassar hair oil that had become fashionable among the remaining royal families of Europe.

The meeting Turner was about to attend in the rooms over Rowland's shop would at least see him make an investment that might one day offer security against his own precarious profession. He was investing in Stephen Drew's Jamaican tontine, the prospectus of which was about to be published.

Stephen Drew was a Jamaican-based barrister who had purchased the Dry Sugar Work estate in Jamaica from William Beckford in 1802. In 1805 he was raising money to re-invest in the business via a tontine. This was an eighteenth-century fundraising formula that saw investors take a life annuity from the business that increased as their co-investors died. The younger the investor, the greater the chance that his or her income from the venture would increase as their fellow shareholders met their maker. Turner, at thirty-one, was a fairly young investor, third out of four types of shareholder graded by age, but not as young as the most celebrated investor, H.R.H. Princess Charlotte, the nine-year-old daughter of the Prince and Princess of Wales.

Let us be quite clear about the nature of the investment that Munn and Turner were about to lend their signatures to. Despite its name, the Dry Sugar Work near Spanish Town in Jamaica was in fact a cattle farm that depended on slavery for its labour. Drew had secured a mortgage to acquire the business from Beckford and he now sought £20,000 to pay off the mortgage and re-invest in slaves and hardware to make the business profitable. He was selling 200 shares at £100 per share. Investors were told they might expect a 15 per cent return, that is £15 a year for each £100 they invested. This was based on the forecast that the works could be turning a profit of £10,000 a year after investment.

The mention of the use of 'negroes' as a slave workforce is more than clear in the published documentation, and the discussion of the fundamental assets on which the business and its profits depended would have formed part of the meeting at the Thatched House. And yet Turner went on, signed his name to the tontine, and handed over £100 for one share that evening. His name was duly published in the prospectus.[2]

Turner's investment in slavery was made at a time when the abolition movement was very well under way and the arguments for the cruelty and immorality of the slave trade well rehearsed. George Morland, a painter with whom Turner was very familiar, had been the first artist to embrace the abolitionists' cause in 1788. Prints of his *Slave Trade*, depicting a black slave being torn from his family, had proved a particularly popular image and were mass-produced, in the workshop of John Raphael Smith, at just about the time that Turner was there.

And even if the thirteen-year-old Turner had somehow managed to miss this popular and much reproduced work of art, the fully grown member of the Academy, who graced London's intellectual establishments and dined with the greatest men of his day, could not have argued ignorance.

In short there is no excuse for this investment. Money was the prime motive behind his interest in the tontine. As artists all around him faced debt and destitution, it was an ongoing concern of Turner to protect his future financial wellbeing. What is more, it is highly likely that he was greatly encouraged to take up the tontine opportunity by one of his patrons. Keen perhaps to begin to extend further his sense of himself as a man of status, Turner may have wanted to make a bolder investment than those he was placing with the Bank of England.

Many have suggested that William Beckford might have proposed the venture to Turner, as the Sugar Work's former proprietor. But Beckford's sale of the works had been prompted by financial mismanagement. Beckford had been cheated by his advisers and consequently forced to sell. This unhappy background to the sale makes it unlikely that he would have encouraged an associate to get involved in the project.

What is more, there was a definite cooling off in the relationship between Beckford and Turner at around this time. In just two years Beckford would sell half the watercolours of Fonthill that he had commissioned from Turner and the major oil of the *Fifth Plague of Egypt*. Beckford's reluctance to follow through Turner's Swiss tour with a commission was not purely financial. He was falling out of love with Turner's work and probably with Turner himself. However, John Julius Angerstein, another of Turner's clients, had an initial interest in the tontine and was asked at one stage to be a trustee of the project, a role he in the end declined. Angerstein may well have suggested the scheme to Turner.

As to the implication of Turner's investment in a business that many of his contemporaries saw as morally bankrupt, it is worth remembering that there were still plenty who were vehemently against abolition per se on economic grounds, though aware of the need to improve slave welfare. Some attempted to find positive aspects to Britain's history of colonial enslavement. Drew would go on to write about the advantages the introduction of Christian values had brought to Jamaica's 'negro' population.[3]

The wealth of the British empire was, crucially, largely dependent upon the Atlantic trade and many could not balance how to maintain economic superiority while doing away with free labour. This attitude chimed with a wider moral paradox that prevailed in the eighteenth century, that saw a paramount belief in the beneficial economic outcomes of free enterprise – from dandy fashion and indulgent excess at one end of the scale, through the tolerance of prostitution, to the maintenance of slavery at the other – in spite of ethical implications.

It is also worth noting that at this stage in his life, Turner seemed unable to see his own experience and career in terms of a wider global picture. He was a deeply self-centred man. Art was the sole motivation in his life. And his contribution to it was dominated by his intense personal experience of the world immediately around him, by his own imaginative response to it. Though his art often resonated and reflected the politics of his day, Turner himself did not actively engage them – at least no politics beyond those of the Academy and the art world. It is notable, for example, that at this very moment a great many other members of the artistic community, painters as well as patrons, were busy training against a feared Napoleonic invasion as part of local militia. But though many artists he was close to, such as Farington, and clients such as Samuel Dobrée, participated in these local military organizations, Turner's name is not included in their roll calls. Turner had scarcely enough time for a family, let alone world affairs. He was never going to fight for king and country and he was never going to march against slavery. He was too busy satisfying his own constant compulsion to keep pencil on paper, and brush on canvas.

Ironically, the tontine proved a disaster for those participating in it. Drew, who planned to travel to Jamaica to begin his overhaul of the works by May or June 1805, did not get there till the end of the year. Within a year proceedings were launched against him as it became clear that, in contradiction to his optimistic forecasts, the scheme could never be profitable. By 1808 the business was in the hands of the receiver.

If 1805 began bleakly with dark canvases of horror and destruction, and investments in pain and misery, these early months were a prelude to a period of happiness and brightness in Turner's life that saw his work become coloured by pastoral landscapes and nostalgic classicism, work that coincided with a new home, on the banks of the Thames.

The stressful politics at the RA, and the overcrowding at Norton Street, must have contributed to Turner's decision to move his family out of town. Perhaps like one of his contemporaries he also found that if he moved out of London he would not be 'liable to have his time invaded by Loungers who in London were accustomed to call upon him to look over his portfolio'.[4]

He realized that with a busy gallery, he needed to seek solace in the countryside on a more regular basis. Escapes to seashores and woods, to Margate and the Sussex coast, had coloured Turner's earlier life and are a reminder that for all his bravura and bluster, there was a constant vulnerability at the heart of his character. He suffered moments of nervous exhaustion throughout his life, for which his personal therapy seems to have been rural solitude. But all these places were some distance from London. He sought a country retreat far closer to town. And he began to think about building himself one.

Country retreats were becoming particularly fashionable among Britain's growing urban population. Apart from Joseph Shepherd Munden's modest 'gentleman's cottage', there were more celebrated examples of men who had sought to get away from it all and had built idyllic homes for rest and repair. Famous at this time were the villas built by Alexander Pope at Twickenham, and that built by William Chambers for Sir Joshua Reynolds at Richmond Hill.

Britain's architects were engaged in a dialogue about the country villa, regularly publishing design templates, and discussing the styles appropriate for rural residences. Just a couple of years earlier the architect James Malton, son of Turner's 'master' Thomas Malton, had published a series of views of rural villas and had followed up this exercise more recently with an essay on *Rural Cottage Architecture* in 1804. Joseph Gandy had equally just released *Designs for Cottages, Cottage Farms, and other Rural Buildings, including Entrance Gates and Lodges*, and the architect William Atkinson had released *Picturesque Views* of the same. In fact the portrayal and promotion of the idea of rural villas for Britain's growing urban population had been regularly rehearsed since the early 1790s when John Soane had presented his ideas on rural retreats in *Sketches in Architecture*.

But though building his own villa was a longer-term ambition, Turner wanted something more immediately available. He thought back to his childhood haunts around Brentford, and began a search for somewhere where he and his family could live away from the bustle of central London, but still within its grasp. It may well have been thanks to the Brentford Hardwicks that he eventually managed to rent Syon Ferry Lodge, on the river at Isleworth. This was an idyllic and large property on the edge of the Syon House estate, owned by Hardwick's client the Duke of Northumberland. The house came with the use of a pavilion where Turner could paint.

The shores of the Thames provided a new source of inspiration for Turner. The Continent that he had sampled all too briefly in 1802 had once again disappeared as Britain and France again engaged in bitter war, after the peace-minded Henry Addington had been replaced again with the fiery William Pitt.

And so Turner had no choice but to revisit those places across Britain he had so assiduously sketched over the last two decades and reconceive his approach to them. The Thames seemed a good place to start. And in returning to it, Turner reimagined it in Arcadian terms.

Syon Ferry Lodge was a house with broad shoulders. Two storeys, double-fronted, with three or four reception rooms and three or four bedrooms, it was large enough to accommodate Turner, his father, Sarah Danby and his baby daughter Evelina. What is more, it had its own little quay and ample grounds. The joy Turner found in this home is reflected in a private watercolour sketch he made in one of his sketchbooks at the time. The house is depicted at sunset, homely against a warm sky. The smoke from the chimney welcomes home Turner, who is sketching from the river, on a boat. A figure is standing on the little quayside, waving. It's Sarah Danby perhaps, wearing a blue skirt with a white apron.

Crucially the house at Syon brought Turner back into close contact with his old friend Henry Scott Trimmer, who lived just a half mile away at Heston, where he was the rector. Henry was a keen fisherman like Turner, an enthusiastic amateur artist, and a classicist. The two rekindled their childhood friendship. Turner borrowed Trimmer's books, and in return for sketching lessons the latter gave Turner some instruction in Greek and Latin. It was with some pride that Turner would display the extent of his erudition in a letter to Lord Elgin in August 1806. Having been invited to see the now famous marbles that Elgin had brought back from Athens, Turner was able to cite Horace when he wrote to congratulate the Lord:

> no one can think of them without feeling the same, your Lordship's collection is perhaps the last that will be made of the most brilliant period of human nature –
> Graiis ingenium. Graiis dedit ore rotundo
> Musa Loqui –[5]

Turner bought a little boat from which he and Henry could fish. It would be a sport for which he never lost his passion. Lord Leicester would go on to joke that Turner spent more time fishing than sketching, and it would become a defining pursuit of his whenever he visited the grand homes of his patrons, inevitably equipped with well-stocked lakes. Images of fish are dotted through his sketchbooks and papers. Turner's relish in their glistening beauty and exquisite colouring is recorded in loving depictions: a trout with its spots, a perch with its orange fins, tench with their muddy brown scales, and silver-striped mackerel.

But Turner's investment in a boat was not just to pursue his passion for angling. It also served as a mobile studio. He began painting from it, dropping anchor mid-stream in the Thames and taking in wide river vistas. He executed a series of oil sketches on the Thames on small panels of mahogany, *en plein air*, a practice that would become more widely associated with his contemporary John Constable. The panels offered a slightly different format from his usual work. At

29 inches long by 14 inches wide they presented a framing of the landscape remarkably close to today's cinematic ratio of 21:9. This wide, panoramic aspect, coupled with the naturalism and immediacy with which they are executed, make these sketches feel particularly modern to a twenty-first-century viewer. And these fresh, happy depictions of an undisturbed rural river informed a number of idyllic views over the next few years.

While Turner's works on wood drew on techniques more associated with preparatory sketches, those on canvas, which sought a misty, indistinct approach to the subject matter, seemed 'unfinished' to many of his contemporaries. The question of finish was further complicated by the fact that Turner also began to show works in his gallery that his contemporaries generally accepted *were* unfinished, and were apparently displayed as a work in progress.

For some this was all proving far too experimental. Turner's generalizations were, according to Benjamin West, who visited Turner's gallery in 1807, 'crude blotches'. But the buying public were apparently less critical. His work was selling well from his new gallery, and even the works that Turner had sketched *en plein air* on to wood found homes with a clientele not beholden to those patrons and Academicians who attempted to guide national taste. A view of Newark Abbey on wood, made with broad generalized strokes, the cows lolling in its shade suggested by mere touches of paint, and the foreground foliage suggested by lines made with Turner's thumbnail, made its way into the hands of the Revd Thomas Lancaster, the curate of Merton in Surrey.

The fact that this very Revd Lancaster was a good friend of Lord Nelson reminds us that despite Turner's attempts to retreat into rural idyll, the wider world was still gripped in bitter war. Nelson was an avid supporter of a school 'for Young gentlemen' in Wimbledon that Lancaster had established in the 1790s. The Admiral even visited the school with his mistress, Emma Hamilton, in September 1805, at which point the school was renamed Nelson House School in his honour. During that visit Nelson agreed to take Lancaster's fourteen-year-old son as a first class volunteer on his ship, the *Victory*, and consequently a month later the boy served at arguably the most famous sea battle of all time, the Battle of Trafalgar.

It was at this battle in October 1805 that Horatio Nelson achieved his defining victory over the French fleet. Twenty-two enemy ships were destroyed and not a single British ship lost. A newly self-appointed Emperor Napoleon had launched a plan for a full-scale invasion of Britain in 1804. But with Nelson's triumph this threat was dismissed. The price Nelson paid for reaffirming British naval primacy was, of course, his own life.

As the *Victory* limped back in triumph, Nelson's body embalmed in a barrel of brandy on board, the British public went wild. For the last year the nation had been in a state of red alert, with home guards ready to engage with the French on English soil. Now the sense of relief and celebration was immense. Everyone wanted to see Nelson's ship, and anyone who had the influence and contacts wanted to secure access to a tour of it. People flocked to Sheerness and Chatham, where the ship was anchored.

For an artist this was a major commercial opportunity. Everyone knew how important it was to turn around an image of the *Victory*, and Nelson's demise, as fast as possible. The news of Nelson's death had reached the British people by 7 November. Within a fortnight many in the artistic community had already determined their response. Benjamin West had entered into a business partnership with the engraver James Heath to make a painting of the death of Nelson that Heath could popularize in print. Meanwhile the sculptor John Flaxman was awarded the commission for a monument to the fallen hero in St Paul's Cathedral. Josiah Boydell, John Boydell's nephew, announced a prize of £500 for the best oil study on the subject of Nelson's death, with a deadline for entries by March. De Loutherbourg of course had a response, as did the other sea painters like Nicholas Pocock and Thomas Buttersworth. Even John Constable threw his hat into the ring on the subject.

Despite his new-found lyricism, Turner was not going to miss this opportunity. At the end of December 1805 he stood on the deck of the *Victory* while she was moored in the Medway. Naturally he had brought his sketchbooks with him. One small book dutifully records views of the ship, from the dock. Details of the deck were duly sketched, as was the uniform worn by the crew. And then Turner, like a reporter, jotted down first-hand accounts taken from those who had been at Trafalgar. In his sketchbook is a hurried plan of the battle, with a note that this account came from the boatswain, William Willmet. *'After the Temeraire passed some other ship with | a white lion Head raked the Vic.'*[6]

Elsewhere he notes members of the crew, their height and demeanour.

Lt. Williams. middle s. small dark Eye. Small rather pointed nose 5 8 | Mr Atkinson. Square. Large. Light hair, grey Eye. 5 11 | Mr. Robins. Midshipman. young Dark Eyes. rather small. good teeth 5 9 | Mr. Adair broad. rather tall and dark. 5 10 |[7]

In the new year of 1806 Turner began to work on his depiction of the Battle of Trafalgar. The sense of urgency was not lost on him, and by June he had his painting on show at his gallery: *The Battle of Trafalgar, as Seen from the Mizen Starboard Shrouds of the Victory.* The first-hand research he had undertaken was presented alongside the painting, with a key indicating who was depicted, and a written account of the battle drawn from the testimonies he had taken.

But the old-guard members of the Academy who came to view the work were once again unimpressed. Farington saw nothing but a 'crude, unfinished performance, the figures miserably bad. – His pictures in general merited similar remarks, when the prices he puts upon them are considered because much more ought to be shown to justify such demand.'[8] The correlation between price and detail or finish that Farington imposes is fascinating, as is his inability to stand back from the work and take it in in its entirety.

If Farington had been able to stand back he would have seen what the younger landscape engraver John Landseer saw – a picture that broke entirely new ground: 'It was the practice of Homer and the great epic poets in their pictures, to detail the exploits or sufferings of their heroes, and to generalize or suggest the rest of the battle . . . and Mr Turner . . . has detailed the death of his hero, while he has suggested the whole of a great naval victory, which we believe has never before been successfully accomplished . . . in a single picture.'[9]

Turner had taken the heroic history painting (the kind of closely focused arrangement of the dying Nelson amid his crew that West delivered) and the traditional sea battle painting, and fused them. The composition of his work is split. A mass of sails, and smoke of ships in mid-engagement, occupy two-thirds of the canvas, while the death of Nelson plays out in the foreground. Turner has placed himself on the mizzen mast – slightly elevated and back from the action. Given the masts of the *Victory* were still in place when he visited the ship, this view suggests he actually climbed the mast rather than imagined this aerial viewpoint. However he achieved this elevated point of view, it places him both in the midst of the events, yet with a perspective upon them. The lofty aspect allows him to perceive the extent to which the vast ships and their clashing sails dwarf the men caught in the chaos of war. He is in fact applying the kind of sublime tactics he used in the Alps, revealing a flimsy mankind, powerless in the vastness of the surroundings.

The price Turner demanded for this brilliantly innovative painting was yet again £400 and perhaps this, combined with the mixed response to it, is why it failed to sell. He continued to work on it for a couple more years, addressing somewhat the criticism about the lack of detail dedicated to the figures, and re-exhibited it at the British Institution in 1808.

Interestingly, despite the insults some of the founder members lobbed at him, Turner worked hard to be embraced by the newly formed British Institution. He could not have remained unaware of the swelling criticism of his work coming from the Beaumont camp. Yet with that characteristic contrariness that defines his life, Turner, on the one hand the bold, modern and determined author of *The Shipwreck* and *The Battle of Trafalgar, as Seen from the Mizen Starboard Shrouds of the Victory*, nevertheless doggedly continued to court the more traditional clients. It is crucial to appreciate that he saw his ability to produce a range of work, and different imaginative responses to landscape, as a defining part of his genius and skill.

And so he produced a classical piece, resonant again of Poussin, to show at the Institution's 1806 show, *The Goddess of Discord Choosing the Apple of Contention in the Garden of the Hesperides*. Alongside it he showed the *Narcissus and Echo* that he had exhibited at the RA but which remained unsold.

The *Discord* is a virtuoso painting in many ways. The subject matter alone suggests a man showing his detailed knowledge of the classics, referring to a moment when the goddess Discord takes a gold apple in an act that will ultimately lead to the Trojan War. But the other virtuoso elements are the inclusion of fantastic rock forms in the distance, surmounted by a dragon, and swirling clouds. It was a painting whose complex references, coupled with an almost fantasy landscape, looked forward to the bizarre mythological paintings of Turner's dotage and suggest the beginnings of an entirely new direction in his art. His finish, which gives an indistinct soft focus effect to the work, adds to the dreamlike quality.

It was well received, though of course Sir George Beaumont was critical. He grudgingly conceded that Turner had good ideas, but saw the soft focus and generalized finish as evidence of a loss of 'power of execution'.[10] But others were genuinely admiring. The younger painter William Havell considered Turner now 'superior to Claude, Poussin, or any other'. Both Thomas Daniell and Farington noted how the deep dark green, coupled with the misty effect, made the work look like tapestry – comments that in the hands of the former were probably a compliment, and in the latter, a criticism.

The *Discord* did not sell. Again it was the £400 price tag attached to it that seemed too much. But if Turner was digging in his heels with regard to his oil paintings, he nevertheless had other commercial ventures at this time that reveal his relentless experimentation and entrepreneurial spirit, as well as his ability to maintain a healthy cashflow.

In 1805 he began a collaboration with the engraver Charles Turner,[11] who had proposed publishing commercial mezzotint prints of *The Shipwreck*. This would be the first of Turner's oils to be reproduced for wider public consumption and would raise his profile yet further.

The two Turners had been at the Academy Schools together and J. M. W. would have seen his namesake become one of the leading mezzotint specialists. This was a technique at that stage associated with portraiture rather than landscape, and it was Charles Turner's mezzotint portraits of both Napoleon and Nelson that had proved very commercially successful. Now Charles Turner had the idea of applying this drypoint technique – which applied tiny dots to a surface to create tonal differences – to *The Shipwreck*.

J. M. W. Turner made it a condition of the deal that, while Charles Turner was to be the publisher of the general project, he intended to supervise and publish coloured versions of the engravings himself. A deal was struck that saw Charles Turner pay Turner 25 guineas for the right to reproduce the painting, while Turner would buy back work at '£1.6 shilling or trade price for all I want to colour' and would undertake not to 'part with any coloured print until 4 months after the publishing of the proofs'.[12]

The painting was retrieved from Sir John Leicester and sent to Charles Turner, who lived in Warren Street, and thus the project was begun. Here he sat in his studio listening to the cries of his two young daughters, who had been born just a year apart, in 1805 and 1806. Every time J. M. W. Turner visited his namesake he must have been grateful for his own domestic arrangements, where the combination of a gallery and rooms in Harley Street and the summer house at Syon Ferry Lodge allowed him to work without interruption.

In January 1807 Charles Turner published the image to much acclaim. The pair had achieved 130 subscriptions at the date of publication, and though the list had the names of many long-time and loyal Turner clients, the collaboration also brought some of Charles Turner's clients to the table. Notable among these was Daniel Lambert, the 50-stone fat man of Leicester, who in 1806 had appeared in London in his specially built, oversized coach.

Taking a house in Piccadilly, a near-destitute Lambert had managed to make a fortune in a moment of typical Georgian enterprise, charging curious Londoners a shilling to come and stare at his girth. And his fame had been secured further by the etching of his portrait, which Charles Turner produced on his arrival in London, the quality of which would not have been lost on Lambert. Leicester's big man had in fact trained as an engraver in his boyhood, and his name among the list of subscribers to *The Shipwreck* is poignant testimony not only to his new-found wealth, but also to an aspiration to reveal his own personal taste and knowledge of art.

The Turners' next project followed quickly. Typical of J. M. W.

Turner, his initial foray into a specific field was followed by an enterprise of unparalleled ambition. This was bound to add further fuel to the fire of Sir George Beaumont's criticism, but also, for the growing number of loyal collectors, offer the prospect of forthcoming delights.

In the autumn of 1806 Turner decided that he would publish, astonishingly, 100 engravings of his landscape subjects. This truly monumental undertaking would be under the title of a *Liber Studiorum*. It would be a venture that would unfurl across twenty parts, with five plates issued in each part. And in order to reveal the full range of his work and his varied approach to landscape, he intended to classify the work under different themes: Historical, Mountainous, Marine, Pastoral and Architectural. These classifications were indicated with the relevant letter, H, M, P, and so on, on the print. This time J. M. W. Turner would be the publisher himself.

The audacity of the undertaking was characteristic of a man who now took it in his stride that he was the greatest landscape artist alive. Even the title acknowledged the parallels that Turner was making between himself and the master artists of the past. Claude Lorrain had embarked on a venture known as his *Liber Veritatis*, in which the seventeenth-century painter had sought to make a catalogue of his work by making tinted drawings of his completed paintings.

At a time when Turner could not find new landscape subjects – such as he had on his tour to Switzerland – this was a brilliant way of continuing to exploit his oeuvre and well-stocked sketchbooks, reworking existing exhibited images in a new form, and working up unseen sketches, for sale.

The idea of the *Liber* arose during one of his regular trips to the Wells household, which was now well and truly installed in Kent. In 1801 William Wells, his wife Mary, and his seven children had moved into Ashgrove Cottage at Knockholt in Kent. Turner's sketches of the cottage reveal the basic conditions that defined rural cottages at that time: a dirt floor and a simple range. And it was perhaps the very unpretentious aspect of life with the Wells that appealed to a Turner who sought little in terms of domestic comfort.

According to his beloved friend Clara, it was here that her father William pressed their guest to embark on the project. 'For your own credit's sake Turner you ought to give a work to the public which will do you justice,' Clara remembered her father railing, 'if after your death any work injurious to your fame should be executed, it could then be compared with the one you yourself gave to the public.'[13]

Recounting the events much later on, it is interesting to hear Clara express the project in terms of democracy. It would offer the public a chance to own works by the great Turner.

Clara claimed that her father's pestering finally crystallized Turner's resolve. 'At last, after he had been well goaded, one morning, half in a pet [Turner] said, "Zounds, Gaffer, there will be no peace with you till I begin, (he was then staying with us at Knockholt) – well, give me a sheet of paper there, rule the size for me, tell me what subject I shall take" – my father arranged the subjects, Pastoral, Architectural, &c., &c., as they now stand, and before he left us the first five subjects which form the first number were completed and arranged for publication greatly to my dear Father's delight. This was in the October of 1806.'

The initial progress of the work was not entirely straightforward, and at the beginning Charles Turner was not attached to the project. Turner wanted to find a way of mirroring the effect Claude had achieved in his *Liber* where outlines were drawn in ink and then a wash was applied. At first he considered that the best way to achieve this was to use an aquatint technique, which Paul Sandby had already effectively used in the reproduction of his views. This was an etching technique that saw a resin applied to create tonal variations and mimic the effect of watercolour or wash.

Initially, therefore, Turner approached one of the leading aquatint specialists of the day, Frederick Lewis, whose suitability for the project would have been suggested by the fact that he was in the process of aquatinting an edition of Claude's work for the antiquary John Chamberlaine, the Keeper of the King's drawings.

But the correspondence between Turner and Lewis reveals an uneasy working relationship, and has contributed much to Turner's reputation for being prickly and ungenerous in his business dealings. The process agreed between the two was that Turner would

supply a watercolour and an initial etching himself, which Lewis
would then take over and aquatint. However, when Lewis pointed
out that the etching did not exactly match the watercolour that was
his guide for the tonal shading, Turner suggested that Lewis etch the
work himself.

When Lewis returned the work etched and tinted, but with a bill
adjusted from an agreed 5 guineas, for just aquatinting, to 8 guineas
for both etching and tinting, Turner grew angry. The increased price
accompanied work that Turner doubted was as of high a quality as
that being produced for the King: '. . . the proof I like very well,'
Turner wrote curtly to Lewis, 'but do not think the grain is so fine as
those you shewed me for Mr Chamberlain – the effect of the Drawing is well preserved, but as you wish to raise the Price to eight
guineas I must decline having the other Drawing engraved therefore
send it when you send the plate, when they have arrived safe, the five
guineas shall be left in Salisbury St where you'll be so good as to leave
a receipt for the same.'[14]

And so, with Lewis haughtily dismissed, Turner returned to
Charles Turner, dropping aquatint for mezzotint.

In June 1807 the first five plates of Turner's great publishing
venture were released. These set the tone for what would come. A
pastoral scene of cows drinking in a river, a rustic wooden bridge
framing them, a watermill just visible beyond and cowherds chatting
on the riverbank. The marine subject was a view of the French coast
with boats grounded on the shore at low tide, French carts wheel-
deep in the shallows, loading and unloading goods. For his historical
subject he depicted Jason, creeping up on the dragon to steal the
golden fleece, basing the design on his painting of the subject shown
at the RA in 1802. For the architectural scene he offered a view of
Basle. Finally he also produced a Claudian scene of a riverbank with
classical figures, which was given an EP – elevated or epic pastoral –
badge by Turner. Turner had set out his stall for all the world to see.
He was the master of many genres. With this business venture, he
was for once the master of his own destiny.

19. *Passage of Mount St Gothard from the Devil's Bridge*, 1804. Turner's pioneering trip to Switzerland in 1802 provided him with stand-out subject matter that none of his contemporaries could match. The imposing, sublime scenery that Turner captured marked him as being in the vanguard of the Romantic movement.

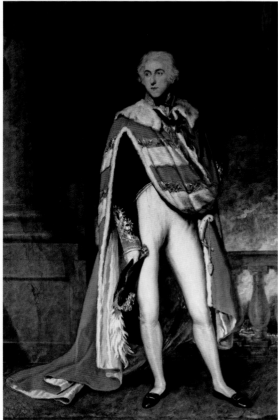

20. *Norham Castle: Morning, c.* 1797. Later in his career Turner would claim that his view of Norham Castle had been important in the growth of his popularity. He would return to this subject matter for his *Liber Studiorum*, for the *Rivers of England* series in the 1820s and again for an oil painting in 1845.

21. English School, *Sir John Fleming Leicester, Bart., in Peer's Robes,* 1789–1826. Leicester was a significant patron of both Turner and a newly emerging British School of painters. His influence and support were crucial in the birth of a modern style of landscape art.

22. *Sion Ferry House, Isleworth: Sunset*, 1805. Turner thrived near water and throughout his life sought second homes with views either of the Thames or of the sea.

23. William Havell, *Sandycombe Lodge, c.* 1814. Turner finally came into his own as a host here. Unwilling to stand on ceremony, he loved the informality of picnics in the grounds of his little villa.

24. Engraving by Charles Turner after J. M. W. Turner, *Jason* from *Liber Studiorum*, Part 1, 1807. 'For your own credit's sake Turner, you ought to give a work to the public which will do you justice.' This advice from William Frederick Wells inspired Turner's ambitious *Liber Studiorum*, in which the painter envisaged the publication of 100 examples of his work as engravings and mezzotints.

25. *Study of Fish: Two Tench, a Trout and a Perch, c.* 1822–4. Turner, an avid fisherman, habitually drew his catch. The beautifully observed detail conveys the joy he found in nature. Mrs Booth noted that he often drew fish bought in Margate before they ate them for their supper.

26. *Cassiobury Park: Reaping, c.* 1807. The vituperative comments Henry Edridge made about a series of harvest scenes Turner was working on while staying at Cassiobury upset him so much they remained unfinished.

27. *Caley Crags with Deer, c.* 1818. The landscape around Farnley Hall in Yorkshire would provide continuous inspiration for Turner until Walter Fawkes's death in 1825.

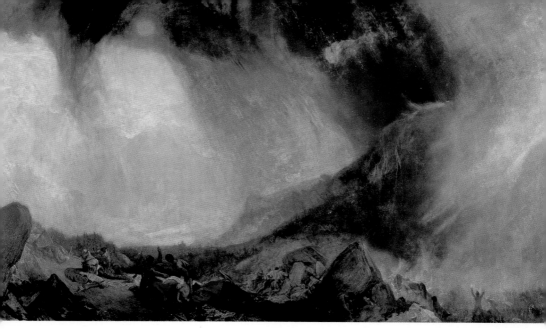

28. *Snow Storm: Hannibal and his Army Crossing the Alps*, exhibited 1812. According to Walter Fawkes's son Hawksworth, it was a storm over Otley Chevin that helped Turner conceive this image. Hannibal's army would also have been seen by Turner's contemporaries as a reference to the ongoing Napoleonic wars.

29. *Rome from the Vatican. Raffaelle, Accompanied by La Fornarina, Preparing his Pictures for the Decoration of the Loggia*, exhibited 1820. Turner may have had the French painter Ingres in his sights when he exhibited this painting.

30. *Dort or Dordrecht: The Dort Packet-Boat from Rotterdam Becalmed,* 1817–18. Walter Fawkes bought this and displayed it in the drawing room at Farnley Hall.

31. *Venice: The Rialto,* 1820–21. Turner's delight in the shimmering city is reflected in his exquisitely delicate palette of watery golds and blues, which provides an otherworldly feel.

32. *The Battle of Trafalgar, 21 October 1805*, 1822–4. Despite Turner's attempts to get royal endorsement for his work, George IV never liked this painting and it was eventually moved to the Naval Gallery at the Greenwich Hospital.

33. Cornelius Varley, *Portrait of J. M. W. Turner, c.* 1815. Varley invented a graphic telescope which projected an image on to paper which he could then trace. Some have argued that this is the most accurate image of Turner aged forty.

34. Unknown artist, *Miniature Portrait of Evelina Turner.* This portrait indicates that Evelina had inherited her father's rather long nose and pronounced top lip.

14.   The eye and the intellect

One of the most unlikely pictures that Turner ever executed was shown at the RA in 1808. It depicts the interior of a dentist's shop, in which a young man, his back to the viewer, is being given a talking to by his father. It is called *The Unpaid Bill – or The Dentist Reproving his Son's Prodigality*. It was a work executed for Richard Payne Knight.

The fifty-eight-year-old jowl-faced and weak-chinned Payne Knight was at the beating heart of London society. Known for his forceful personality and strong beliefs, he was a confirmed radical, a passionate advocate of Charles James Fox, a scholar, philosopher and collector. He was also seen by some as a dangerous libertine, who managed to corrupt Lady Oxford (who would go on to have extra-marital affairs with many men, including Lord Byron) 'by filling her head with innumerable vain conceits and teaching her to exclaim against institutions especially that of marriage'.[1] Others considered him a crucial arbiter of taste who wrote extensively on the subject. Turner would have perhaps first encountered him as the person who paid for John Robert Cozens's care when that artist was being treated by Dr Monro.

The rather odd picture that Turner delivered for Payne Knight was intended as a pendant for a Flemish Old Master in his collection, *The Alchemist's Laboratory*, which at the time was attributed to David Teniers. An extant oil sketch of *An Artist's Colourman's Workshop* discovered in Turner's studio suggests that he may have proposed a number of subjects that could complement the Flemish original. Quite why the final choice was dentistry remains a mystery, unless it was simply the spectacle of bottles and potions associated with this new kind of surgeon that appealed.[2]

That Turner was suggested at all for the commission was probably because of another depiction of everyday life, *A Country Blacksmith Disputing upon the Price of Iron*, which he had shown in 1807. The origin of this genre piece from a Turner otherwise deeply involved in Arcadia, tempests and classical landscape is worth recounting. Because in an act that is yet further evidence of Turner's intense competitiveness, he had painted it as a response to a newcomer, a young Scottish painter called David Wilkie, who had stolen the show at the RA in 1806 with his *Village Politicians*. This portrayed a group of countrymen huddled around a tavern table, deep in debate over the newspapers. While this group put the world to rights, village life continued around them: dogs licked out discarded bowls, wives peered through doorways seeking their errant husbands, and other men huddled around a fire discussing matters of less significance.

Wilkie was the surprise success of the year. His ability to convey a complex narrative around a scene of common life enchanted the public. Turner had always invested in the characters populating his scenes, but the close-focus, concentrated story-telling in the busy scenes Wilkie depicted was something quite else.

Turner, for all his talents, could not quite meet Wilkie in his own genre. When the meticulously observed dentist's shop was exhibited, it was not its human story that the critic of the *Examiner* praised, but its 'colouring and effect', which 'is not only exceptionable but inestimable. The blaze of sunshine bursting through the window received increased splendor for the profusion of bottles and other apparatus of the dentist's shop. His is admirably qualified by a secondary sunshine seen through the door of another room.'[3]

Though not a complete success, the commission of the *Dentist* brought Turner other benefits. With it he gained access to Payne Knight's private gallery full of antique coins and bronzes, as well as his freezingly cold, but uniquely fireproof library at 3 Soho Square. The library, with an iron roof and skylights, housed many treasures that held particular appeal for Turner. Here he could view Payne Knight's collection of Claude drawings, just as he was preparing his own *Liber*, and he could enlarge his knowledge of the work of John Robert Cozens. But here Turner also had access to Payne Knight's collection of classical erotica and priapic statuary, as well as his books on antique subjects, and his own controversial but deeply influential work on the subject of pantheism.

Payne Knight's firm espousal of pantheism had surfaced in a particularly controversial manner over twenty years earlier, when he had published a *Discourse on the Worship of Priapus*. This well-researched, highly academic document managed to cause a stir even in the context of the free-thinking, free-loving eighteenth century. It suggested that an ancient universal theological system, known as pantheism, was in fact the origin, or reflected in, all subsequent religions including Christianity. For Payne Knight all religions were essentially oriented around the forces of generation and life, and destruction and chaos, and were all expressions of a common theology. The most recent, tantalizing proof of this had been witnessed in Italy in a village in Isernia, where as part of a 'Christian' ceremony villagers were seen buying wax ex-voti in the form of male organs, which women kissed before dedicating to the local saint. Clearly a relic from a Roman era priapic ceremony, Payne Knight argued that the rituals celebrated 'the active or male powers of creation'.

Payne Knight pointed out that the ancients extended this symbolism of creation and destruction to the universe itself. Fire was at the heart of both creation and destruction in a universe that was in a constant cycle of conflagration and renovation, determined by a Creator. Payne Knight suggested that in the ancient world the sun had been held up as the symbol of this great destroyer and renovator.

It is easy to grasp how Payne Knight's thesis must have struck a chord with Turner. Impressed, he jotted down some of the terms he was unfamiliar with in a sketchbook, noting 'Worship of the Lingam or Phallus – Priapus'.[4]

To see the world not in terms of religion but in terms of chaos and generation made total sense to a man who had so immersed himself in the study of nature. His own fascination with the sun, and with the power of the elements, was now sanctioned within a belief system that saw ultimate truth in Nature.

It is unlikely that Payne Knight's thesis was new to Turner, however. Payne Knight was the high-profile, scholastic embodiment of views that were in fact widely held in Turner's time. Pantheism was a popular eighteenth-century subject, and those who found sympathy with it were more often than not also associated with radical or

'Jacobinical' politics. One only need look at the membership of the
London Corresponding Society, a body that sought political reform,
where the vast majority of its 150-odd petty-bourgeois members
were confirmed 'deists', rejecting conventional religion and seeing
Nature as the conduit for spiritual experience.

It is within this band of petty-bourgeois men with radical views
that Turner firmly sat. The influence of his Wilkesite uncle, his exposure to the Jacobinical and radical thoughts of the Covent Garden elite,
even Thomas Coleman's Methodist teaching, had all in their own way
put him in perfect alignment with the kinds of beliefs the Corresponding Society's 'deist' and society's libertines also espoused.

But what Payne Knight delivered Turner was a thesis that would
allow mythological figures to become potent symbols reinforcing
underlying truths. He revealed a symbolic language to which both
Turner's classical and landscape works could equally contribute.
Returning to the painting of *The Goddess of Discord Choosing the Apple
of Contention in the Garden of the Hesperides*, through the lens of Payne
Knight, one now sees this as also the Garden of Eden. The looming
chaos about to be visited upon man is suggested in the thunderous sky
and the violent jutting rocks, and the broken tree in the left of frame.

Payne Knight also had strong views on the potency of colour. In a
recently published treatise on the subject of Taste he had dealt with
the senses one by one, and in his section on sight he dwelt on the psychological and sometimes physical effect colour could have on the
beholder. Red, a colour which Turner used so deftly, he noted could
actually be painful for some viewers. Payne Knight also attempted his
own redefinition of the picturesque, which he suggested was a dialogue between art and nature, framed within memory. For Knight,
picturesque 'objects recall to the mind the imitations, which skill,
taste and genius have produced; and these again recall to the mind the
objects themselves, and show them through an improved medium –
that of the feeling and discernment of a great artist. By thus comparing
nature and art both the eye and the intellect acquire a higher relish for
the productions of each; and the ideas excited by both are invigorated
as well as refined, by being thus associated and contrasted.'[5]

If ever there was an epithet for Turner, it was 'the eye and the intellect'. And in terms of intellectual pursuit, at this period Turner was firing on all fronts. His exploration of classics and mythology fuelled his love of poetry, and his own pen erupts at this time. A 'verse book', still in the Turner family, provides his voice loud and clear. Sometimes playful and satirical, sometimes earnest, sometimes erotic, the painter's dogged determination to write verse is clear. A poem on 'The Origin of Vermillion' seems to be a response to Payne Knight's theories on colour and the picturesque. Here Turner's poem suggests that an early artist is inspired by the blush on the cheek of a sleeping girl and that

> Her modest blush first gave him taste
> And chance to Vermil first in place
> As Snails trail oer the morning dew
> He thus the lines of Beauty drew.[6]

That Payne Knight's scholarship also went hand in hand with a very liberal attitude towards sex and marriage would not have been lost on Turner either. He had now been living with Sarah Danby for several years without resorting to marrying her. The continuing presence of erotic drawings in Turner's sketchbooks (including in the same book as the preparatory sketches for *The Dentist* one depiction of a woman with her legs spread wide to reveal all, her shoes still firmly on) suggests that Turner's appetite for the opposite sex continued to extend beyond the mother of his daughter. Given the sketchbook is otherwise filled with images of the Kent coast and Margate, it is fair to suppose that on one of his sketching trips he availed himself of one of those leisure pursuits that had been associated with that seaside resort since his boyhood. Was it here that he encountered the 'Molly' to whom another of his poems is dedicated? This Molly was a woman who he urged to

> Be still my dear Molly be still
> Nor more urge that soft sigh to a will
> Which is anxious each wish to fulfill
> But I prithee Molly – be still.
> By thy lips quivering motion I ween

> To the center where love lies between
> A passport to bliss is thy will
> Yet I prithee dear Molly be still

Before imagining the ultimate act and assuring his girl that

> By the touch of thy lips sure loves band
> By the critical moment no maid can withstand
> Then a bird in the bush is worth two in the hand
> O Molly dear Molly – I will.[7]

The eighteenth-century slang for a prostitute was, of course, 'molly'. And this poem, together with his erotic sketches, suggests that Turner continued to avail himself of 'mollies' since he was so rarely at home. He was always on the move. It was not just his sketching trips around Britain that took him away from home, but even when he was in town it remains clear that, after a day at work at the easel, he would rarely head back to Isleworth. Turner was a regular dinner guest in the London homes of his patrons, as well as a man also much in demand among the intelligentsia of London. When he was not meeting clients, or potential clients, he attended exhibition openings and Academy events and dined with his colleagues as an important part of his professional life. He crops up in diary after diary at the time. Pick a name from Hazlitt to Farington to Soane, somewhere Turner will be noted as a dinner guest. After these events a bed in Harley Street would have been the obvious option.

With such a hectic self-imposed schedule, Turner relied more and more on his father to perform every necessity, from assisting with preparation of materials and canvases, to overseeing deliveries, to helping with correspondence and financial affairs, to buying and delivering clothes to him while he was away. William could also double as a butler who would serve at the few dinners Turner hosted himself.

But Turner had several concerns now. With a second home at Syon, in addition to the rooms and gallery in Harley Street, it became clear that yet more domestic help was needed. This was eventually provided by another member of the Danby clan, Hannah. She was the daughter of Charles Danby, who had lodged with Turner for a while in town, and the niece of the deceased John Danby. It is unclear exactly when she joined the Turner household, though in time she would take firm tenure as his housekeeper in town.

Despite the clear pleasure Turner took in life at Syon Ferry Lodge, his was not a lasting tenancy. In 1806 his stay there concluded and he sought new solutions for his increasingly complex lifestyle. High among his priorities was the need of a place where he might be able to live and work away from both the gallery *and* the family.

In 1807 he purchased land in Twickenham in an area called 'Sand Pit Close', with plans to build his own country villa with a fine view of the Thames. If there had ever been an intention for this house to be large enough for a family, the final design would be for an extremely modest property, similar in concept to Joseph Shepherd Munden's 'gentleman's cottage', Croft Lodge in Kentish Town. Pages of sketches in a book generally dated between 1809 and 1811 reveal a plan for a building that could never comfortably accommodate a large family. Instead Turner repeatedly worked on a scheme for a modest classical villa with three reception rooms on the ground floor and as few as two bedrooms above. Whereas Munden's Lodge had not benefited from a wine cellar, Turner did at least plan a kitchen and cellar at a lower ground level, but the name that he first bestowed on the property, 'Solus Lodge', clearly reflected the purpose of this house as a getaway where he could sojourn and work without interruption.

But Solus Lodge was a while away. So in 1806 he took two significant steps: he bought a small cottage at Lee Clump, a tiny hamlet just outside the village of Great Missenden in Buckinghamshire, and within days he also took a lease on 6 West End, Upper Mall, Hammersmith Terrace. While the small property at Lee Clump would remain in his ownership for the rest of his life, he rented the house in Hammersmith until 1811.

The property at Hammersmith was another house that fronted the river. Many of the houses on Upper Mall were prestigious, the premium properties in an area that was becoming known as an out-of-town enclave for artists, writers and theatrical folk. Turner took one, its garden down to the river, which the Victorian artist and critic Fred Stephens, who would live just a few doors away later in

the century, described as 'moderate but comfortable'. The property
had a summerhouse overlooking the river where Turner could paint.
This became his natural habitat – at the water's edge. It would be one
to which he would be drawn again and again.

With these two properties, along with the gallery and its attendant
rooms in Harley Street, Turner now had options. The cottage in Lee
Clump could serve as a bolt-hole for him or a retreat for Sarah and the
girls (though at some point he leased it to a John Fletcher). The girls
at least were reducing in number. In 1806 Sarah's daughter Louisa
was apprenticed to a schoolmistress in Wimbledon, and by 1810
another, Marcella, had found a similar position in Hammersmith,
with a Mrs Wyatt.

Turner's letters which are addressed from both town and Hammersmith suggest a pattern of life that saw him work between those
two bases over the next few years. That Turner himself was often in
the habit of picking up Sarah's pension from the Royal Society of
Musicians suggests that she and the girls were based between Hammersmith and occasionally Buckinghamshire.[8]

Hammersmith Terrace had other attractions in addition to its
riverside aspect. Philip James de Loutherbourg was a neighbour
there, and it is hardly surprising that Turner, always so keen to share
his spare time with fellow painters, quickly made his colleague aware
of his proximity. Mrs de Loutherbourg, however, disliked Turner.
His perseverance and doggedness annoyed her. She found him continually on her doorstep and shut the door in his face on at least one
occasion.

It was de Loutherbourg's books, as much as his company, that
Turner sought. His new project to build his own house fired up an
already strong interest in architecture. Turner already had a vigorous
grasp of architectural rules. Having worked in the studios of Hardwick and Malton as a young man, he had been introduced to the
language of architecture. What his masters did not teach him, his
own endless observation of buildings had given him an encyclopedic
knowledge of. Nevertheless he continued to read around the subject
as his plans for his own project evolved.

Again his pocketbook of composed verse gives a sense of the

thoughts running through his mind. He read, or re-read, an early architectural text by Henry Wotton, a seventeenth-century politician and writer who published *Elements of Architecture*, in the spirit of improving British taste. The work prompted Turner to consider the extent to which British builders had misapplied the golden rules of classical design. His own sketches for his proposed villa reveal his reverence for classical principles and order, a respect that would continue to be expressed in the classical furniture he would buy for this and his other properties later. Despite the gothic adventures of William Beckford and the emergence on the market of models for gothic cottages when it came to building, Turner was a classicist. This aspect of his taste that reflected a respect for order and tradition stood in stark contrast to the chaos of his private life. While in the latter a degree of mayhem seemed the norm, when it came to the matter of the built environment, Turner had a strong sense of propriety. This encouraged him to spell out annoyance at seeing classical rules abused in another of his poems.

> Sir William Wootton often said
> Tuscan like to the labourer is made
> And now as such is hardly used
> Misplaced moulding much abused
> At Gateway corners thus we find
> That carriage wheels its surface grind
> Or placed beneath some dirty wall
> Supports the drunken cobblers stall.[9]

In 1807 Turner was given his own unique platform to express his views about art and order. In December 1806 the Academy's teacher of Perspective, Edward Edwards, died and the Academy decided to replace his role with a new professorship, bringing the total of these most senior positions the Academy could offer its members to five. John Soane had just become the Professor of Architecture, and Henry Tresham Professor of Painting. Professor of Sculpture was not a position that would have been offered to Turner, and the Anatomy professorship was one offered to surgeons. So, aware that another opportunity was not likely to arise for considerable time, it comes as little surprise that Turner, always ambitious, always seeking to enhance his professional status, and also with a desire to give something back to the institution that had nurtured him, quickly put himself forward. A year later he was voted into the role, barely contested. Twenty-seven Academicians put their cross next to his name, and only one raised an objection.

The appointment came with significant demands. Professors were required to deliver six lectures a year. Though ostensibly for the benefit of the students, these lectures had become national events, often attended by the press and intelligentsia, and often published. They were occasions of particular importance that could enhance or crush a reputation. That Turner did not manage to deliver a single lecture for the first four years of his tenure of the role is revealing. The man had quite simply overstretched himself.

It was not for want of trying. Turner attacked the responsibility with typical determination and scholarship. He gathered at least thirty published treatises on perspective. Henry Scott Trimmer brought over the book that he and Turner had pored over as children in Brentford: Joshua Kirby's *Dr Brook Taylor's Method of Perspective Made Easy*. Turner read everything, annotating texts as he went.

But his commitments elsewhere were now so vast that Turner was just unable to gather his mind to write lectures. Despite his attempts at poetry, his skills were not literary and his struggles were profound. A year after his appointment, the Academy reminded him of his obligation to lecture with a polite note asking whether 'he proposes to lecture this season'. When Turner did finally climb up on to the podium in 1811 he confessed that 'Alacrity should have appeared earlier in my behalf, but when the continual occurancies and ardours of the profession crowd around it too often happens that they prevent the completion of greater concerns . . .'[10]

The 'continual occurancies' of his profession were indeed considerable. As if his new *Liber* project and an increasing stack of commissions were not enough, Turner was also painting speculatively for his own gallery and the annual R A and British Institution shows, as well as to order.

Typical of Turner, when he found a set of subjects that sold well, he repeated them. This was a golden commercial formula. Clients bought, and then, when he painted something similar to what they had bought once, they bought again. The group of ardent Turner fans, Sir John Leicester and the Earl of Essex, Walter Fawkes, Samuel Dobrée, Thomas Lister Parker, and others, just could not get enough.

And so after the successful sale in 1807 of Arcadian views of *Walton Bridges* to both the Earl of Essex and Sir John Leicester, with the latter also buying a depiction of *Newark Abbey on the Wey*, Turner made sure that in 1808 similar poetic views of the Thames were available again. This time he offered delicate observations of *Pope's Villa at Twickenham*, and *The Thames at Eton*. Both presented careful compositions that saw light, water, nature and man in a calm, warm, idyllic harmony.

Leicester came to the table again for *Pope's Villa*, while Lord Egremont bought the *Eton*. In this last, night is falling. Boatmen and their punt, already in dark shadows, are tying up, as the fading sun reflecting on the water keeps the river alive. A group of white swans glows against darkening foliage, and Eton College shimmers in the dusk.

Lord Egremont, of Petworth House in Sussex, would prove a massively important client over the forthcoming years. He had bought *The Thames at Windsor*, another sunset scene, just a year earlier, and a sea piece, *Ships Bearing up for Anchorage*, before that.

In 1808 Egremont went on a shopping spree at Turner's gallery. It was not just *The Thames at Eton*, but he also made sure he had examples of the other genres Turner had made his own. *The Forest of Bere* was a gentle landscape scene based on woods that Turner had passed through on a trip he made to Portsmouth the previous October. Egremont also picked two seascapes, a view of *Margate* from offshore and *The Confluence of the Thames and the Medway*.

The Medway picture was one of a series of images that Turner painted around this time of the stretch of the Thames estuary around the Nore, where the river meets the North Sea. It was a place that had strange resonance in Turner's era. It was an important anchorage for the fleet, and it was where the British public had flocked to get a first glimpse of the *Victory* on her return from Trafalgar. Here William Beatty had famously performed an autopsy on Nelson's body to remove the fatal musket ball from his shoulder before his burial. It was a treacherous piece of water thanks to a perilous sandbank, and was famously the site of a 'lightship' that had been invented specifically to warn incoming ships of the shallows. In addition to the view bought by Egremont, Turner also sold Nore paintings to his other regular clients, a view of Purfleet to the Earl of Essex and views of Sheerness to both Thomas Lister Parker and Samuel Dobrée.

Turner had explored the notion of series in the past when he had painted and displayed multiple views of the same subject – for example Fonthill Abbey. But he had never been able to display these views with any degree of control. His own gallery gave him a new freedom to display series of paintings in the form of a narrative experience for the visitor. The engraver John Landseer noted how, in 1808, Turner had arranged his views of the Thames, beginning with the Arcadian images of the upstream river and then travelling in order down to the open water of the Nore. It was yet another innovation that made his work and its presentation stand out from his contemporaries. His creativity was boundless.

The group of patrons who bought from Turner's gallery in the immediate years after its launch stand out not just for their powerful enthusiasm for Turner's work, but because without exception they also embraced him as a friend. This too was a departure for the once shy, awkward boy. The mature man had become a much requested companion in the great houses of England, a privilege that Turner would from now on enjoy and take full advantage of.

15. The overturner

July 28th. 'Papa, Mama, Sally and Sophy dined at Cassiobury. Mr Eden there and Turner. Mr Capel passed by . . .'[1]

Dr Thomas Monro's son Edward scribbled this note in his diary in 1809. The Monros had acquired a country 'cottage orné' at Bushey, close to George Capel-Coningsby, the Earl of Essex's, Hertfordshire seat, Cassiobury, two years previously. The Essex and Monro families were firm friends, and much of Bushey's appeal was its walking distance from the larger estate.

The summer routines saw Edward and his younger brother Henry walking to Bushey from Adelphi Terrace, their belongings going on ahead in a cart, in much the same way that a younger Turner and Girtin had walked to the Monros' previous country house in Fetcham. For the first two summers of their occupancy of the cottage, the Monro family worked hard making extensive improvements to the house. Edward's diaries describe a particularly active 1808 when even the hottest summer in fifty years, boasting 96 degrees in the shade, could not stop their progress: curtains were hung, grates installed, a well was cleaned and a lake cleared. The rooms were papered, Dutch tiles were laid and doors and floors fitted. Dr Monro's precious drawings were hung in the ante-room. Gravel went down in the drive, and plants and turf were delivered from Elstree to lay around the house.

While his family was in situ, Monro dashed back and forth from London in a carriage or a smaller one-horse whiskey, so called because it could whisk around another vehicle. While at Bushey he indulged his favourite pastime: drawing. This, along with haymaking and cricket, were the main diversions offered at both Bushey and nearby Cassiobury during the long summer days.

By the summer of 1809 the house was fit for guests and Dr Monro began to bring friends with him. The painters Thomas Hearne and Henry Edridge were regulars, as was Joseph Farington.

The group of men drew all sorts of things. Edward noted that Henry, keen to become an artist, sketched his father on 2 July 1809. On the 5th, Edridge made a portrait of Hearne. On the 7th, Edridge, Hearne and Farington returned to town and 'Henry mimicked Farington'. It was not long before they were back again. Typically they walked and sketched in the grounds at Cassiobury; they went to Harrow Weald and drew there, as well as at Bushey Mill and the lecture house at Watford. These were summers defined by conviviality and camaraderie.

Turner visited the Monros at Bushey too. His warm feelings towards Monro and Bushey are suggested by his ownership of four charcoal sketches by Monro from this period, today still in the possession of Turner's family. One a landscape with trees, another featuring sheep, a third a view of a cottage and another a landscape with shepherds and sheep, all suggest days out in the fields, under a summer sun.

During these excursions, conversation returned again and again to art. When Turner was not one of the party, it was the discussion of his work that brought out strong opinions.

Farington records one such incident in his diary of that summer, when, at 2 p.m. on 5 July, Monro took the party to see Cassiobury for the first time. There, alongside historic pictures, many painted 'from the reign of Henry 4th', were three landscapes by Turner. They were Essex's most recent acquisitions. The *Falls of the Rhine at Schaffhausen* (which Turner had exhibited at the RA in 1806 and Essex had bought the following year), *Walton Bridges*, acquired in 1807, and *Purfleet and the Essex Shore as seen from the Long Reach*, which had been purchased in 1808.

Farington, ever the diplomat, does not reveal his own view of the works, but records the venomous response his friend Hearne had to them. The sky in one was 'painted by a mad man', the sea piece was 'raw'. Hearne's fury could not be contained. When the party returned to Bushey later in the afternoon and sat down to dinner, Hearne continued to rail at the state of British art.

'There is now an established false taste and the public mind is so vitiated that works simple and pure would not be relished,' he argued. This state of affairs was largely down to the terrible influence of

Turner on other contemporary artists. Hearne's former pupil had lost sight of the fine talent he had once shown and instead 'has neither sublimity or dignity when he attempts those characters, nor sentiment and pastoral simplicity in his rural scenery'.[2]

Three days later Hearne was still on his high horse. Farington notes yet another heated debate about Turner during their Bushey sojourn, this time about the prices he was achieving. 'For a person a full admirer of His pictures fifty guineas,' Hearne grumpily decreed, 'but for myself I would not give fifteen.'[3]

The subject of Hearne's criticism had been spending quite a lot of time at Cassiobury over the last few hot summers, making a series of drawings of estate life, capturing the workers in sun-drenched fields. He began a couple of works in oil on wood, using the broad loose brushwork that characterized those pictures made *en plein air* around the Thames that had so riled Hearne. One was of farm workers reaping in the fields. Another was of the harvest celebration in a huge barn, from which the Cassiobury lands were visible through a great door.

Turner was using his relationship with Essex not just as an opportunity to make drawings, but to enjoy some form of extended vacation away from home. It would be a pattern that he would follow from this point on, seeking sojourns out of town with those patrons who were happy to throw their doors open to him.

This new freedom of access was a significant development. He was no longer necessarily working on the estate to commission – his status had changed. Rather, the resources of the great houses of England were now placed at his disposal, for work or for pleasure.

When, at the end of July, Hearne returned to Cassiobury to discover Turner there, the old artist could not stop himself repeating his views on Turner's work, to the artist himself. Perhaps it was *because* Hearne had tutored the boy in Adelphi Terrace that he felt he had licence to criticize his work to Turner's face. He made no secret of his opinion of Turner's new loose technique in the harvest and reaping scenes of Cassiobury. He also laid into the huge sums Turner was demanding for his work.

It was an incident that bit deeply. Years later when a young woman befriended an elderly Turner,[4] it was a confrontation he could still summon. He never sold those paintings. He never properly completed them. For Turner they had become poisoned.[5]

Hearne's outburst in 1809 is evidence of the success Sir George Beaumont was having in what was fast becoming a fanatical campaign against Turner and a group of younger artists influenced by his work. Hearne was after all a good friend of Beaumont, for whom the rules of taste and good art were fixed in a firmament of tradition, exemplified by the Old Masters. And it is true that Turner was developing techniques that went way beyond anything that these painters explored. Turner always shook off an attempt to pin down his approach to technique, as Farington had noted in his diary years earlier. Certainly where watercolour was concerned 'Turner has no settled process but drives the colours about till he has expressed the ideas in his mind.'[6]

It was exactly this open-minded approach that made Turner so revolutionary. Not constrained by a need to stick to accepted methods of painting, his constant desire to achieve new effects led him in search of difference. He learned from the scientists of his generation, for whom trial and investigation were key.

Since his return from France and Switzerland, these points of difference were becoming glaringly obvious to the old school painters such as Beaumont. The latter coined a phrase for Turner and his followers: *the white painters*.

The term referred in part to Turner's use of bright white, high tones in his seascapes, Beaumont preferring the mellower lights of the Old Masters.

But it wasn't just the flecks of white Turner and his followers used in their seascapes. Turner had also turned to using a white ground for his oil painting, rather than the traditional dark-coloured base that most painters used in imitation of the Old Masters. This was consistent with his search for luminosity in his work and it was clearly taken from watercolour practice where a white ground beneath transparent washes could achieve a sense of space and airiness that had eluded oil painters. He also thinned his oils to make them behave in a manner closer to watercolour. This transgression, or transference between genres, was typical of Turner's lateral thinking, but to Beaumont, who had a sense of the order of things, this was the disgraceful borrowing of a technique associated with a lower genre, applied to a higher one. It was as if the new democratical politics rushing through Europe were infecting the arts.

But there was more. Turner was attracted to the new brighter pigments that inventive colourmen were bringing to the market, and the application of these over his pale base meant that Turner's palette was at once more vivid and highly coloured than just about any other of his contemporary artists. And his careful use of piquant accents, of a spot of red or streak of bright blue, served only to amplify his colour schemes. This was yet another affront to Beaumont's sensibilities. For it inevitably meant Turner's work, placed in a public exhibition, killed the muted and mellow palettes of the artists that Beaumont admired. Their work simply paled next to Turner's.

Perhaps it was no wonder that the younger Wilkie was so prepared to agree with Beaumont's position, since his own painting, *Blind Fiddler*, suffered this very fate when, in 1807, the hanging committee at the RA placed Turner's *Country Blacksmith* close to it. One contemporary remembered how Wilkie's work was 'flung into eclipse by the unmitigated splendour of a neighbouring picture'.[7]

As if to add salt to Wilkie's wounds, Turner had emphasized the high colouring of his own work with finishing touches added during the so-called 'varnishing days'. This was a closed period between selection and the opening of the exhibition when Academicians could complete and varnish their work. It was noted of Turner's *Blacksmith* that it was '. . . painted into its overpowering brightness, as others more bitterly said in the varnishing time which belongs to Academicians between when the pictures are sent in, and that on which the exhibition opens'.[8]

As if the colouring and other transgressions were not enough, the final torment for Beaumont was Turner's brushwork. The latter was far from polite in this regard. In fact he was the prototype for the physical painters of the late nineteenth and twentieth centuries in his particularly corporeal approach to work, sometimes scratching away paint with his nails and stopping it out with a sponge or shirt sleeve.

Impatient, working fast, a drop of saliva on the canvas often served its purpose. James Wyatt told Farington he had seen Turner 'spit all over his picture, and, then taking out a box of brown powder, rubbed it over the picture'.[9]

He would use absorbent grounds that could soak his diluted oil into the warp and weft of the canvas, and then, rather than apply consistent fine brushwork, he might apply different types of brush effect to different areas of canvas, using different rhythms of paint for different subjects. This inconsistency was another affront to Beaumont's expectation of a uniformity of approach. This, plus his speed of execution, flouted the virtues of hidden and time-consuming labour that Beaumont undoubtedly put into his own work, and believed to be essential in good art.

'Turner . . . is perpetually aiming to be extraordinary,' Beaumont furiously declared when he saw the *Falls of the Rhine at Schaffhausen* on show at the R A's 1806 exhibition. This product of Turner's Swiss trip conveyed the drama of the waterfall with white and grey paint, scraped diagonally across the canvas with a palette knife, the solidity and mass of the water conveyed by the thickness of the paint.

But the picture could not convince Beaumont. It was another example of a Turner who 'produces works that are capricious and singular' rather 'than great'. The nation had lost a painter of once great promise. 'His former pictures were better than his present,' he concluded.[10] No wonder Beaumont's friend Hearne was so agitated when he saw this very picture again three years later, hanging on Cassiobury's walls.

That some younger artists painting in the manner of Turner were benefiting from being seen as heirs to the virtuoso must have also riled Beaumont. Notably, Turner's friend and firm supporter Augustus Wall Callcott was considered part of the 'White School' by Beaumont, and attacked in similar vein. That the most active collectors of contemporary art, Sir John Leicester, Richard Payne Knight, Viscount Lascelles of Harewood House, and even minor patrons like Thomas Lister Parker were buying Callcott's work could have only further fuelled Beaumont's resentment.

It is around this time that the accusation of insanity begins to be levelled at Turner by some members of a press that was split in its approach to the painter. The critic of the *Oracle*, James Boaden, declared that the painting of the Schaffhausen Falls was 'Madness' and that therefore by default Turner must be 'a madman'. The *Sun*'s John Taylor on the other hand would prove a supporter of Turner, writing so favourably about his Perspective Lectures when they were finally delivered in January 1811 that Turner felt moved not only to thank Taylor for his 'kind and honourable notice of my endeavours'[11] but also to write a him a poem, which begins:

> Thanks gentle Sir for what you sent
> With so much kindness praise – 'besprente'
> Upon a subject which forsoothe,
> Has nothing in it but its truth . . .

Beaumont had managed to establish the idea that Turner was a controversial painter. This would be a status he would never shake off, and it is significant that in a sale in 1807 Beckford disposed of most of the Turners he had commissioned, and also that Beaumont's other old friend and co-founder of the British Institution Richard Payne Knight did not follow up his purchase of the *Dentist's Shop* with anything else by Turner.

The accusations of madness would take hold in time, and would gather a literal interpretation that would prove the foundation for the erosion of his reputation in later life. Such vituperative and damaging criticism had its personal effects on Turner too. 'No one felt more keenly the illiberal structures of the newspapers,' Henry Syer Trimmer would remember, 'and I have seen him almost in tears, and ready to hang himself, though still only valuing their opinions at their worth.'[12]

And so as criticism and debate about his work intensified in the second decade of the nineteenth century, it is hardly surprising that Turner sought out respite on the estates of those whose passion for his work helped expunge the toxic atmosphere that could often follow him around London.

But for a Turner who had as a younger man been used to being treated as a form of staff, his new social status as guest of the great and the good was initially hard to navigate. In the summer of 1808, when Turner visited Sir John Leicester's seat at Tabley in Cheshire, while executing views of the house for his host, he behaved much like the other house guests, spending time fishing and enjoying other comforts and recreations. As part of the normal social and recreational exchanges that occurred when guests were staying, Sir John asked Turner to critique his own amateur painting and Turner duly provided some lessons. Unsurprisingly, Sir John was rather astonished to later receive a bill for tuition from Turner, which, though he duly paid it, nevertheless rankled with a man who had spent hundreds of guineas with the painter already. Interestingly, Leicester only bought one more Turner after this.

One relationship that Turner managed far better was that with Walter Fawkes. Since Turner's trip to Switzerland, Fawkes had commissioned thirty watercolours based on the tour, an exceptional quantity not lost on John Raphael Smith, who, painting Fawkes's portrait in 1809, did so showing the Yorkshire man with a Turner portfolio at his feet. In this same year Fawkes bought an oil from Turner's gallery, *Shoeburyness Fisherman Hailing a Whitstable Hoy*. It was the second oil he had bought, the first being a view of *The Victory Returning from Trafalgar* that Turner had shown at his gallery in 1806. It would not be his last.

The Fawkes' seat, Farnley Hall, in West Yorkshire, is remote, placed high on the hills of Wharfedale, looking over a deep valley on to the bleak bluff known as Otley Chevin. It took some determination to reach it in the era before the train, representing a five-mile journey west from the comfortable home of Turner's other patron Edward Lascelles at Harewood House, near Leeds, across remote countryside.

Farnley was not on the scale of Harewood. Its architecture was more unusual and homely. A Jacobean building was joined to a newly built classical wing, designed by John Carr of York, which faced outwards over the Wharfe Valley and spoke much of the Fawkes family, deeply rooted in Yorkshire history but also at the cutting edge of current cultural aspiration.

From 1808 Turner was a regular visitor to Farnley, a habit

encouraged not just by the Yorkshire landscape that he found so inspiring but also by the master of the house, who became one of Turner's closest friends. He typically arrived for the shooting season in mid-August, an indication of one of the pastimes that he made sure to enjoy during his stay.

The two men got on well. Fawkes was a man of extremes, profound feeling and not a little eccentricity. He was a compulsive collector and a passionate radical. He was a very close friend of Francis Burdett, a reformist and supporter of John Horne Tooke. Fawkes had a deep love of landscape, was a more than competent amateur landscape artist and was keen on the country pastimes of fishing and shooting. Like Turner he was also hungry for knowledge and keen to contribute with his own projects. Over the next decade, Turner became engaged in a set of very personal schemes for Fawkes that reads like a diary of their time spent together at Farnley. He had his own paint-spattered table at the Hall, and on it he created depictions of all aspects of life there.

The enthusiasm for shooting at Farnley is captured in Turner's sketchbooks and in a series of finished watercolours that he made during his August trips to the estate. He depicts shooting parties of different sizes and degrees of formality. One sketch, ultimately worked up into a watercolour for Fawkes, shows a major shoot on the moors, where Fawkes's estate staff have erected several tents and brought cart-loads of equipment with them, including a barrel of beer. For Fawkes's neighbour, Sir William Pilkington of Chevet Hall, near Wakefield, Turner made a misty view of a group on horseback, *Grouse Shooting on Beamsley Beacon*, and he depicted a solitary gunman on a wooded escarpment in *Woodstock Shooting on the Chevin*. Turner sketches members of a hunting party snoozing in the hot grass under the August sun, their dogs curled around their legs. Another watercolour shows a party returning through the back gardens of Caley Hall, part of Fawkes's estate. Fawkes stocked Caley Park with an unusual and eccentric farrago of game including red and fallow deer, and wild hogs, but also exotic animals, zebras and a species of deer from India. Leaving their wild safari behind them, the party return to a scene of British horticultural domesticity: a well-kept garden complete with a lawn roller that had just been put down, and a watering can standing in the garden path next to a basket for flower cuttings.

Turner also made a series of gouaches of the house and its grounds over the next few years. He painted a view of the Oak Staircase at Farnley, along the walls of which were mounted antlers. He drew most of the major rooms: drawing rooms and morning rooms; the library with a portfolio on the floor; the conservatory; a memorial window, the old hall; an old dairy; the West lodges guarding the entrance to the estate, and the East ones which Turner himself designed for Fawkes. And of course he made view after view across the Wharf and its valleys, the parklands and lakes.

He joined in with Fawkes's undertaking to create an Ornithological Collection of Birds, based on those shot or otherwise discovered on the estate. The feathers were mounted and accompanied by watercolours. Turner contributed more than a dozen exquisite depictions of birds that are a powerful reminder, just like his images of fish, of his deep ability as an illustrator of natural history, his eye for detail and technical prowess quite simply breathtaking. These are evidence enough that the broad, loose, atmospheric and indistinct effect he was moving towards in his painting was entirely intentional, and never for a minute indicative of a loss of ability to paint with utter precision should he have wanted.

And then there is also Fawkes's *Fairfaxiana*. Walter Fawkes had a fanatical interest in the civil war and in particular in the Cromwellian general Thomas Fairfax, a one-time MP for Yorkshire. His interest in this moment in history was closely linked to his own radical beliefs in the need for parliamentary reform. A number of relics supposed to have belonged to Fairfax and Cromwell, including the latter's watch and hat and the former's drum, had found their way to Farnley Hall. And as a means of celebrating this collection Turner and Fawkes compiled an album of illustrations, many accompanied by texts that display an almost childish glee in the subject matter, and an often playful approach to it.

In the album Turner drew a complex frontispiece featuring the various items of civil war ephemera held in Fawkes's collection. Then he designed a series of vignettes that moved through British history. One depicted the Coronation Throne and the Stone of Scone. He framed a gold coin found at Agincourt with images of armour. There is a vignette of the Reformation in which Turner depicts someone being burned at the stake. He illustrates the King Versus Parliament; The Civil War; The Protectorate of Cromwell. And at the very end of the album is a drawing of the oak cabinet in which Fawkes's precious *Fairfaxiana* was stored. Turner cut out little paper doors that opened to reveal the Fawkes treasures drawn in miniature within.

Turner had become a part of the Fawkes family, with attendant nick-names. Fawkes's second wife Maria referred to him affectionately (though possibly condescendingly) as 'little Turner', while the 'overturner' was another sobriquet applied after an incident involving Turner and a carriage on the Yorkshire estate.

Apart from his annual August visit to enjoy the shooting season, Turner would dine with the Fawkes family almost every Sunday when they were in London, along with members of Thomas Lister Parker's family who, equally, were part of the intimate circle. Walter's son Hawksworth developed a warm friendship with the painter that survived his father's death. The childish and playful side of Turner's character that often creeps into his correspondence with close friends, evidently enjoyed the company of children. Or at least other people's children.

Hawksworth, whom as a child Turner taught to draw ships, provides one very vivid description of Turner gripped with the spectacle of a storm over Otley Chevin one day in 1810. Walter's son would have been no more than thirteen when he witnessed the painter begin to make notes about what he saw on the back of a letter: 'I proposed some better drawing block but he said it did very well,' Hawksworth remembered. 'He was absorbed – he was entranced. There was the storm rolling and sweeping and shafting out its lightning over the Yorkshire hills. Presently the storm passed and he finished. "There," he said, "Hawkey, in two years you will see this again, and call it Hannibal crossing the Alps." '[13]

The precision of the date was perhaps a detail Hawksworth added to the tale with the benefit of hindsight. Indeed, in 1812 *Snow Storm:*

Hannibal and his Army Crossing the Alps was exhibited at the Royal Academy show. The reference to Hannibal would, for Turner's audience, conjure up Napoleon's more recent campaign to conquer Italy. But the dual reference was important. For it implied the cycle of victory and destruction that ran through history. Turner made sure that his storm dominated three-quarters of the canvas: a great arch of rain about to release on to men and mountains below. In the far distance an elephant, rendered minuscule by the great wide world, can just be made out in silhouette. A yellow sun glows dimly through the weather, a reminder of one constant power.

In this painting the influence of the popular pantheism of the day is again in full force. As if to make his point further, Turner wrote some lines of poetry to accompany the piece. Apart from displaying his erudition and grasp of Classics – since the lines draw on accounts of Hannibal by Polybius and Livy – they are intended to convey the pointlessness of man in the great cycle of creation and destruction that overcomes all human endeavour. Turner indicated that his poem was an excerpt from a work in progress of his own called *The Fallacies of Hope*. And in it he describes how the Carthaginian general Hannibal and his men

> look'd on the sun with hope; – low, broad, and wan;
> While the fierce archer of the downward year
> Stains Italy's blanch'd barrier with storms.

The fierce archer of the downward year is a reference to Sagittarius, and the winter storms that accompany him. But despite his destructive forces, Hannibal still looks forward to his victor's prize, 'Campania's fertile plains'.

'But the loud breeze sob'd, "Capua's joys beware",' Turner warns, for history reveals that in the warm and fertile land of Campania, Hannibal's men gave in to decadence and idleness. The Carthaginian empire died as part of the great cycle of life. As Turner hoped Napoleon's empire would too.

The story of Turner's *Hannibal Crossing the Alps,* conceived perhaps as he stood on the steps of Farnley Hall, reveals Turner's fascination for the history of Carthage and the myths associated with this ancient

empire. This interest would lead to the evolution of a series of paintings, which would be completed over the next seven years. Because
in 1815 Turner provides a prequel to his *Hannibal* in the form of
Dido Building Carthage: or the Rise of the Carthaginian Empire, and then at
the RA show of 1817 he showed the sequel to *Hannibal*, *The Decline of
the Carthaginian Empire*.

Turner paints the series of paintings depicting the story of the
rise and fall of Carthage within a wider series of paintings he would
make throughout his career alluding to Virgil's *Aeneid*. This is the
epic tale of Aeneas's flight from Troy to found Rome, and his doomed
love affair with Dido of Carthage. The Aeneas series had in fact
started with his earliest admiration of Claude, and his depiction of
Aeneas and the Sibyl, based on the drawings he had seen by Sir Richard
Colt Hoare. This wider piece of story-telling across a career was
intended to play off his audience's sense of empire at a time when the
warring French and British empires were fragile.

Despite the obvious allusion to Napoleon's own trajectory across
the Alps in the Hannibal painting, Carthage was in fact more widely
associated with the British empire in nineteenth-century popular
culture. Napoleon Bonaparte had consciously modelled his empire
on Rome and had adopted its language. He heroized Julius Caesar
and provided his army with battle standards featuring eagles modelled on the Roman legionary aquilae. In consequence the French
dubbed the British 'the new Carthaginians', a badge intended as an
insult but one worn with pride over the Channel. When Lord Nelson
died, the cartoonist James Gillray described Nelson's mistress as
Dido. But over a decade before that the publisher John Murray had
had some success with a publication that likened 'Great Britain and
Carthage' and another aligning France with Rome.[14]

The reference to popular culture aside, Turner's pursuit of the
Carthaginian story reveals a man whose sense of the vastness of time,
and the powers operating across it, was deeply felt. That a storm
above Otley might feed into the huge saga of Turner's imagination is
also indicative of a man whose sense of greater truth was constantly
triggered by the world about him.

The poem *The Fallacies of Hope,* which Turner associated with the painting, was yet another saga which he would continue across the course of his career. From this moment on, snippets of an apparently epic endeavour appear attached to various paintings, to suggest an heroic work in progress. Did this poem actually exist? Or was the *Fallacies of Hope* in fact an imaginary poem, fragments of which Turner summoned from time to time to represent his world view? Apart from his poetry book, which remains with his family today, there is another reference that suggests that this question concerned Turner's own contemporaries.

Not long after Turner's death the Royal Academy's librarian, Solomon Hart, wrote to the fanatical collector James Hughes Anderdon on the subject of poetry. Anderdon regularly scoured the sales rooms for material relating to Turner, and bought some items from Turner's long-time friend the engraver Edward Bell as well as from his later colleague Dawson Turner (no relation). Hart was writing on behalf of Turner's first biographer, the journalist Walter Thornbury. 'I know you have several matters pertaining to the late departed magician "Turner",' he wrote, 'particularly a poetic effusion which exhibits his aspirations to be as serious and famous with his pen as with his pencil.'[15]

Turner used Farnley as a stopping point on a trip further north to Cockermouth in the summer of 1809, this time on commission for Lord Egremont of Petworth, whose family owned the castle there. After his spending spree the previous year at Turner's gallery, Egremont had commissioned views of both Petworth and the northern estate. The commission marked the beginning of another very important friendship in Turner's life, though it was one that had a false start.

The third Earl of Egremont, George O'Brien Wyndham, was a hugely generous man. He did not stand on ceremony, and laid open his home, Petworth House, to artists whom he sought to patronize and encourage, clearly enjoying the Bohemian atmosphere that their presence brought to his cavernous drawing rooms. His generosity extended to his estate workers, to whom he became known as a kind, fair employer, and innovative agriculturalist. He was also a canal builder extraordinaire. And a renowned lothario who, when Turner encountered him around the turn of the century, had already sired seven children by his mistress Elizabeth Iliffe before marrying her. The marriage did not last. Elizabeth left her newly-wed when she realized that he could not remain faithful to her. In fact Egremont maintained about fifteen mistresses and had a raft of illegitimate off-spring outside those produced by the woman he married.

The appeal to Turner of this art-loving, liberal-minded libertarian seems obvious. That hunting and fishing were recreations also pro-vided alongside pretty women and erudite conversation, and a wonderful collection of Old Masters that Egremont and his forebears had amassed, meant Petworth soon became another favourite haunt.

And of course in visiting Petworth, Turner could extend his circle of contacts yet further. It was during one visit there that he may well have encountered John Fuller, Egremont's neighbour, who lived at Brightling in Sussex and was known colloquially as 'Mad Jack'. Fuller was also a patron and friend of Turner's colleague the sculptor Francis Leggatt Chantrey. All three men shared common attributes. Chantrey – who would go on to make a bust of Fuller – was known for being a vivid raconteur, and had a propensity to use overly strong language. This last, along with a down-to-earth ability to call a spade a spade, could have been equally applied to either of the others. Fuller turned down a knighthood on the basis that he had been born plain Jack Fuller and wished to die the same.

Turner was invited to make views of Fuller's estate at Rose Hill, and with this invitation he embarked on a series of pastoral scenes of the most breathtaking warmth and beauty.

One, *The Vale of Pevensey, from Rosehill Park*,[16] which Turner painted in around 1816, is achieved in a golden palette and depicts a pastoral scene in a rounded valley, with beautifully observed sheep in the foreground and shepherds or estate workers in the mid-ground, and a folly in the far right. As so often in his work, Turner adds a little smoke in the middle distance, and then in the deep distance melts the blue vale into a creamy sky. He leads the eye towards the centre of the composition with a small winding sheep path; there is the faintest hint of it – possibly a thumbnail mark – winding onwards through the vale, which continues to be dotted with sheep of diminishing size. In tone it shares, with the sun-drenched views he made of reapers and harvesters at Cassiobury, a sense of warm calm and wellbeing, and of harmony between the season, the land and those sustained by it. Set against his depictions of foaming seas and angry storms, these images of fecundity and peace offer the counterbalance to destruction and chaos.

But just as Turner overstepped the mark with Sir John Leicester, John Fuller enjoyed recounting the tale of how when Turner delivered his oil view of the park to its new owner, he charged Fuller for the carriage fare. It remains one of the contradictions in Turner's character that in one moment he could see the good business sense of sending small works gratis to patrons with large commissions, and yet in another charge them for small services rendered.

A faux pas that Turner made with Lord Egremont, however, had more drastic consequences. The relationship with George Wyndham was progressing so well that after he commissioned views of Petworth and Cockermouth, the third earl went on to purchase a further two works from Turner's gallery in 1812.[17] Yet by the end of 1814 the promising friendship had broken down. It would take a decade before the two men once again appreciated one another's company.

It was Turner's nemesis, Sir George Beaumont, who was at the root of the falling out. Beaumont was the driving force behind the British Institution, the new organization that purported to promote contemporary art alongside Old Masters. Many of Turner's fellow artists considered that the Institution was destroying contemporary art rather than supporting it. Its emphasis on the guiding importance of the taste of aristocratic connoisseurs for Old Master values, the expectation that contemporary artists should strive to paint like their forebears and to the order of patrons, and the constant assertion that they were failing in this obligation, were giving rise to much unease and anger in the artistic community.

Turner had doggedly sent work in for the BI's exhibitions, carefully picking his most 'classical' pieces. But since he had been personally singled out by Beaumont as the painter who exemplified everything the Institution was striving to eliminate, he was becoming weary of abuse. And in 1814 he began to fight back.

In this year the Institution was offering a prize for the best work of art submitted as a companion to a work of Claude or Poussin. These proposed pendants should be 'proper in point of subject and manner'. Turner was already showing a depiction of *Dido and Aeneas* at that year's RA show, Claudian in spirit and in subject matter; nevertheless it was a totally original piece of work, with Turner revisiting sketches he had made of the Thames around Richmond for his idyllic Carthaginian landscape.

To the Institution, however, he sent an almost carbon copy of a Claude in the ownership of Lord Egremont. In a picture he titled *Apullia in Search of Appullus,* Turner had quite simply taken Claude's *Jacob with Laban and his Daughters,* copied it as exactly as he could, then simply changed some figures in the foreground and the architectural detail of some buildings in the mid-distance. In spite of the not inconsiderable effort such an act of direct imitation must have taken, it was clearly proposed as a comment on the Institution's, and particularly Beaumont's, fetish with the superiority of Old Master works. Turner was effectively suggesting that if Beaumont wanted Old Master values, then why paint anything original? Why not just *copy* an Old Master?

Turner's satirical gesture was heightened by his title, subject, and proposed price. The subject matter and the title have, for starters, a comic ring. It is a pantomime version of one of the myths related in Ovid's *Metamorphoses*, in which the shepherd Appullus is turned into a tree for mocking some dancing myths. Turner has an invented wife come looking for her naughty husband. 'Sir, I have sent you one Picture subject Apullia in search of Appullus,' he wrote. And then, as if they hadn't yet got the joke, he suggests this work might be so important that he should charge more than double his standard fee for it, 'the price 850 guineas . . .'[18]

Turner's gesture initially backfired. For a start, the press failed to get the joke, and instead accused Turner of plagiarizing the Egremont Claude. But what was far more unfortunate was that Turner failed to take into account the views of Lord Egremont, who had allowed him such freedoms with his home and art collection. Lord Egremont had links with the Institution and had been invited to judge the very competition to which the *Apullia* had been submitted.

His subsequent failure to attend to this commitment must have reflected the compromising position in which he felt he had been placed by Turner. Petworth's doors closed. For a while at least.

Turner's joke was, however, in the vanguard of a victory of sorts secured the following year.

The summer exhibition of Old Masters at the British Institution declared its intention 'to gratify the public taste, and to animate the British artist to exertion'.[19] The members of the Royal Academy, many of whom failed to share Beaumont's vision for British art, took exception to this presumption, and refused en masse their invitations to the show. It was not merely the question of taste that concerned them, but also that the promotion of works by dead artists was seen as commercially detrimental to those who were trying to make a living. Beaumont could not have been more surprised by this declaration of 'War against the British Institution'.[20]

But this was a mere prelude to the greater blow that was soon dealt: an annotated catalogue of the exhibition, published anonymously, and serialized in the radical paper the *Morning Chronicle*. To this day the author of a piece of work that laid out brick by brick the failings of the British Institution and its members, and took a hatchet to the assumed influence of patrons and their preferences, has remained unconfirmed. But many of those who had accompanied Walter Fawkes around the show, and had heard his running commentary on it, were in little doubt that he had penned the invective. Given Turner and Fawkes's tendency to work jointly on projects, along with Turner's shot over the bows in the previous year, Turner may have been the co-author.

The tone of the pamphlet was satirical and bitter. It accused the directors that: 'On the mere strength of a most mischievously superficial acquaintance with old pictures, do ninety-nine out of a hundred set themselves up as arbiters in art . . .' before going on to add that '*Their* ONLY standards are old pictures; hence if the new production fails to remind them of somewhat they have seen before, it is instantly condemned.'[21]

The pamphlet picked on Beaumont in person, posing the question 'On what principle could we pretend to explain the abuse with which the noble Director . . . pours forth on the greatest landscape painter of the present day . . .' before suggesting wickedly that it was 'jealousy and the despair'.

It is too easy to portray Beaumont as a total demon. In fact, all the evidence is that he was a charming, passionate man who was generous to his artist friends and was only acting out of strongly felt beliefs that belonged to their time. It was a genuine shock to him to discover the extent to which he was out of step with so many of the men he considered friends and colleagues. The sustained public attack in the summer of 1815 was beyond anything he had anticipated. As Farington recorded in his diary in June 1815: 'He appeared to be quite broken up in constitution. His countenance fallen; His spirits gone, He seemed to be fast declining towards dissolution.'[22]

Sir George Beaumont may have felt that he had lost a battle, but for the British Institution the war was not over yet, and others rallied round him. At the end of July 1815 the *Morning Post* conveyed news that the Institution planned to repeat its success with an exhibition of Italian Old Masters in 1816, and, in another direct challenge to the RA, the paper revealed that some patrons had agreed to allow their Dutch Old Masters to remain in Pall Mall 'to serve as a school' for Britain's artists.

What is more, the effect of Beaumont's persistent attacks had managed to irreparably damage Turner's reputation. For years he had stubbornly dug in his heels on the price of his work. But by 1815 the market for his oil paintings had collapsed. When in February 1815 Sir Richard Colt Hoare took delivery of an oil by Turner, *Lake Avernus: Aeneas and the Cumaean Sibyl,* he did so having paid just 150 guineas, a price only slightly higher than that fetched by Turner's largest watercolours.[23] The price for Turner's work in oils never properly recovered, something that pained him for the rest of his life.

16.   Summertimes

Napoleon Bonaparte lost the Battle of Waterloo on 18 June 1815, and in doing so his seat at the pinnacle of the French Empire. London erupted with joy and the artistic community was thrust yet again into a mad race to benefit from the ensuing commercial opportunities. This time it was not just the British aristocracy who packed their trunks and headed for Calais. Now Britain embarked on what Mary Shelley describes as an 'incarnate romance' with the Continent as 'a new generation' of youthful travellers, with 'time and money at command', yet heedless of 'dirty packets and wretched inns', headed over the Channel.[1]

Many of those rushing across La Manche were the new middle class keen to see a world recently prohibited by war, and traditionally the reserve of society's privileged. One writer observed his countrymen 'pouring in swarms over every part of the Continent, carrying with them their sons fresh from College, and their daughters full of romance, and eager for composition – when countries which, two or three years ago, were wholly locked up from our inspection, or only accessible to persons of a more than ordinarily adventurous spirit, now lie as invitingly open to the sober citizen and his worthy family, as Margate or Brighton'.[2]

And to get a sense of the new rush, compared to the 12,000 British visitors to Paris in 1802, it was estimated that in 1815 more than *15,000* British tourists went to enjoy the fruits of a city denied them for so long.[3]

Turner, however, stayed put. It is a measure of the extreme workload he had taken on that the man who loved travel and adventure more than almost anything else was just too committed to go. The 'to do' list was growing and growing. Alongside an enlarging number of clients wanting oils and watercolours, and the *Liber* project, in 1809 Turner had become involved with an Oxford-based printseller, art dealer, carver and gilder called James Wyatt, who commissioned an oil view of the *High St, Oxford* which he intended to engrave. Turner had completed this and shown it to such success that Wyatt went on and commissioned a second view of *Oxford from the Abingdon Road*, which he had executed by 1812. Wyatt and Turner got on well, and the small tokens of their friendship are hinted at in some of their surviving correspondence, not least a thank-you note from Turner for 'the Sausages and Hare' that were 'very good indeed'.[4]

There were other publishing ventures. The engravers George and William Cooke had commissioned *Picturesque Views on the Southern Coast of England*, a publication of Turner's watercolours intended to run to forty-eight plates published over four years, though in the end thirty-nine were achieved up to 1826. Turner's relationship with William Cooke was fractious. It was not only the complex process of getting proofs corrected and annotated while Turner was moving around the country, but also the tight deadlines that the production had set that endlessly presented organizational challenges. His letters to Cooke are fraught with instructions about where and when to send material, when to meet, surprise or concern at failing to meet, or not having received correspondence. Other difficulties that needed to be navigated by both sides were Turner's captions for his work, which were rejected by the journalist William Combe, who had been asked to edit the series. Turner's sharp sense of intellectual property in an era before the copyright laws is revealed when he insists, in a tortuous correspondence, that if his words are not to be used, then Combe's rewritten words must in no way 'seem to approximate' them 'as any likeness in the descriptions must compel me to claim them − by an immediate appeal as to their originality. Moreover, as I shall not charge or will receive any remuneration whatever for them, they are consequently at my disposal, and ultimately subject only to my use . . .'[5]

If the logistics of the *Southern Coast* project were onerous, the sketching tours that Turner had taken to the West Country and its coasts across the summers of 1811, 1813 and 1814 were by contrast deeply pleasurable.

In 1811 he made a tour around the south-west coast, necessarily passing through the bustling port of Plymouth. The port was one of the main berths of the Channel fleet and, as a particular target for French invading forces during the Napoleonic wars, was always heavily guarded by great gunships. As usual Turner made careful preparations before visiting the town, eager to get the best out of his time there. The Devon-born Charles Eastlake, then still just a student at the RA, had been alerted to Turner's impending visit and had written ahead to his father, an Admiralty lawyer, that 'What he wants is to go on board some large ship, and I daresay George will be very happy to take him on board the Salvadore,[6] and perhaps into the Dockyard, &c. He is the first landscape painter now in the world . . . I hope all at Plymouth will be attentive to him.'[7]

Alongside Eastlake's brother George, there were plenty of others in Plymouth keen to entertain their eminent visitor. The town had a thriving cultural life and an established artistic heritage. Sir Joshua Reynolds had hailed from Plymouth. There was the bookseller Benjamin Haydon, whose premises housed various soirées for the town's thriving artistic and literary community. Haydon's son of the same name had already gone to London to study at the Royal Academy, as had another son of the city, the watercolourist Samuel Prout. But there were still painters in situ, not least a landscape painter, Ambrose Johns, with whom Turner soon became firm friends. The local mayor, Henry Woollcombe, was sufficiently proud of Plymouth's ability to produce painters that he would, in 1812, found the Plymouth Institution. The fecundity of Devon was not lost on Turner who, as part of the tour, had been paying visits to members of his family in the region, and was subsequently quick to point out his own connections to Barnstaple.[8]

Two years later Turner was back, this time determined to spend longer in and around Plymouth. His 1813 trip coincided with Charles Eastlake's presence in his hometown, and so inevitably Turner, Eastlake and Johns organized some sketching trips together. 'As he wished to see the scenery of the river Tamar, I accompanied him, together with Mr. Ambrose Johns . . . to a cottage near Calstock, the residence of my aunt, Miss Pearce, where we all stayed for a few days,' Eastlake later recalled. 'From that point as a centre, Turner made various excursions, and the result of one of his rambles was a sketch of the scene which afterwards grew into the celebrated picture of *Crossing the Brook*. The bridge in that picture is Calstock Bridge; some mining works are indicated in the middle distance. The extreme distance extends to the mouth of the Tamar, the harbour of Hamoaze, the hills of Mount Edgcumbe, and those on the opposite side of Plymouth Sound. The whole scene is extremely faithful.'⁹

Though Eastlake's recollections are somewhat summary, one man who met Turner that summer has provided some of the most vivid and insightful accounts of him. Cyrus Redding was the editor of the *West Briton and Cornwall Advertiser* when he first encountered Turner at one of the twice-weekly open houses held by the Plymouth merchant John Collier. Turner and Redding forged a friendship that saw the latter accompany the painter on a number of adventures over the next few weeks.

Redding instantly grasped that Turner had a photographic memory, for which his most sparse sketches were a prompt. 'In his observations on the scenery, Turner seemed to command at a glance all the main points of view and all that was novel in it, and to receive the whole in his mind reflected as in a camera,' Redding observed. 'What he committed to paper . . . seemed often quite unintelligible to the stranger. From these pictorial memoranda, he worked out his landscapes . . . He must have borne in his memory much of the details of what he saw, for his sketches frequently did not present many of the objects that are found both in his pictures and in the reality. His sketches seemed, therefore, to be a species of short-hand which he deciphered in his studio.'¹⁰

One thing that impressed Redding was Turner's hardiness, at sea, and when it came to travel generally. 'One day, a fine old seaman, a Captain Nicols, who possessed a good sized Dutch boat, with outriggers and undecked, proposed to run round the coast to Bigbury Bay. In the bay is an island called Burr or Borough Island, on which there was then a fishery,' Redding recalled. 'It was proposed that we should make for the island, to eat hot lobsters fresh from the sea. The morning was squally and the sea rolled boisterously into the sound, the breakwater having been scarcely begun. We worked out between the Mewstone and Rome Head to obtain an offing.'¹¹

Turner and Redding embarked on this adventure with an army
officer, and Mr Collier. Another friend of Turner's, James de Maria,
a specialist in scene painting and panoramas (whose panorama of
Paris had so eclipsed poor Thomas Girtin's attempts a decade earlier),
was also part of the party.

'As we ran out, the sea continued to rise, and off Stake's Point
became stormy,' Redding remembered.

> Our Dutch boat rode bravely over the furrows, which in that low part
> of the channel roll grandly in unbroken ridges from the Atlantic.
> Turner sat motionless, quietly watching the scene around. He was not
> at all affected by the sea, though two of our number were ill. The sol-
> dier officer, in scarlet faced with white and gold lace, looked dismal
> enough, drenched in spray. He wanted to throw himself over board.
> We were obliged to keep him down among the rusty iron ballast, with
> a spar across him. Mr. Demaria bore his suffering with patience. In
> this state we made the island, got through the surf with some diffi-
> culty under the lee of the rocks, and were once more upon terra firma.
> Turner was all the while quiet, watching the troubled scene, and it was
> not unworthy his notice. The island, the solitary hut upon it, the bay
> in the bight of which it lay, and the long gloomy Bolt Head to sea-
> ward, against which the waves broke with fury, seemed to absorb the
> entire notice of the artist, who scarcely spoke a syllable; While the fish
> were getting ready, Turner mounted nearly to the highest point of the
> island rock, and seemed writing rather than drawing. The wind was
> almost too violent for either purpose; what he particularly noted
> he did not say. We now commenced our lobster pic-nic, and soon
> became merry over our wine, on a spot where quaffing the juice of the
> grape could hardly have been expected.

As the wind only increased during the course of the day, the party
decided to wade back to the mainland at low tide and stay over at
Kingsbridge. And here Redding sampled Turner's habit of rising
early. 'Early in the morning before the rest were up, Turner and
myself walked to Dodbrooke, hard by the town, to see the house that
had belonged to Dr. Walcot, (Peter Pindar), and where he was born
. . . We walked much of the way back to Plymouth.'

It would not be the last time that the intrepid and unflappable Turner showed his Devonshire colleagues his mettle. 'Mr. Collier, a couple of friends, and myself, had on one occasion accompanied Turner along the shores of the Tamar, and, having been out all day with a scanty supply of provisions, Tavistock being distant about three miles, it was proposed we should go there and pass the night, returning to the same spot in the morning,' Redding recounted.

There was, indeed, a small country inn, with a spare sitting room and sanded floor, but no beds. Turner had a great desire to see the country round at sunrise. It was, therefore, agreed that three of the party should go over to Tavistock; and, as I did not mind 'planking it,' to quote the sailor's phrase, I agreed to remain with Turner. It was uncertain, while our friends were feasting in clover at the inn in Tavistock, whether we should get any fare at all. Turner was content with bread and cheese and beer tolerably good, for dinner and supper in one. I contrived to feast somewhat less simply on bacon and eggs . . . In the little sanded room we conversed by the light of an attenuated candle and some aid from the moon, until nearly midnight, when Turner laid his head upon the table, and was soon sound asleep. I placed two or three chairs in a line, and followed his example, at full recumbency. In this way three or four hours' rest were obtained, and we were both fresh enough to go out as soon as the sun was up, to explore the scenery in the neighbourhood, and get a humble breakfast, before our friends rejoined us from Tavistock . . .[12]

Redding confirms that for all Turner's gruffness he could be a generous host – particularly when a picnic avoided standing on ceremony. 'On the foregoing occasion, he provided his picnic in excellent taste, and, on that beautiful spot, we spent the best part of a fine summer's day,' Redding said. 'Cold meats, shell fish, and good wines were provided on that delightful and unrivalled spot. Our host was agreeable, but true, blunt, and almost epigrammatic at times. Never given to waste his words, nor remarkably choice in their arrangement, they were always in their right places, and admirably effective.'

Redding's accounts of Turner, apart from being wonderfully vivid, are also uncannily psychologically perceptive. Sure enough he spotted that degree of insecurity in the artist, particularly with women, that makes sense of so many of his choices in life. Redding noticed something on another occasion that many would have considered of little consequence.

> He was once at a party where there were several beautiful women. One of them struck him much with her charms and captivating appearance, and he said to a friend in a moment of unguarded admiration, 'If she would marry me, I would give her a hundred thousand.' I have no doubt that he felt his own personal disadvantages, and, perhaps, the thought might have aided in leading him still more arduously to build up a great name in his profession.[13]

Ambrose Johns made a fuss over Turner during his stay in Plymouth. So keen was he that the artist should capture the local scenery that he made a portable painting-box for him, 'containing some pre-prepared paper for oil sketches as well as the other necessary materials. When Turner halted at a scene and seemed inclined to sketch it, Johns produced the inviting box, and the great artist, finding everything ready to his hand, immediately began to work . . . Johns accompanied him always.'

The warmth of his welcome in the West Country was not lost on Turner. Charles Eastlake recalled that when he returned home Turner sent Johns a gift: 'long afterwards the great painter sent Johns in a letter a small oil sketch as a return for his kindness and assistance.' [14]

Turner dashed back to the West Country in 1814 and the dialogue on art continued with his new friends. He discussed Opie's and Reynolds Discourses with Johns, and subsequently offered to send copies of the works to him. It may well have been Turner who encouraged Johns to submit a work for that year's R A show. But the difficulty of nineteenth-century communications between the West Country and London presented consistent hurdles. Turner related that in returning to London, he 'got rid of my cold by catching a greater one, at Dartmouth, being obliged to land from the boat half drowned with the spray as the gale compelled the boat men to give up half way down the Dart from Totnes'. Meanwhile, just as Turner left Plymouth, yet more proofs from Cooke had arrived, too late as usual, and now he had to ask Johns to track down the parcel at the Mail Coach office and 'let me have it for him when it may be convenient for you to send'.[15]

These Devon trips undertaken between 1811 and 1814 bore yet more fruit. Turner's relationship with Cooke was not so troubled as to prevent a further venture. In 1815 Cooke went on to commission a *Rivers of Devon* series; though it was never delivered in its initially imagined form, Turner nevertheless made six watercolours for it, which were produced elsewhere.

As if he had not enough on his plate, during all this Turner had also been working on a major refurbishment of his Harley Street gallery. The lavishness and extent of this reworking of his professional space is revealed by his note that while he might set aside £500 for Solus Lodge, he was prepared to invest £1,200 in his premises in town. Having acquired a lease on a property in Queen Anne Street that adjoined his gallery and gave him a site across the corner of the two streets, in 1811 Turner began works to make an entrance to his gallery from Queen Anne Street and improve the gallery itself. The chaos that followed as he attempted to continue to work amid the building rubble is conveyed in a note to James Wyatt when he insists, 'let me call upon you, for really I am so surrounded with rubbish and paint that I have not really at present a room free'.[16]

Turner reopened his gallery the following year, in 1812, though with a degree of tardiness according to the diary of Edward Monro. Twice Edward and his younger brother Henry attempted to visit the reopened and refurbished rooms, on 7 May and a week later, on the 14th. Henry's note is quite clear in both instances: 'Then to Turner's, not open.'[17]

It is Henry Monro's diary that gives us another brief glimpse of Turner at this time. Henry had enrolled at the Royal Academy Schools, and in 1812 observed Turner teaching as 'Visitor' at the Academy. He clearly presented a rather ominous figure to the young students and Henry recalls that his acquaintance 'Mr Joseph[18] spoke to Turner who answered in a brutal manner – told him not to talk and to look at the rules'. Despite his gruff manner and his determination to see students hard at work, Turner was not a savage critic. 'In going

round the Royal Academy he never made any severe remarks but his
favourite method of calling attention to any specially bad work was to
put his thumb upon it, and say, "That's a poor bit, isn't it?"'[19]

It is no wonder that with so much work and so many commitments Turner soon realized that his dream of splitting life between
London and his gentleman's cottage at Twickenham was never going
to be properly realized. Turner's builder, a Mr Tayler, had completed
Solus Lodge in Twickenham by 1813. The new property was quickly
renamed more cheerfully Sandycombe Lodge, probably after its location in Sand Pit Close. But within two years of the property being
finished Turner was admitting to friends and colleagues that he was
hardly ever there.

'I have just now received your Note from Richmond,' Turner
wrote wearily to George Cooke in May 1815, as they struggled to get
another proof for their publication ready on time. 'I am so much in
Town now that sending there makes it longer in regards to time.'[20]

Just a few months later a similarly resigned tone is employed in a
letter to his boyhood friend Henry Scott Trimmer, when he is forced
to admit: 'I lament that all hope of the pleasure of seeing you or
getting to Heston – must for the present wholly vanish. My father
told me on Saturday last when I was as usual compelled to return to
town the same day, that you and Mrs Trimmer would leave Heston
for Suffolk as tomorrow Wednesday . . . After next Tuesday . . . a line
will reach me at Farnley Hall . . . and for some time . . . until November therefore I suspect I am not to see Sandycombe. Sandycombe
sounds just now in my ears as an act of folly, when I reflect how little
I have been able to be there this year, and less chance (perhaps) for the
next . . .'[21]

In fact one letter suggests that Turner was even prepared to sell his
brand new home, if only one person who was hinting an interest in
it, would just make an offer. 'If Miss – would but wave bashfulness,
or – in other words – make an offer instead of expecting one – the
same [Sandycombe] might change occupiers . . .'[22]

Frustrated with its lack of use, Turner nevertheless enjoyed Sandycombe very much when he was able to. It is still standing today,

and though a little altered it remains an expression of quiet, elegant classicism.

The little villa originally stood on a triangular two-acre plot, had a fish-pond and vegetable garden, and also a meadow nearby where Turner could keep his horse, Crop Ear. It had views over the Thames, and this was a crucial requisite for an artist who drew so much inspiration from this river in particular.

His evident pleasure in the property is signalled by some of the touches he made to its grounds. He enlarged an existing pond so he could stock it with his catch from Thames fishing expeditions, converting the original natural kidney shape into a square. Notes of expenses in his sketchbooks indicate he spent £100 on planting up the garden.[23]

He also made a point of taking a cutting from a willow tree in the grounds of Alexander Pope's former villa at Twickenham. Lady Howe had demolished the villa in 1807, much to Turner's revulsion, but his determination to take something from the poet not only indicates his sentimentality, but also his sense of himself among a line of great men who had found pleasure close to the Thames.

Sandycombe itself was simple. It had a two-storey central block, with two single-storey wings on either side. The plan was cruciform, allowing for an entrance porch facing the road, while the central block stood proud of its wings at the rear, giving prominence to a central feature window and a balcony that looked over the garden, which sloped down towards the river.

The exterior ornamentation, in its restrained classical simplicity, was reminiscent of the work of Turner's friend, and the R A's Professor of Architecture, John Soane. It is no coincidence that Turner owned a copy of Soane's *Sketches in Architecture, containing Plans and Elevations of Cottages, Villas and other . . . Buildings.*

Turner designed the interior details of the house, though again the hand of Soane is suggested. A sketch for a fireplace in one of his sketchbooks reveals his plan for restrained Soane-style ornamentation. Fluted mouldings around the front door are reminiscent of Soane's designs for his own Pitshanger Manor. The entrance hall is also resonant of Turner's colleague, where pairs of arches gather up the entrant. Similarly the steeply winding stair, interrupted by an alcove, and lit from above by a glass skylight, takes typical Soane style and rewrites it on a modest scale.

Inside the house there was a central sitting room which probably doubled as a studio, with a large north-east facing window, where Trimmer recalled that 'Turner used to refresh his eye with the run of the boughs from his sitting-room window'.[24] And this was flanked by two smaller rooms, one a small dining room, the other possibly a library or study. Again the delight Turner took in furnishing his project is indicated by the commission for a small frieze to sit above the fireplace in the dining room from the sculptor Chantrey, who lived close by and had become a regular fishing companion. Above this simple ground floor were just two bedrooms, and below a kitchen.

The new house became his father's main residence, with Hannah Danby installed as housekeeper in town. The Twickenham locals soon found their own nickname for the short, beaky-nosed and bright-eyed painter who they saw popping in and out of Sandy-combe. The boys who plagued Turner by stealing fish from his pond and blackberries from his hedge called him 'blackbirdy'.

The lifestyle at Sandycombe was as modest as the architecture. Henry Scott Trimmer's son remembered visiting the house with his father, and that 'everything was of the most modest pretensions: two pronged forks, and knives with large round ends for taking up the food . . . the tablecloth barely covered the table, and the earthenware was in strict keeping.'[25]

The engraver John Pye remembered being fed a simple supper of 'cheese and porter'. And the basic stock held by William senior is also indicated by a recollection from the young Trimmer, who recalled Turner saying one day, '"Old Dad", as he called his father, "have you not any wine". Whereupon Turner senior produced a bottle of currant, which Turner, smelling, said "Why, what have you been about?" The senior, it seemed, had rather over done it with hollands, and it was set aside. At this time Turner was a very abstemious person.'[26]

Released from the bustle of inner-city London, William senior became a keen gardener, and quickly discovered that the most cost-effective means of getting in and out of town was on the back of the vegetable cart of a local costermonger. Despite the lack of provision for fine dining, nor indeed room for larger parties inside the house, there is plenty of evidence that Sandycombe became a place in the summer where Turner enjoyed hosting picnics in his garden and could provide refreshment after group outings along the Thames. A brief glimmer of these fun occasions is suggested in a note to his fellow painter Abraham Cooper in the summer of 1821.

'The *second* meeting of the Pic-nic-Academical Club will take place at Sandycombe Lodge, Twickenham, on Sunday next at about three o'clock,' Turner gleefully wrote. 'Pray let me know in a day or two that the Sec y may get something to eat.'[27]

The figure missing from Turner's life during the early Sandycombe years was Sarah Danby. There was literally no room for her and her girls in the new house. But neither was there room for her in Turner's wider life. In 1813 she emerges in London's records as living in Warwick Row in Southwark.

The end of Turner's relationship with Sarah Danby came despite the fact that she had given him another daughter. Though well into her forties, Sarah had given birth to Turner's second daughter, Georgiana, in 1811, a decade after Evelina's arrival. The event is shrouded in mystery, though a trip to Hastings at this time is recorded in the sketchbooks, where some jottings read 'Guestling call'd 3 Oaks'.[28] Guestling was where Evelina had been born and it may well have been that Turner and Sarah Danby returned to the same place.

There is another possibility. Might Georgiana Danby in fact have been *Hannah* Danby's child? After all, Sarah, in her late forties at least, was unusually old even by twenty-first-century standards to be having another child. Getting her niece pregnant would have been reason enough for Sarah to pack her bags.

Certainly plenty of Turner's contemporaries were under the impression that Hannah and Turner were lovers at some stage during their life together.

'There is no doubt that he habitually lived with a mistress. Hannah Danby, who entered his service, a girl of sixteen . . . and was his housekeeper in Queen Anne Street at his death, is generally considered to have been one,' wrote William Cosmo Monkhouse.[29] There may be some confusion here between the two Danbys, but the very personal gifts Turner made to Hannah – such as the very first self-portrait in oils that he made – may suggest a degree of intimacy between the two that went beyond the relationship of loyal housekeeper and her master.

But if Hannah was the mother of Turner's second child, clearly an accommodation was reached that suited all concerned. Sarah Danby left with Georgiana as well as Evelina and continued to oversee their care alongside her other daughters. Sarah and Turner also parted on good enough terms. There is the fact that she attended his funeral, and after his death it became evident that she was in possession of a good number of works by him, tokens of affection perhaps, or part of an informal separation deal.

There is some meagre evidence that Turner continued to see his daughters from time to time and that he had some concern for their welfare. Apart from their appearance in early versions of his will, Henry Trimmer remembered seeing a young girl in Queen Anne Street. In 1813 Turner's beautiful depiction of a *Frosty Morning* was shown at the RA, showing a man and a young girl standing on an ice-bound road watching workers clearing a ditch. 'My father told me that when at Somerset House it was much brighter and made a great sensation,' Trimmer's son remembered. '. . . The girl with the hare over her shoulders, I have heard my father say reminded him of a young girl whom he occasionally saw at Queen Anne-street and whom, from her resemblance to Turner, he thought a relation.'[30]

That Evelina had inherited the Turner genes is not only suggested by Trimmer's account of her, but is also evident in a small portrait that has survived and remains with her descendants today. It depicts a dark-haired woman with a long nose and dark wide eyes. But it is her mouth, with its lower lip receding below a fuller upper lip, that matches the descriptions and youthful profiles made of her father.[31]

Frosty Morning depicted a scene that Trimmer claimed Turner had seen while travelling by coach in Yorkshire. In 1816 Yorkshire was once again a destination.

But this time his trip to visit the Fawkes occurred during what would become known as the 'dark summer'.

On 5 April 1815 Mount Tambora on the island of Sumbawa in Indonesia began to splutter. Five days later these volcanic labour pains were followed by the largest ever recorded eruption in history. The explosion was so huge it could be heard 1,600 miles away, and reduced the 13,000 foot mountain to half its original size. But it was the 140 billion tonnes of ash and debris that was spewed into the atmosphere that had a worldwide effect. Reducing the warming power of the sun, and producing dark days across the summer period, the weather in Europe in the following year was some of the worst ever recorded, and crops once again failed in wintry conditions.

This climatic anomaly coincided with a major new commission from Turner's former patron Dr Whitaker, who wanted to follow up his *History of the Parish of Whalley* with a seven-volume *General History of the County of York*.

'Turner told me He had made an engagement to make 120 drawings views of various kinds in Yorkshire, – for a History of Yorkshire for which he was to have 3000 guineas,' Farington wrote on Friday 17 May 1816. 'Many of the subjects required, he said, he had now in his possession. He proposed to set off very soon for Yorkshire to collect other subjects.'³²

These other subjects in mind, Turner made his way to Farnley a month earlier than normal so that he could take his sketching trip ahead of the shooting season. On Wednesday 17 July 1816 a group set off from the Fawkes estate which included Walter and his newly-wed second wife, Maria. It is Maria who takes up the tale in her diary, which recounts that other members of this intimately acquainted touring party were family – 'Amelia, Ayscough [Fawkes's son and daughter]' and 'Richard [Fawkes's brother]' – and best friends: 'John Parker' joined 'at Skipton where we slept and saw Skipton Castle'.³³

The group went on to Browsholme, the seat of the Parkers, but were instantly hemmed in by heavy rain. It 'rained all day' on Friday the 19th. 'Sat in the house,' Maria wrote gloomily. 'Late in the evening walked a short way with John Parker and Mr Turner.' The party stayed at the Parkers' for a few days, taking trips out to the valley and high pass known as the Trough of Bowland, and local places of interest such as Waddington church. But the heavens did not relent.

'Obliged to take shelter in a farmhouse,' Maria noted for Tuesday 23 July. The party made Malham village under 'dreadful rain' and visited the nearby Gordale waterfall, again with 'heavy rain' beating down on them. The Fawkes gave up finally on 25 July and returned home, but Turner determined to venture onwards.

Turner's sketchbooks testify to what extent he roamed around during these outings despite the appalling conditions. His sketchbooks feature subjects sketched repeatedly from different viewpoints and distances. He works solely in pencil, making outline drawings and not pausing to apply colour nor to make notes regarding weather or coloration. It may have been the consistently bad weather that dictated this approach, which continued throughout his Yorkshire trip, but it also signals Turner's growing independence from circumstance. While outlines provide an aide-memoire of the basic structural qualities of the topography and landscape around him, the Turner who was sketching in 1816 had already begun to cut loose from a straightforward depiction of reality in his work, using the immediate world merely as a beginning from which to explore his own imaginative responses to it. These were images that he might reuse now in imagined classical landscapes. And though Whitaker's commission had a clear factual remit, such was Turner's grasp of weather, season, and time that he was more than capable of reworking these visual notes later with an imaginative rendering of them in a different period, under a new sky or at an alternative hour.

After leaving the party on 25 July, Turner headed through Wensleydale and Swaledale to Richmond. Here he stayed for a few days and wrote to the watercolour painter James Holworthy. Holworthy was an admirer of Turner's work who had already subscribed to the *Liber*, and he was a fellow fisherman. Some of Turner's warmest and most amusing letters are written to this chum, with whom he had become particularly friendly, and the pair had planned to liaise in Yorkshire at the home of Henry Gally Knight, an author, antiquarian and architectural historian whose country residence was Langold Hall. Knight had, exceptionally, travelled to Spain, Sicily, Greece, the Holy Land and Egypt in 1810, and had made extensive sketches that Turner was keen to see. Turner had, however, decided to extend his journey and explore more of Lancashire in spite of the down-pours, a mark that the intrepid and hardy side of his character that had been so apparent as a young man had not altered.

'Weather miserably wet,' he exclaimed to his friend. 'I shall be web-footed like a drake, except the curled feather, but I must proceed northwards. Adieu!'[34]

Whereas the Farnley party had had carriages at their disposal, Turner headed north on horseback in appalling conditions. After Richmond he made for the village of Greta Bridge and the market town of Barnard Castle. Beyond these Turner headed into Upper Teesdale to see the great waterfalls of High Force and Cauldron Snout. He then trudged across the High Pennine moors to Appleby; 'the passage out of Teesdale leaves everything far behind for diffi-culty,' he recounted later, '– bogged most completely Horse and its Rider, and nine hours making eleven miles.'[35]

After Appleby came the picturesque town of Kendal and a visit to Morecambe Bay, which Turner followed as far as Ulverston. To make Lancaster he had to cross the treacherous Morecambe Sands, where quicksand and fast-flowing tides presented a notorious peril. So fam-ous was this dangerous crossing that Turner made it the subject of a view for his *Picturesque Views in England and Wales*. He depicts a coach lurching dangerously as it veers slightly from the safe passage marked out by the local guides with laurel twigs.

Turner got back to Farnley in time for the shooting season, of course. The relief must have been immense. Farnley was buzzing with guests and on 12 August Maria Fawkes recorded that 'all the gentlemen' went to the moors.

But if Turner had hoped that the misery of 1816 had concluded, he was to be disappointed. On the very next day disaster struck when Fawkes's brother, Richard Hawksworth, was wounded in a gun accident.

At first the party seemed to think there was some hope for the injured party, with Maria recording in her diary that he was 'pretty well'. But by the 15th problems were becoming evident. 'Richard pretty well until evening,' Maria related glumly. But then the family sent for the doctor, 'who said he was dying'. This opinion proved all

too correct. 'Poor Richard died at 5 oclock in the morning' the very
next day. It is significant that as the house party broke up with the
tragic news, 'Turner and John Parker remained . . .' In fact Turner
stayed for a full month with the family, plunged into grief.

The summer had proved a dark one indeed. It was a tragic end to
an era in which Turner had otherwise found great joy and calm in the
British countryside and his friendship with the Fawkes family. All
was about to change. It is hard to know whether Turner already knew
that his great friend and patron faced yet more troubles, in the form
of mounting debts. And Turner's own fortunes would only become
more mixed.

But at least with the downfall of Napoleon the packets were sailing the Channel once more and the wonders of Europe were again
available. Though he had resisted a trip earlier, it was only a matter of
time before Turner would pack his belongings and head overseas
again. After the misery of the summer of 1816, that time had now
come.

17. Waterloo

On the spectacularly bright and sunny morning of 18 June 1817 London was in a state of excitement. In the early hours of the morning the banks of the Thames were growing fuller and fuller and the city's population poured on to every available quayside, terrace and wharf. Adelphi Terrace, right outside Dr Monro's residence, was particularly packed. Across the river, the south bank had been transformed. The entrepreneurial owners of London's wharves had erected raked seating and were making good money providing ringside views of the day's activities. The proprietors of the coal and corn barges that crowded the Thames, supplying the city with its fodder, had been similarly smart, and for once these river work-horses had been washed down to accommodate the numerous spectators.

The object of this mass excitement was the new Strand bridge, complete, impressive, and about to be officially declared open under a new triumphal name: Waterloo Bridge.

Deep crowds watched as the heroes of Waterloo amassed. Members of the Horse Guard, veterans of the great battle, many wearing medals, went on to the bridge at ten that morning. Members of the Foot Guard and Royal Horse Artillery followed. At three in the afternoon the Prince Regent arrived at Whitehall steps, where the artist John Constable was embedded in the crowd and watched him embark on the golden Royal Barge. There was a non-stop discharge of artillery as the barge set sail, and until it, and the flotilla of other official barges following it, tied up again at a flight of steps to the south-east of the bridge, where the Prince was met by Wellington himself.

Since the Battle of Waterloo, the British victory, the French defeat and the image of the disenfranchised Napoleon had become the staple fare for many British artists and entrepreneurs. Turner's young acquaintance Charles Eastlake had had his first real success with a portrait of the fallen dictator that he had managed to paint on board the *Bellerophon* when it docked in his home town of Plymouth in July 1815. By January 1816 central London saw both the opening of the Waterloo Gallery, featuring artefacts retrieved from the battle, and Henry Aston Barker's new panorama featuring a recreation of the battle.

Two months after the celebrations for Waterloo Bridge, Turner finally headed to the Continent to see Waterloo for himself – it had been fifteen years since he had made an overseas trip. On 11 August he boarded a vessel at Margate, headed for Ostend. He had left London the night before and may have taken advantage of the new steam packet service that was now newly running between the metropolis and that seaside town.[1]

For a painter who had only been abroad once, Turner's choice to visit Waterloo, as part of a wider plan to also tour the Rhine, is deeply significant. After all, for many, Rome, the city almost literally worshipped by western artists, would have been the first choice for a post-war destination. However, the Rhine had found a new advocate in 1816 in the form of Lord Byron, who had himself visited Waterloo and then followed the course of the Rhine, publishing his response to both the battlefield and the great river in the third canto of his *Childe Harold's Pilgrimage* in the same year. And it was the potency of this poem that seems to have persuaded Turner to explore the Rhineland in the first instance.

As Turner set sail from Margate and found himself 'Once more upon the waters! yet once more!'[2] he followed in the footsteps not just of Lord Byron, but of many inquisitive British travellers who had made the very same trip immediately after the battle. In August 1815, weeks after the fighting had concluded, Turner's direct contemporary Henry Crabb Robinson had made his way to the battlefield, though he was disappointed with what he found.

'Not all the vestiges of the conflict were removed,' he noted, 'there were arms of trees hanging down, shattered by cannon balls . . . Ruined and burnt cottages in many places and marks of bullets and balls on both houses and trees.' Something of the human tragedy was still visible too. Robinson became aware that a woman in a local inn 'was come on a vain search after the body of her husband slain there'. But despite the evidence of slaughter, Robinson felt the place lacked atmosphere. Generally flat and featureless, it might have been any field in Cambridgeshire, he thought. This offered little promise for an artist in search of inspiration.³

Turner had prepared for his trip with the level of care and research that characterized the man, and had in his luggage the latest guide-book to the region, Charles Campbell's *The Traveller's Complete Guide through Berlin and Holland . . . with a Sketch of a Tour in Germany*.⁴ Land-ing at Ostend on the 12th, he made Bruges the same day, then Ghent on 13 August, Brussels on the 14th and Waterloo just two days later. The fact that his sketchbooks have detailed drawings that trace this route with enthusiasm suggests not only an artist who was able to work accurately at terrific speed, but also one who must have been up at first light every day to capture this new world.

He noted the famous medieval belfry in Bruges, and the Grand Place in which it stands, complete with the carts and barrows being trundled along by the citizens of the city. He sought out the church of Notre Dame and the Chapel of the Holy Blood, and found the Minnewater or 'Lake of Love' in the south of the city, where an arched bridge over the water conformed to one of his favourite motifs. In Ghent his pencil captured the densely populated Quai au Blé and Quai aux Herbes, and their steep gabled buildings. In Brus-sels he was quick to draw the cathedral of St Michael and St Gudula and the Palace of Laeken.

When he finally made Waterloo he walked the field in the order proposed by his guidebook. He made seventeen sketches, annotated here and there with battle notes gleaned from one of the local guides who made a living repeating key facts and figures to tourists. The emptiness and flatness of Waterloo is captured by Turner in some sketches that amount to no more than a single line, tracing the out-line of the horizon. What is evident in the annotation, though, is that, despite the apparent lack of atmosphere of the field two years after the event, nevertheless Turner saw death everywhere.

After Waterloo, Turner travelled by diligence to Cologne but then relied on his own two feet to measure out the middle Rhine. Moving at his own pace, along the west bank of the Rhine along a road newly laid for Napoleon's army, he managed to make a huge number of depictions of the region, its villages and castles. He walked the Rhine as far as Mainz before travelling back downstream along the river itself by boat.

Turner's enthusiastic response to the landscape is suggested not only by the number and level of detail in his sketchbooks, but also by a new tendency to divide his pages to capture several scenes and views on one page while he is travelling by boat. Sometimes he drew across two pages in 'strips', capturing the linear narrative of the river.

But above all it was the intensely gothic aspects of the riverscape that so clearly enthralled Turner. The unique geology of the middle Rhine creates astonishing drama. The first section that Turner encountered between Bonn and Coblenz already featured a range of hills surmounted by exotic medieval fortified castles with suitably mythical names. Though he had been using just two small sketch-books for his trip up to this point, when he reached the impressive volcanic Drachenfels or Dragon Rock, the highest peak in the region, surmounted by a ruined castle, Turner had to open a larger sketch-book to draw again and again what Byron would later recall as a 'castled crag . . . oe'r the wide and winding Rhine, whose breast of water broadly swells, between the banks which bear the vine'.[5] After this, as he moved south, Turner found himself with a vast wealth of material. He sketched castle after castle: the fortified Burg Rheineck, looming high above the village of Brohl; the exotic-looking watch-tower in the town of Andernach, and the castle of Marxburg sitting high on a steep-sided hill. He was fascinated by Ehrenbreitstein, the fortress that the French had destroyed after holding siege to it for a year before it fell to their revolutionary forces in 1799. Between Coblenz and Bingen the river is noted for a steep gorge and the dens-ity of medieval castles, forty in all, concentrated along the river. Here he was presented with a cornucopia of subjects, emerging one after another as the river took another turn.

Turner travelled light. He wore a 'wallet', or rucksack, on his back in which he carried a basic traveller's wardrobe of 'a Book with Leaves, ditto Cambell's Belgium, 3 Shirts, 1 Night ditto, a Razor, a

Ferrule for Umbrella, a pair of Stockings, a Wais Coat, ½ Doz of pencils, 6 Cravats, 1 Large ditto, 1 Box of colours'.[6] That he managed to lose this wallet and its precious contents during the course of the trip and yet bring home his sketchbooks suggests he must have had his working sketchbooks and pencils either in his pockets or in a secondary day bag.

Losing luggage was a Turner failing. Years later Clara Wells would warn her friend Robert Finch about asking Turner to convey a parcel for him in his luggage. 'He would be quite sure to lose your books, as he invariably does, more than half of his own baggage in every tour he makes, being the most careless personage of my acquaintance.'[7]

Losing his travel bag was not the only calamity on the trip. Foreign food and water also had its effect on Turner's stomach. Jotted down in a sketchbook is a remedy for diarrhoea or vomiting which, like many of Turner's notes, allows the reader to almost hear the directions being provided by a fellow traveller. A particular substance must be 'm[ixed] in weak warm water washed off with W Gruel If costive a Glyster Drink 2 of water whey or Gruel to each quart a tea spoon full of cream of tartare if lax motion No other medicine or food until the P becomes cooler Bleeding to be avoided.'[8]

After the Rhine he had spent the first few days of September travelling through Holland via Antwerp, and Dordrecht to The Hague. From here he took a boat to Harwich. Despite the minor disasters, Turner arrived back from his adventures in early September. He had only been away a month but the material he had gathered was phenomenal. But he did not stop. In fact he may have transferred directly to a collier to head north to Newcastle, before moving on to Lord Darlington's seat, Raby Castle. He had scheduled work at Raby, with a commission in hand from Darlington for a view of the castle, as well as another to sketch views in Durham for a proposed history of the region by the antiquary Robert Surtees. In addition Turner must have been keen to share with Darlington news from his trip to the Rhine, and may have been hopeful that he and his former travelling companion Newbey Lowson would be some of the first to commit to Rhine views, since the pair had made their own trip up the Rhine in 1816.

William Harry Vane, the third Earl Darlington, like so many of Turner's well-heeled clients, was a man defined by eccentricity. Described in a popular song as 'Darlington's peer with his chin sticking out and his cap on one ear',[9] he had become infamous as a passionate and dedicated huntsman, as well as a devil-may-care character who threw social caution to the wind when, as a second marriage, he wed his mistress, the daughter of a market gardener and the former mistress of the banker Thomas Coutts. His children by his first wife changed their names in protest.

Turner's sketchbooks employed during his stay at Raby combine views of the building with studies of the hunt, its dogs and horsemen. The bustle of Raby and its enthusiasm for outdoor sports must have reminded Turner that he would normally have been at Farnley at this time of year.

It was not just Darlington's commission that was delaying Turner's travel to Farnley. Turner's sixteen-year-old daughter Evelina had become engaged to an ambitious civil servant, Joseph Dupuis, and their marriage was to take place on 31 October at St James's in Piccadilly. This must have been a relief for a father for whom a sense of parental responsibility lay greatly in the shadow of his first and foremost commitment to his art.

With Evelina's impending nuptials in mind, perhaps, Turner had planned to head south in mid-October, aiming to liaise with Henry Gally Knight at Langold Hall en route to London. Knight, who had been encouraging Turner to visit him since the previous year, had suggested Turner visit 'e're the leaves do fall'[10] and Turner had provisionally suggested a window between 23 and 29 October. This would still allow him to attend the wedding, since the coach travel trip between Nottingham and London necessitated just two days, with a customary stopover at Leicester.

And yet at some point during his stay at Raby, Turner's plans changed. Instead of attending a wedding, he pursued yet more work. 'Lord Strathmore . . . took me away to the north,' he explained sheepishly in a letter to Holworthy.[11] John Bowes, the tenth Earl of Strathmore, had commissioned three watercolours of his properties at Gibside and Hylton Castle. Sarah Danby found herself witnessing her daughter's marriage without her one-time common-law husband by her side.

Staying north did at least mean that the doors of Farnley were reached with greater ease. On 15 November, a day once again characterized by heavy rain, the Fawkes 'returned home and found Mr Turner and Greaves here'.[12]

Turner had with him fifty-one worked-up watercolours based on his Rhine trip, rolled up under his arm.[13] The speed with which he had worked on them, partly during his stays at Raby and Gibside, and partly while on tour, was evident in the particularly loose brushwork employed. He had painted them on paper which he had washed grey. In contrast to the yellow ground in his 'Claudian' or 'Wilsonesque' works, or the white ground shining beneath his other recent pieces, this grey wash gave the series a sense of melancholic mistiness and cool northern light.

If Turner had expected Fawkes to pick a number of views from this selection, which he could then work up to an even more finished state (as had happened with his Swiss series), he must have been astonished that instead Fawkes simply offered to buy all fifty drawings in their current form. It was a gesture typical of the largesse and enthusiasm of the man.

'The transfer of these precious things from Turner to Fawkes's collection was the work of a few minutes friendly talk', according to one near-contemporary, and nephew of Turner's friend Augustus Wall Callcott, who also related the story that 'Turner, being much gratified with the rapidity of the business settlement, said, "Now I must mount them for you." To this end he walked down to the neighbouring village, went to the one shop of the place, bought a quire of that strong sugar-paper in which saccharine matter is supplied to purchasers, and some wafers of the period, about the size of a shilling, and with this material the two devoted friends set to work and mounted all the sketches, putting a wafer at the four corners of each, and cutting the paper to the size of each drawing, leaving a good margin all round. I believe they so remained for several years, and when they were properly mounted there was still some trace of the wafers to be seen.'[14]

Fawkes had offered £500 for the whole series, which, at just under £10 a watercolour, was substantially below Turner's market rate. This must in part reflect the quantity and immediacy of the purchase and Turner's friendship with Fawkes. But it also suggests another possibility – that these were sold as loose drawings, closer to sketches than highly finished watercolours, in what amounted to a new commercial enterprise for Turner, and a new category under which collectors might acquire work.

There was no real recognized market in preparatory 'sketches' per se in the first half of the nineteenth century, outside those of the Old Masters bought by connoisseurs. For the contemporary artist working during Turner's life, value was ascribed to finished pieces, whether in watercolour or oil, though there was also a limited interest in pencil drawings. But in the way Turner was beginning to blur the lines between traditional watercolour technique and oil techniques, and in line with his exploration of different levels of finish in his presented work, he and Fawkes may have felt that there was an intermediary place for colour sketches that captured the essence of their subject matter without subjecting it to detailed completion. That Turner would go on to create more traditionally 'finished' views of the Rhine adds some weight to this notion. Turner was loosening the traditional definitions of art. And it was the fact that Fawkes was prepared to accept, love and ascribe some value to a work that offered an imaginative reflection on a subject rather than finely finished depiction of it that was in itself a departure. The emphasis on the response to the subject rather than the subject itself was gradually becoming more and more important in Turner's work.

Turner was finally back home in London for Christmas, and instantly immersed himself in Academy life. The following spring of 1818, further fruits from his overseas trip went on show at the Royal Academy to mixed results. His visit to Waterloo had resulted in an oil, *The Field of Waterloo*. Accompanied by lines from the third canto of Byron's *Childe Harold's Pilgrimage*, the painting was a near-literal visual interpretation of Byron's poetry: 'The thunder clouds close o'er it, which when rent, The earth is covered thick with other clay Which her own clay shall cover, heaped and pent, Rider and horse – friend, foe, in one red burial blent!'

Turner depicted a night-time nightmare, where the piled-up bodies of the dead and dying are momentarily illuminated by an angry flash of sheet lightning in the distance. A group of women are in the immediate foreground, looking for what is left of their husbands. The painting harks back to the dark biblical scene he had painted for Beckford so much earlier in his career. But its boldness lay in a narrative angle that, rather than celebrate Waterloo as a crowning victory, saw it only as carnage and tragedy. Though the nation was continuing to celebrate Wellington's victory, the reality was that the battle represented the greatest slaughter of men on European soil, with 40,000 men killed across just nine hours. In his determination to acknowledge this epic loss of life, Turner made a genuine, bold break from the tradition of presenting the battle in purely victorious terms. And it once again marks out Turner as a painter who never tired in his attempt to be original, to move art onwards, and to explore its potential over and above public expectation and common practice. Above all the painting is another reminder of Turner's constant quest to take the actual, and through its depiction and reinterpretation reveal a greater universal truth. In this instance the tragedy of war.

Turner's ally John Taylor, in the *Sun*, instantly grasped the innovative and brave aspect of Turner's work, praising it as a 'terrific representation of the effects of war'.

But most of the art community could not see beyond the unconventional technical aspects of Turner's work. The unrepentant darkness of the canvas, its determined indistinctness in its treatment of a place rendered intangible amid smoke, cloud and nightfall, and the treatment of the bodies as a writhing mass, read as a nonsense. The *Annals of Fine Arts* was without mercy, reporting that 'we really thought this was the representation of a drunken hub bub on an illumination night, and the host as far gone as his suffering and scrambling guests, was, with his dame and kitchen wenches, looking with torches for a lodger and wondering what was the matter.'[15] The picture did not sell.

In contrast to the overall poor reception for *Waterloo*, however, there was widespread praise for Turner's depiction of a ship he had seen in the harbour at Dordrecht, *Dort or Dordrecht: The Dort Packet Boat from Rotterdam Becalmed*. Reflecting his recent travels in the way his *Calais Pier* of 1802 had reflected his journey of that year, the turbulence of the earlier piece is replaced by sheer calm in the most recent. This in itself may have been Turner's way of alluding to the more permanent sense of peace and calm in a post-Napoleon era.

Sitting in a golden light, on glass-smooth water, the Dort packet boat hangs to the left of the composition, a noble presence mediating the chasm between water and sky. Its composition anticipates *The Fighting Temeraire tugged to her last berth to be broken up, 1838*, which Turner would paint twenty years later. Its strong intense colour also looks towards that painting.

But it is also a human painting. The packet is crowded with travellers. A row-boat full of passengers heads out towards the stranded ship, while another, already alongside it, is engaged with hauling people and provisions on board.

In this picture Turner was knowingly continuing his robust dialogue with the British Institution. The Dutch Old Master Aelbert Cuyp had been a seventeenth-century resident of Dordrecht and had painted many scenes in its harbour. One, *The Maas at Dordrecht*, had found its way into the collection of Sir Abraham Hume, who had lent the work to the British Institution for its Dutch Old Master show in 1815, where Turner had undoubtedly studied it. That Turner painted his view with Cuyp's in mind is also without doubt, and that he may have hoped that Hume would purchase it as a pendant is a possibility suggested by Turner's weighting of the picture's composition to the left of the canvas, while Cuyp's view features a ship to the right of the frame. There are other narrative echoes in the pictures. Cuyp's original features a troop carrier full of Dutch soldiers, a row-boat of Dordrecht dignitaries rowing towards it to greet the returning heroes. The play with scale, the larger boat in dialogue with its smaller dinghy, is clearly echoed in Turner's *Dort*, and again anticipates the *Temeraire*, where the great fighting ship is compared to the miniature tug pulling it.

The press could not have been more positive about the work. The *Morning Chronicle* considered the *Dort* 'one of the most magnificent pictures ever exhibited'. Its sublime, rich colouring was a complex composition of complementary blues and yellows, cool and warm tones, and juxtaposed a horizon laden with misty marble clouds, and a wider sky full of golden light. 'It almost puts your eyes out,' one contemporary noted to Farington.[16]

Henry Crabb Robinson managed to sum up the general reaction to Turner's offerings to the 1818 RA show in his diary: 'Turner's *Field of Waterloo* is a strange incomprehensible jumble,' he noted, but 'The *Dort* . . . has a richness of colouring unusual in water scenes, and perhaps not quite true to nature; but this picture delights me, notwithstanding.'[17]

Despite the dent Sir George Beaumont's brickbats had made in his prices, Turner asked an unprecedented 500 guineas for the *Dort*, a new benchmark. And, astonishingly, he got it from Walter Fawkes, the enthusiasm of his friend and patron apparently boundless.

It was Fawkes's inability to assuage his appetite for the things he loved that had, by 1818, got him into considerable financial difficulties, though. He was careering towards bankruptcy. Perhaps it was the agreement to buy the *Dort* for such an exceptionally large sum, hot on the heels of the purchase of all the Rhine views, that forced Fawkes to reveal the true state of his affairs to his friend. In an unprecedented move Turner loaned him £3,000, a massive sum of money. It was a move that is hard to imagine of the hard-nosed, penny-counting, modest-living young painter who would charge patrons for the price of a carriage and drop engravers who asked above an agreed rate. Or of the man who might put a commission above a daughter's wedding. But, as this gesture reveals, the forty-three-year-old Turner of 1818 was showing signs of generosity and concern, of a new humanity and empathy, that could play out alongside the gruff or undemonstrative versions of himself.[18]

Turner had been biding his time, but he was a man with a deep sense of community, and as he reached his forties he began to express this, materially. After all, his own early life had benefited greatly from community. The community of his father's clients, who had taken up the young boy and supported his ambition to be an artist; the community of friends and family in Tonbridge, Bristol and Brentford, who had provided food and board for the young man; the community of barbers and Covent Garden residents who had rallied around his father and provided their signatures and bonds when his mother had to be admitted to hospital. The Royal Academy had provided a community of artists and patrons that would help Turner's career. In fact eighteenth-century society more generally functioned around the necessity for generosity and philanthropy, as any brief glance at the front page of *The Times* in this era, with its advertisements for subscriptions to philanthropic causes, would attest.

In his fourth decade, and a very wealthy man indeed, Turner no longer saw himself as a beneficiary, and understood his duty as a benefactor. And so in 1814 he, and a number of other leading artists including his friend Sir John Soane and the painter Thomas Phillips, founded the Artists' General Benevolent Institution. It was intended as a body which raised and invested money to provide for 'Decayed Artists of the United Kingdom whose works have been known and esteemed by the public'. This initiative represented a step on from another scheme, the Artists' Fund, which had been set up four years earlier but which was a joint stock fund available only to those who had invested in it.

The financial support that Sarah Danby had received from the Society of Musicians' Benevolent Fund must have served to heighten Turner's interest in a similar scheme for his profession. It is a rich irony that in the year that he became the chairman of the latter, Sarah, separated from Turner, applied once again to the former for assistance.

Turner took on his new role with a strong degree of commitment, and one letter suggests he routinely solicited donations from friends. In June, when he failed to attend a subscribers' dinner, his apologies were accompanied by 'a second donation of three guineas . . . with a donation of two guineas from J. J. Wheeler Esq and an annual subscription of five guineas from Mr Fawkes of Farnley esq'.[19]

It was Fawkes's constant support in everything that Turner brought to him, right down to his campaign for decayed artists, that must have contributed greatly to Turner's determination to help his friend in his own moment of crisis. And the gesture was reciprocated. Fawkes almost immediately embarked on a project that would prove hugely beneficial to Turner's career.

In April 1818 Sir John Leicester, Fawkes's friend and the man who had bought ten Turners in as many years, opened his private picture gallery in his London home to the general public. Private galleries had been opened in the past, but when the public entered the bespoke gallery at 24 Hill Street, Mayfair, top-lit through an elegant circular skylight, they were witness to the first exhibition of a collection solely comprising the work of British artists.

The gallery was a sumptuous experience. Leicester's second wife Georgiana, whom he had married in 1810, when she was just sixteen, had furnished it in the style of Paris's Madame Récamier, with elegant chaises-longues, some framed by curtains, so that visitors might enjoy the paintings in a newly informal manner. The popularity of the gallery was instant. On the first day it opened 500 visitors poured through the doors, and traffic in Hill Street ground to a halt amid a jam of carriages.

In the following year Leicester repeated the initiative and this time Fawkes, taking a leaf from his friend's book, also mounted an exhibition of *his* collection at his London home in Grosvenor Place. But there was a spirited difference in Fawkes's exhibition. For his collection was not only largely based around his now extensive number of Turners. It was also a collection of watercolours. In one single gesture the show was intended as a tribute to Turner, but also a piece of advocacy for watercolour as a genre, revealing how Turner had achieved a new level of sophistication and brilliance within the once-overlooked medium.

The Fawkes family headed down from Yorkshire in March to prepare for the show, which was hung, not in a picture gallery, but through four rooms: their front drawing room, small bow drawing room, large drawing room and music room. The moment they were in London, Turner, of course, dined with them, Mr Parker inevitably another guest at the same Sunday evening supper.

The exhibition opened on 13 April in advance of the Royal Academy show on what Maria Fawkes pointed out was yet again a 'very wet day'.[20] There were a total of sixty Turners across all the rooms. The progress through the event saw a range of artists on view in the front drawing room and then '20 Sketches by Turner' in the small drawing room. The music room showed twenty drawings by, again, a mix of artists, and the finale was the large drawing room where finished large-scale watercolours by Turner were on show, representing the full range of his work. Alongside Swiss views were London views such as *Flounder Fishing at Putney Bridge*. There were views of Yorkshire spectacles, such as the High Force waterfall, drawn during one of the many summer stays at Farnley; a view of Loch Fyne; another of Coniston Water; a seascape featuring a *Man of War, making a signal for the pilot, off the Tagus*, and even a view of the *Field of Waterloo*, quite different from the oil that had been shown in the previous year, this time with the slaughtered men seen in daylight, lying on a bank above a road . . . the horizon line that Turner had marked so carefully in his sketchbook now quite visible. In effect it was a display designed to show the range of Turner's work, and the mastery he enjoyed across so many subjects.

At the same time that Fawkes and Leicester were presenting their exhibitions, Turner also had two oils at the annual RA show. One of the aspects of Turner's work that is almost impossible to grasp some 200 years after the event is the humour and wit he often wove into his titles, and his delight at the interplay between title and image. Turner's contemporaries would have better grasped the wry pun in his convoluted title *Entrance of the Meuse: Orange-Merchant on the bar going to pieces, Brill Church bearing S.E. by S., Masensluys E. by S.*

The painting shows a Dutch ship breaking up on a sandbar, its cargo of oranges spilt into the sea. In the distance Brill church is still visible on the mainland. The pun is on Orange, not only signifying the cargo of the vessel, but its nationality, since the Dutch Royal Family were part of the House of Orange. That this Royal Family had suffered recent investment losses during the Napoleonic wars is also implicit in the conceit.

In terms of composition and subject matter it is similar to a watercolour that probably had its origin in that blustering trip out to Burgh island with Captain Nicols, Mr Collier, Cyrus Redding and others in 1813: *A Ship against the Mew Stone at the Entrance to Plymouth*, which was engraved for *Picturesque Views on the Southern Coast*. As such it is typical of Turner's tendency to repeat popular motifs, to rework successful compositions, and to create series. The nautical coordinates in the title must also serve to reinforce the viewpoint that both the *Meuse* and *Mew Stone* pictures share – one in which the viewer is thrust into the midst of the ocean waves, bobbing in his own unseen boat.

Crabb Robinson saw this *Entrance to the Meuse* in June. He was underwhelmed and simply noted that 'Turner has fewer attractions than he used to have'.[21] Turner must have been disappointed that members of the public such as Crabb Robinson failed to appreciate his oils at the RA. Particularly since one of them was the largest-scale oil he had ever painted: *England, Richmond Hill on the Prince Regent's Birthday*. A massive eleven feet in length, this idyllic scene of partying on the banks of the Thames was a conscious follow-up to the *Waterloo* of the previous year. After the carnage and sacrifice, England was enjoying peace.

The *Annals of the Fine Arts* probably best summed up the issue with Turner's latest RA submissions. They were both very fine paintings, but both in their own way resonant of existing work. Turner was treading water, while the expectation was that he should surprise year on year. The *Annals of the Fine Arts*[22] thought the *Meuse* 'Too scattered and frittered in its parts to be reckoned among Turner's happiest productions. Compared with himself, this picture suffers, – compared with others, it maintains Turner's rank uninjured.'

But if Turner's representation at the RA failed to reveal new wonders, Fawkes's exhibition of watercolours at Grosvenor Place did just this. Suddenly there were sixty works by a single hand, most completely unknown to the public, and showing a range and variety of subject and approach that defied expectation.

Compared to the crowded walls of the RA, where paintings, like cattle in a truck, jostled for position with their neighbours, in the Fawkes' ample town house Turner's watercolours were presented like

an array of carefully selected jewels, set in an environment designed
to complement them. Here, in airy sand-coloured rooms, gilt wood
furniture was upholstered uniformly in Regency blue stripes. Amid
this glittering composition of gold, beige and blue, each painting sat
in splendour, its colours accentuated by the surroundings. Fawkes
was so delighted with this view that he commissioned Turner to
make a watercolour of it. Turner did this, and also made a view out
of the drawing room window as a little companion piece.

The press understood instantly the achievement of both the collector and the artist.

> . . . it is among the proud distinctions of the British School of Art that
> in its bosom painting in Water Colours has arrived at greater excel-
> lence, and has united more of the qualities of painting in oil, with
> qualities peculiarly its own, than in any other age or country – To use
> the expression of Mr Shee, 'It now rivals the most finished produc-
> tions of the easel'. The degree of pre-eminence has been acquired
> within a very few years . . .[23]

> Turner is perhaps the first artist in the world in the powerful and
> brilliant style peculiar to him; no man has ever thrown such masses
> of colour upon paper; and his finest works have been collected in Mr
> Fawkes' house . . . the singular style and extraordinary powers of
> observation, selection, combination and execution of Mr Turner are
> neither subject to the ordinary rules of art, nor perhaps to be duly
> estimated by the superficial observer of the common and every day
> appearances of nature. By the magic of his pencil, we are brought to
> regions of such bold and romantic magnificence, and introduced to
> effects of such rare and awful grandeur, that criticism is baffled . . . for
> design, for colouring, for strength of conception, for depth of feeling
> and felicity of execution – for originality, truth and variety, it places
> him indisputably in this department of the art, at the head of all Eng-
> lish . . . artists . . . [24]

The success was not lost on the artist. While Fawkes's doors were
open, Turner revelled in the reception to his work. 'Turner generally
came alone,' one contemporary observed, 'and while he leaned on the

centre table in the great room, or slowly worked his rough way through the mass, he attracted every eye in the brilliant crowd, and seemed to be like a victorious Roman General, the principal figure in his own triumph.'[25]

So delighted was Fawkes with the outcome of the show that he knew it had to be recorded for posterity. He had a catalogue made, the frontispiece by Turner himself. In it he reproduced the ecstatic praise the venture had received in the press and penned his own generous and devoted dedication to his friend. Fawkes also decided to open the show again the following year, 1820.

After such success Turner must have felt more than ready for his next expedition. It would be undertaken on a scale greater than anything to date. Turner finally decided it was time to visit Italy. He would spend six months there.

18.   Earth and Heaven

'The only person who comparatively could do [Rome] justice would be Turner,' scribbled the portrait painter Thomas Lawrence to his friend the engraver and publisher Samuel Lysons almost the instant he arrived in the eternal city in May 1819. 'It is an injustice to his fame and to his country to let the finest period of his genius pass away . . . without visiting those scenes which if possible would suggest still nobler images of grandeur and of beauty than his pencil has yet given us, and excite him to still greater efforts.'[1]

Lawrence was turned fifty, but, like Turner, had never managed to visit the well-spring of western classical art. He had rushed to Rome from Vienna, where Europe's dynasties had been convening and where he had managed to execute a large number of portraits as part of a commission for the Prince Regent, who wanted to commemorate those who had helped quash Napoleon. So great was Lawrence's sense of urgency to get to Rome after this commitment that he kept his carriage on the road twenty-four hours a day, sleeping in it en route. But the instant he arrived, the need for his compatriot to join him became an obsession with him.

'Take some opportunity, with my respects to him, of pressing this on his attention . . . as one who has never been insensible to the superiority of his talents,' he begged Lysons.

It is unlikely that poor Lysons ever got the chance to exploit his recent appointment as Antiquary at the R A to track Turner down on Lawrence's behalf, for he died unexpectedly just two days after Lawrence had written.

A few weeks later, Lawrence found his anxiety undiminished, expressing again his deep desire that 'Turner should come to Rome'. This time he was writing to Joseph Farington. 'His genius would here be supplied with new materials, and entirely congenial with it. It is one proof of its influence on my mind that enchanted as I . . . am whenever I go out, with the beauty of the hues and forms of the buildings, with the grandeur of some, and variety of the picturesque in the shapes of the ordinary buildings of this city, I am perpetually reminded of his pencil; and feel the sincerest regret that his powers should not be exerted to their utmost force.'[2]

'He has an elegance and often a greatness of invention that wants a scene like this for its free expansion; whilst the subtle harmony of this atmosphere that wraps every thing in its own milky sweetness, (for it is colourless compared with the likes of France & England) and . . . this blending I say of Earth and Heaven, can only be rendered according to my belief by the beauty of his tones.'

Lawrence's sense that Turner would respond well to the milky atmosphere and that only Turner's brilliant handling of tone could grasp 'this blending of Earth and Heaven' was prophetic. The effect that Italy would have on Turner in the future would prove transformative. It changed his palette irrevocably, and from the moment he stepped on to its soil, a greater dreamlike quality would pervade his work. But Turner would bring a new aspect of Italy to Britain too. For, while his compatriots were piling headlong into Rome, it would be his discovery of Venice as a subject for nineteenth-century painters that would prove crucial in the development of the wider story of art.

Italy had been much in Turner's mind in 1818 and 1819, and the subject of his pen too. In the summer of 1818 James Hakewill, an entrepreneurial architect and traveller, had approached him with the proposition of publishing a *Picturesque Tour of Italy*. Hakewill had visited the country in 1816 and drawn extensively. Anticipating that tourism would only increase there after the Napoleonic episode, he saw an opportunity. Turner saw the potential of the project too and went in with Hakewill, working up a series of watercolours from the pencil studies made by his associate, for a book that would be published by John Murray in 1820.

Drawing from Hakewill's impressions, Turner must have felt keenly the need to see Italy for himself. The combination of this and Lawrence's pleading missives must have strengthened his resolve. By August that year he was en route.

As with all his other trips, Turner made sure he had done his research. His friend James Hakewill wrote down guidance on places to see and the best route to take. Hakewill took considerable time and care in this service for his friend, filling several pages of a new blank notebook with practical information for a route through France, over the Alps at the Simplon Pass, and then through Milan, Turin and Genoa to Florence, and then Rome.

'After leaving Dijon enter the Jura Mountains at Poligny – good Inn,' Hakewill wrote. 'Continue to Morez. good Inn – Geneva –. Eau de Genève. good – Best view of Geneva, said to be from Secheron. In the Route of the Simplon, when at Martigny you are at the nearest point to Chamouny & Mont Blanc. Stop at Sion, the Capital of the Vallais. At Tourtimagne, is a good waterfall. Don't go to Brig but to Glise at the foot of the Simplon. Go leisurely over the Mountain. The descent on the Italian side the finest. Good inn at DomoDossola and at Baveno.'[3]

But despite these clear notes and the temptations of a 'good water-fall' and the 'finest' descent into Italy, Turner did not follow his friend's suggested route.

Turner's decision to avoid Simplon seems at first glance counterin-tuitive. This pass had not been in existence in 1802 when he had last been in the Alps. Built by Napoleon's armies, it was renowned as a feat of exceptional engineering. But more than that, crossing the Simplon had become an experience sought by those poets and adven-turers seeking heightened romantic experiences and dramatic views.

Nevertheless, typically Turner had also carried out extensive research using sources other than Hakewill. His notebook also con-tains a long list of alternative routes into Italy, their length and cost of travel, gleaned from Reichard's *Itinerary of Italy*, published in 1818. In the end Turner took the Mont Cernis pass into Italy instead. He had, after all, copied John Robert Cozens's view of the pass when he had been a young man in Monro's 'Academy', and perhaps the temptation to see what Cozens had seen was too great.

From here Turner headed to Milan, but now, instead of taking the diligence south to Rome as Hakewill had suggested, he headed north to view Lakes Como, Lugano and Maggiore. And then, as if he had realized his folly in not taking the Simplon Pass in the first place, Turner took a detour into Switzerland and headed for the pass. As he approached the mountains he washed his sketchbooks grey, scratching away the wash to imply highlights or snowy peaks. The pages of the book are spattered with raindrops and suggest the difficult conditions he encountered.

Turner then turned about and retraced his steps to Milan, but instead of heading for Rome, where Lawrence so eagerly awaited him, he took another detour and headed east to Venice. He reached it in early September. He was one of the first British artists of his generation to set foot in the city, and its impact on him was immediate.

The unique architecture and the constant play between light and the water on which the city seemed to float instantly struck any traveller who arrived. And yet Venice in 1819 was not quite the commercial nexus witnessed nearly 100 years earlier by Canaletto, who had seen a republic at the height of its power. The Venice into which Turner stepped was one of faded splendour, its exotic architecture pockmarked by war, and its former riches diminished. Having passed from the hands of Napoleon into Austrian rule, it was the embodiment of an empire in decay, at the end of its life, yet replete with the memories and legacies of a past built on maritime power and trade. For a man obsessed with the fallen empires of the past, walking into Venice must have been like walking into a version of Carthage.

And yet amid the diminished grandeur of a defeated nation, Turner discovered a people alive with a sense of fun and liberty. It was a city that barely slept, its cafés and piazzas open and bustling all night, its inhabitants often up until sunrise. There was lightness to existence there. The traveller William Berrian, who was there a year before Turner, felt something of this too as he witnessed people 'promenading in the arcades, or sitting under them, and taking ices, coffees and other refreshments. The gay and sprightly Venetians were mixed with Frenchmen, Englishmen, Germans, Armenians, Greeks and Turks. The last were distinguished by their oriental costume . . . the vivacity of the Italians . . . the curious and inquisitive look of the strangers, the varying physiognomy and dress . . . the flutter of passing groups; the easy air and unconstrained mirth . . .' all offset against 'the vastness and splendor of all the surround objects . . .'[4]

In Venice Turner made a series of colour sketches that feel entirely different from his work to date. Captured in the early morning, in the moments after the city folk finally faded to their beds, they have a uniquely quiet and ghostly sensibility. Defined by their supreme economy, they are also the first instances where one feels that the painter, so used to conveying the interplay between dramatic mass and reflective water, dedicates himself to capturing everything other than the tangible. In this handful of sketches Turner used the most delicate tones, sparsely applied, to indicate the city on the water. So pale and slight is his work that one gets the sense that it is less a real city he conveys, than a ghost or palimpsest of the original. On paper washed with a pale yellow he uses grey-blue brushstrokes to imply Venice's spires seen from across the lagoon, the palest wash of the same colour over this implying the haze over the city and the water on which it rests; a touch of pink and darker grey implies the early morning sun. And yet so light is his touch, and so fragile his image, that one is given the sense that it is less Venice per se that he is depicting, than a projection of it caught in vapour. For the first time one senses that in Venice Turner dedicates his vast talent to depicting not stuff and matter, but the negative attributes of experience: air, and space. Not so much the city but the particles of light which allow it to be perceived.

If artists were still lured to Rome, poets and writers at least had ventured to Venice after the Napoleonic wars. At the time of Turner's arrival Lord Byron had been living in the city, benefiting not only from its warm waters, in which he swam regularly, but from the city's climate of sexual leniency. It is tempting to consider that as Turner produced his dreamlike sketches of a phantom city just glimpsed over the water he had Byron's lines in mind, for certainly there is a close relationship between Turner's otherworldly images of Venice and Byron's description of his protagonist Childe Harold in the city, who considered Venice 'a fairy city of the heart, Rising like water-columns from the sea'.

Venice had, according to some accounts, as many as 20,000

prostitutes and Turner may well have availed himself of their services. Certainly on his subsequent visits to Venice, erotica forms part of Turner's sketching enterprises. One watercolour sketch reveals two women leaning out of a window, one with a sheet clinging to her body, her companion apparently topless. Another depicts a figure on a rumpled bed.

While Turner was in Venice, he remained the subject of correspondence between Lawrence and Farington. The fashionable young man who had painted his self-portrait two decades earlier had vanished. Turner was now thick-set and red-faced. He had also begun to disregard his appearance. Described as looking 'somewhere between a Dutch captain and a journeyman carpenter' by this time in his life,[5] it seems that his language and manners now matched this demeanour.

'You have given Mr T's character with very happy discriminations,' Lawrence wrote to Farington. 'I wish it were placed before him, though I fear he would not know it. His standard of Vulgarity must be so different to ours. He fancies himself I suppose the Gentleman of the Old Comedy "A Man of Wit and Spirit About Town".'[6]

In spite of his reservations about Turner's curmudgeonly tendencies, Lawrence was nevertheless thrilled when the small beady-eyed painter finally saw the eternal city.

'Mr Turner is come,' Lawrence wrote to Farington on 6 October, at once ecstatic and a little disappointed. 'I had the sincerest pleasure in seeing him for he is worthy of this fine City, of all the Elegance and Grandeur that it exhibits!' the portrait painter excitedly reported, before adding with a degree of disappointment: 'He is going immediately to Naples, but his longest stay doubtless will be here.'[7]

A rumbling Vesuvius was a temptation too great for Turner, the painter of the sublime. Only four years earlier he had exhibited an oil, *The Eruption of the Souffrière Mountains, in the Island of St Vincent*, and even more recently had made a series of watercolours of Vesuvius for the publisher W. B. Cooke. These had necessarily been based on the observations of others and drew on the image of the volcano as a terrifying agent spouting fire and brimstone. But when he sketched in the Bay of Naples he dismissed the dark tones of terror in favour of

the limpid palette of Venice, reducing Vesuvius's ire to a wisp of distant smoke. While the numerous pencil sketches Turner made of
Naples testify his enrapture with the location, his colour studies
speak of an awakening to new possibilities in colour after the experience of Venice. Using a white background, the thinnest washes and
brightest rainbow colours, to effect a glittering translucent finish,
Turner in one swift move took his sense of brilliance to a new level.

Turner's host in Naples was Sir William à Court, the British Envoy
there. 'You may depend upon my paying every attention to your
friend Mr Turner during his stay at Naples,' he had assured Thomas
Lawrence on 12 October. 'His merits as an artist are well known to
me, & I was very glad to make his personal acquaintance.'[8]

In fact Turner's presence in Naples at that moment proved quite
useful for à Court, since he was in the process of attempting to acquire
pictures there for the King, via his private secretary, Sir Benjamin
Bloomfield. Turner's expertise in assessing the prices being asked
would prove useful, a service for the Crown that the painter would
have been keen to accept. A Royal Commission still eluded Turner
and in the forthcoming years he would embark on a mission to
achieve one.

Once returned to Rome, Turner made his enthusiasm for the quality of light and the countryside clear. 'He feels the beauty of the
atmosphere and scenery as I knew he would,' Lawrence wrote,
delighted. 'I hope he will paint some fine works while remaining in
Italy, for the want of knowledge of the present state of the arts in
England is very singular . . . Many perhaps may agreeably represent
the scenery that I have witnessed but none but Turner or after him
Mr Callcott can (as far as human means go) do it justice.'[9]

The Rome Turner discovered had been much changed by
Napoleon. Unlike the British travellers on their grand tour in the
eighteenth century, post-Napoleonic travellers benefited from the
extensive excavations that the French dictator had made. Ruins once
buried were newly revealed. Since Bonaparte's demise others had
continued his work, not least Lady Elizabeth Foster, the Duchess of
Devonshire, who since 1816 had been funding excavations of the
city's antiquities.[10]

The Duchess was yet another of the aristocrats Turner would encounter who defined an age characterized by liberal attitudes and a sense of adventure. She had lived in a ménage à trois with the Duke of Devonshire and his wife Georgiana, bearing him illegitimate children, before marrying the Duke after Georgiana's death. A great beauty, she had been immortalized by Sir Joshua Reynolds.

Now the Duchess took Turner in hand. 'My dear sir,' she wrote to Thomas Lawrence, 'Mr Turner will come at three to dinner & you shall decide what we go to shew him in the evening.'[11]

Whether it was that evening or not, that the Duchess gave Turner a personal tour of the Forum is suggested by the contents of his sketchbook. During the Napoleonic era the Forum had been greatly dug out and the past was literally rising up before the people of Rome as never before.

In one sketch of the Forum, made with the huge attention to architectural detail that he was so uniquely capable of, Turner shows the great arch of Septimius Severus still half buried, with a fully excavated Corinthian column to its right. The Duchess had been responsible for the excavation of the base of the Column of Phocas herself, and one imagines she showed Turner her discovery with some pride. Her endeavours had exposed an inscription dedicating the Column to the Byzantine emperor whose statue once surmounted it. Turner made a point of sketching a detail of this base and the inscription on a separate page in his sketchbook.

The British in Rome were very social. In addition to the Duchess and Lawrence, Turner benefited from having other friends and acquaintances there at the time, including the sculptor Francis Leggatt Chantrey, the poet Thomas Moore, the scientist Sir Humphry Davy and his wife and another Academician, John Jackson. But if in the evenings he allowed himself to benefit from the dinner parties on offer, during the day he cast a solitary figure. He is glimpsed from afar, hard at work. Thomas Moore related that his friend Colonel Camac, caught in windy conditions with the Princess of Denmark on the tower of the Capitol, saw Turner sketching there and grabbed his umbrella to protect her, much to Turner's displeasure. Another account is from Sir John Soane's son, also called John, who described his father's friends in the most derogatory terms. 'At Rome a sucking blade of the brush made the request of going out with pig Turner to colour – he grunted for answer that it would take up too much time to colour in the open air – he could make 15 or 16 pencil sketches to one coloured, and then grunted his way home.'[12]

Neither account presents Turner favourably, but neither are the accounts contextualized. The presumption by Colonel Camac that he could just take Turner's umbrella may well have been considered by Turner as yet another example of the kind of social prejudice that some continued to extend to his profession even in the nineteenth century, regardless of the need of a princess. While the unattractive account of a 'pig Turner' comes from a young man who, apart from enjoying a strained relationship with his father, one contemporary described as a 'censorious and intolerable bore'.[13]

But what both accounts do give a sense of is that Turner was highly sensitive to anything that might slow his progress. He made an astonishing 2,000 sketches in the city, meticulously studying everything from the inscriptions on monuments, to details of antique ornamentation, vistas of the Forum and other Roman sites, breathtakingly detailed views and panoramas over the city itself, as well as the surrounding campagna. Turner absorbed every facet of Rome with every waking moment of his day. For him there was no time to waste, and his annoyance at the loss of an umbrella that afforded him protection from the elements while he sketched, or the encumbrance of a hanger-on who wanted to paint with him, was duly expressed.

His sketching aside, while in Rome Turner also made a point of familiarizing himself with the work of the Old Masters associated with the city as well as those contemporary artists working there. In the nineteenth century Rome was Raphael's city. His work and the myth of his life and loves pervaded the city and provided tourists with a specific tour of places associated with him.

At the time of Turner's stay, the scientist Humphry Davy was investigating – at the request of concerned members of the RA – Raphael's huge frescoes in the Vatican, which were in a concerning state of decay. Apart from these and the highly decorated 65-metre-long arched loggia he also designed in the Papal city, there were many other locations to see. One extraordinary experience was to go to the house the artist occupied at the end of his life, the Casino de Raffaello, where one could seek the permission of the then owner, Signore Nelli, and walk in and see the frescoes Raphael painted in the bedroom of his mistress, La Fornarina. That Turner walked through both Raphael's loggia, meticulously noting the decorations, and to Signore Nelli's home is evidenced by his sketches at both locations. He also sketched the Statue of Jonah in the Chigi Chapel, at that time attributed to Raphael.

As well as tracing the footsteps of artists long dead, Turner made a point of seeking out landscape painters from all over Europe who were working in Rome at the time, listing their names in one of his sketchbooks and doubtless making a point of seeing their work. Turner also visited the famous sculptor Antonio Canova. As part of the cultural exchange in the aftermath of Waterloo, Canova had visited London and had been taken to Turner's studio by Benjamin Robert Haydon in November 1815. Now Canova arranged for Turner to be awarded an honorary membership of the Roman Academy of St Luke, of which he was the President. The tribute delighted Turner, who on 27 November wrote from his rooms in the Palazzo Poli offering 'the most sincere thanks for the distinguished honour of your Nature in recommending me'.[14]

At that time the Villa Medici was home to the French Academy in Rome, where a range of portrait and history painters were also at work. This Academy had introduced the sensational French classical painter Jean-Auguste-Dominique Ingres to the city in its Napoleonic era. Ingres stayed on post-Napoleon, until 1820, in rooms at the Villa Gregoriana. He made his money painting the new breed of tourist who came to scramble over the ruins in the Forum. Though there is no direct evidence of Turner meeting Ingres, it is likely he at least saw some of his work in Rome. Ingres's fascination with Raphael had led him to make a series of imaginative portraits of Raphael and La Fornarina, one version of which he had shown at the French salon in 1814.

Turner's stay in Italy far exceeded any other trip he had made. For years it had been his routine to be back from tour and in London for

the Academy's winter term, but for once his own studies took prec-
edence over Academy business. He knew, however, that were he to
have a canvas ready in time for the annual show, he would have to get
back in early spring. And so as the January snows began to fall, Turner
chose this most precarious time to make his return.

It was a long and arduous return, and one that could have proved
fatal. The standard coach services across the Alps were cancelled
because of the weather, and so in mid-January Turner threw his hat in
with another traveller and hired a coach privately to attempt the Mont
Cernis Pass, despite the knee-deep snow. It was a foolhardy move.
'We were capsized on the top,' Turner later recounted with some
mirth, adding 'very lucky it was so', the implication being that had the
carriage turned over on the narrow road, Turner and his companion
would have crashed down the side of the mountain: '. . . the carriage
door was completely frozen that we were obliged to get out at the
window – the guide and Cantonier began to fight, and the driver was
by process verbal put into prison, so doing while we had to march or
rather flounder up to our knees nothing less in snow, all the way down
to Lancesbyburgh [sc. Lanslebourg] by the King of Roadmaker's
Road, not the Colossus of Roads, Mr MacAdam, but Bonaparte, filled
up by snow and only known by the precipitous zig zag . . .'[15]

Turner arrived back in London by the beginning of February. To
his delight the Fawkes were there earlier than usual and within a fortnight of his return he was dining with them. Of course Fawkes was
eager to see the sketches Turner had made in Italy, and as usual Walter's heart overruled his head. Despite his financial situation, Fawkes
commissioned a series of watercolours, including views of Venice,
Rome, Naples and Mont Cenis.

Turner's watercolours of Italy were virtuoso. His view of the
Rialto for Fawkes, for example, not only employed the new vibrant
colour scheme of blues and golds he had explored in his colour
sketches out there, but now combined fine architectural drawing and
the most detailed depiction not only of the palazzos along the Grand
Canal, but the gondolas and the people busying themselves on the
water, and leaning over balconies. The lightness and playfulness
Turner felt in Venice is indicated in his own moment of fun, where he

writes his signature on a gondola in the right of frame and sees it reflected in the shimmering water below.

But for Turner the more significant outcome of his Italian trip was an oil painting for the RA. His public had been lukewarm about his efforts in oil at the most recent shows. They expected to be surprised by Turner again.

He set to work on a view of Rome seen from the Vatican, featuring none other than the artist who had haunted Rome's streets: Raphael. 1820 was, after all, the tercentenary of Raphael's death. Taking a leaf from Ingres's book, and perhaps knowingly in competition with his French counterpart, he also depicts Raphael's mistress. The painting's title is quite clear in this respect: *Rome, from the Vatican. Raffaelle, Accompanied by La Fornarina, Preparing his Pictures for the Decoration of the Loggia.* In the foreground is the loggia in which Raphael, surrounded by famous works, looks up towards the ceiling. A few steps away from him his mistress, her back to the viewer, gazes out over a panorama of Rome, stretching almost to the horizon, under an azure sky and hot sunshine. In Ingres's work the viewer is focused on his characters captured in a domestic interior: Raphael looking at his own depiction of his mistress on his easel, his mistress staring back at the viewer. In Turner's picture, the viewer and La Fornarina gaze out over Turner's depiction of the city, the architecture and depth of field rendered in exquisite detail. Together they experience the magical version of Rome Turner has conjured. Only Raphael is locked in his own time. The city beyond him features Bernini's colonnades, built after Raphael's death, an anachronism which renders Raphael and his lover as ghosts. The presence of Raphael's mistress is a reminder of his fate. The tradition is that Raphael died after a night of passion, a fact not lost on Byron, who wrote of the painter, 'Italian beauty did thou not inspire Raphael who died in thy embrace.'[16] The seductive qualities of Rome were clearly not lost on Turner either.

The viewing public, however, were not overly impressed by a work that attempted to comment at once on the nature of art, the alchemy of the artist, the danger of love and the influence of time. The *Annals of the Fine Arts*,[17] while conceding the 'grandeur of conception', insisted that though 'Turner has not gone back', nevertheless 'he only stands where he did', before attacking the 'excessive yellow-ness, which puts everything out of tune that hangs by it'. The painting did not sell, and like so many of his oils from this time onwards went back to Queen Anne Street to be stored.

But if nothing more, with his third overseas trip now complete, Turner realized how much he enjoyed the experience of new people and places. From this point onwards he would cross the channel regularly, most years exploring another part of Europe. In the next five years he would revisit France, Germany, Belgium and Holland before returning to Italy in 1828.

One gets a sense that travel also provided relief from the grind of work. At home he had continued to place himself under extreme pressure. In 1818 he had embarked on a project to illustrate Sir Walter Scott's *Antiquities of Scotland*. The following year Robert Stevenson commissioned him to design the frontispiece for his *Account of the Bell Rock Lighthouse*. Turner's work for Cooke continued alongside this – the relationship between the two men as fractious as ever – with Cooke following the commission for the *Picturesque Views on the South Coast* with, in the next few years, *Views in Sussex*, then *The Rivers of Devon*, *Rivers of England* and *Marine Views*. Meanwhile in 1824 Turner embarked on another ambitious series of topographical water-colours for engraving, *Picturesque Views in England and Wales*, for Charles Heath.

Private commissions continued, as did his Academy work. He served on the RA council in 1819, and became the organization's auditor in 1824. Between times his Perspective Lectures were still delivered.

As Turner became busier and busier, the public's appreciation of the work of British artists generally was increasing. On 18 May 1821 Christies held a sale of paintings from the collection of Sir Joshua Reynolds's niece, the Marchioness of Thomond. The sale comprised works by Reynolds himself as well as Old Masters. Benjamin Robert Haydon saw a significantly increased interest in Reynolds's work over that by the Old Masters. 'Nobility and men of property seem really to be open to the merits of native genius,' he declared trium-phantly to his diary.[18]

A week later Reynolds's unfinished works and sketches went on sale, and this time Turner and his friend John Soane, among others, were bidding. It was yet another breakthrough moment, that preparatory and incomplete work was attributed the considerable value that to date had largely been reserved for Old Master work alone. The polymath and astronomer Sir John Herschel paid a massive 100 guineas for a sketchbook from Reynolds's tour of Italy. Soane paid 25 guineas for another book, and Turner bought Lot 10 – three unfinished pictures by Reynolds. One of Admiral Keppel, another a self-portrait of Reynolds himself and the third of Lady Elizabeth Foster, the Duchess of Devonshire, who had only recently paid such kind attention to him in Rome.

As the shift in the perception of the value of British art gained momentum, more entrepreneurs moved to meet a growing demand for the home-grown school. William Cooke played his part in the promotion both of British contemporary painters, and of works on paper: watercolours and engravings.

In April 1821 Cooke mounted exhibitions of Turner's prints and then, over the following three years, between 1822 and 1824 he held a series of three loan exhibitions of Modern English Masters at his premises at 9 Soho Square. The catalogues of these exhibitions reveal new clients buying and subsequently loaning Cooke Turner's work to show. The vast majority, far from being members of the aristocracy, represent a mix of the new moneyed merchant class, and those working in the evolving art and publishing industries, some of whose connections to Turner went right back to his youth. Times were changing. The stranglehold on art that the nobility had exercised for two centuries was finally loosening.

There were, of course, those adventurous patrons among the nobility who cared deeply about the new British school. In 1823 Sir John Leicester offered to sell his entire collection of British art to the nation in order to create the beginning of a National Gallery. Astonishingly his offer was rejected on the basis that he did not have a similarly impressive collection of Old Masters. This could not be said of the collections of Sir George Beaumont and of John Julius Angerstein, however. Now the former offered his collection to found a

National Gallery, on the condition that Parliament purchased Angerstein's too. The banker had died in January 1823. Beaumont's lobbying
proved successful, and in 1824 the statutes for a National Gallery
were finally proposed. Angerstein's collection was acquired for
£57,000, his house at 100 Pall Mall serving as the gallery while plans
for a bespoke public building were drawn up.

Just prior to this, Turner had reconsidered his own gallery on the
corner of Harley Street and Queen Anne Street and yet again embarked
on a set of improvements. The works got under way around the time
Turner returned from Italy and the building remained in a state of
transition until 1822. The refurbishments were on a major scale, with
a complete remodelling of both the interior and exterior spaces, and
the construction of a new state-of-the-art picture gallery. Turner
reoriented the building to have a main entrance now on Queen Anne
Street.

He played architect again down to the tiniest detail. He designed
a glass roof for the gallery, as well as the moulding for the ceiling.
The Revd William Kingsley described it as 'the best lighted gallery'
he had 'ever seen'.[19] True to Turner's neo-classical taste, it was painted
Pompeian red. But his renovations and decorations extended beyond
the gallery to the house in general. He introduced a heating system
and a water closet. He designed and commissioned furniture
which revealed his restrained classical taste: a fine sideboard and hall
chairs made to his specification, Wedgwood vases, and a beautiful
front door.[20]

The work added yet another level of turmoil to Turner's already
frantic life. 'Aladdin's palace soon fell to pieces,' he told his friend
William Wells in a letter in November 1820. 'I am turning up my eye
to the sky through the chinks of the Old Room . . . it rains and the
Roof is not finish'd. Day after day have I threatened you not with a
letter, but your mutton, but some demon eclypt Mason, Bricklayer,
carpenter &c & c & c . . . has kept me in constant oscillation from
Twickenham to London, from London to Twit, that I have found the
art of going about doing nothing.'[21]

Turner paid the same level of scrutiny to houseworks as to his
engravings and one imagines the tradespeople coming and going at

Queen Anne Street were subject to the same kind of criticism and comment that his engravers endured. 'Whenever I have been absent either something has been done wrong,' Turner grumbled to Wells, 'or my wayward feelings have made me think so, or that had I been present it would not have occurred, that I am fidgety whenever away. When this feeling has worn itself away, at least, I shall become a better guest.'[22]

Wells was keen that Turner should stay with him and Clara during the refurbishments, at their new home in Mitcham Common. The friendship with William Wells was now close to three decades old, and their lives had much in common. Wells's wife had died in 1807 and he had quickly taken up with a wealthy thirty-seven-year-old, Susanna Thrale, living a 'modern' unmarried life together, as Susanna's disapproving mother, Mrs Piozzi, had put it. But much like Turner's relationship with Sarah Danby, Wells and Susanna had separated and while she retained Ash Grove Cottage, William and his family had sought pastures new.

But in the end Turner moved into his friend James Holworthy's house at 29 York Buildings, New Road, Marylebone, while Holworthy himself was out of town. This was close enough to Queen Anne Street and would enable Turner to keep an eye on his builders' progress. The property came with its own inconveniences, though. Here he discovered himself much visited by Holworthy's neighbour. 'The garrison is well in the New Road,' he related to his chum just before Christmas 1820, 'only besieged Morning and Night . . . by General Miss Croker who has not forgotten the sweets of that delicious wine you gave her at Nine at night, which appear the favourite hours of attack . . . hasten home Dear General or your weak Aid de Camp may be forced to capitulate.'

In the very same letter to Holworthy in which the unwelcome attentions of Miss Croker are related, Turner also broke bad news to his friend. First he related that 'Alas. Poor Sir John Thoroton is no more. Stegler the frame-maker, called yesterday evening to tell you Sir John died last Friday.' But once on the subject of death his mind followed a grim train of thought. 'Again, in the catalogue of death is Naldi, the prima buffa of the opera,' Turner related. 'Visiting his friend Garcia, and inspecting the cooking by steam, he stopt the valve, when the boiler burst and the fragments carried away the upper part of his skull; instant he became a corpse.'[23]

Death loomed larger in Turner's life as the nineteenth century commenced its third decade. The list was growing of those who had nurtured the painter and who had now died. It was not just Angerstein who had gone; of Monro's school both Edridge and Hearne had also departed. Benjamin West had died too, in 1820, and in 1821 Joseph Farington fell to his death down a flight of stairs in a church.

There were tragedies even closer to home too. In 1820 Turner's uncle Joseph Marshall passed away. He ended his days in Sunningwell, where Turner had sketched the local church as a boy.

This death dealt an unpleasant blow. Marshall, who had had no children himself, failed to remember the boy he had nurtured in his will, leaving his entire estate, including four properties in Wapping, to his second wife Mary for the duration of her life. This was the price Turner paid for a dedication to work at the expense of his family. It was not, however, a forfeit Turner was prepared to make without a fight.

Not content to wait for his uncle's wife to die before he might benefit, Turner and his cousin, the solicitor Henry Harpur, immediately challenged the will, pointing out their immediate rights as 'heirs at law' based on the will of their great-grandfather. Within a year a Deed of Partition and Feoffment had been drawn up by the pair that saw Marshall's four properties in New Gravel Lane, Wapping, which had come into the family so many years ago through Joseph Mallord, divided between his two descendants.[24] Turner took properties Nos. 7 and 8, and Harpur Nos. 9 and 10. Marshall's widow meanwhile relinquished the properties in favour of an annuity from them of £20.

Turner's properties included a tavern, the Ship and Bladebone, located at No. 8. Just a month after he had secured their ownership, Turner received his first payment of £36. 15s rent from their tenant, Isaac Hodgeson.[25] The widowed Mary Marshall had evidently given up an annual income far greater than the annuity she settled for.

Turner was assiduous in making sure that his part of the payment to her was made. In the following year he asked his publisher William Cooke to take the money to Mrs Marshall for him while en route to Oxford. A hand-drawn map still exists which was designed to show Cooke how to find Mary Marshall at Sunningwell, where she was living with the Revd Benet's old butler, Mr Lovegrove. Turner's instructions to Cooke are still clearly legible. 'Mrs Marshall; Mr Lovegrove 20 L to pay her,' Turner had noted down for Cooke. Though he also pointed out that Cooke should, before handing over the money, suggest that Turner might invest it on her behalf, asking 'first to say how JMW Turner should do with it for her'. But, crucially,

> if she takes the money she to give you a receipt for the same viz recd of JMWT our lady's day last for 2 years annuity for the Estate at Wapping – signed by Herself and to say how the money is to be sent to her in future – but she must in each year or application send me a letter to that purpose.[26]

Turner and Harpur were not so unusual in the course they took over their uncle's will. Wills were regularly challenged in this period, and the rise of the 'heir at law' who could claim a blood line to supersede the wishes of those who died without issue often served as the subject of caricature and humorous cartoons.[27] But there is huge irony in the fact that Turner's own family would in future adopt the same legal arguments in challenging *his* will as he did his uncle's.

Another man who had treated Turner as his own son, and subsequently resented the painter's lack of attention, was John Narraway in Bristol. Turner's father's great friend was ailing in 1822. News of his demise reached London, and Turner's father made a special visit to Bristol, being 'the last friend who paid a visit to his house'[28] before John Narraway died on 9 December. The hugely successful business he had built was equally doomed. It failed soon after Narraway's death, with his son John declared bankrupt in 1824.

Amid all this miserable news, the hardest blow for Turner however was undoubtedly the death of Walter Fawkes. Debt had proved a hard burden to bear. As early as 1820 there were signs of Fawkes's failing health, which may have been a factor in limiting access to his exhibition in its second year. 'I but yesterday received a card from Mr Fawkes who is very unwell,' Turner had explained to Clara Wells back in the spring of 1820, 'the view of the works . . . is but a private one this year of course . . .'[29]

Turner spent close to a month in Farnley in the winter of 1824, between 19 November and 14 December. The Fawkes followed him back to London just three weeks later, where they took up residence in a new property in Baker Street. They had only been in town two days before 'Mr Parker and Turner came to dinner'. That was a Saturday. The very next day, Sunday 9 January, was foggy and 'nasty' and Turner returned for dinner again.[30] From this point on, a routine developed that saw Turner dine most Sundays with the family. There were moments of greater entertainment. A dinner party to celebrate Fawkes's birthday in March, and then in April the marriage of his son Hawksworth was followed by a wedding party. But by June Fawkes sensed his own end was nigh.

'Walter was this evening condemned to his bed,' his wife recorded on 3 June. 'He kissed me and cried bitterly. Came back several times to kiss and said he knew he never more should get out of it. I passed a wretched night.'[31]

On Sunday 27 August Turner dined at Baker Street for the last time. He left on a trip to The Hague the very next morning and failed to return before Fawkes died on 25 October. Fawkes left seven oil paintings and some 200 watercolours by Turner.

The demise of Fawkes left Turner with a gaping hole in his life. It was not just that he had lost his very greatest patron (and it would not be long before the generous patronage of Leicester would be gone too), but the trudges over Wharfedale, the convivial days at Farnley, the shared projects and the discussion of art that he had enjoyed for more than fifteen years had now also vanished.

'Alas! my good Auld lang sine is gone . . . and I must follow,' Turner wrote bleakly to James Holworthy in January 1826, soon after Fawkes's death.[32] The weight of his grief seemed to be reflected in everything he saw around him: the world was in deep winter and the foolhardiness of mankind all about. Britain's economy was in sudden decline, having suffered what is regarded as the first modern financial crisis, not caused by war nor fashionable speculation, but by deeper rooted market forces. 'The Thames is impeded below bridge [sic]; St James' and the Serpentine both frozen in spite of every attempt to keep them open by folly and rashness,' he informed Holworthy. 'Look at the crash in the commercial world of mercantile speculation, and the check which must follow.'

Turner's relationship with Fawkes's widow and son continued, of course. He still dined with Maria Fawkes from time to time, and Hawksworth remembered Turner every Christmas until the end of his life with game pies, hares or pheasants sent to Queen Anne Street. Turner meanwhile made sure Hawksworth Fawkes was invited to the RA dinners 'in the place of his late father; first because he has uniformly expressed himself in the favour of the Arts . . . but that any mark of attention to the present Mr Fawkes might induce him to give his thoughts likewise to the patronage of the Arts'.[33]

Turner's determination to see the son receive those invitations that the Academy used to extend to his late father bore fruit. In 1827 Turner presented a figure painting at the RA show, *Rembrandt's Daughter*. A study in the juxtaposition of darkness and light, it suggests the painter hovering in the shade, while his daughter reads a letter in a shaft of light, her white dress and the sheet on a bed behind her creating a gash of brilliance in an otherwise darkened room. The press were deeply unimpressed, with Colburn's *New Monthly Magazine* asking whether this was in fact a 'joke upon Rembrandt and upon the taste of his admirers'. Nevertheless Hawksworth Fawkes bought it, the last work by Turner to be added to the Farnley collection. But despite this important gesture, with Walter gone Turner felt unable to return to Wharfedale and instead he took stock of his own situation.

For a start, William senior was showing his age. Sandycombe was now too remote for an old man living alone. In the summer of 1825 there was still some entertaining to be had there. Edward Monro mentioned in his diary of that year that on 9 May he 'Saw Mr Turner's house with Sarah',[34] but the winter of 1825 was a bitter one and Twickenham would not have been easily reached on a frozen river or across snowed-up roads. And so, in 1826, the house was sold and

William Turner senior was installed in Queen Anne Street – it was the end of an era.

Turner's sense of his own mortality began to change around this time. Although the renovations to his gallery had begun with the commercial aspects of his work in mind – a new improved sales room – in due course Queen Anne Street became less a selling exhibition space, and more a museum. It began to assume the role of a repository for a collection of work that, like Beaumont's and Angerstein's, would be left to the nation. This perceived new role for the gallery is also suggested by Turner beginning to buy back his earlier work around this time.

In July 1827, after Sir John Leicester became the next of Turner's great patrons to pass away, Turner bought back two pictures of his own work from the sale of the nobleman's collection. One, described in the catalogue as *View of Dutch Fishing Boats, Sun rising through the Mist*, was without a doubt his *Sun Rising Through Vapour*, originally exhibited in 1807 and sold to Leicester a decade later. The celebrity of the work was such that it was received in the sales room with a round of applause. Turner would have no one buy it but himself and he paid 490 guineas for it. The other painting he bought back was his *Country Blacksmith Disputing Upon the Price of Iron*.

Turner's desire to reacquire his own work is deeply significant. His sense of the importance of his role in the story of art was acute, but whereas up to this point in his career he had been focusing on establishing the value of his work in the present, from this point onward he also set his sights on being remembered in the future.

19.   In search of the King

In the British Library in London, there is a drawing of Turner's friend the chubby sculptor Francis Chantrey, without his trousers on. The sketch was made by the twenty-seven-year-old painter Edwin Landseer, son of the engraver John Landseer and already an Associate of the RA.

Chantrey's déshabillé was the result of a watery encounter. The sculptor was fishing on the River Test in Hampshire, near the village of Houghton, when he 'captured a monster' and a 'bustle of six minutes ensued'. His fellow fishermen followed the action. 'He was however subsequently seen washing and drying some of his undergarments – at last he proceeded slowly towards the Tent, covered with his waterproof cloak, and on arrival stated that he had tumbled in and was obliged to dry his clothes, and the party were bound to believe, that this was the ONLY ACCIDENT that had happened. At all events he dined this day without certain inexpressible conveniences which custom sanctions and decency enjoins.'[1]

This account of a day's fishing and its amusing events is in the Houghton Fishing Club Commonplace book. Its tone is typical of the entries club members regularly made: prankish, full of humour and warmth. It is a reminder of the camaraderie and boyish larks that the middle-aged members of the Royal Academy circle could still enjoy when they chose.

Turner, unlike Chantrey, did not belong to the Houghton club, but his love of fishing took him there as his friend's guest from time to time. Certainly for a few days in the last week of July 1829 Turner joined a party – including ladies – that installed itself at the Boot, a local thatched inn where the beds were described by members of the club as uncomfortable for those without much flesh on their bones, and where one might find oneself suffering from what the local farmer, Brett, referred to as 'the Bum Ague'.

Turner contributed a little sketch to Houghton's book. Almost intentionally childish in its execution, he shows himself fly-fishing in the river, clad in a brown overcoat and a hat, with two onlookers in mid-ground and a couple in the far distance.

However, the fishing was not particularly successful during his holiday. As another guest, Mr Goodenough, recorded, '. . . Gentlemen come to Stockbridge in July thinking that trout and grayling must be as hungry as themselves; not remembering that the fish have not had the benefit of change of air, scene and occupation.' The reason for the poverty of the catch was revealed by one of the club's founders, Mr Barnard, who showed his party 'the nature of a trout's larder'. 'Under his guidance you will pull up a handful of pondweed & find it swarming with the most delicate shrimps,' Goodenough explained. 'You will turn up a board that has been lying in the water, & find its underside studded with lovely little snails . . . Now to suppose that when a trout has the accumulation of epicurean dainties always before him . . . He will for your gratification condescend to take your compound of wool, fur and feather, which you dignify with the appellation of a fly, is to suppose him a far greater simpleton than he really is . . .'[2]

But even if the fish were not biting, it was the companionship and sense of escape that Turner sought at Houghton. For the author of the *Fallacies of Hope*, fishing also offered Turner perspective. For all the hopelessness of human endeavour, the 'trouts will be found in the pool and the gudgen in the shallow', he had once told his friend Holworthy.[3] And in August 1829 Turner had some cause to consider *his* endeavours had been in vain. For by 1829 it must have been clear to him that his ten-year campaign to woo the endorsement of the new monarch George IV had been entirely lost.

His quest to win the patronage of George had begun when the latter was still Regent, a title he had acquired in 1811 when George III succumbed once again to insanity. In 1819 Turner had exhibited his enormous canvas depicting *Richmond Hill on the Prince Regent's Birthday*. But that painting proved as unsuccessful in hooking its intended as that 'compound of wool, fur and feather' of which the trout in the River Test were so disdainful.

The Prince Regent was a controversial figure. He was a man whose lavish and indulgent lifestyle had, by the end of the eighteenth century, contributed to his vast debts as well as his huge waistline. He was a serial womanizer, and his association with the pleasure gardens and gambling dens of Brighton, where he had converted a modest lodge into a Marine Pavilion, marked the apex of Georgian libertarianism. The Regent's taste for opulence and the exotic would inform his vision for the British monarchy more generally. His ambition was for a court with a grandeur and vivacity akin to Louis XIV's at Versailles. Hand in hand with his desire to recreate something of the Sun King's glamour came a penchant for pre-revolutionary French art and furniture. George collected French art on a scale unprecedented by a British monarch: he acquired furniture from Versailles and artefacts including a clock and pieces of Sèvres porcelain that had once belonged to Madame de Pompadour.

There was sufficient patriotism in Turner, and certainly enough of the businessman in him, to understand the opportunity that George presented. As George became monarch in 1820, the potential benefit to the creative communities became apparent. He began an ambitious refurbishment programme of the royal palaces that saw the architects and artists of the day clambering over one another to win major commissions. The new King's purse seemed bottomless: he was spending hundreds of thousands of pounds restyling his palaces in a new English rococo manner, replacing early Georgian restraint with bright textiles, and embellishing rooms with gilded curves and scrolls.

Turner decided against depicting the lavish Coronation in 1821, the pageantry of which was marred by the fact that the King's estranged wife, Queen Caroline, was refused admittance, a public humiliation so great for her that it prompted her almost immediate decline and subsequent death. However, Turner did join the group of artists who travelled to Edinburgh in August 1822 when the King's visit was the highlight of a festival of Scotland, orchestrated by Sir Walter Scott.

Afforded special access by Scott and his associates, Turner began a speculative series of commemorative paintings featuring the King's progress through various events, from the Provost's banquet to his attendance at a service at St Giles. But he left the project incomplete when an actual commission from the King was forthcoming later that year, thanks less to his own endeavours and more to the continuing admiration of the R A's new president, Sir Thomas Lawrence.

As part of his refurbishment scheme the new King was restyling St James's Palace and, on the advice of Lawrence, Turner was chosen to make a pendant to an existing painting of *The Glorious First of June 1794* by de Loutherbourg. It was to be another depiction of the Battle of Trafalgar.

The resultant huge canvas, *The Battle of Trafalgar, 21 October 1805*, was delivered to the King two years later. But it was not met with the kind of praise that Turner had hoped.

He had worked hard to present a multi-layered picture, wrought with symbolism. One of the ship's masts, bearing Nelson's white vice-admiral's flag, is falling as Nelson himself lies dying below. Meanwhile the code flags spell 'd-u-t-y' – famously the theme of Nelson's Trafalgar signal and his final words.

But much like his other depictions of battle, Turner chose to foreground the tragic toll of war, rather than emphasize its heroic aspects. The *Victory* is placed in the centre of the canvas, its billowing, shredded sails illuminated by a golden sun. The vast ship dwarfs the human action played out on its decks. The death of Nelson is depicted in miniature here. But the terrible death throes of the ordinary sailors in the water are seen clearly, in the lower foreground of the canvas. When the picture was hung, it was these writhing bodies that thrust up against the plane of vision.

Turner compresses time in the picture, showing events that occurred at different stages of the battle in one single sweep. On the right the French *Redoubtable,* from which Nelson was shot, is already sinking, although she in fact went down in the storm after the battle.

But there is something else quite strange about the work. And this is the very still nature of the *Victory* herself. She is high and almost static on a glassy sea, movement created only by the thrashing of other ships around her, and her own billowing canvas. For a painter more than able to capture a sea and ships in violent motion, this is as if she were a ship in a bottle, quite frozen, just her sails folding and swirling in a dance around her.[4]

The officials at St James's found themselves in knots over the accuracy of the work. Turner's compression of time was considered inappropriate by some. Others saw fault with the accuracy of the depiction of the ship. And there was concern with the issue that ignited Sir George Beaumont – Turner's finish.

The matter was delicate. Turner was after all acknowledged to be the greatest painter of his day by many, and was the recommendation of the Royal Academy. And so it was to Lawrence that the King's officials wrote.

'My Dear Sir Thomas,' wrote Sir Charles Long, Baron Farnborough, 'I do not know whether you have seen Mr Turner's picture during its progress – I had not seen it for some time till I came to St James yesterday – I do not know whether he considers it finished, but it appears to require more to be done to it, & particularly to want force & effect.'[5]

It is not insignificant that Farnborough had been a founder member of the British Institution with Beaumont. But he was not the sole member of the King's entourage picking fault with the painting. Across eleven days Turner made adjustments to the painting in a bid to meet the comments of various members of the nobility and admiralty.

The British Institution was quick to capitalize on the controversy. In June 1824 it launched a competition offering prizes of £200 and £100 for the two best sketches of the Battle of Trafalgar, and the following year a further prize of £500 for the best finished picture, an initiative that at least one painter of the day suggested was designed purposefully to pique Turner.[6]

Lawrence found himself playing piggy-in-the-middle, not just in having to handle the concerns of the client, but also in having to deal with the terms of the painter. Turner had delivered a particularly large canvas and, as ever, was keen to be paid at an appropriate level. 'I have now received a letter from the Lord Chamberlain's Office's stating that the amount for my picture will be paid upon demand,'

Turner had informed Lawrence. 'I therefore feel the necessity of
again asking you if you do authorize me in demanding the 600 gs you
mentioned, or if on your warmth for the service of the Arts you wd
exceed (in your wishes) the terms proposed: Do pray have the goodness to tell me . . .'[7]

In the end actions spoke louder than words. The King expressed
his desire to remove Turner's *Trafalgar* from St James's Palace
altogether. This was politically sensitive. It would be read as a humiliating rejection of Turner and the Academy. But the King was
apparently oblivious to the fact that the act might also fuel concerns
among *his* critics, since it could be seen as yet another example of
wasteful behaviour. Baron Farnborough employed a deft piece of
diplomacy. He came up with a solution that put all parties in a favourable light.

Farnborough suggested that not just Turner's painting, but de
Loutherbourg's too should be 'removed from the Place where they
hung' and 'that they should be placed in some public institution'. And
he identified a brilliant opportunity. In the wake of the foundation of
the National Gallery in 1824, a National Gallery of Naval Art had
been opened in the Painted Hall of the Royal Naval Hospital at
Greenwich. The King's donation of two major pieces placed him in
the vanguard of a new spirit of public patronage.

In spite of this elegant solution, however, Baron Farnborough still
had reservations about Turner's painting. 'I cannot help submitting
to your consideration whether before Mr Turner's picture goes to the
Hospital it would not be desirable that he should just look at it & consider whether it would not be very advantageous to the Picture to
give the ships a little more solidity – I leave the matter? entirely to
your judgement – but as you know I think highly of his talent I could
not help supporting what appears to me would be a great improvement . . .'[8]

The *Trafalgar* was not transferred to Greenwich until 1829. The
uncertainty over its fate had hovered over Turner for half a decade.
After the triumph of Fawkes's exhibition of his watercolours in 1819,
and the excitement he felt about Rome and Venice in the same year,
the 1820s generally represent a less satisfactory time for Turner. Even

his kinder critics were conceding that his work had hit an impasse, and was failing to progress. Turner's tours to the Continent in the mid-1820s seemed to bear little fruit. His visit to Holland in 1825, for example, on which he made *hundreds* of small pencil sketches, failed to result in an immediate finished work. And yet he must have been all too aware of the rise in this decade of John Constable, who many considered was making the gains in landscape painting that had once been attributed to Turner alone. The ascendance of his rival culminated in 1831, when Constable, serving on the Academy's hanging committee, actually removed one of Turner's paintings – *Caligula's Palace and Bridge*, to replace it with his own *Salisbury Cathedral from the Meadows* – an act for which Turner teased Constable unmercifully at dinner with General Phipps in Mount Street, his mirth probably concealing a more deep-felt concern.

What one does see in the 1820s, however, is Turner's conscious engagement with those involved in the new aesthetic wave that the King was spearheading. He reinforced his friendship with the architect Jeffrey Wyatville, the nephew of Turner's former employer James Wyatt. Wyatville was one of the pioneers of the English rococo style which the new King was so keen to promote.

Wyatville was Turner's next-door neighbour at Harley Street. He had also worked on the Cassiobury estate, where he had designed 'cottages ornés' for Lord Essex. The painter and architect must have known each other well, and Turner had certainly made a point of sketching one of Wyatville's buildings, a picturesque 'cottage orné' on the Duke of Bedford's Devon estate, Endsleigh Cottage, during his West Country tour of 1814.

But significantly in 1824 Wyatville won the commission for one of George IV's massive refurbishments, the remodelling of Windsor Castle. He had been given a set of rooms in the Winchester Tower at Windsor Castle and from 1824 was installed there. From the moment Wyatville took up his residency, Turner made a habit of visiting him annually, his sketchbooks testimony to the days strolling in the environs.

Turner, so attuned to the changes in taste going on around him, had been making attempts for some time to arrange a visit to Belvoir

Castle, where another of the new rococoists, and member of the
Wyatt dynasty, James Wyatt's son Matthew Cotes Wyatt, had decorated the Elizabeth Saloon entirely according to the new revival Louis
XIV fashion. Turner's contact there had been the Revd John Thoroton,
who, despite being a man of the cloth, had overseen the fanciful
designs of Belvoir for the Duke of Bedford. But 'alas, poor John
Thoroton is no more', Turner had written to Holworthy in December 1820, 'so adieu to all my prospects again at Belvoir'.

But there were yet more exponents of the new wave, not least the
architect John Nash, who had been working for the new King since
1815. He had been responsible for the redevelopment of Brighton
and specifically the conversion of the Regent's Marine Pavilion, into
the yet more flamboyant, lavish, and exotic Royal Pavilion. He
was also the architect of Regent's Park and Regent Street, and in
1825 he had won the prestigious commission to refurbish Bucking-
ham Palace.

In the summer of 1827 Turner visited Nash on the Isle of Wight,
where the architect had built himself a fanciful neo-gothic mansion,
East Cowes Castle.

His decision to return to the Isle of Wight at this particular
moment was opportune. It coincided with a royal event. The August
of 1827 would see the second ever Cowes regatta, but it would be the
first time that the King had endorsed the event, by presenting a cup
there. As such it was an event with strong topical appeal.

George IV was a passionate yachtsman. He had joined the Yacht
Club in 1817, two years after it had been founded in that well-known
establishment the Thatched House Tavern in St James's. When
George ascended to the throne, the club rose with him to become
known as the Royal Yacht Club.

Cowes was a favourite haunt of the Royal Yacht Club, whose
members included the son of one of Turner's earliest patrons, Lord
Yarborough, who died in 1823. The Second Baron Yarborough was
in the habit of holding court at the clubhouse and was certainly there
when Turner made his way to the island for a second time, an occasion when the whole place was buzzing with excitement.

On Monday 13 August 'his majesty's cup was sailed for', the *Mirror* keenly reported. The streets and homes of the island were totally deserted early in the morning, as everyone on the island headed 'on the road to Cowes', where the harbour was 'filled with the sails of divers countries and studded with anchored yachts, decked in their distinguishing flags'. So spectacular was it that the *Mirror* even published a poem to commemorate the event, which began:

> The crowded yachts were anchor'd in the roads
> To view the contest for a Kingly prize
> Voluptuous Beauty smiled on Britain's Lords,
> And fashion dazzled with her thousand dyes;

Turner sketched the day's activities avidly. In addition to drawing in his sketchbook, he made more than forty chalk sketches on loose sheets of paper that charted the events. His attention to fact was typical. He jotted down the names of some of the boats, their colours and owners. At some point he joined the throng of spectators who were offshore in little boats and drew from there.

Though Turner had clearly understood the opportunity the Cowes regatta might offer him, he had perhaps not been prepared for the level of excitement and sense of moment that he encountered there. The event was so thrilling that he persuaded Nash to commission two oil paintings, apparently spontaneously. This is suggested by a letter Turner sent his father shortly after the event, asking for more supplies since suddenly and unexpectedly he was extending his stay.

'I shall want more light Trouzers,' he wrote, '– and so I do of White Waistcoats. I ought to have 4, but I have but 2, and only 1 Kerseymere [woollen twill trousers].'[9]

It was not just clothing that Turner was going to need, but canvas to work up a series of proposals for Nash. And so once again his father found himself in receipt of another instruction, this time for canvas 'size 6 feet by 4 ft . . . I want the canvas only. I don't want the stretching frame . . . I want some scarlet Lake and dark Lake and Burnt Umber in powder from Newman one ounce each.'

When the canvas arrived, Turner cut it into two and, in a painting room that Nash made available to his guest, painted on each half a series of oil sketches that provided different options for him and his client to discuss. From the start he was proposing two scenes, one featuring the regatta in full flow on the sea, another featuring the mouth of the River Medina, where the regatta begins, and where the public assembled to see it. But as a tribute to his new patron he made sure that Nash's home is featured, though distantly, in both. And when he came to title the finished picture he was clear to mention his patron's home.

In *East Cowes Castle, the Seat of J. Nash, Esq.: the Regatta Beating to Windward* the main subject of the painting is a stream of yachts leaning sharply, their sails exaggerated as they move through a choppy sea on which Turner, typically, has imagined himself also afloat. The seat to which the painting's title alludes is only faintly visible. The sails of the yachts part to reveal it, sitting high on a promontory, minuscule and distant. *East Cowes Castle, the Seat of J. Nash, Esq.: The Regatta Starting for their Moorings* is Claudian in its composition. The Medina has been transformed into a serene harbour, a high sun reflected in its waters, framed by a throng of spectators sitting on the banks and crammed into little rowing boats.

The enjoyable social atmosphere at East Cowes Castle was a real tonic for Turner. Earlier that year he had been complaining to Holworthy about a sudden weight loss, and one gets a sense that for all his continuing business and social engagements, he was missing a degree of informal companionship. But the company at East Cowes Castle revived him, and a new-found energy and lust for life is reflected in the sketches he made of the house party there. Significantly these sketches reveal an artist immersed in the subtle tenor of his time. There is undoubtedly a rococo sentiment in these drawings, quite unlike Turner's earlier work, that seems utterly of that moment.

As he strolled through the castle's wooded grounds, Turner took blue paper and sketched – with black ink and white chalk – house guests picnicking and lounging beneath gothic crenellations and fanciful towers. He depicted his impressions of the convivial goings-on inside the castle too. Again on blue paper, but this time using gouache in vivid reds, blues, bright whites and sharp blacks, he depicts ladies in the drawing room and music parties in the library. From these at once slight and yet deeply potent images Turner conjures the swish of

35. *East Cowes Castle, the Seat of J. Nash, Esq., the Regatta Beating to Windward*, 1828. Turner witnessed the Cowes Regatta in 1827, the first year in which George IV endorsed the race with a cup.

36. William Parrott, *J. M. W. Turner at the Royal Academy, Varnishing Day*. Turner became known for making considerable changes on varnishing days. Here he is working on, probably, *Mercury and Argus* in 1836. His trusty umbrella is in the left of the frame.

37. Engraving by H. R. Cook after Thomas Phillips, *George Wyndham, 3rd Earl of Egremont*, 1835. Egremont became another great patron of Turner.

38. *Boulevard des Italiens, Paris, c. 1832.* This view was published in Turner's *Annual Tour, 1835: Wanderings by the Seine.* It reminds us of the delight Turner could take in people and cityscape despite his overriding relationship with landscape.

39. *Lowestoffe Lighthouse, c. 1827.* This vignette of the lighthouse at Lowestoft was part of a series of eight engravings that Turner made of the Norfolk and Suffolk coast but never published.

40. *The Old Library: a Vase of Lilies, Dahlias and Other Flowers, 1827.* In his 'rococo' moment Turner delivered a vibrant series of interior sketches of Petworth House that revealed a new palette of bright and often primary colours.

41. *The Lighthouse at Marseilles from the Sea, c.* 1828. The heat in the south of France was almost too much for Turner, who may have been asthmatic. The few coloured sketches he made, however, reveal how strongly the colours and landscape impressed him.

42. *Dudley, Worcester,* 1830–33. British industry was clearly a source of pride for Turner, who celebrated the energy and toil of the Black Country in this view.

43. *Ulysses Deriding Polyphemus – Homer's Odyssey*, 1829. Preparatory sketches in a book dated 1807 suggest that Turner mulled his subject matter over for a good twenty years before he finally executed this painting.

44. Engraving by Francis Hall, after George Richmond, *John Ruskin*, 1857. Ruskin described Turner's work as the 'entire direction of my life's energies'. However, even he found Turner's late mythological paintings problematic.

45. Richard Doyle, *Turner Painting One of His Pictures*, 1846. In the 1840s the negative criticism of Turner's work reached its zenith. He was regularly accused of daubing.

46. *Undine Giving the Ring to Massaniello, Fisherman of Naples,* exhibited 1846. The story of the water nymph Undine, who marries a human and takes on the burdens of the world, was written by the German Friedrich de la Motte Fouqué.

47. *Falls of the Rhine at Schaffhausen – Distant View,* 1841. When he was sixty-six, Turner returned to Switzerland and made a series of watercolours that revealed a new freedom of expression. He found a new fragility in the landscape around him, yet his sense of wonderment at the jewel-like beauty of the world is perhaps at its most intense in these later works.

48. *Peace —Burial at Sea*, exhibited 1842. Referring to the death of his friend and rival the painter David Wilkie, Turner again returns to an exploration of the creative legacy of the artist.

49. *War. The Exile and the Rock Limpet*, exhibited 1842. Exploring the
legacy of a man of war, Turner observes that for all his empire-building,
Napoleon's final dominion was a mere rock pool on St Helena.

50. Alexander McInnes, *House near Battersea Bridge (The Residence of J. M. W. Turner, RA)*, 1852. In this depiction of the home Turner shared with Mrs Booth in Chelsea, the artist has imagined Turner at the property's gate.

51. George Jones, *Turner's Body Lying in State, 29 December 1851*. Turner's dear friend captured the image of the artist lying in state in the Queen Anne Street Gallery, Jones suggesting light emanating from the coffin itself. The woman sitting in the left of canvas is perhaps the heartbroken Hannah Danby.

silk dresses on the warm velvet of chaises-longues and there is a palpable sense of joy.

These images reveal the distance Turner has already travelled from
the meticulous, less populated, and highly detailed interiors he had
made of Farnley. The Georgian classicism and no-nonsense honesty
associated with Farnley is replaced by something far more flamboyant. There is an abandon in these sketches, evocative of rooms
resounding with laughter and games of hide-and-seek. The lack of
attention to actual detail, and Turner's reliance on the turn of his
brush simply to suggest, is indicative of the route his art was now
travelling.

Just weeks after Turner left John Nash's gothic home he was at
another huge country seat, this time Petworth House, the late seventeenth-century mansion of Lord Egremont, where he arrived in
October 1827. Turner had met Lord Egremont in July of that year at
the sale of the recently deceased Lord Leicester's effects. While Turner
was there to buy back his *Sun Rising Through Vapour*, Egremont bought
Turner's view of Leicester's home, *Tabley, Cheshire, the Seat of Sir J. F.
Leicester, Bart.: Calm Morning*. It was perhaps at this meeting it was
suggested that Turner should return to Petworth.

It had been a good decade since Turner's last major visit. Petworth's
reputation as a cultural 'open house' where artists might spend time
enjoying the third Earl of Egremont's hospitality and use of his generous home and estate to paint and draw had become legendary. The
penniless Benjamin Robert Haydon stayed there in November 1826
and wrote in his diary something of his experience.

After being received by Egremont in a manner that was 'frank and
noble', Haydon 'sketched and studied all day'. Haydon was overwhelmed by Egremont's lack of ceremony and egalitarian attitudes.
'He has placed me in one of the most magnificent bedrooms I ever
saw! It speaks more for what he thinks of my talents than any thing
that ever happened to me! The bed curtains are difft, coloured velvets
let in on white satin. The walls green damask, sofas, easy chairs, carpet, & a beautiful view of the Park out of the high window . . . There
is plenty, but not absurd profusion – good wines, but not extravagant
waste. Everything solid, liberal, rich & English. At 74 he still shoots

daily, comes home wet through, and is as active & looks as well as many men of 50.'[10]

In many ways Egremont and Turner were cut from the same cloth. They shared a down-to-earth lack of fuss, a love of outdoors, a delight in female companionship, and above all spoke their minds and stuck to their guns.

Egremont's wealth was of course on an utterly different scale. His inherited estate was enormous, his home huge, and his stables housed 300 horses. For all his lack of ceremony, there was no doubt that Egremont was an aristocrat, with a sense of grandeur, who 'reigned . . . with great authority and influence'. He was a man who in his own way held court.

Turner realized that the rococo abandon, the courtly style inspired by the King that he had explored at East Cowes Castle, was also pertinent to Petworth, with its liberal atmosphere and handsome interiors. Across the course of a month, he embarked on a series of sketches with a fervour, enthusiasm and industry that – even by his remarkable standards – seems exceptional. Continuing the spirit of the series of interiors he had begun in Cowes, and with varying degree of detail, he depicted the major rooms of the sumptuous mansion. Turner found new pleasure in ornament and decoration. In depicting the White and Gold Room with its Van Dyck portraits, he lovingly picked out the gilded plasterwork, the red chairs and the huge mirrors. With a new freedom he expressed the charm of the White Library, its far red walls giving way to a sunlit enfilade, the beading picked out in its white vaulted ceiling. Turner's depictions of the house go on and on: the Somerset Room, the Red Room, the Grand Staircase, the Square Dining Room and the North (Picture) Gallery. In all cases he meticulously recorded the paintings on the walls, the architectural details, and the decorative motifs. He picked out items that lent themselves to the particularly bright, pure palette that he was employing: two huge blue and white Chinese vases framing a console table, or a joyous vase of flowers with gaudy red and yellow dahlias complemented by white lilies. He showed the early morning light flooding into the house, and the picture gallery at night, with Flaxman's statue of *Michael Overcoming Satan* hauntingly caught in a shaft of moonlight. He depicted the house-guests: a woman at a piano, a group of men playing billiards; a vicar with his back to the fire; a man in a red uniform.

Compared to the hunting, shooting and fishing that had been on offer in Farnley, both Cowes and Petworth offered a different country house experience. One gets a sense of how much Turner enjoyed the female company available, particularly in Petworth. He notes a lady in black seated on a pink sofa; a woman in a yellow dress; a man and woman engaged in a game of backgammon; a lady in red reclining on a couch and chatting to a companion.

In these images the people take on a ghostly, insubstantial aspect. It is a phantom-like quality that emerges more fully in his later work, but is already suggested in the Petworth sketches. Turner offers the house and its furnishings as robust, solid and timeless, while those inhabiting the rooms seem like mere colourful shadows, just passing through.

But in his work at Petworth, Turner also provided a very strong sense of two worlds, one downstairs in the public rooms, another upstairs, behind closed doors. It was in the old library, up a rickety and unadorned back staircase, that those artists staying at the house often erected their easels and were allowed to study some of the treasures from Egremont's collection. Here Turner captured some of his peers, peering over prints and canvases. And here he shows one painter, standing at an easel before the huge, arched north-east-facing window in the old library, a gaggle of women looking on.

The attention of women was not something Turner was inclined to rebuff, and some have considered this another example of Turner depicting himself – though this suggestion is at odds with other accounts of Turner's habit of locking the old library door when he was working there, unless it was Egremont himself who wanted to come and see him.

'I was always at my grandfather's heels,' one of Egremont's granddaughters recounted years later. 'As he went along the passage to the rooms set apart as Turner's studio, his slow sliding step (to say nothing of the innumerable train of dogs that always accompanied him) informed the great painter of the approach of his host, and he then unbolted the door, which he always kept locked against other visitors.'[11] This account would also lend credence to another story about a practical joke that Chantrey played on his friend while also staying in the house. He apparently imitated Egremont's strange slow sliding step so well that Turner opened the door, much to the amusement of both the perpetrator and butt of the jest.[12]

Turner captured far more of the goings-on upstairs at the grand stately home than when painting in the old library. He also made a series of studies of the bedrooms at Petworth, sometimes empty, sometimes not.

He reveals one room with a bed hung with green curtains. An empty armchair awaits, some clothes hang from the door of a wardrobe. In another it is a bed hung with red curtains, its crumpled white sheets recently vacated. A bed hung with yellow silk is also apparently empty. But not the blue bed Turner painted, where the sugar pink skin of its incumbent is all too evident, as are the piles of clothes carelessly discarded on a sofa. Then Turner returns to the green bedroom to find it occupied by a lady in black, her back to the artist, another man hovering in the doorway. And then he peers beyond the yellow-curtained bed to discover a naked woman sitting at her mirror, tying up her hair.

These astonishingly intimate depictions of bedroom scenes are the successors to the watercolour sketch Turner made in Berne. Did he peep? Was he the recipient of hospitality that included local prostitutes? Or were these open-minded high-class female guests who took men to their beds in the bohemian atmosphere of Petworth? Perhaps these sketches were examples purely of Turner's imagination, running wilder.

There is something reminiscent of the work of the French early eighteenth-century Antoine Watteau in the sensibilities of both the Cowes and Petworth drawings. It is not just the fascination with social gatherings that the French artist produced, which became defined as *fêtes galantes*. It is also a new interest that Turner seems to be displaying in fashion and surface detail: the shimmering silks and the sugar-pig colours, a composition of social interaction that is symphonic in its balance of colour, gesture and the arrangement of figures. Again it seems to be a resonance that speaks to the prevailing aesthetic of the moment, not least because Watteau was an artist collected by George IV.

The work of Antoine Watteau, which had largely gone out of favour by the mid-eighteenth century, was enjoying a renaissance in the second quarter of the nineteenth, thanks to the influence of George IV. When he was still Regent, George had lent two Watteaus to the Royal Institution in 1818. And he had bought a third, *La Surprise*, just a year later.[13]

Turner's admiration for the French rococo painter was expressed in a homage to the artist he painted in 1822, entitled *What You Will!* It took from the French painter the juxtaposition of a rich autumnal landscape with white statuary and women in silk gowns, the highlights of which were also depicted in white. Watteau's expressive use of white – a trait in Turner's own work that had regularly seen him scolded by critics – was part of the appeal of the artist to him. And Turner must have been delighted when his friend Chantrey bought the painting.

A number of Turner's circle were also collecting Watteau,[14] including the banker poet Samuel Rogers, who owned five paintings by the French artist. Turner would collaborate with Rogers from 1826 until 1834, providing vignettes for his collections of poems: *Italy*, for publication in 1830, and a further publication, *Poems*, published in 1834. The other illustrator Rogers used for these projects was Turner's colleague the painter Thomas Stodhard – another huge admirer of Watteau's work.

Poor Thomas Stothard, who had recently illustrated Boccaccio's *Decameron* in Watteauesque manner, found himself the subject of Turner's wry sense of humour in April 1828. This was when Turner showed work quite specifically referencing Watteau: *Boccaccio Relating the Tale of the Birdcage*. Turner had produced genre paintings to rival David Wilkie years earlier, and now felt the need to remind Stodhard just who was the real heir of Watteau.

It is hardly surprising that in the genre for which he was arguably most famed, marine art, Turner would also be keen to put newcomers firmly in their place. And this is exactly what he did in 1827 when Turner also fired a shot over the bows of the younger painter Clarkson Stansfield. Stansfield, a former sailor who had served with the Royal Navy and the East India Company, was working as a set painter. But his ambitions and talent were clear. In 1826 he attempted an oil called *Throwing the Painter* (the painter being a nautical rope) but had failed to finish the work in time for submission to the RA show that year. In a gesture that reveals how one might take painters out of the schoolroom but discover that the schoolroom never quite leaves some painters, Augustus Wall Callcott, Turner's friend and follower, had rather childishly referred to this failure by extending the title of his own picture that year: *Dutch Fishing Boats running foul in the endeavour to board, and missing the painter rope.* In 1827 Turner contributed to the joke, submitting a painting depicting a group of women in a little row boat heading out to a larger vessel, *Now for the Painter (Rope.) – Passengers Going on Board.* The reference to his own status was immediately appreciated by the press, with the *London Literary Gazette* declaring, 'Now for the artist!'

Despite the *Gazette*'s praise, many of the critics that year saw *Now for the Painter* as representing Turner's increasing tendency to depart from what was considered credible. His heightened colour, and desire for effect, were placing imagination over observation. The sensibility that placed the artist's response to the subject above the faithful depiction of it was considered inappropriate by many, not least the *New Monthly Magazine and Literary Journal*, which noted that 'Mr Turner's pictures are everything they should be except natural.'

To the twenty-first-century eye *Now for the Painter* looks far from a departure from what can be considered a credible reality. But there were other paintings that Turner began to produce around this time that nearly 200 years later still feel like an adventurous response to the natural world – they were far closer to the loose, suggestive techniques he was using in his colour sketches, and with an emphasis on certain colour schemes that suggest a specific agenda. Paintings he made for the Carved Room at Petworth fit into this category.

While at the estate in late 1827, Egremont commissioned Turner to make a series of unusually shaped paintings to fit in bespoke panels in

Petworth's Carved Room, where Grinling Gibbons's delicate carvings curl around huge full-length portraits. Each panel was a particularly long and narrow landscape format, measuring 24 by 57 inches, thus extending the aspect width ratio Turner had explored in his Thames views painted on wood nearly two decades earlier. The paintings were to be estate views, continuing the work Turner had begun in 1809 when he painted *Petworth, Sussex, the Seat of the Earl of Egremont: Dewy Morning*.

Turner delivered two views of Petworth's parklands, and two views associated with Egremont's achievements outside his own estate: a view of the Chichester Canal and one of Brighton Pier, ventures in which he had been an investor.

Different versions of the works reveal that Turner delivered an initial series that was installed in the room for a trial period, before a final, amended set of pictures was delivered. One painting from this series, *Petworth Park, Tillington Church in the Distance*, suggests the artist experimenting with the unique shape of canvas he had to work on. Turner depicts the view from the Carved Room, out over the terrace towards the park beyond. He shows Lord Egremont's faithful dogs launching out from the house after their master, while the light casts long shadows from the deer grazing nearby. But the terrace itself curves upwards at the left and right of frame, suggesting that Turner may have used a scioptic ball, a kind of early wide-angle or fish-eye lens and a camera obscura to capture this image and project it across the unusually wide, panoramic format. Certainly Egremont's neighbour 'Mad' Jack Fuller, whose purpose-built observatory at Rose Hill was complete by this time, and which Turner had visited around 1818 for Cooke's *Views in Sussex*, had this kind of equipment, and Turner's natural inclination to problem-solving might have seen it as particularly useful for the task in hand. The convex lens in the scioptic ball also intensified the brightness of the colour of the image projected, providing a reflection more intense than the reality itself, while the aperture admitting the light to the camera obscura governed the level of clarity with which the image was conveyed. These attributes were utterly pertinent to Turner's fascination with and exploration of sunlight and his experiment with distinct versus less distinct imagery.

The different versions of the views for the Carved Room reflect the vigorous discussions Turner had with Egremont, sometimes erudite and sometimes playful. While the latter's granddaughter remembered a conversation that went 'far above' her head, the pre-Raphaelite painter George Price Boyce recounted an anecdote regarding the depiction of Brighton Pier. Turner had introduced some floating vegetables into the sea and a debate between the painter and his patron saw a bucket and some vegetables being summoned to test the painter's science.

In the end the versions that were chosen had some alteration to detail. The dogs were removed from the view over the park in favour of a cricket match, and the number of deer were multiplied to reflect their genuine abundance. In the later version of the view of the lake, a stag is also introduced, drinking its waters. Those Egremont chose were also defined by the dominance of yellow. Compared to the other versions that Turner presented, which used a varied palette with skies a mix of creamy blues, gold and pink – paler versions of the bright preparatory gouaches he made in his sketchbook of the parkland – the chosen works are in effect studies in yellow and as such adhere as a group, but were consequently disliked by some visitors. Boyce for one thought they were of a 'crude yellow sort'.[15]

However, the emphasis on yellow in these paintings may well reflect Turner's growing interest in the properties of light and the latest scientific thinking about optics at the time. Back in 1822 when Turner had followed the new King on his progress through Edinburgh, he had made the point of acquainting himself with the optical theories of the Scottish scientist David Brewster, the recent inventor of the very popular kaleidoscope. He had actually attempted to meet Brewster in person, but though he had failed, the company he was keeping while in Scotland, particularly the circle of intellectuals associated with Turner's friend John Thomson of Duddingston, had acquainted him with the latter's latest scientific discoveries.

Brewster believed that there were three primary colours in light, red, blue and yellow, none of which could be decomposed. The discovery of yellow as a primary colour was a recent one, and what is more Brewster had suggested that it had a particular prominence in the spectrum. Turner had begun experimenting in his watercolours with the interplay of primary colours, and their combination to make secondary hues, particularly in his dealing with sky and water around this time. And it may well have been Brewster's theory about the spectral significance of yellow that reinvigorated Turner's own interest in giving dominance to that colour in his palette.[16]

The dominance of this pervading golden light in the Carved Room paintings may also have simply reflected Egremont's personal penchant for the colour. Certainly after these paintings were delivered Egremont became associated with a love of yellow, as his granddaughter would recount. This love prompted a challenge to Turner to paint a figure study in yellow, which he duly did in the form of *Jessica*, a reference to the character in Shakespeare's *Merchant of Venice*, reaching out to close the shutters of a window.[17]

But Egremont's predilection for yellow to one side, Turner's sketches at Cowes and Petworth reveal an artist otherwise experimenting with a highly coloured palette and unmediated primary colours. Turner was pushing the coloration in his finished canvases to a new height. And in order to do so further, Turner craved the vivid light and bold colour of the south once again. It was time for him to return to Italy.

20. Brilliance

Since Turner's first visit to Rome in 1819, British artists had continued to visit the city with enthusiasm. So just as Thomas Lawrence had been able to make arrangements for him previously, Turner had no shortage of colleagues in situ willing to do the same again. The family of Turner's friend and follower Augustus Wall Callcott had used an apartment in the Piazza Mignanelli for some years, close to the Spanish Steps. Turner's friend Charles Eastlake was making use of it in 1828, and Callcott's wife Maria had already 'given such a remarkable account' of it that Turner was looking forward to staying there with Eastlake. He planned to arrive in Rome again at the beginning of September 1828.

This was the earliest possible date that Turner could envisage getting away that year. As he had noted previously, 'in the Spring when the trout begin to move, I am fixed by Exhibition's log', and only in the summer could he 'oil my wings for a flight'.[1]

Turner set off in early August 1828 and reached Paris by the 11th, when he wrote ahead to Eastlake whom he jollily addressed as 'Signor Carlo', reporting happily that he was 'at last off from the loadstone London'.[2]

The roads to Paris were packed that summer, as were the rivers, now the main European arteries for that popular addition to modern travel, the steamboat. Turner probably went from Dieppe to Rouen by coach, before availing himself of steam along the Seine to the French capital. He would have found himself in good company. The British love affair with France had not abated. If anything it had grown and the public transport was packed with tourists. 'Our passage to Rouen was extremely amusing,' an American traveller had noted that July, 'although we had a crowded boat, such numbers of English flocking to Paris'.[3]

Turner had been in Paris briefly just two years earlier in 1826, after a sketching trip along the Loire, and had made several sketches there. But his exploration of the city had not yet been exploited from a commercial point of view. And in 1828 he had no intention of recording the city further. His stopover at Paris was purely practical, and was probably determined by his inclination to once again follow the family tradition of not spending money unnecessarily. British travellers at the time could bypass the expense of paying for a British passport to France and Italy by acquiring a French one from the French Ambassador in London, 'at whose house they are obtained gratis, a trifling present to the porter excepted'.[4] This cheaper alternative did, however, necessitate a stop in the French capital, where further signatures for passage on to Italy had to be obtained from the British, Sardinian and Austrian Ambassadors, as well as the Pope's Nunzio and official stamps at the Préfecture de Police and the Office Ministre des Affaires Étrangères. Turner may have felt this extra bother worthwhile, given he had a number of colleagues in the city at the time, including the painter David Roberts. He had also befriended the once-exiled Louis Philippe, Duc d'Orléans, when both men were living in Twickenham, and it is likely that the latter would have provided Turner with plenty of potential introductions to Parisian society should he have wished.

Typical of Turner, by the time he reached Paris he had already changed his plans and had decided to take a detour. He broke the news to Eastlake sheepishly. 'I venture to apologise for not being with you by the time I expected to be in Rome and likewise with you and no 12 Piazza Mignanelli,' he wrote. 'I cannot say when I can arrive in Rome owing to my passing . . . by way of Antibes.'

It is clear why southern France should have appealed to Turner. It was undiscovered by artists, and tourists for that matter, and generally considered a wild and inhospitable area, far too hot and remote in the summer for civilized folk. The British love affair with the area as a winter health resort was still some years away. For the man who had discovered the romanticism of the Alps and was in the vanguard of the discovery of Wales and the Scottish Highlands, the opportunity to experience yet another rugged wilderness was too tempting. And for a man who was in search of vivid colour, one wonders whether Turner had been intrigued by an account of the astonishing light in the region.

His sketchbooks relate the route he took south – Lyons, Avignon, Arles, finally hitting the coast at Marseilles. But Turner soon found out just why this part of France had remained largely off the tourist path. 'The heat was so intense, particularly at Nismes [sic] and Avignon,' Turner later related, that it 'almost knocked me up'.[5] He 'got a plunge into the sea at Marseille'. His delight is noted in two brilliant colour sketches he made of the port in bright gouache on blue paper. In one, he records the deep red coloured rocks of Marseilles, its red lighthouse chiming with the vermilion sails of a fishing boat, bobbing on a vivid blue sea. As so often in his work he must have found a little boat to make this observation, since the point of view of the sketch is from offshore.

As Turner moved east along the coast, through Cannes, Antibes and Cagnes-sur-Mer, towards Nice, the conditions he encountered became if anything more challenging. At that time the stretch of coast here was a plain bisected by the great Var river, which only a few years earlier travellers had had to ford at their peril. In 1828 a wooden bridge had been built across the torrent which at least afforded a safer passage. Nevertheless the lack of shade in an area where, instead of trees, Turner would have only found 'hedges of pomegranates, myrtles and aloes'[6] left him exposed to the beating sun.

He dropped his use of colour entirely and reduced his impressions of the region to quick pencil sketches of the sharp rugged mountain scenery and the towns and villages perched therein. 'I felt so weak that nothing but the change of scene kept me onwards to my distant point,' he confessed.[7]

It is another instance of Turner's health failing, and a reminder that for all his work ethic and lack of care for comfort, he had an asthmatic susceptibility that could cause problems. Perhaps this was why William senior still fretted about his son, despite the fact that his fiftieth birthday was behind him. That parental concern, founded in the ill-health of a young Turner dispatched to Bristol, Brentford and Margate, had never properly abated. Just two years previously, in 1826, when Turner senior heard news of an explosion at Ostend that happened to coincide with when he believed Turner would be there,[8] the elderly man suffered such a paroxysm of panic that his despair even emerged in the press 'that J.M.W.T. not having written home since the affair at Ostend . . . great fears are entertained for his safety'.[9] Now in 1828 Turner wrote to his friend George Jones and urged him to call on his father and reassure him 'that I am well . . . for I fear young Hakewell has written to his father of my being unwell'.[10]

If Turner's health in the south was adversely affected by the climate, at least he began to see the potential of the region from an artistic point of view. After Nice, the coastal topography becomes more pronounced, with the red cliffs descending sharply and directly into the sea. Turner, who seems to have been walking the coastal path, noted to George Jones that 'Genoa, and all the sea coast from Nice to Spezzia is remarkably rugged and fine'. The scenery made him think of 'That fat fellow Chantrey' and the 'thousands he had made out of those marble craigs which only afforded me a sour bottle of wine and a sketch . . . he did give me a fit of the spleen at Carrara.'[11]

But despite Turner's laborious trudge, it would not be he who would immortalize the cypress- and pine-strewn cliffs of the French Riviera. The region would have to wait for the Impressionists a half century later. It seems strange that a man so invigorated by colour failed to capture the blazing tones of the south more fully. And though Turner would return a few years later to the region, its potential was never properly realized by him. A painter such as Turner still needed a client. Whereas he had found interest in the Alps from men such as Fawkes, the mysteries of the south of France apparently remained unappealing to his wider audience.

Turner finally arrived in Rome in October. On his first trip there in 1819, Rome itself had been his subject, but this time he sought something different. It was the ambience of the place that Turner required as much as its views. He arrived with an agenda already set and paintings in mind. In fact, so clear was he about what he wanted to paint in Rome, he had even written ahead to get Charles Eastlake to order two canvases, '8 feet 2½ by 4 feet 11¼ inches'. Turner wanted to paint something for Lord Egremont, 'a companion picture to his beautiful Claude'.[12]

In the end Turner's arrival came hot on the heels of that of his
studio-mate Eastlake. Turner's concerns that he might have incon-
venienced the younger painter by failing to arrive on 1 September as
planned must have vanished when he discovered the latter had taken
his own detour en route to Rome, and had himself only arrived in
mid-September. But now, at last, the two companions set to work.
Eastlake began a picture featuring the local bandits that were so notoriously dangerous in the countryside outside Rome. Later he
remembered that while he strove studiously on his Banditti, 'Mr Turner
used to laugh at me for my fastidiousness (he began several pictures
and finished three long before I had done one).'[13]

'He has worked literally night and day,' Eastlake continued in a
letter to Thomas Lawrence that December; 'one of his finished pictures, a sea port, is exquisite, and equal to his best efforts'.[14]

The seaport referred to was *Regulus* – a work now so typical of
Turner. As he had so often before, Turner placed the sun almost central in the composition, its rays playing on the waters of a seaport,
around which grand buildings basked in the sunlight, the masts of
ships silhouetted in the foreground. Yet this time Turner avoided
charges of repetition by taking the familiar kind of Claudian scene
and giving it a new dramatic dimension.

The wit of the work lay in the subject matter. Regulus was a
Roman general who was captured by the Carthaginians and had his
eyelids removed. In depicting the tortured Regulus setting sail into
the brilliant sunshine, and perhaps drawing on his own recent discomfort under the burning skies of Provence, Turner provided a new
narrative twist on his continuing fascination with the sun.

In terms of colour and drama, *Regulus* also diverges from other
earlier seaports. If Turner did not paint the south of France per se, he
brought its brutal climate and vivid colour to this image of the classical past. Compare it to his *Dido Building Carthage* of 1815. In the
earlier work the palette is cool, and the mood of the work is calm.
The soft golden glow of the sun lacks power and instead simply offers
a warm counterpoint to grey stone classical buildings, the deep green
foliage of shady trees in the foreground, and the dark green, still harbour waters. The air is crisp and the detail of the architecture is clear.

The *Regulus* offers a richer, more intense palette reflecting the red/blue contrasts Turner had recorded at Marseilles. His sun is powerful, pulsing white rays through a blue sky; the buildings are red and cannot be clearly seen for the heat haze enveloping them. Turner intensifies the picture by depicting choppy waters in the harbour, where the white spume of waves worries the shallow waters and complements furrowed clouds overhead. All the prows of the ships in the harbour are pointing towards the powerful punishing sun, directing the viewer's eye towards a molten white focal point. It is a painting full of anxiety, where the tiny population of the imagined seaport are drawn towards the sun like moths to a flame.[15]

Turner completed three other canvases in Rome, all of which feel at once familiar and yet also innovative. He painted a *View of Orvieto* which, while alluding to classical landscape tradition, incorporated contemporary figures at a well. The most striking aspect of this painting, however, is the crisp, bright palette used to realize a vivid blue sky and the strong golden tones in the sun-drenched Italian countryside below. The early morning mists rising around the city of Orvieto in the distance place it in an indistinct dreamlike realm that makes reference to the backgrounds that occur in Renaissance painting. And of course Turner's determination to create images that emerge from his canvas without lines or borders bears comparison with Leonardo da Vinci's development of sfumato techniques, where his subjects emerge smokily and seamlessly in the imagined space.

The other paintings Eastlake saw finished were *Vision of Medea*, and possibly also a view of *Palestrina*. The latter, which most scholars today consider to be the painting Turner had earmarked for Lord Egremont, complements *Orvieto*. It shares its palette of bright blue and gold, and the theme of taking an ancient landscape and peopling it with contemporary Italians. The *Medea*, on the other hand, is a violently imaginative rendering of a witch mid-incantation, which harks back to *A Subject from the Runic Superstitions*, an oil that Turner had painted so many years earlier when he was living in Hammersmith Terrace. But again, the two works make interesting comparison. The darkly gothic scene that Turner painted in his Hammersmith moment seems a million miles from the bright, airy yet violently chaotic image of spell-making he conjured in Rome. His palette is, like the other works of 1828, a careful balance of blues and golds, the colours rich and light and crisp, but where there was previously gothic gloom and stasis, now his witchery is depicted with a rococo sense of abandon, as Medea's pale pink garments float and twist around her flailing arms, as leaves rustle around her, and bubbles float mysteriously in the air.

Turner's reputation had preceded him in Rome and he described in one letter home a sense of the 'gabbling' going on around him as to whether he was going to show any work while there. He gave in to those who nagged him to do so and, just before Christmas, hired a room to exhibit three finished canvases.

'More than a thousand persons went to see his works when exhibited,' Eastlake later related, 'so you can imagine how astonished, enraged or delighted the different schools of artists were, at seeing things with methods so new, so daring and excellences so unequivocal.'[16]

The Italian critics were damning of Turner's work, however. Being less familiar with it than the British press, its effect was all the more shocking for them. In fact such was their horror that one newspaper depicted the painter farting into a trumpet directed at St Peter's. 'The angry critics have, I believe, talked most, and it is possible you may hear of *general* severity of judgment,' Eastlake continued, somewhat underplaying the reaction.

When Thomas Lawrence heard about Turner's reception by the Italian press, he was not surprised. 'When I found him in Rome I proclaimed to the Conclave, Nobility and People of Rome the glorious works they would see by him before his departure,' he remembered from the time he and Turner had been together in the city, 'and from that moment I kept myself exceedingly snug from the dread of being . . . whipt and stone'd by them for my impudent play on their credulity . . .' [17]

As far as Eastlake and Lawrence were concerned, however, Turner represented the very heart of British ingenuity. He was their hero. And even if they chose to work differently from him, his bravery and imaginative force was only to be admired.

'I long to see the Seaport – the two other Pictures, and the two or three hundred sketches,' Lawrence wrote from London to Eastlake. 'I breakfasted yesterday morning with our mutual friend Mr [George] Jones . . . Our principal talk was of our absent genius, his worth & increasing power and fame.'

'I am disposed now to think that the excellences which belong to and characterize painting are more understood in England by a few men than anywhere else,' Eastlake would write back from Rome later. 'Of these it is my opinion that Turner is the first – without going the length of admiring all his extravagances – though his very exaggerations have opened my eyes to his real merits.'[18]

Turner headed back from Rome in the new year of 1829, with plans to return the following year. He took several unfinished works with him, rolled up, but sent the finished canvases by ship. It was a poor decision yet again to travel in the deep winter, and the lesson from a decade earlier had clearly not been learnt. Turner related his adventures to Eastlake.

> . . . the snow began to fall at Foligno . . . that the coach from its weight slide about in all directions, that walking was much preferable . . . so I soon got wet through and through, till at Sarre-valli the diligence zizd into a ditch and required six oxen, sent three miles back for, to drag it out; this cost 4 Hours that we were 10 Hours beyond our time at Macerata, consequently half starved and frozen we at last got to Bologna . . . But there our troubles began instead of diminishing – the Milan diligence was unable to pass Placentia. We therefore hired a voitura, the horses were knocked up the first post, sigr turned us over to another lighter carriage which put my coat in fll requisition night and day, for we never could keep warm or make our day's distance good, the places we put down at proved all bad till Firenzola being even the worst for the down diligence people had devoured everything eatable (Beds none) . . . crossed mount Cernis on a sledge – bivouacked in the snow with fires lighted for 3 hours on Mont Tarate while the diligence was righted and dug out, for a Bank of Snow saved it from upsetting – and in the same night we were again turned out to walk up to our knees in the new fallen drift to get assistance to

dig a channel thro' it for the coach, so that from Foligno to within 20 miles of Paris I never saw the road but snow![19]

Not returning to British shores till February, Turner had left things rather late in the day to get ready for the major event in the arts calendar, the RA show, and a sense of panic sets into the few letters that remain from the spring of that year. He had planned to exhibit a whole series of canvases originated in Rome, but many were still just beginnings. His need to press on fast with unfinished work was, however, interrupted by a flurry of social interest. First there were the friends and relatives of those painters still in Rome who began calling at Queen Anne Street. They included the Eastlakes, keen for news of Charles, and the Wyatts wanted to hear about Robert Wyatt, the sculptor.

Meanwhile, those close friends who had not seen Turner since the previous September put in their invitations for dinner. Turner despaired at not being able to see Clara Wells, and apologetically offered her a little ink sketch of a spilt pot of paint. In his attempts to rush he had simply put himself further behind. 'I must not allow myself the pleasure of being with you on Saturday to dinner,' he wrote in March. 'Time Time Time so more haste the worse speed.'[20]

Some engagements, particularly those with a commercial aspect, could not be declined, however. Samuel Rogers's brother Henry had to be let down because of a prior invitation at Blackheath. Here Turner's former client, the magistrate John Green, had just died in possession of two oil paintings from the turn of the century, *Bonneville, Savoy, with Mont Blanc* and *Venus and Adonis*.

Chantrey meanwhile booked him into a turtle supper at Purfleet with the rich industrialist W. H. Whitbread, who owned extensive chalkpits there. The visit took up a whole weekend but two drawings of Purfleet were commissioned as a result.

Meanwhile the canvases Turner had sent on from Rome by sea had not arrived. Despite plans to exhibit a magnificent series, he had just three finished oils to show. Two, a view of Loreto called *The Loretto Necklace*, and a view of *The Banks of the Loire*, had similar qualities to the *Orvieto* and *Palestrina* views, their palettes informed by a hot sun and blue skies.

The third, *Ulysses Deriding Polyphemus*, is not so much a reflection of the other work executed in Rome but a climax to it. It took Turner's flights of imagination to a new height, building on the *Medea* and *Regulus* to present a classical narrative where natural and supernatural elements collided in a mesmerizing symphony of vibrant, fiery colour.

The work is a seascape. Two ships are shown, deep red under a rising sun. Around them the sky is a kaleidoscope of colour ranging through mauves and pinks, to creams, golds and blues. The sea is a still mirror reflecting back these fiery colours. The classical hero Ulysses stands on one ship mocking the great giant Cyclops Polyphemus, whom he has tricked and blinded. The giant is spectral, barely flesh – his body rises like a huge bruised cloud hunched in the sky above the ships. He cannot see the Horses of the Sun that Turner depicts rising up on the horizon. Nor can he see the translucent water nymphs and sea monsters emerging from the dark waters of the sea to watch the spectacle.

After seeing the new work on show at the Academy, Charles Eastlake's former teacher, the embittered Benjamin Robert Haydon, who had become by this time a stern critic of the Academy, voiced the case against Turner in his diary.

> Turner's pictures always look as if painted by a man who was born without hands, and having contrived to tie a brush to the hook at the end of his wooden stump, he managed by smudging, bungling, scrawling, twisting and splashing to convey to others a notion of his conceptions. His pictures and drawings have this look – they are the works of a savage, suddenly excited to do his best to convey to his fellows his intense impression of the scenery of Nature – without the slightest power in the world of giving the forms, he devotes himself solely to the effects & colours of what he sees.
>
> On what metaphysical principles genius can be proved to exist in a Picture because every rational person mistakes an elm tree for a cabbage, I have yet to learn . . . The Landscape Painters stand up for Turner with an heroic adhesion, conscious if they don't what becomes of them.[21]

If *Regulus* represented the eye-watering power of Turner's alchemy on canvas, the *Ulysses* was surely its pendant, commenting on the blindness of those, like Haydon, unable to see the brilliance.

No one bought either canvas. But Turner made these paintings without a client in mind and in the full knowledge that their innovative aspects were more likely to reduce marketability rather than secure a sale. This work anticipated the Turner who would, in the last twenty years of his life, throw all caution to the wind and pursue a course that no other artist of his day had the courage to take.

Turner changed his plans to return to Rome in the following summer of 1829 and had to send another grovelling, last-minute letter to Eastlake there. Having paid up-front for rooms at the Piazza Mignanelli, the latter was now required to 'do the best for me to lessen the [cost]'.[22] Turner's health was poor again and it was almost certainly this that deterred him from subjecting himself yet again to the heat.

Travelling to a cooler France to enjoy the more temperate climate of Normandy, Turner traded heat for rainstorms and returned in September soaking wet 'though much better in health'. But on his arrival in London he was the recipient of worrying news. His great friend and patron Lord Egremont was ailing. 'Most accounts of L E are not so well as I could wish,' Turner wrote, concerned, to Chantrey in early September. 'I must go to Petworth for a day or two.'[23]

Turner's trip to Petworth was unfortunate. In his concern for his client he had failed to notice the condition of his own father. His dear old 'Daddy' William Turner senior died on 21 September 1829, aged eighty-four. Despite Turner's realization several years earlier that his father was growing too frail to be alone in Twickenham, his death must have been sudden and unexpected.

The loss of the man that Turner still referred to in such affectionate childlike terms had a profound effect on him. Apart from the painful absence of a man whose life had been dedicated to his son's success, his love and companionship, it also threw a stark light on Turner's own mortality, and heightened yet further his sense of human transience. When Clara Wells lost her sister Hannah just a couple of months later, Turner's expression of grief reveals his own suffering:

'Earthly assurances of heaven's bliss possest, must pour their comforts and mingle in your distress a balm peculiarly its own – not known, not felt, not merited by all . . . Alas I have some woes of my own which this sad occasion will not improve.'[24]

Only a day after he had buried his father, Turner wrote his first will. The theme of legacy is paramount. In it he makes provision for a Chair of Landscape at the Royal Academy and a gold Turner Medal for landscape painting. He leaves instructions for a picture gallery that will continue to show his work, and for almshouses for 'decayed English artists (landscape painters only) and single men' on a patch of land that he had retained in Twickenham after the sale of Sandycombe Lodge. And he wanted two of his pictures to be hung with works by Claude at the National Gallery.

In early January 1830 another great blow was delivered. His ally and admirer Thomas Lawrence also died, quite suddenly. What had begun as a pain in his chest proved the end of him. Turner's despair is all too clear in the note he wrote to George Jones.

'Alas! Only two short months Sir Thomas followed the coffin of Dawe[25] to the same place. We were then his pall-bearers. Who will do the like for me, or when, God only knows how soon. My poor father's death proved a heavy blow upon me and has been followed by others of the same dark kind. However it is something to feel that gifted talent can be acknowledged by the many who yesterday waded up to their knees in snow and muck to see the funeral pomp swelled up by carriages of the great.'[26]

Added to his sense of the transience of human life, then, Lawrence's funeral, much like that of Reynolds before, reminded Turner of the importance of endeavour – the poignancy of human achievement against the backdrop of inevitable death, this in turn set against the great cycles of history.

The spate of deaths marking the arrival of the 1830s heralded a noticeable change in Turner's behaviour. Throughout the 1820s his commitment to the Royal Academy summer exhibitions had been patchy, to say the least. In 1821 and 1824 he did not show work there at all. In 1820, 1822, 1823 and 1825 he only offered a single work. In 1826 just four of his canvases were on show. But then, as the decade turned, the number of pictures being sent in by the Academy's most notorious son more than doubled. Between 1830 and 1840 he exhibited fifty-one works.

In the 1830s, then, Turner effectively returned to his Alma Mater. True, he had never left. He had remained an important member of the institution, a teacher, lecturer and councillor, but the distraction of his own commercial gallery had certainly reduced his contribution to the public-facing side of the organization. There were limitations to showing in Queen Anne Street, after all. The gallery was run poorly. Access to it was unreliable. Though a convenient and important space that allowed people to view his work outside the art season, it was never going to be able to provide an alternative to the highly important RA show. If his own personal endeavours were to be properly recognized before his own demise, Turner needed to redouble his presence at what was still unquestionably the main event in the arts calendar, and to re-engage with the brotherhood of painters that the institution represented.

21. Industry

Turner had had plenty of quarrels over the years with his associates. But he was a man who, as he aged, sought reconciliation. Taking a leaf from the master of such things, Joseph Farington, he had made sure that his influence on who was accepted into that important fraternity of the Royal Academy was felt. He had been keen to see the engraver Charles Turner made an Associate, and he put aside a nineteen-year rift he had had with his former business partner to make sure the latter was elected in 1828. The two had fallen out in 1810 over a rights issue regarding *The Shipwreck*. In that year Turner found some coloured engravings of the painting that breached his contract with his namesake. Charles Turner had coloured the reproduction despite the fact that Turner had reserved the rights to colour his work.

Once the election was over he had the opportunity to renew his friendship with the engraver. What 'a shame the clamour of the love of money caused' he wrote to Charles Turner straight after his election, urging the engraver to 'dismiss it now . . . you see I am acting again the Papa with you but it is the last time of asking'.[1] The pep talk was received in good grace, since the two became so close once again that Charles became an executor of Turner's will.

It was all very well Turner lecturing Charles Turner on being too focused on money. He was a man who sat with more than £10,000 in the bank in 1830 – and this merely his investment in 3 per cent consols, making only a part of his portfolio. Turner's speculations had by and large done well. A great many of his contemporaries, particularly publisher engravers, had fared far worse. Indeed Charles Heath, who had borne the risk in Turner's latest adventure with engraving, the ambitious *Picturesque Views in England and Wales*, was already in financial difficulties, since the series was not performing as had been hoped.

The market for engravings had transformed rapidly over the 1820s.

A new fashion for 'annuals' had begun to emerge. The public had got a taste for collecting these yearly publications that often combined literary contributions with illustrations. Heath now published a number of titles such as *The Keepsake* and *Heath's Picturesque Annual*. But what is more, he had also broken new ground in publishing by using steel plates for the engravings in them. More durable than copper, a steel plate could generate a larger print run at a lower cost. The burgeoning middle class loved these affordable publications, which established a new popular market.

The issue with Heath and Turner's hugely ambitious *Picturesque Views in England and Wales* was threefold. Not only was the project entitled traditionally, with a banner that harked right back to Henry Boswell's *Picturesque Views of the Antiquities of England and Wales*, which Turner had so assiduously coloured as a boy. It was also published in an old-fashioned manner, inviting subscriptions for parts, which were to be published at the rate of three a year, each part including four engravings. And then, on top of all this, Turner had insisted that the vast project should be engraved traditionally on copper, which had meant that his work seemed expensive compared to much on the market.

It is no wonder that Heath began a campaign to boost sales. In the summer of 1829 he put on a show of some forty of Turner's watercolours for the series at the Egyptian Hall, in Piccadilly. The show was designed both to promote the series and to sell the watercolours themselves in order that Heath could recoup some of his costs. Not since Walter Fawkes had shown his collection of Turner watercolours a decade earlier had the public had a chance to see so many of Turner's drawings side by side. The public reaction reflected the transformation in his art over that period. Delighted though many were, there was a general astonishment at Turner's palette, his choice of colours, revealing a world so much more vibrant and brilliant than that which they themselves perceived.

Turner returned to many of the subjects portrayed in Boswell's eighteenth-century tome. Compared to his earliest topographical views, which he had executed somewhat in the vein of that influential publication, his views of England and Wales as exhibited in 1829 revealed a rebalancing of subject matter. In the past he had depicted men and women dwarfed by the edifices of the past. But now the series foregrounded contemporary life. It showed the British of that moment crammed in boats, fishing in rivers, enjoying wedding picnics, crossing sands, shooting game, or bartering over the price of a horse on a busy market day. The great castles, abbeys and cathedrals of the past are always present, but more often than not they form part of a misty backdrop, sometimes marking distant horizons.

And the colour, like his paintings executed in Rome, draws on a new delight in the harmonies Turner could achieve between bright blues and golds, sometimes mauves and damson purples, occasionally accentuated with spots of vivid, pure red or green. The sheer exquisite beauty of the bright colour schemes contributes to the general optimism of the series. Turner sees a bright world of golden hills and sparkling waters, seas full of fish and hills replete with sheep and rabbits. This world is a jewel to be admired, and a resource to be enjoyed while one can.

The response to the original watercolours for his *England and Wales* revealed a reaction to his work that Turner would solicit again and again from the 1830s onwards. Those encountering it could not deny its brilliance, and its emotive effect on them. And yet nineteenth-century viewers struggled to align their emotional responses with their intellectual requirement that representation should better approximate a more objective reality. At the heart of their struggle with Turner's work was the issue of 'truth'. His own heightened response to the world around him was forcing a debate on the meaning of truth in art. But it was a debate that few at the time were equipped properly to enter.

This focus on contemporary life that Turner chose to display in the series provided him with new material. And nothing reveals this more than his decision to include in the *England and Wales* a depiction of the industrial town of Dudley.

'The Black Country is anything but picturesque,' the engineer and inventor of the steam hammer James Nasmyth recounted. He had travelled to the region that surrounded the town of Dudley in 1830 and described it as a place where 'The earth seems to have been turned inside out. Its entrails are strewn about; nearly the entire surface of the ground is covered with cinder-heaps and mounds of scoriae. The coal which has been drawn from below ground is blazing on the surface. The district is crowded with iron furnaces, puddling furnaces, and coal-pit engine furnaces. By day and by night the country is glowing with fire, and the smoke of the ironworks hovers over it. There is a rumbling and clanking of iron forges and rolling mills. Workmen covered with smut, and with fierce white eyes, are seen moving about amongst the glowing iron and the dull thud of forge-hammers.'[2]

This account of the place certainly agrees with Turner's depiction of it, which was finally published in 1835. He headed for the Midlands in the August of 1830 having once again failed to return to Rome, and leaving Charles Eastlake yet again in charge of personal belongings that he had left in their studio there two years previously. This time it was France's July Revolution that had put paid to a continental visit. After three days of rioting in Paris, Turner's former neighbour in Twickenham, Louis Philippe d'Orléans, was put on the French throne as a constitutional monarch, replacing Charles X, who had ruled as a hereditary monarch post-Napoleon. The regime change with its pursuant chaos was enough to frustrate travel.

So instead of turning his face again to the southern sun, Turner found himself heading north, with Birmingham, Dudley, Coventry, Warwick and Kenilworth on his itinerary. He had not been to the Midlands since 1794, but in the intervening years he had forged significant friendships with painters with strong Midlands connections. There was his friend James de Maria, who had accompanied Turner in Devon years previously, and with whom he had remained on warm and friendly terms. De Maria had been attached as a scene painter to the theatre in Birmingham, where he had trained the younger Birmingham artist David Cox. Cox was a passionate follower of Turner, and a fervent advocate of watercolour, whom Turner affectionately nicknamed 'Daniel'. He had an almost religious adoration for Turner's work, and made a point of visiting Turner's gallery annually. Cox had shown at Birmingham's Society of Artists for the first time in September 1829, and he and de Maria may have provided the encouragement for Turner to also exhibit in that year five water-colours from the England and Wales series.

The image that Turner conjured of Dudley for his *England and Wales* was one of fiery industry. The waters of the canal glow red from the reflections of the furnaces and smelting works on its banks. In the mid-ground grey smoke weaves upwards into a sooty sky from smudged black buildings, and the whole of the ancient town of Dudley, and its castle, on the hill beyond, is enveloped in grey black smoke. And yet it is not a picture of gloom. Far from it. It shares the same level of fascination in the activity occurring there that Turner applies to his other subjects. Turner shared with Nasmyth a sense of marvel in what he saw around him.

'I went into some of the forges to see the workmen at their labours,' Nasmyth recalled.

> There was no need of introduction; the works were open to all, for they were unsurrounded by walls. I saw the white-hot iron run out from the furnace; I saw it spun, as it were, into bars and iron ribbands, with an ease and rapidity which seemed marvellous. There were also the ponderous hammers and clanking rolling-mills . . . I lingered among the blast furnaces, seeing the flood of molten iron run out from time to time, and remained there until it was late. When it became dark the scene was still more impressive. The workmen within seemed to be running about amidst the flames as in a pandemonium; while around and outside the horizon was a glowing belt of fire, making even the stars look pale and feeble. At last I came away with reluctance . . .[3]

After the rococo Regency era, in his image of Dudley Turner had already captured the new emergent tenor of the next, Victorian era. Even before the young Queen had ascended the throne, Turner had encapsulated one of the dominant themes of her reign: the supremacy of industry, the march of progress. From now on this would be his new subject material.

Of course Turner had noted industry before, on his previous extensive explorations of Wales and the north, when he had drawn kilns, forges and watermills. But the invention of steam provided a new impetus to British industry that was now becoming manifest. If Britain had once conquered the world through sail, its route to a new kind of empire was through steam.

Dudley was particularly associated with the development of the steam engine, which was first operated near Dudley Castle in 1712. Less than a decade earlier the first iron steamer, with its funnel a massive 47ft tall, had been built at the nearby Horseley works, a point that would not have been lost on Turner's enquiring mind. This ship, named the *Aaron Manby* after the owner of the works, had been sailed to France in 1822 to begin its work ferrying passengers along the Seine to Paris. Just two years after his Black Country tour, Turner made a point of making a watercolour of the *Aaron Manby* on the Seine for engraving.[4] From this point on steam would become a recurrent theme in his work and the subject of four of his most famous works, *Fingal's Cave, Staffa,* which he would paint in 1831, the *Temeraire*, which would be exhibited in 1839, *Snow Storm – Steam-boat off a Harbour's Mouth*, three years later, and his reaction to steam trains in 1844, *Rain, Steam and Speed*.

Steam also assisted Turner in his travels to Margate. Since 1815 the Margate Steam Packet Company had been providing fast passage there. Turner had made trips back to the seaside town of his childhood across the 1820s. In 1822 he painted a fine watercolour of *Margate from the Sea, Whiting Fishing*, which had been bought by the Tottenham businessman Benjamin Godfrey Windus. It was exhibited the following year at W. B. Cooke's gallery in Soho Square and was finally included in Cooke's *Marine Views* in 1825. The year before that, Cooke's *Picturesque Views on the Southern Coast of England* had included another view of the seaside town, and his sketchbooks suggest yet another trip there in 1829 or 1830, not long after the death of his father.

Turner had had plenty of opportunity therefore to encounter Sophia Caroline Booth, who ran a guest-house that overlooked the sea at Margate. Next to the main harbour was a small beach, framed between the old stone pier and another landing jetty that had been built to cater for the steamers that had tripled tourism to the resort since their inception. Over the beach a road known as Cold Harbour led up to the old fort that sat above the town. Here was Mrs Booth's house, and here at some point Turner knocked on the door and was admitted as a guest.

Sophia Booth was just a year older than Turner's eldest daughter, Evelina. She lived with her elderly second husband, who was reasonably financially comfortable, and she was not the type of woman to rely on others for her own wellbeing.

Sophia Nollte, as she had been before marriage, was a local girl from Dover who had been born early in 1799. Her parents were of German immigrant descent.[5] With little education and a soft Kentish accent, she had married her first husband just as she turned nineteen, on 3 February 1818 in St John's Margate, the church Turner had drawn as a schoolboy. He, a young fisherman called Henry Pound, was only a little older than her, having just turned twenty-two the previous December. The Pounds were an established Margate seafaring family. An uncle was the harbourmaster, while Henry's father, Daniel, was a master mariner in charge of one of the passage vessels out of Margate, the *Britannia*.

Sophia and Henry had a honeymoon baby. Their first son, Joseph Henry, was born just before Christmas in the same year. And their second son followed less than a year and a half later, on 23 April 1820. The Pounds called their younger child Daniel, after Pound's father and his elder brother.

But their marriage was to prove short and tragic. Barely a year after the arrival of their second child, in the small hours of 22 March 1821, Henry Pound set out in a small fishing vessel called the *Queen Galley* with six other fishermen, one of whom was his older brother Daniel. The scene would have been all too familiar to Turner, who had so often watched the fishermen climbing into their boats in the dark of night to make an early morning catch. And the *Queen Galley* could not have been much different to the vessel that Turner depicted in his own *Fishermen at Sea*, where he shows a similar number of men rowing out into waves under the moonlight.

But that afternoon tragedy struck. On its return, the *Queen Galley* was caught on the treacherous Margate Sands, a notorious spot where many ships had been wrecked. But the breaking-up of the fishing boat was particularly dreadful. All her crew were drowned. Henry

Pound's father lost both his sons that day. They were just twenty-five and twenty-six years old. The oldest crew member, Jarvis Holness, was only twenty-nine, and the youngest just twenty-three. All in all seven infants were left without fathers that Thursday, four of which were in the Pound family. Margate sank into despair and grief. The local newspaper, the *Kentish Gazette*, related the news two days later, along with a plea for charitable donations. 'With a view of alleviating the distress of the surviving relatives which in several respects is very great, the contributions of the affluent and charitable are earnestly entreated,' the newspaper advised, 'and the appropriation of the sums subscribed will be at the discretion of such of the subscribers as may be pleased to meet for this kind purpose at the Town Hall, on Tuesday 1st May.'

The troubles of the recently widowed Sophia Pound did not end here. Her little boy Joseph died three years later, in November 1824. He would have been not quite six years old.

It is then little wonder that when a man who described himself as a gentleman of Margate in his will expressed an interest in the widowed and bereaved Sophia Pound, it seemed like a godsend. John Booth had been born in 1762. He and Sophia married in 1825. They must have seemed an odd couple, he sixty-three and she just twenty-six. But it was more than a marriage of convenience. Within a year John Booth had sired a son whom the newlyweds called John Pound Booth.

John Booth took his responsibilities towards his new family seriously. As he turned seventy, he drew up a will in April 1832, and divided his estate generously, leaving his property to his young wife along with the income from his investments and a lump sum of cash. He left £300 to his son and £200 to his stepson. On Sophia's death they were entitled to further payouts of £600 and £400 respectively. Aware of his own age, he made sure that the popular and well-respected doctor in Margate, his friend Dr David Price, was not only the executor of his will but the named guardian of both John Pound Booth and Daniel Pound. John Booth was aware his own chances of seeing these boys become men were slim.

The will was timely. Britain was being swept by a terrifying epidemic. In the autumn of 1831 cholera outbreaks began to be recorded in the UK. They began in London, a fact not lost on Turner, who watched with concern. The newspapers began publishing daily tallies of deaths, alongside new instances of outbreaks, and generally charting the disease's progress through the country. Given there was no known cure, a degree of panic set in among those wanting to protect themselves. Cartoons began to appear depicting withered patients surrounded by some of the 'remedies' that were being promoted. The caricaturist Robert Cruikshank worked up a scene he entitled *Random Shots*, where a desperate patient is seen surrounded by alternatives: emetics, blue pills, and a starvation diet, all propped up on a table with a skeleton serving as its legs.

Turner too was eager for something to protect him from the menace. Writing to the publisher he was working with on some illustrations for Walter Scott, Robert Cadell, he keenly enquired after new treatments. 'In regard to the cholera,' he wrote in February 1832, 'I will thank you to send me the paper which your medical-men printed as to the treatment & c. or if anything has been discovered during the progress of the disease in Scotland . . . Here the dispute runs high and no treatment made known or Cholera Hospitals established . . .'[6]

Cadell did at least send Turner an article published by Sir Matthew Tierney, the physician to the King, and Turner assiduously transcribed his proposed remedy into a sketchbook, noting that he should apply '25 Drops of Cajeput oil in glass of Water, if not relieved in 5 min take 50 more'.[7]

In the summer of 1832 Turner, en route to northern France to make sketches for a publication for Charles Heath, ran headlong into the cholera epidemic that had just broken out in the Channel Islands. After a sustained drought the weather broke on 5 August, and by the 6th the diarrhoea that presented as the initial symptom of the disease struck many of the inhabitants of Jersey. Soon it was widespread. Arriving on the islands in mid-August, Turner again sought advice on how to protect himself from the scourge. On the back cover of his sketchbook he noted a potion to treat diarrhoea that included cinnamon water, epicackuana (*sic*), laudanum, spirits of lavender and two drams of tincture of rhubarb.[8]

No such remedy helped Sophia Booth and her family. In the spring of 1832 the cholera swept into Margate. Given the traffic of people from boats and steamers, it is hardly surprising that the town was particularly badly hit. Little John Pound Booth succumbed in July 1832. He was six. Sophia also may have contracted the disease, for in a state of grief and concern John Booth amended his will in early 1833, his words conveying the grave worry he had for his wife's welfare. 'In consideration of the bad state of my wife Sophia Caroline Booth's health and in consequence of the lamented death of my son John Pound Booth . . . I wish the sum bequeathed for the use of my late son to be given to my wife . . .'[9]

Two weeks after making this amendment to his will, John Booth was also dead. Sophia Booth was thirty-four and had already lost two husbands and two sons.

Mrs Booth and William Turner found one another when they were both physically fragile and recently bereaved. After the death of John Booth there was nothing to stop their liaison. Margate was now an easy reach from London and Turner found himself taking the Saturday morning steamer to see her. It was known as 'the Husband's Boat', so called since it was full of men who had sent their families to live healthily by the seaside and would join them at weekends.

Charles Turner would later describe Sophia Booth as being 'like a fat cook' with no discernible education; he was to her '. . . Muster Turner instead of Mr Turner'.[10] But Turner's love for the younger Sophia Booth was deeply romantic. He wrote her poems and, as he had with Sarah Danby, gave her drawings.

In return Mrs Booth asked little. The fact that the two lived for so long without marrying is testimony enough to her lack of ambition in this area – perhaps Sophia Booth felt she had lost too many husbands already. And as she was financially independent after the death of her second husband, she presented as a delightfully undemanding prospect for a man with so little room in his life for anything but work.

Sophia took over where William senior had left off, making Turner's wellbeing a focus of her concern. Though Turner had a London physician in the form of the Academy's Professor of Anatomy, Sir Anthony Carlisle, she made a point of introducing him to Margate's Dr David Price. Price loomed large in her life. Not only a guardian of her children, Sophia had also given him the responsibility of looking after her substantial inheritance. Price would later arrange for Daniel Pound to study in Leipzig when his own son David Simpson Price went there in the 1840s.

At the time he was getting to know a doctor in Margate, another doctor who had played such a huge role in Turner's life passed away. Dr Thomas Monro died on 14 May 1833 in his cottage in Bushey, having suffered a stroke three days earlier. He had retired to Bushey in 1820. Here he had finally given himself up entirely to his art collection. Without patients to administer to he spent hour upon hour in the octagonal room there, poring over his drawings under the natural light provided by an overhead skylight.

A sale of Monro's 'very capital collection of drawings of . . . principal artists of the modern school' was held across five days in June and July 1833. Turner acquired a number of drawings by Edward Dayes, as well as two albums of the watercolours he and Girtin had made after John Robert Cozens as boys.

In looking back over his juvenilia it is tempting to wonder if Turner was reminded of some of the drawing exercises that he and Girtin had pursued under the supervision of Monro and his colleagues. Robert Cozens's father, Alexander, had developed a 'blot' technique for watercolourists where he encouraged students to make random blots of ink and then look for a suggestion of a landscape within these forms.

A technique that exercises the imagination rather than techniques of observation seems to sit uncomfortably within the eighteenth-century requirement for artists to be true to the natural world, despite the other requirements for them to be inventive and original. But in the nineteenth century, when Turner was exploring his inner imaginative response to the outside world with a greater vigour than perhaps any other artist, it seems highly appropriate that he began to revisit this.

Certainly around 1836, perhaps inspired by his life with Sophia

Booth, he began a series of erotic blot technique sketches. Across a couple of leather-bound sketchbooks he began to explore the suggestive potential of apparently random, and often very wet, watercolour marks. A watery wash of grey is manipulated into the form of a ghostly woman; another wash of grey, when two fingers are drawn through, suggests the raised knees of a recumbent figure; a brownish wash is manipulated to suggest a naked seated woman with her leg raised, another figure at her feet. In these monochrome improvisations the figures might be rising through mist or water, or part of some fantastical landscape populated by ethereal beings. They could be mermaids reclining on rocks, sea nymphs rising up through dark waves or water sprites huddled in dark caves. They are reminiscent of the ghostly figures in the sea that Turner painted in his *Polyphemus*, or the image of Polyphemus himself, which seems to be part cloud, part rock. But at other times the addition of second or sometimes third loose patches of colour creates scenarios more reminiscent of the Berne or Petworth erotica, where Turner is clearly suggesting curtained beds and crumpled sheets with couples peering out.

If these were not purely imagined scenarios inspired by Sophia Booth, were they improvisations inspired by what he saw in Wapping? The Ship and Bladebone inn, of which Turner was now the landlord, was a place with a dubious reputation to say the very least. A lodging house for coal whippers, dockworkers loading and unloading the coal barges, entertainment there was likely to include the services of local mollies.[11]

'I am assured on the best authority,' Turner's first biographer, Walter Thornbury, wrote, he would 'paint hard all the week till Saturday night; and he would then put by his work, slip a five-pound note into his pocket, button it securely up there, and set off to some low sailors' house in Wapping or Rotherhithe, to wallow till Monday morning.'[12]

The tantalizing question remains, for whom were they executed? Are these works purely personal? Or are they preparatory scenarios with a client in mind? One of Turner's clients who had an obvious penchant for erotic nudes was Hugh Andrew Johnstone Munro of Novar, the son of a diplomat and Scottish landowner. Turner had been friendly with Munro since around 1826, and the latter bought his first Turner oil at auction in 1830, a *Venus and Adonis* which Turner had painted back in 1803. Then in 1833 he bought *Rotterdam Ferry Boat* from the artist himself, having seen it at the RA show. Munro remains a somewhat mysterious figure. He was nervous and stammering, and yet beneath an awkward exterior there lay a deeply thoughtful intellect and a lover of beauty. He never married but was reputed to have enjoyed what his contemporaries referred to as a 'sensuous life', and to have fathered illegitimate children. In this respect he falls in line with the long list of libertine men who populated Turner's career and might have sought more unusual private commissions from the artist.

The drawings could of course have also been a development of those Turner had started at Petworth, and perhaps been made as proposals for a private series for the lord of that great house. Turner was now a regular visitor at the estate, but this was a tenure that would not last that much longer. Egremont was ailing, and in November 1837 he died at the age of eighty-five, to Turner's huge distress. It was the end of another era; another second home from home had run its course. Turner went on a cold wet winter's day and walked behind the coffin along with a great throng of mourners. Meanwhile Egremont's private papers were consigned to the bonfire, and perhaps along with them works by Turner that were only ever designed for his eyes.

22. Indistinct, unintelligible, unstoppable

Egremont was truly the last of the old-style patrons. Now Turner found himself in a new world. There was no more aristocratic patronage to be had, for him at least, but the number of wealthy businessmen prepared to invest was growing. These were men who lacked the inherited wealth and assumed authority of the British aristocracy, but either considered art the currency that would buy a new kind of status, or had enough money to invest in a genuine passion for art. The Leeds cloth merchant John Sheepshanks had begun to buy Turners, and the horse trader Robert Vernon had also commenced his collection. Add to this list the pen-maker Joseph Gillott, the chemist and instrument-maker John Maw, the textile manufacturer Henry McConnell, the wine merchant John Allnutt, the Liverpool tobacco merchant John Miller and others. Between them, this group of new collectors secured Turner's fortunes and encouraged his output as he entered a new phase of creative outpouring.

Vernon is a fascinating case in point. He had made his money supplying the livestock for the cavalry in the Napoleonic wars. And by the 1830s he was on a dedicated mission to build a collection of modern British artists that he could donate to the nation and in doing so secure his enduring fame.

He may have been inspired by that other groundbreaking collector, Sir John Leicester. Vernon's business was based in Mount Street in Mayfair, a street parallel to Sir John's home and gallery in Hill Street. Like Turner, Vernon attended the sale of Leicester's collection and bought a number of paintings. But Turner's connection with Vernon was strengthened by the influence of Turner's great friend the painter George Jones, who began to advise him, probably in the late 1820s, about what he should buy. In 1832 Vernon bought a house in Pall Mall with the specific intention of creating a gallery of British art that he could open to the public. And from the 1832, 1833, and 1834 RA shows he made sure that he acquired three of Turner's latest works.

The works that Vernon bought had drawn mixed reviews. One of the issues that the viewing public was having with Turner's work in the 1830s was actually *seeing* it properly. The tradition of the exhibition that had begun in the eighteenth century had been one where paintings were hung close together and viewed at close quarters. There was no precedent for placing a picture in a spacious environment with the viewer observing it from some distance. The eighteenth- and early nineteenth-century viewer walked towards a painting and leaned in. It took the *Literary Gazette* to beat away criticism of the painting Vernon bought in 1834, *The Golden Bough*, which it argued was, far from being slovenly in execution, a gem.

'What other hand could have produced such streams of rich and lucid colour over the canvass or have filled it with such masses,' the Gazette opined, '– indistinct and unintelligible when closely inspected, but, when viewed at proper distance, assuming shape and meaning, and delighting the eye with the finest poetical and pictorial beauty?'[1]

In light of the debate around Turner's work, Vernon was a brave man to pay out good money for a Turner painted in the 1830s. The growing critical assessment across the decade was that Turner's greatest work lay behind him, and while that was well worth collecting, his more recent output, which continued to split opinion, was a risk. In fact the exposure to risk in collecting works by Turner was not huge. Turner was aware that there was now a ceiling in the market for his work. Across the 1830s his canvas sizes remained modest, reflecting the correspondence in pricing and dimension. As such the price of his work therefore remained relatively suppressed, effectively reducing the risk to investors. In 1833 Vernon paid 200 guineas for an oil painting of the *Bridge of Sighs* measuring 20 by 32 inches. A decade later he paid the slightly higher rate of 250 guineas for another Venetian view measuring a slightly larger 24 by 36 inches. Given Turner could realize 300 guineas in 1803 for *The Festival Upon the Opening of the Vintage of Mâcon*, which measured 57 by 93 inches, and 500 guineas in 1818 for the similarly sized *Dort*, the price of his work had at best plateaued across his career.

Amusingly, though, there was a careless aspect to *The Golden Bough* that serves as a good reminder of the degree of chaos that was constantly at play in Turner's life. A man who took on far too much work, with far too little assistance, whose organizational skills were limited and who was in a constant rush could make the odd oversight.

A couple of years after he had bought the picture, it was brought to Vernon's attention that a figure in the foreground was peeling off. Turner was invited to view this phenomenon and on seeing it explained, 'Why, this is only paper! I now remember all about it. I determined, the picture being all but finished, to paint a nude figure in the foreground, and with this intention went one night to the Life School at the Royal Academy, and made a sketch in my note-book. Finding, next day, that it was the exact size I required my figure to be, I carefully, by its outline, cut it out of the book and fixed it on to the picture, intending, when I had time, to paint the figure in properly. But I forgot this entirely, and do not think I should have remembered but for you.'[2]

Much of the chaos in Turner's life was down to the fact that he continued with extensive engraving projects. An important source of income, such commissions also gave him an excuse to keep travelling, which he so loved. Never before had this workaholic been so busy as he was across the 1830s, when during the summers he headed to Scotland, to France, to Germany, to Prague, Vienna and Venice, to Denmark and Bohemia, and returned to the Val d'Aosta.

The erosion of public sympathy that his paintings and watercolours had suffered had not transferred to his engraved work. Here the clarifying and mediating hand of the engraver and the translation of his highly coloured watercolours into monochrome print served to highlight the aspects of Turner's work that the public still loved: his brilliant sense of composition, his witty human narratives, his astonishing attention to detail and the sense of depth he brought to views.

The quantity of watercolour he produced to be engraved in the 1830s is extraordinary. He illustrated an edition of Byron's *Life and Works* and Milton's *Poetical Works*. There were editions of Sir Walter Scott's *Waverley* novels, his *Poetical Works*, *Prose Works*, and *Life of Napoleon*. There was extensive work for Samuel Rogers. In addition to Rogers's *Italy*, Turner took on his *Poems* too. He illustrated Finden's Bible, as well as editions of Thomas Moore and also John Bunyan. Many of these illustrations were vignettes – but their association with the most popular literary names of the day brought Turner to vast multitudes of the English people.[3]

His letters convey the complex schedule these commitments presented and the sense of urgency that pursued him. 'Oh for a feather out of Times' wing,' he wrote to Sir Walter Scott in the spring of 1831. Scott had asked Turner to visit his home, Abbotsford, to collect views. 'How long do you think it will take me to collect the material,' Turner asked, '. . . my bad horsemanship puts your kind offer of Poney I fear out of the account of shortening the time and when I get as far as Loch Kathrine shall not like to turn back without Staffa Mull and all. A steam boat is now established to the Western Isles so I have heard . . . and therefore much of the difficulty becomes removed but being wholly unacquainted with distances &c will thank you to say what time will be absolutely wanting.'[4]

For the *Life of Napoleon*, part of Scott's *Prose Works*, Turner suggested to the publisher Robert Cadell how he might work up some views without visiting the actual locations, drawing on his own cache of past sketches and using his wits and contacts elsewhere: 'As to the battles I have made sketches from the pictures painted by order of Bonaparte of Marengo and Eylau, Lodi I can get in London – Waterloo I have – but I desired a German bookseller in Paris to obtain any print of the above places . . .'[5]

Compared to the relatively limited metropolitan exposure his paintings had in London, his engraved works gave him access to a much wider, national market. His illustration of Rogers's *Italy* alone made Turner a household name when, by 1832, 68,000 copies of the book had been printed. The seventeen-volume edition of *Byron's Life and Works* produced by the publisher John Murray was, according to Murray, 'a success unprecedented, it is believed, in the annals of British literature, except in the instance of the Waverley novels'.[6] This was reproduction on a scale far beyond the engravings he had made in the two previous decades.

The vignette form played its own role in the evolution of Turner's art, because rather than adopting the standard rectangular landscape or portrait format of the rest of his work in oils and watercolour, the vignettes were executed as ellipses – oval compositions, arguably mimicking the optical form in which the eye captures light. The oval and sometimes circular format he explored gave Turner the opportunity to yet further the intensity of his composition around a central distant sun, in his depictions of landscape. We find him whirling storm clouds around a sun in his *Hurricane in the Desert* illustration for Rogers's *Poems*, or, in the same publication, wrapping rising waves over a boat in *A Tempest – Voyage of Columbus*. The circular form also invited him to explore the idea of painting without boundaries. Whereas the rectangular format offers clear delineation, Turner's circular and oval vignettes have no clear frame but experiment with merging the white snow of the Alps into the paper, or allowing cloudy skies to vaporize into the page. These illustrations re-engaged him with poetry and fantasy in a newly direct and intense manner, giving him the opportunity to conjure fantastical imagery for Milton's *Poetical Works*, replete with armies of spectral angels and river nymphs.

He also finally properly embraced the new market for annuals, publishing his own series of *Turner's Annual Tours* with Charles Heath. This was a hugely innovative move. In the same way that years before he had been one of the few artists with the confidence that their name might carry their own gallery, now he and Heath ventured that the popularity of his engravings was such that he could be the first artist to create an annual marketed entirely on the strength of his name. And finally these annuals were to be engraved on steel, not copper.

The first annual of a trio, published in 1833, was *Wanderings by the Loire*, with the annuals in the subsequent two years covering views of *The Seine*. Like the *Picturesque Views in England and Wales* for Heath, Turner made a point of foregrounding contemporary life in many of the views he made. But he also drew on the full history of his repertoire to depict different aspects of the rivers. So the Seine at Le Havre, at that time a popular resort, is given a Claudian treatment, with passengers and revellers crowded along the harbour where ships line up to take them upriver. Paddle steamers are shown on several occasions in the Seine book, the tall chimneys offering trails of smoke. But in this series Turner also draws on his unparalleled ability to render complex architecture with breathtaking detail. The fairy-like gothic cathedral at Rouen dominates the people of the city, as Turner reminds his audience that no one can portray the marvel of medieval architecture quite like he can. And finally he gives us his version of Paris in this series, staying there again in 1832 to make studies for depictions of the *Pont Neuf*, of the city from the *Barrière de Passy*, of the *Hôtel de Ville* and the *Marché aux Fleurs*. Most magnificent of all his Parisian views was one of the *Boulevards* – a tour de force of a city view that is reminiscent of the earliest work he did for Malton, yet speaks of the years of experience that have intervened. It sums up the world of the elegant Parisians, promenading in the early evening. The architectural rigour of the student of Malton, who can depict the wide streets and framing buildings with panache, is combined with the *joie de vivre* and compositional elegance of the admirer of Watteau, who could make crowd scenes seem like delightful choreographed symphonies.

It is with some irony that the royal appreciation he had always sought from the Georgian British monarchy was finally delivered, with apparent genuineness, by the French. Making a point of re-acquainting himself with his former neighbour, if not when he was in France in 1829, then perhaps in 1832, Turner sent King Louis Philippe a set of these engravings of his French views and received first a medal of honour in 1836 and later a magnificent gold snuffbox and an invitation to dinner.[7]

But despite prestige and praise for *Turner's Annual Tours*, Charles Heath sank financially. It was not this endeavour but the *Picturesque Views in England and Wales* that had proved too great a risk and brought his entire company down. The reusable steel plates for the French rivers series were sold on to another London publisher, Longman, who reprinted the three annual tours as a single edition in 1837. The *England and Wales* series meanwhile was offloaded by Heath in 1831 to another publishing house, Jennings and Chaplin. Over the next few years the project passed from J. & C., through Moon, Boys & Graves of Pall Mall, until it too ended up with Longman in 1835.

The range of work, breadth of ability and endless inventiveness that Turner expressed across the watercolours he made for engraving in the 1830s is mirrored in the range of his work that he sent to the Academy during that period for exhibition, though with less immediate commercial success. His redoubled efforts to engage with the Academy's audience saw him also presenting a variety of work intended to show his multi-genre virtuosity.

Seascapes make up a large proportion of the show-pieces of those years, including *Helvoetsluys; – the City of Utrecht, 64, Going to Sea*. This depiction of a sixty-four-gun ship heading out for sea was one of four seascapes sent to the RA show in 1832. Though by this time he was becoming notorious for his use of vibrant colour, this picture employs a cool palette of greys, blues and browns, associated with a much earlier version of Turner. This cooler work may well have been the result of an ongoing exchange of dares and practical jokes that Turner and his friend George Jones were trading at the time. Jones had told Turner 'that if he did not paint some cool and grey pictures the world would say that he could not do so. He said "I will prove to the contrary." '[8]

But it was in the very year in which Turner offered this more muted palette that the hanging committee decided to place John Constable's vast, 7ft long, highly coloured view of *The Opening of Waterloo Bridge* next to Turner's *Helvoetsluys*, which was half its size. Constable's work was vigorous and animated. He worked his surface with thick impasto paint and applied brilliant red and green to the boats he depicted on the Thames. Turner's smaller, cool work might have been lost next to it had the older artist not taken up the challenge, as he had done several times in the past to the amusement of his contemporaries, and rectified the situation during the varnishing days. The painter Charles Leslie watched on bemused as Turner applied a round spot of red to the *Helvoetsluys*:

> . . . somewhat bigger than a shilling, on his grey sea, [and] went away without saying a word. The intensity of the red lead, made more vivid by the coolness of the picture caused even the vermilion and lake of Constable to look weak. I came into the room just as Turner left it. 'He has been here' said Constable, 'and fired a gun' . . . The

great man did not come again into the room for a day and a half; and then in the last moments that were allowed for painting he glazed the scarlet seal he had put on his picture and shaped it into a buoy.⁹

Many of Turner's submissions across the decade reflected his continuing fascination with travel. Importantly, he presented views of Venice in oil for the first time. Closer to home, the trip to Fingal's Cave and Staffa that he mentioned in his correspondence with Sir Walter Scott is brought to life in a work that also offered his first depiction of a steamer in oil.

Turner and his fellow tourists, inspired by the Ossianic myths that were popular at the time, had been dropped in choppy weather on the tiny island of Staffa, and 'after scrambling over the rocks on the lee side . . . got into Fingal's cave. It is not a very pleasant place when the wave rolls right in,' Turner recalled later.¹⁰

Despite the impressive cave, it was not this that Turner chose to share with his audience, but rather the experience of the struggle to get home. For Turner the drama of the day lay not in the appreciation of the geology, but in man's battle against the prevailing elements.

When the captain picked up his passengers again, the elements were stacked against their speedy return. There was 'such a rainy and bad looking night coming on', Turner remembered, '. . . the sun getting towards the horizon burst through the rain-cloud, angry, and for wind; and so it proved for we were driven for shelter into Loch Ulver.'

Turner painted the steamer battling against the wind, the plume of smoke from its funnel blown back in a horizontal swathe towards the great purple-grey basalt cave it struggles to leave behind. Both headland and ship are dwarfed beneath dark threatening rainclouds through which the sun barely glimmers. With an extremely loose, visible and vigorous handling of paint, Turner invokes a complex symphony of vapour – rain, sea spume, cloud and steam, and in doing so *Staffa, Fingal's Cave* looks forward to *Snow Storm – Steam-boat off a Harbour's Mouth*.

Staffa was the first of Turner's paintings to go over to America, thanks to his colleague Charles Leslie, who bought it more than a decade after its exhibition for a New York collector, James Lenox. Lenox had Scottish ancestry and had spent time in Britain. But like so many faced with one of Turner's works from his middle and later periods, when he unpacked the work he wondered initially if it had been damaged, since it seemed to his eye rather 'indistinct'. Lenox overcame his initial prejudice against the work, though, and went on to buy another 'indistinct' piece, *Fort Vimieux*, which Turner had displayed a year earlier than *Staffa*. This too had sat quietly in Turner's gallery for nearly fifteen years until it found a client adventurous enough to purchase it. This time the purchaser was the British industrialist Charles Meigh, a pottery manufacturer from Staffordshire. When Meigh sold it five years later, in 1850 at Christie's, Lenox stepped in for it.

Fort Vimieux is a picture that describes the cusp on which Turner's Britain stood in the 1830s. The painting is of an incident that had occurred off the French coast when the British were at war with France a quarter of a century earlier. Turner describes the incident in an accompanying quotation from *Naval Anecdotes* that he supplied with the painting: 'In this arduous service of (or reconnaissance) on the French coast, 1805, one of our cruisers took the ground and had to sustain the attack of the flying artillery along shore, the batteries and the fort of Vimieux, which fired heated shot, until she could warp off at the rising tide, which set in with all the appearance of a stormy night.'

Turner's canvas is a blaze of fiery golds, oranges and reds. The ship is seen beached and on its side in the mid-distance. In the immediate foreground its redundant anchor is proud in the damp sand. In the far distance the sun sets in a bright red sky.

When Turner painted *Fort Vimieux* in the early 1830s, he sensed that the glorious era of British naval history was over. The disabled ship, silhouetted against a setting sun, though ultimately victorious invites a sentimental reflection on times past. It is a painting that combines a sense of melancholy with pride.

Turner understood the power of shared public sentiment. Ever since he had painted his view of the *Pantheon the Morning After the Fire*, back in 1792, he would leap on the opportunity to depict a scene that could unite his audience. For him the power of art was its ability to capture in an image not just his own personal response to events, but a common sensibility. In this way he was not just presenting to his viewers, but embracing them, anticipating and reflecting what bound together the people he saw around him, whether that was national pride, a delight in the experience of steam, terror at the power of nature's elements or delight in the beauty of landscape. When the old Houses of Parliament burned down on the night of 16 October 1834, Turner knew instantly that this was a subject that he must deliver.

The whole of London was up that night, watching awestruck a blaze that lit up the night sky so brightly that people could read a newspaper half a mile away from Westminster. Turner and his younger colleague Clarkson Stanfield launched a small boat into the Thames and from it sketched the flames devouring the sky. Turner delivered two oil paintings of the fire in the following year. One he showed at the British Institution, depicting the view of the blaze from the south side of the Thames, close to Westminster Bridge. The canvas is an essay in indistinctness, with Turner wrapping the bridge and specta-tors in a pall of night and smoke all the better to give contrast to the furnace of colour on the north side of the river. At the RA he showed a different version, taken from a view farther down river. Here the inferno is fanned by the night's south-westerly wind, the wide river reflecting the full magnificence of the vast tower of flames. And in this view Turner shows a seemingly tiny floating engine being towed by steamers towards the disaster, so that it might pump water from the Thames and finally bring the fire under control.

But despite the commitment of the handful of bold new collectors, around half of the exhibited works Turner presented across the 1830s did not sell for a decade, when it would take the insight of yet another wave of patrons like James Lenox to come forward for them.

Some paintings, however, he *never* sold. One such was arguably the greatest, and certainly the most famous painting that Turner ever painted – *The Fighting Temeraire tugged to her Last Berth to be broken up, 1838.*

It is a painting that combined a number of themes, sentiments and responses that Turner had been exploring in his recent depictions of British naval glory, in his leverage of topical events, and his fascination with the power of the new steam technology. It hits a note between sentimental melancholy and nationalistic pride, but also strikes a new note of hope. But for Turner's audience it offered yet another level of pertinence lost on us today.

Ever since the great fire that Turner and Stanfield watched consuming the Houses of Parliament, Britain had been engaged in a national debate about how best to define itself. The Reform Bill had been introduced in 1832, opening up Parliament to a wider pool of MPs and loosening the grip of the aristocracy on political power. Should therefore the new Parliament building be classical, a style with connotations of republicanism, or gothic, a style suggestive of deep-rooted conservatism and old power? By 1835 it had been decided that the style would be gothic or Elizabethan, and Charles Barry, in the following year, submitted the winning designs to this brief.

Yet a year later, when the teenage Queen Victoria ascended the throne, another opportunity arose to debate the state of Britain. With her accession, Parliament had been dissolved and an election fought. The Whig Lord Melbourne – an alleged illegitimate son of Turner's great friend Lord Egremont – saw in the young Victoria the embodiment of a new generation, a monarch who could stand for *new* British values: progress and reform. This depiction of the young Queen was quickly espoused by the hopeful working classes, and it was a depiction that carried the Whig government back into power. When Lord Melbourne arranged Victoria's Coronation in June 1838 there were noticeable changes. More money was spent on displaying the Queen to her wider public, with an extended progress to Westminster Abbey for all those who could find a space on a pavement or a perch on a windowsill. But some of the more medieval aspects of the ceremony were consciously dropped, specifically the ritual of the Queen's champion riding in full armour.

This caused an outcry among the old guard, to such an extent that one member of the threatened aristocracy, the Earl of Eglinton, mounted a full-blown medieval tournament as a response. Such was the massive public interest and widespread publicity surrounding the

Eglinton Tournament that it became a national event when it was finally staged in the August of 1839.

In this moment, when factions in Britain were passionately reviving images of a glorious past while industry, science and political reform were suggesting a different future, Trafalgar Square was also being conceived. The area around St Martin's church had, until the 1830s, been a maze of seamy alleyways and courtyards, colloquially named after the islands that had built Britain's fortunes in previous centuries: the Bermudas, Caribbee and Cribbe Islands, and Porridge Island, famous for its low-grade cook shops. These had been systematically cleared away to accommodate a scheme by Turner's friend John Nash, which created a large open space where not only the new National Gallery would be built, but a memorial to Nelson could be placed. In February 1838 the committee was formed for the selection of an appropriate monument to the great naval hero and the debate was well under way.

How timely then it must have seemed to the new Victorian public that between 5 and 6 September 1838, *Temeraire,* one of the most famous veterans of Trafalgar and one of only nine remaining ships that had served at the battle, was towed up the Thames from Sheerness to be broken up in Beatson's Yard at Rotherhithe. The legendary 98-gun ship of the line was slowly pulled by two little steam tugs, the *London* and the *Sampson.* And the press was quick to note the significance of the occasion.

There remains doubt whether Turner actually saw this event, despite several accounts that place him at different locations on the river. Certainly if he had seen the ship towed, it was in a sorrier state than that which he recreated on canvas – a mere hulk without its magnificent masts.[11] But Turner's imagination was sufficient to revive the ship to her former glory.

Turner's painting of the scene went on show in 1839, at just the second annual exhibition that the Royal Academy had held since it had moved from the building it had occupied in the Strand to the newly built National Gallery, in an embryonic Trafalgar Square. It arrived a year after the Coronation of the new young Queen, which marked the dawning of a new era of progress.

Turner depicted the old ship fully masted, the sun setting brilliantly in the distance. The paddles of a single black tug, pulling the
old wooden ship of the line behind it, churning an otherwise glassy
and near-empty river.

For once the press and public were unanimous. For all his eccentricities, this was Turner back on form. The work was a masterpiece
in which the 'gorgeous horizon poetically intimates that the sun of
the *Téméraire* is setting in glory'.[12] The writer William Makepeace
Thackeray, who regularly disliked Turner's work, pointed out that
most of Turner's submissions to the 1839 show remained 'quite incomprehensible' and 'not a whit more natural, or less mad, than they used
to be in former years'. And yet even he, writing under the pseudonym of Mr Titmarsh, was overcome by a picture that at once
combined so many elements in a uniquely timely and timeless vision.

> I must request you to turn your attention to a noble river-piece by J.
> W. M. Turner, Esquire, R.A., 'The Fighting *Téméraire*' – as grand a
> painting as ever figured on the walls of any Academy, or came from
> the easel of any painter. The old *Téméraire* is dragged to her last home
> by a little, spiteful, diabolical steamer. A mighty red sun, amidst a
> host of flaring clouds, sinks to rest on one side of the picture, and
> illumines a river that seems interminable, and a countless navy that
> fades away into such a wonderful distance as never was painted
> before. The little demon of a steamer is belching out a volume (why
> do I say a volume? not a hundred volumes could express it) of foul,
> lurid, red-hot, malignant smoke, paddling furiously, and lashing up
> the water round about it; while behind it (a cold grey moon looking
> down on it), slow, sad, and majestic, follows the brave old ship, with
> death, as it were, written on her. I think . . . we ought not, in com-
> mon gratitude, to sacrifice entirely these noble old champions of ours,
> but that we should have somewhere a museum of their skeletons,
> which our children might visit, and think of the brave deeds which
> were done in them. The bones of the *Agamemnon* and the *Captain*,
> the *Vanguard*, the *Culloden*, and the *Victory* ought to be sacred relics,
> for Englishmen to worship almost. Think of them when alive, and
> braving the battle and the breeze, they carried Nelson and his heroes

victorious by the Cape of Saint Vincent, in the dark waters of Aboukir, and through the fatal conflict of Trafalgar. All these things, my dear Bricabrac, are, you will say, absurd, and not to the purpose. Be it so; but Bowbellites as we are, we Cockneys feel our hearts leap up when we recall them to memory; and every clerk in Threadneedle Street feels the strength of a Nelson, when he thinks of the mighty actions performed by him.

It is absurd, you will say (and with a great deal of reason), for Titmarsh, or any other Briton, to grow so politically enthusiastic about a four-foot canvas, representing a ship, a steamer, a river, and a sunset. But herein surely lies the power of the great artist. He makes you see and think of a great deal more than the objects before you; he knows how to soothe or intoxicate, to fire or to depress, by a few notes, or forms, or colours, of which we cannot trace the effect to the source, but only acknowledge the power . . . Mr. Turner and his 'Fighting *Téméraire*' which I am sure, when the art of translating colours into music or poetry shall be discovered, will be found to be a magnificent national ode or piece of music.[13]

Yet for all his rare praise Thackeray could still not see the true brilliance in Turner's painting. Because far from depicting a 'demon of a steamer', Turner's little steamboat, like all his steamers, and like the furnaces of Dudley, represented the next phase of human graft and progress. He reduced the actual number of tugboats from two to one specifically to emphasize the wonder of this vessel, which despite its diminutive size could haul the great hulk of the past along the Thames. Far from just celebrating and mourning the past, Turner's picture simultaneously applauds the potential of the future.

With a sun and a moon simultaneously on the canvas, the one rising in the sky, the other setting over the water, it is the greater cycle of life that he sees. The breadth of his vision stretches far beyond the moment of his own time. Turner's *Temeraire* is an expression of his own profound understanding that beyond the triumphs of empire he had witnessed in his own time, more was to come in the endless revolution of time. Rise and fall. Night and day. Rome and Carthage. Chaos and creation. Life and Death. Old victories and brave new worlds.

That the *Temeraire* remained in Turner's studio was not, for once, down to debate or controversy over its quality. The picture that won the hearts of its audience in 1839 remained unsold simply because Turner refused to part with it. Much later the American Lenox would offer a simply astonishing £5,000 for it, almost as much as the ship-breaker Beatson had paid the Royal Navy for the right to dismantle the old warhorse. But Turner would not sell a piece that he knew was already priceless.

23.   To please himself

'The work now laid before the public originated in indignation at the shallow and false criticism of the periodicals of the day on the works of the great living artist to whom it principally refers.'

These words poured from the pen of an indignant John Ruskin when he was in his early twenties. The son of John James Ruskin, who had become very wealthy through his sherry importation business, Ruskin, Telford and Domecq, this was a young man whose brilliant intellect had been indulged all his life. Now, having graduated from Oxford, he was writing the preface for a book that, on its publication in May 1843, launched a career that would lead to him being recognized as the greatest critic of his generation.[1] Called *Modern Painters*, it was the result of his pent-up fury at the increasingly regular and ferocious criticism that Turner's work was attracting. Despite the success of some canvases, not least his *Temeraire*, the tide of disapproval was consistently rising against the artist as the 1840s got under way.

Ruskin's robust advocacy of Turner was crucially timed. It came on the cusp of change for an artist who, already controversial, was about to embark upon a final quest for freedom in the last decade of his life. Turner's search for a new level of personal expression coincided with the physical deterioration of his gallery in Queen Anne Street. Hannah Danby, suffering from the detrimental effects of her skin condition, gradually lost a grip on the house and her master turned a blind eye. The house became filled with cats which she encouraged off the street. The dust began to gather, the glass skylight in the studio weathered and the paint began to peel. It is as if a new-found agenda to explore total artistic liberty became so consuming for Turner that it could not accommodate the mundane concerns of maintaining a building.

Ruskin's devotion to Turner had begun when the family home in Denmark Hill became one of those bestowed with a copy of Rogers's

Italy. His father's business partner, Henry Telford, bought him a copy for his thirteenth birthday, an incident which Ruskin himself confessed 'determined the main tenor of my life'. 'This book was the first means I had of looking carefully at Turner's work: and I might, not without some appearance of reason, attribute to the gift the entire direction of my life's energies . . . I could understand Turner's work when I saw it; . . . Poor Mr Telford . . . was always held by papa and mamma primarily responsible for my Turner insanities.'[2]

Modern Painters was not just a defence of his beloved Turner, but Ruskin's wider manifesto for modern art, a determined riposte to the arguments that continued to be made, even in the nineteenth century, that British art should aspire to the past. 'It was intended to be a short pamphlet,' Ruskin continued,

> reprobating the matter and style of those critiques, and pointing out their perilous tendency, as guides of public feeling. But . . . I found myself compelled to amplify what was at first a letter to the Editor of a Review, into something very like a treatise on art . . . The reputation of the great artist to whose works I have chiefly referred, is established on too legitimate grounds . . . to be in any way affected by the ignorant sarcasms of pretension and affectation. But when *public* taste seems plunging deeper and deeper into degradation day by day, and when the press universally exerts such power as it possesses to direct the feeling of the nation more completely to all that is theatrical, affected and false in art...it becomes the imperative duty of all who have any perception or knowledge of what is really great in art . . . to come fearlessly forward . . . to declare and demonstrate . . . the essence and the authority of the Beautiful and True.

The proposed letter to which Ruskin alludes had been intended for the editor of *Blackwood's Magazine*, which in 1836 had published a scathing review of the paintings Turner showed at that year's Royal Academy show. *Juliet and her Nurse*, *Rome from Mount Aventine*, and *Mercury and Argus* had all drawn the scorn of the publication's art critic the Sketcher, aka the Revd John Eagles, who took up the mantle that Sir George Beaumont had worn in a previous generation. 'We should be almost inclined to believe that there was some truth in the remark we have often heard, that there is no use in painting other than the lightest pictures for the London Galleries, which are said to be half the year obscured by our fogs, did we not, in addition to a dislike of this malevolent satire upon our climate, see in the numerous collections of fine Italian masters in our metropolis a contradiction to the assertion,' Eagles wrote, before going on to destroy each of Turner's canvases.

His argument was the same for each work: they were simply too bright. The hazy, indistinct forms Turner was exploring simply infuriated Eagles further. Of Turner's reimagining of Shakespeare's Juliet, not in Verona but looking out from a balcony across St Mark's Square in Venice, he spewed out a venomous commentary that finally summarized the painting as a 'higgledy piggledy' mess where streaks of 'blue and pink' were 'thrown into a flour tub'.

Rome from Mount Aventine was no more than an 'unpleasant mixture with childish execution', while *Mercury and Argus* was 'all blood and chalk', where 'there was not the least occasion for Mercury to put out Argus' eyes', for 'the horrid glare would have made him shut the whole hundred'.

'Turner has been great,' Eagles accused, 'and now . . . he chooses to be great no longer, he is like a cunning creature that having lost its tail persuaded every animal that had one, that it was a useless appendage.'[3]

This assault, not just on Turner, but on anyone who dared to follow him, prompted a counter-blast from a young Ruskin prepared to wage war in the name of progress. He sent his proposed reply to Maga – the nickname for *Blackwood's* – to Turner himself for the latter's approval.

'I never move in these matters,' Turner responded. 'They are of no import save mischief and the meal tub which Maga fears for by my having invaded the flour tub!'[4]

But for all Turner's protests that he took no notice of criticism, he felt sufficiently impressed by Ruskin's positive interpretation of his work that he sent it to Munro, who had bought the painting.

Ruskin was capable of ecstasy when viewing a work by Turner.

He saw instantly the visual poetry that Turner wrought, transform-
ing mere depiction into an imaginative response to place. Ruskin
understood that the space Turner conveyed on his canvas could be
multidimensional. He, like Thackeray, had grasped that 'He makes
you see and think of a great deal more than the objects before you.'
But where Thackeray could see time and history behind Turner's
depiction of place or event, Ruskin saw even more. Ruskin found the
evocation of dreamworlds and spiritual planes. Far beyond the classical reference he used, Ruskin recognized a new range of motifs,
peculiar to the artist, in which the elements such as mist or sunshine
took on supplementary, often holy meaning. For Ruskin, far from
streaks of blue and pink, Turner's depiction of Venice was one of
'many coloured mists . . . as you might imagine to be aetherial spirits,
souls of the mighty dead breathed out of the tombs of Italy into the
blue of her bright Heaven and wandering in vague and infinite glory
around the earth they have loved'.[5]

And the city itself could be seen as an offering to God, its spires
rising 'indistinctly bright into those living mists like pyramids of
pale fire from some vast altar; and amidst the glory of the drama,
there is as it were the voice of a multitude entering by the eye . . .' For
Ruskin Turner's 'own special gift was that of expressing mystery and
the obscurities rather than the definition of form'.

It is hardly surprising that the precociously talented teenager
soon persuaded his rich merchant father to begin a collection of
Turner's work.

The very first purchase the Ruskins made was a watercolour of
Richmond Hill and Bridge, Surrey that Turner had made for *Picturesque
Views in England and Wales*. Ruskin and his father probably first saw it
when it was on show in the gallery of Messrs Moon, Boys and Graves
of Pall Mall in 1833. A year in which the father and son, inspired by
the illustrations in Rogers's *Italy,* made a point of seeing Turner's
work in the flesh as it came up for exhibition. But it was not until
around 1837 that admiration commuted into transaction. After this,
the pair invested further, buying two more watercolours from the
same *England and Wales* series, *Gosport* in 1839, and in 1840 a view of
Winchelsea, Sussex.

Thomas Griffith was the man who sold the Ruskins their Turners. He had been appointed by Charles Heath to sell on the watercolours Turner had made for the *England and Wales* series, and had bought a large number himself in the process. With the death of his father, Turner's ability to represent himself via his own gallery was under yet more strain. Griffith, the wealthy son of a successful auctioneer, presented a convenient compromise.

With the demise of aristocratic patronage, and the rise of the art-buying nouveau riche, art dealing had begun to emerge as a distinct profession in the nineteenth century. For example, in 1817 the carver, gilder and frame-maker Thomas Agnew and his partner Vittore Zanetti had set up business in Manchester to sell frames, mirrors and barometers. However, finding themselves in the heartland of industry, their business quickly shifted emphasis to cater for the appetite for contemporary art that was growing among moneyed industrialists. It would not be until the 1850s that the commercial galleries we recognize today, solely dedicated to selling paintings, emerged discreetly from the related business of publishing or frame-making. But those whose names would preside over the doors of these enterprises were already operating as dealers.

Artists and clients alike were sensitive to the profit lines this new breed of dealer was adding to the sales of contemporary art. Griffith, however, sought to introduce clients to artists direct, for a far more modest remuneration. The *Art Union Journal* related that compared to the 'ad libitum profits' applied by most dealers, Griffith allowed artists to set the price of their work and took a small commission to cover his own expenses. It was an approach that garnered Griffith a large following among contemporary artists such as Clarkson Stanfield, George Jones, and Copley Fielding, and would clearly appeal to a Turner sensitive to those who exploited his talent.

Clients also warmed to Griffith, who had a particularly informal style of presenting work. One letter to Griffith from the nephew of Samuel Taylor Coleridge, the Revd Edward Coleridge, expresses just how beneficial Griffith's brokerage was considered.

'I cannot help finding a few moments from my pulpit to assure you that I entirely approve of your gallant endeavours to rescue the really deserving artists from the tender mercies of the dealers,' wrote Coleridge. He appreciated how Griffith brought 'the artists into more immediate contact with their admirers, without any of the disagreeables generally attended to such meetings . . .', inviting him to spend an evening with him and 'bring a good fat portfolio, some new Turners and a warm pair of slippers'.[6]

Griffith introduced the Ruskins to Turner in person in June 1840 at his ample home in Norwood, then a country residence. They partied in his garden, much to Ruskin's delight.

'Everybody had described him to me as coarse, boorish, unintellectual, vulgar,' Ruskin recalled. 'This I knew to be impossible. I found in him a somewhat eccentric, keen-mannered, matter-of-fact, English-minded gentleman: good-natured evidently, bad-tempered evidently, hating humbug of all sorts, shrewd, perhaps a little selfish, highly intellectual, the powers of his mind not brought out with any delight in their manifestation, or intention of display, but flashing out occasionally in a word or a look.'[7]

The young critic and the painter had many things in common despite the difference in their age and education. Apart from the fact that Ruskin was also a very fine watercolourist, the two also shared a love of travel and specifically of the Alps. A passionate geologist, John Ruskin had first glimpsed the great mountains when he was a boy in 1833, and had instantly considered them not only 'the revelation of the beauty of the earth, but the opening of the first page of its volume'.[8] As they sat chatting in Griffith's garden the two discussed their mutual adoration of mountain scenery and found themselves 'talking with great rapture of Aosta and Courmayeur'.[9]

That meeting may well have also included a discussion of one of Turner's latest submissions, *Slavers Throwing Overboard the Dead and Dying – Typhoon Coming On*, an oil painting which had just gone on show at the annual RA exhibition.[10] Given Turner had once invested in a Jamaican tontine, the picture reveals that despite his former financial interest in the economics of slavery, from a narrative and topical point of view he could see the subject's potential. Slavery had finally been abolished in the British empire in 1833 but in 1839, when Turner perhaps conceived this work, the British and Foreign

Anti-Slavery Society had been formed to continue a global fight. In the very year that Turner showed *Slavers*, the organization held its first convention.

The victims of Turner's ruthless slavers are presented within a maelstrom of paint that conjures an angry sea and a tempestuous sky, expressed with the rough loose brushstrokes that had become typical of Turner's later work in oil. But it is the pathetic hands and manacled feet grasping vainly through the foam, and the frenzy of fish rising to the surface in anticipation of their imminent meal, that convey Turner's sense of the tragic obscenity of the event, and makes it reminiscent of his Waterloo and Trafalgar pictures. Though, perhaps with the folly of his own failed investment in the dreadful business in mind, the lines of poetry from his *Fallacies of Hope* present an observation that asks his audience to consider the fact that merchant empires and man's financial markets can be broken by natural disaster just as much as armies or armadas.

> Aloft all hands, strike the top-masts and belay;
> Yon angry setting sun and fierce-edged clouds
> Declare the Typhon's coming.
> Before it sweep your decks, throw overboard
> The dead and dying — ne'er heed their chains.
> Hope, Hope, fallacious Hope!
> Where is thy market now?

For Ruskin *Slavers* was the greatest painting Turner had painted, and he wrote a passionate account of it. It would be the first oil painting that the Ruskins would buy by Turner, and it would be Griffith again who would broker the sale.

A friendship grew between the Ruskin family and Turner. He became a frequent guest at their home in Denmark Hill, and would become a regular at the Ruskin annual New Year's party and at John Ruskin's birthday party on 8 February.

To visit the Alps with Turner would have been an exquisite delight for the passionate John Ruskin, but it was a dream that was not realized. It must have piqued Turner's self-proclaimed greatest admirer that the painter had last visited the Alps in 1836 with Hugh Munro.

Ruskin would grow to mistrust Munro, and would soon rightly conceive him as his main rival, both in the affections of the artist, and as a collector of his work over the next decade – though in truth the Ruskins never really managed to rival the huge collection Munro built of Turner's work – at least not during Turner's lifetime.

In spite of this irritation, Ruskin certainly hoped that he and Turner might enjoy some foreign experiences together. Ruskin found himself in Naples in the spring of 1841, from where he wrote to Griffith for news of Turner.

'As for Turner, I dare not speak about him in society now, for fear of being thought decidedly non compos . . .' he wrote, explaining that he had been following in Turner's footsteps, 'down the Loire from Orleans to Tours'. Despite what others were saying about Turner, the experience had done nothing but reinforce Ruskin's admiration. 'One of his feats – and even you would have been astonished to observe the minute and naturalist like accuracy with which he had noted every apparently contemptible detail – the shape of the vine sticks – of pruned tress – of rudders – oars – cartwheels . . . but touched in with the early accidental happiness – the perfect incorporation with the whole spirit of the scene . . . the ne plus ultra of truth – wherever I go – I find that other painters only reach the corporeal point – the cold, marked exterior of nature – he alone has reached her heart.'[11]

'I had hoped to have met him in Italy,' Ruskin confessed, asking, '. . . has he not been abroad at all – or is he returned?'

Turner had in fact already returned. Across his career he felt strong impulses to revisit places and continue a dialogue with them, adding to the sense of his life's work as a collection of series. In 1840 he revisited Venice. He had last been in the city in 1833, but that magical capital of a lost empire had been on his mind more recently, since in the spring that year he had painted two oils of Venice for exhibition at the RA. These had been painted for the cloth manufacturer John Sheepshanks, from which he was to pick his favourite as part of a commission worth 250 guineas.

Sheepshanks had moved from Leeds to Blackheath, just outside London, in the mid-1830s. He had been collecting Old Masters and fine prints for some time, but his interest in modern art was growing. When Turner's friend the architect John Nash died heavily in debt in 1835, it was Sheepshanks who picked up at the sale of his effects those views of the Isle of Wight that Turner had so enthusiastically painted back in the 1820s. Not long after acquiring these, the industrialist attempted to meet the painter himself, inviting him over to his home, Park House, to view his art collection. He did so via a mutual acquaintance, the Scottish portrait painter Andrew Geddes, who was an associate at the RA. The initial contact with Turner was apparently unsatisfactory, though, as Geddes found himself having to apologize for not responding to Sheepshanks's invitation with sufficient alacrity.

'I delayed writing to you,' Geddes explained apologetically, 'as after I saw Turner and mentioned your most kind manner of invitation he left me uncertain when he could make a day, but said he was certainly engaged all last week and if he had any day it was only a day or two before Christmas . . . any man who thinking himself exempted from the common courtesies of Life makes a great mistake let his situation be what it may.'[12]

Perhaps the industrialist appreciated the image of a man so totally occupied in his work that he had literally no time to spare, since Turner's 'mistake' was overlooked sufficiently for Sheepshanks to place a commission.

It was as if in the process of remembering and conjuring Venice for Sheepshanks, Turner was motivated to see it again. Certainly he packed his bags and headed there soon after his Venetian views had been brought down from the Academy walls.

The watercolour sketches of Venice that Turner made in that summer of 1840 reinvigorated his depictions of the city. They marked a definite move away from the often playful, human views that he had developed for his *Picturesque Views in England and Wales* and his comprehensive views of the Loire and Seine. They also represented a distinct change in tone from the view he had made in oil for Sheepshanks. *Venice, from the Canale della Giudecca, Chiesa di S. Maria della Salute*,[13] presented a city placed firmly on water, located beneath a high blue sky with white whipped mare's-tail clouds. But in his new watercolour sketches, the distinction between sea and sky is less evident. It is as if Turner is painting not the firm stuff of the physical world, but the far more elusive reflection of it captured in particles of light.

The result is a set of sketches at once highly atmospheric and dreamlike. Harking back to the brief, translucent notes he had made in 1819, Turner paints Venice with a melancholic delicacy. Ghost-like people and phantom buildings are caught floating in an insubstantial golden world. The passage of gondolas is smudged on to the watery lagoons and canals, the red outlines indicative of Venetians at work and play, by their very cursory and incomplete nature, suggesting something transitory and remembered.

This trip to Venice in 1840 proved transformative. Turner worked there without a commission or a premeditated series. For once he was working purely for pleasure. As if unburdened, he painted a number of the deeply impressionistic works, on spec and *en plein air*. It was a liberating experience that would set the tone for the last decade of his life.

Three oil paintings of Venice that Turner delivered to the RA show of 1841 were not as wildly atmospheric nor as impressionistic as his watercolour sketches. They were, however, boldly modern in their own way, using a bright, reduced palette of gold, white and blue and playing with the discrepancy between the linear clarity of beautifully observed gondolas in the foreground, and the hazy mirage of the city rising over the water in the distance. Turner must have been delighted when his great friend Chantrey bought one of these even before the public had a chance to see it. *Ducal Palace, Dogano, with part of San Giorgio, Venice* was snapped up by him on one of the varnishing days.

En route to Venice Turner had been accompanied some of the way by Henry Harpur and his wife, Eleanor.[14] But the Harpurs would not have witnessed Turner sitting in his gondola, brush in hand. After tracing the Rhine to Bregenz with him, the couple branched off to explore the Swiss Alps before descending to Italy via the Lakes, to Milan. While Turner was in Venice, Harpur wrote to him, raving about their Swiss trip.

'After you left us at Bregentz we soon found ourselves amongst the Mountains, and from the fineness of the sky anticipated a clear day for the Splugen . . . taking all the passes I have yet seen, this [the Splugen] is by far the best . . . the Via Mala is a gorge so close that the Rhine is chased between the Rocks so close that a piece of wood of the size of a foot cannot descend and in consequence when the Rains fall, the Water rises 400 feet.'[15]

Their account of the Alps may have played a part in Turner's decision to return to Switzerland the following year. His Swiss watercolours forty years earlier had been defining, and now Turner had a desire to revisit the Alps and respond to them anew. After the airiness and space of the floating city, and his experiments with painting in situ, the mass of the mountains proposed an enticing counterpoint. Turner wanted to experiment with the dramatic scenery. And again, his mission while there was to paint free of clients' requests, publishers' briefs or market influences; he wanted, as Ruskin later put it, 'to please himself'.

It is something that at the age of sixty-six Turner's desire for adventure and experiment still defined him. Resilient to the abuse his oil painting in particular was attracting, the creative impulse could not be repressed. As he explained to his namesake, the antiquary Dawson Turner, 'after all my determination to be quiet some fresh follerey comes across me and I begin what most probably never to be finish'd'.[16] His innate compulsion to work aside, such 'follerey' may also have been encouraged by the fact that suddenly Turner found himself with no more major print series to complete. At the dawn of the 1840s his workload was becoming lighter.

Despite his desire to explore complete creative freedom, Turner hoped that there might nevertheless be a market for this work done to please himself. For a man who had seen the influence of patrons gradually slackening across his lifetime, and the voice of the creative artist slowly growing stronger, such a thing would mark a triumph.

So he headed abroad again that summer of 1841 intending to make a series of watercolours for the handful of clients who had proved his most ardent supporters. Munro's and Ruskin's interest in a new series of Alpine watercolours would be easily raised. Apart from these two, there were other passionate watercolour collectors that Turner had in his sights.

One was the whaling magnate Elhanan Bicknell, a close neighbour of Ruskin, who lived near Denmark Hill. Bicknell had made his considerable fortune out of sperm whale oil, which his company, Langton and Bicknell, processed. The lighthouse builder Robert Stevenson used their oil and swore by it. And in addition to illuminating the northern shores of Britain, it was also widely used in street lighting and the manufacture of candles.

Bicknell already had plenty of artistic associations. His son, Henry, had married the Scottish painter David Roberts's daughter, Christine. In addition, his brother-in-law was the illustrator Hablot Knight Browne, who under the pseudonym of 'Phiz' became famous for illustrating Dickens's works. Bicknell had bought his first two Turner watercolours in 1838. But given the shared friendship of Roberts, he may have known Turner personally earlier. Either way, Bicknell had been in Switzerland in 1836, touring in the Alps with his brother-in-law Browne at just the same time as Turner and Munro, and so his interest in Swiss views may also have been canvassed by the painter.

Another potential buyer was Benjamin Godfrey Windus, whose fortune came from a coach-building business, as well as from the manufacture of a miracle cordial made from morphine and treacle that Victorian families bought, unsurprisingly, in their droves. Windus had not only been collecting since the 1820s, but had been displaying Turner watercolours at his home in Tottenham. He had had a library specially built in which, by the mid-1830s, he displayed a huge number of Turner watercolours,[17] and to which interested parties could gain admittance every Monday. In fact Windus's home had become a place of pilgrimage to the artists of the day, keen to get a sense of contemporary art, and John Ruskin had certainly taken advantage of Mr Windus's gallery in the 1830s to better acquaint himself with the work of his hero. Here he saw 'walls beset . . . with Turner drawings of the England series; while in his portfolio-stands, coming straight from the publishers of books they illustrated, were the entire series of the illustrations to Scott, to Byron, to the South Coast, and to Finden's bible'.[18]

Turner knew Windus extremely well and considered the client a firm friend. The similarities that the former shared with Walter Fawkes may have been part of his appeal to the painter. Windus had been an ardent supporter of the reformist Francis Burdett, for example, and his passion for music and poetry was also profound. Windus's daughter, Mary de Putron, relates how Turner and George Jones were in the habit of attending her father's annual birthday party on 15 January throughout the 1830s, an occasion on which Turner was always in the habit of examining the little landscape motifs on Windus's pink-edged Worcester dessert-ware.[19]

But for all the birthday parties and kind invitations, Windus, like John James Ruskin, and like most of the other wealthy collectors that Turner was dealing with from the 1830s onwards, was a businessman. He, like Sheepshanks and Vernon, Gillott and others, had become successful through smart negotiation and strong-minded behaviour. These men may have been passionate art-lovers, but they were not necessarily easy. If early in his career Turner had to negotiate the whims of an aristocracy who had grown to expect artists to come at their beck and call, in his later career he was dealing with a set of difficult businessmen who also expected a degree of compliance for their money, knew their own minds, and could be financially cautious.

With these potential clients in mind, Turner headed out to Switzerland at the end of August 1841. His plan was to make a series of up to twenty watercolours, for which he began preparatory sketches.

Once again he took a steamboat up the Rhine as far as Coblenz, then revisited the falls at Schaffhausen that he had drawn previously. From here he continued east to Constance, then headed south down towards the Splugen Pass, which had been so vividly described to him by Harpur. Next he headed back towards Zurich. Near Lucerne he spent time sketching the great mountain, the Rigi, which drew tourists to that lake. He then headed to Thun and Lake Geneva, returning to Lausanne and Geneva before heading for the Rhine again to take him home.

As in Venice, Turner worked *en plein air*, and as in Venice his work offered a new kind of response to scenery.[20] He did some ten sketches

of the Falls of Schaffhausen for example. But whereas he had sought
to find mass and weight in the huge volume of water in his depiction
of it in oils forty years earlier, now in watercolour it is the vaporous
mist thrown up by the waterfall that Turner captures, a mist which,
originating in the white churn of water, envelops the countryside all
around it. But what is a real departure in his 1841 watercolours of the
Alps is the colour scheme Turner employed. Using the most translucent washes, his depictions of the mountains work through rainbow
schemes of purplish greys through to salmon pinks and pale yellows,
with towns and villages hinted at with faint lines in red ink. The
thinness of the wash suggests a distant, fragile world that stands in
strong contrast to the imposing substantial drama Turner was able to
find in Alpine scenery previously.

Turner showed Griffith the sketches immediately on his return
and asked him what he might be able to secure for finished watercolours. When Griffith suggested 80 guineas for worked-up versions,
Turner wondered if they were not worth more.

'Says Mr Griffith to Mr Turner (after looking curiously into the
execution, which you will please note, is rather what some people
might call hazy): "They're a little different from your usual style" –
(Turner silent, Griffith does not push the point) – "but – but – yes,
they are worth more, but I could not get more".'[21]

Turner felt that there might be a market for the watercolours even
in their most immediate sketch form. After all, Walter Fawkes had
been prepared to take his earlier, sketch-like Rhine watercolours in a
first rather than a finished state. On this basis Turner reworked a
range of sketches on different sizes of paper into a series of ten
sketches on same sized paper, retaining them, however, in a 'primi-
tive state'. Aware that some clients might prefer something more
conventionally finished, however, he also provided four samples of
how the sketches might then evolve into more finished pieces. This
done, Griffith set about bringing the buyers to the table.

But Griffith's sense that the new work might be harder to sell was
right. Even the proposed 'finished' versions were significantly different from Turner's work of the 1830s, with misty atmospheric effects

combined with this newly bright and delicate palette. And Windus, for one, was having none of it.

In fact Griffith's attempts to sell Windus Turner's new Swiss watercolours brought rumbling antagonism to a point of rupture. Back in the summer of 1840, Turner had got word that Windus was annoyed that the painter had resolutely failed to respond to two of three proposed commissions from him. No doubt the man who had so extensively bought Turner's work 'off the shelf' felt he had earned the right to have something painted bespoke. A right that perhaps Turner was reluctant to acknowledge, given the considerable amount of unsold work he harboured in Queen Anne Street.

'I feel very much distressed in your being displeased with me,' Turner wrote at the end of July 1840. 'I hope to loose [sic] no time . . . to express my regret that any apparent backwards on my part should have occurred respecting the commission you gave me and that the 2 or three inquiries on your part had not been satisfactorily answered by me!!!'[22]

The fact that just a year after this frustration Griffith turned up with a new proposition from Turner must have riled Windus further. Windus didn't like having his arm twisted by an agent, and he felt aggravated that rather than being able to satisfy his own personal agenda, he was being asked to satisfy Turner's. He wrote some stern letters to the painter on the matter. Only Turner's responses remain. Nevertheless the accusations that Windus made are clear from Turner's riposte.

'Your letter of Saturday last gives me much concern and pain in that I have caused you in any way such annoyance,' Turner wrote on 14 March 1842, 'most particularly so in your concern of my doing any more Drawings.'[23]

Part of Windus's grievance seemed to be the fact that he was offered a proposition from the artist into which he could have no input, and a price which seemed set rather than negotiable. This is again suggested in Turner's attempts to pull his client around. Four days later, on 18 March, he wrote: 'Mr G offered . . . to ascertain how far my employ for my own use when out upon my . . . trips might be . . . approved of [by] my admiring friends in being carried on or left in their chance state when done from nature thus.' In the finished works, 'opinions [from the client] might be shown,' he suggested, insisting further that he was 'not fixing any price'.[24]

But despite his attempts to heal the rift, Windus's nose was out of joint. In addition to the presumptions of the artist, he was also particularly suspicious of Griffith who, apart from selling Turner's work, was building his own collection. Bumping into John Ruskin's father, John James Ruskin, in April 1842, Windus expressed his concern at the manipulative influence Griffith might have on the market for Turner's work. 'Be on your guard,' Windus warned Ruskin. 'I myself have kept to the best Turners and am safe.'[25]

Though Windus was still refusing to buy, Turner managed to sell ten finished watercolours of the new Swiss series and a number of the sketches to his other clients. Of the finished versions, Bicknell bought two, Griffith took one as his commission in kind, Ruskin took two, and Munro took an astonishing five. It remained a point of envy and irritation on Ruskin's part that Munro took the finished version of Turner's view of the Splugen Pass, a painting that Ruskin particularly craved but had not been quick enough to secure.[26]

The sale of these ten watercolours was a watershed moment. From this point on there is the most definite sense that Turner gave himself permission, in the last decade of his life, to be himself. They mark a moment from which his painting in both oil and watercolour becomes even more purposefully experimental.

Significantly it is in the 1840s that Turner also quite clearly embarks upon a personal life. Unlike the man who had been married to art and the demands of his order book when Sarah Danby had had his daughters, now Turner found a way to find time for a life with Mrs Booth. His trips to Kent became more regular, and his investment in a life with her more profound.

The strong sense of his own mortality must have had some bearing on his behaviour. Death was the hovering angel that Turner seemed to have consistently in his sights now. Not only did James Holworthy, with whom Turner had been so close, die in 1841, but in June that year David Wilkie also passed away during a trip to the East. When returning from the Levant he fell ill at Gibraltar, and he was buried in the bay. For all their rivalries as younger men, Turner was very upset indeed by the death of a man who had become a good friend, and was only midway through his fifties. He could barely bring himself to talk about Wilkie's demise without betraying his sense of loss. John Ruskin's friend the amateur painter and cultural hostess Lady Trevelyan, who first met Turner shortly after the event, could never forget 'the tone of feeling with which he alluded to it'.[27]

But in November 1841 Turner's heart broke when his dearest friend, Francis Chantrey, died quite suddenly aged just sixty. 'He came to the house of our deceased friend,' George Jones later remembered. 'He asked for me; I went to him; he wrung my hand, tears streamed from his eyes, and he rushed from the house without uttering a word.'[28]

Significantly, Chantrey had left the vast portion of his estate to the nation for 'purchase of works of fine art of the highest merit . . . that can be obtained'. Works by British artists were to be bought for 'liberal' prices. It was a specific stipulation in Chantrey's bequest that the works were not to be commissioned, nor influenced, but must be completed by the artists before purchase. He, like Turner, had been looking towards a day when artists might be able to produce work that was entirely of their own conception, unmediated, and free.[29]

With his own life so clearly entering its last chapter, the sentiments posthumously expressed by his great friend must have spurred Turner's own pursuit of this utter freedom. In 1842, 1843 and 1844 he returned to the Alps with his little leather wallet of portable watercolours, purely to continue his experiments. Meanwhile, dauntless, his work in oil ventured into new realms.

In the 1842 RA show, alongside two more typical scenes of Venice that Bicknell and Vernon bought respectively, were other highly unusual paintings that marked Turner's new agenda. *Peace – Burial at Sea* and *War. The Exile and the Rock Limpet* were offered as a complementary pair, and stood out instantly for their highly unusual format. Both were delivered as squares but were then worked further into octagons during the varnishing days. Both paintings were accompanied by verse. *Peace*, which was a tribute to David Wilkie, was a

symphony of dark blue-greys and charcoal blacks. It showed the silhouette of the steamship *The Oriental*, on which Wilkie had died, with
huge black soot clouds erupting from its funnels, and its sails unfurled
like dark funeral palls. A narrow sliver of golden light is cast down
the side of the ship as torches illuminate Wilkie's body being lowered
into the water. *War*, by contrast, was painted with blood-red a dominant colour. Alluding to the ashes of Napoleon, which had just been
brought back from St Helena, where he had been exiled, it features
the solitary figure of the former emperor alone on a watery beach.
His arms are folded and he contemplates a tiny limpet in the rock
pool at his feet.

As so often, Turner had his contemporaries in his sights with this
painting. The painter Benjamin Robert Haydon had made a rare
impact with his own *Napoleon Musing at St Helena*, which featured the
general, his arms crossed, looking out to sea. The tragic hero in Haydon's version is belittled by Turner, who mimics the pose Haydon
had used for Napoleon. But rather than offering him a vast ocean to
contemplate, Turner gives his Napoleon a rock pool. For all his conquests, his empire has shrunk to Lilliputian proportions. In contrast
to his farewell to Wilkie, where Turner manages to evoke a sense of
loss, as a body so tiny against the vast ocean is nevertheless bestowed
with a heroic glow, the sense of loss in *War* is reserved for Napoleon's
own feelings of failure. There is little heroism in Turner's belittling
depiction of the exile. There is, however, when one takes the two
works together, the suggestion that the achievement of the artist
might be considered greater and more enduring than that of the
emperor.

This interest in the legacy of the artist was of course something
Turner had explored from the very early days of his career, beginning perhaps with his homage to Pope's villa at Twickenham. And as
he got closer to death, it was a subject that grew in his consciousness.
The very next year Turner submitted *The Opening of the Wallhalla,
1842* to the R A, a painting that reprised the subject of war, peace and
the endurance of art.

Back in 1840 when travelling in Germany, Turner had made a
point of visiting King Ludwig of Bavaria's ambitious monument to

Germanic talent – the Walhalla, which had still been under construction on the banks of the Danube near Regensburg. Fashioned on the
Athenian Parthenon, this temple to German genius would eventually
house some 130 busts not just of Germanic military heroes, but also
of scientists and artists. Turner had made plenty of sketches of the site
and the building high on its promontory above the Danube. When
news reached British shores that the building had been opened in
October 1842, Turner set about imagining the opening using the
sketches he had already made.

The painting is an essay in his 'indistinct' approach to the physical
topography of the view, the temple bleached by sunlight in a hazy
mid-distance, groups of people in the foreground and their discarded
belongings all leaning in towards the centre of the canvas, to guide
the eye to the monument to human achievement, amid a landscape
that has been worked into a single misty symphony of golden tones.

Alongside the work, Turner submitted, as he had done so often
before, some more lines from the apparently unending *Fallacies of
Hope*. His verse acknowledges that after the ravages of war, and when
peace has returned,

> . . . – the morning ray
> Beams on the Wallhalla, reared to science, and the arts,
> For men renowned, of German fatherland.

In the year that Ruskin's *Modern Painters* was launched, this painting
was actually met with little resistance from a British public who had
grown used to Turner's recent style. Not so its German counterpart,
who saw the painting when Turner submitted it to the Congress of
European Art in Munich in 1845. To the German press and public,
not used to the 'eccentricities' of his late works, and familiar only
with pristine engravings of his work, the painting was interpreted as
a hideous satire on good art and an attack on the monument itself. It
was sent back, rudely, to Queen Anne Street, where Munro happened
to be visiting with Elizabeth Rigby – the young woman who would
marry Turner's friend Charles Eastlake.

'His splendid picture of "Walhalla" had been sent to Munich, there
ridiculed as might be expected, and returned to him with 7[£] to

pay, and sundry spots upon it,' Rigby wrote in her diary on 20 May 1846. 'On this Turner laid his odd misshapen thumb in a pathetic way. Mr. Munro suggested they would rub out, and I offered my cambric handkerchief; but the old man edged us away, and stood before his picture like a hen in a fury.'[30]

Turner's frustration at the public's inability to grasp his message in *Wallhalla* is palpable. Not least because the painting acknowledged Ludwig's honouring of German *art and science*. In the last decade of his life, as he saw science and industry rise to define the modern world, Turner sought to synthesize and align these disciplines in his work in newly adventurous manner. Science had always been part and parcel of Turner's craft, of course. From his earliest drawings, his exploration of natural science is evident in his acute and detailed observation of clouds; of his sketching of the rhythm and patterns of waves and, as Ruskin had testified, his unparalleled depiction of geology. His attempts to incorporate the physical attributes of colour and optics into his work in the 1820s were an extension of this. And now in the 1840s he attempted to incorporate into this work the discoveries of the nineteenth century's new science – magnetism and electricity.

Operating in London's intellectual elite as he did, Turner found himself fairly regularly in discussion with those scientists exploring these phenomena. It was not just that the Royal Academy and the Royal Society had been housed alongside one another in Somerset House, and that these scientists often performed public lectures and experiments to the delight of London's public, but it was at the coffee houses, breakfast and dining clubs and dinner parties that Turner attended so regularly and with such enthusiasm that he had the opportunity to meet and become acquainted with the scientific luminaries of his era.

Turner had certainly attended some of the soirées that the pioneer of computing and investigator of electrodynamics, Charles Babbage, had held. Both Turner and Babbage were also regular guests at Samuel Rogers's famous gatherings. In fact Babbage had had the unique privilege of returning the umbrella that Turner was rarely seen without, which he had left at Rogers's. Babbage discovered that despite its rather well-worn appearance, Turner had a dagger concealed in the handle, presumably as a precaution against the many bandits that still plagued intrepid tourists on the Continent.

When the Athenaeum Club was founded in 1824 as a place where artists and scientists could meet, Turner was invited to join as a founder member, an invitation that he took up with relish and a facility and privilege that he used well, becoming a familiar figure seated in the south-east corner of the Drawing Room.

It is worth noting that the chemist Humphry Davy was the first chairman of the Athenaeum, and the man who explored electromagnetism, Michael Faraday, was its first secretary. But significantly, Turner had already encountered both these men through the web of friends and patrons that had always served him so well.

Davy had been in Rome with Turner in 1819. The Faradays, meanwhile, had first met Turner around the dinner table of the lithographer Charles Hullmandel, a friend of Turner's stockbroker, Charles Stokes. Perhaps it was inevitable that this meeting would lead to a proper friendship, since Faraday and Turner shared a delight in storms and skies. 'Storms excited his [Faraday's] admiration at all times,' the latter's brother-in-law would later relate, 'and he was never tired of looking into the heavens. He said to me once, "I wonder yon artists don't study the light and colour in the sky more, and try more for effect." I think this quality in Turner's drawings made him admire them so much. He . . . often had applications from him [Turner] for chemical information about pigments. Faraday always impressed upon Turner and other artists the great necessity there was to experiment for themselves, putting washes and tints of all their pigments in the bright sunlight, covering up one half, and noticing the effect of light and gases on the other . . .'[31]

In 1829 the doctor William Somerville had been a dinner companion at that turtle supper Chantrey and Turner had attended at the home of chalkpit owner W. H. Whitbread in Purfleet. Somerville and his scientist wife Mary were very friendly with Turner. Mary recounted in her own memoirs how, in the 1820s, she 'frequently went to Turner's studio, and was always welcomed. No one could imagine that so much poetical feeling existed in so rough an exterior.'[32]

Alongside her astronomical research, it was Mary Somerville's experiments with the magnetizing property of violet light within the solar spectrum that Turner, the painter of light, found so fascinating. This was alongside Faraday's researches into the relationship between electricity and magnetism, where he had shown how magnetic force could be revealed by moving a magnet over iron filings.

But in 1839 the work of Turner's friends was taken a stage further when the Astronomer Royal, George Biddle Airy, presented a paper at the Royal Society that discussed the forces of magnetism and electricity at sea. The new iron steamships that had been introduced were discovering that their compasses were deviating, and Airy suggested this was due to the fact that the ships were becoming magnetized by the electrical current being produced by the motion of the waves.

Snow Storm – Steam-boat off a Harbour's Mouth Making Signals in Shallow Water, and Going by the Lead. The Author was in this Storm on the Night the Ariel left Harwich was a major canvas that Turner showed in 1842. In the work the painter took on board Airy's thesis and depicted an iron steamer as the black heart of a vortex of energy and motion. The circular composition Turner employs draws on the experiments he made in his vignettes, though here the ship at the centre of a whirlpool of clouds, waves, rain and spume is also informed by magnetic theory. It was an unparalleled attempt by Turner to depict not only his own personal perception of the maelstrom of the storm, but also represent the greater forces of science and nature and to see beyond the experimental world a far greater system of divine or fundamental powers.[33]

The long and detailed title of the work was designed to emphasize the point of view of the painter. That Turner had made a point of experiencing storms and that he was an intrepid sailor is without doubt. He would go on to relate that for this particular picture he lashed himself to the mast of a ship, a myth that has stuck fast. But it is dangerous to take literally the words of a man who was mining the most profound recesses of his imagination and memory, for whom titles were often complex conceits drawing on contemporary references, and whose wry sense of humour often prompted him to tease people about the meanings of his pictures.

The work is a bubbling cauldron of potent allusions designed to muster emotion, hold his audience spellbound, and confound and tantalize his public and critics.

Those visiting the Royal Academy when the painting hung there for the first time were better placed than those viewing it today, as they knew that it was the *Fairy*, not the *Ariel*, that had been famously wrecked off Harwich in the winter of 1840, with the tragic loss of her entire crew. However, the evocation of Shakespeare's powerful *Tempest*, which also dashed ships, must have been irresistible for the painter, who converted *Fairy* into the Shakespearean sprite *Ariel*. In doing this he simultaneously alluded to the *Ariel* steam-packet that had equally famously encountered bad weather when it brought Prince Albert over to marry Queen Victoria in February, an incident that was recorded in many popular prints of the time.

Meanwhile, Turner's claim that he tied himself to a mast remains evidence that the painter's wry and erudite sense of humour was intact in his sixty-eighth year. The legend that the great sea painter Joseph Vernet had lashed himself to a mast to better understand a sea storm would also have been better known to nineteenth-century painters than it is today. Vernet's painter grandson, Horace, had commemorated the event in a painting in the 1820s, and there was even a statue of Vernet lashed to the mast in the Louvre at the time.[34] But whether Turner actually followed the example of the painter he so admired, or simply enjoyed the legend, remains wide open to debate.

The *Snow Storm* picture was the natural precursor to two paintings he showed in the following year: *Shade and Darkness – the Evening of the Deluge* and *Light and Colour (Goethe's Theory) – The Morning After the Deluge, Moses Writing the Book of Genesis*. Here the centrifugal composition that he explored in the *Snow Storm* of the previous year is repeated and intensified in two weather-related pictures, which also combine science and biblical themes. Like his unusual reveries on death in the previous year, these were also displayed in octagonal frames.

The theory of Goethe that Turner referenced was one in which the German writer explored the psychological effects of colour. The fact that his friend Charles Eastlake had recently translated Goethe's work into English gave Turner a good opportunity to bring this long-held belief to public attention. Goethe depicted colour on a wheel of plus and minus values, with the red end of the spectrum associated with happiness and the blue-green end of the spectrum associated with anxiety. Appropriately then, Turner exploited the negative range of the wheel in his depiction of pre-deluge storm clouds spiralling around a distant ark, a peppering of jet black birds swooping down towards it, and pairs of animals casting long shadows marching through a murky fog. *The Morning after the Deluge* by contrast depicts God's promise of salvation not as a rainbow but as a circle of rosy hope, translucent angels rising heaven-bound as if in a bubble.

For Turner these and the *Snow Storm* of the previous year marked the culmination of a body of work that had consistently sought to communicate the ultimate truth about the world of which he was a part: whether through direct observation of the natural world, or by referencing mythologies that could communicate the patterns of rise and fall that he saw to be fundamental to existence. In these late paintings Turner used every ounce of his painterly virtuosity to depict a complex, mysterious world and contain it within a single round holistic emblem. As if encouraging his viewer to peer through a multidimensional telescope, he shows time, science, different worldly planes and natural phenomena at once in a mysterious kaleidoscope.

His public were appalled. After vicious reviews of *The Storm* in the previous year, the condemnation of the *Deluge* paintings was practically unanimous. The *Morning Chronicle*, 9 May, considered them 'perfectly indescribable', while *The Times* critic saw nothing other than a 'ridiculous daub' and 'a wretched mixture of trumpery conceits, involving an anachronism that the meanest scholar at a parish school could rectify'.[35]

Meanwhile a Hungarian artist, Miklós Barabás, got his first glimpse of Turner's work at the show and was dumbfounded. 'Turner's is not a picture at all,' he wrote, '– it is just a piece of canvas smeared with colours, without any reason, meaning, or thought. A painting like that would not be accepted for an exhibition anywhere else in the world . . .'

Barabás's friend the watercolour painter William Leitch attempted to offer some perspective on why Turner's work did still manage to get shown.

'Leitch told me that Turner used to paint very beautifully 25–30 years before, but his mental state had deteriorated to such an extent that he had become childish. The pictures he had painted in the last 25 years were not worth looking at, and even his best friends were not taking them seriously. But his reputation used to be great . . . There were many people who, being ignorant about the arts, were only after big names – and were thus ready to buy his daubs.'[36]

The fury and pain Turner felt when faced with thoughtless criticism was not just witnessed by Elizabeth Rigby and Munro, but also by John Ruskin. Turner was at Denmark Hill in October 1844 at a time when a series of interviews with the recently deceased William Beckford had been published in the *New Monthly Magazine*. The magazine's reporter related how, when he and Beckford were looking at one of the watercolours of Fonthill that Turner had executed, Beckford complained how much changed Turner's late work was from that of his early years. 'He paints now as if his brains and imagination were mixed up on his palette with soapsuds and lather,' Beckford declared. Turner must have picked up this article at the Ruskins' home, for John Ruskin relates that '. . . after dinner, sitting in his armchair by the fire I heard him muttering to himself at intervals "soapsuds and whitewash! What would they have? I wonder what they think the sea's like? I wish they'd been in it." '[37]

For all those prepared to condemn Turner in print in the 1840s there remained a passionate few, however, often painters, who continued to uphold even his late work as the embodiment of artistic freedom. 'His latter style, though possibly extravagant, was only excess in development of nature,' George Jones reminisced, 'he exaggerated what he saw, but the foundation was truth; the vivid and warm colouring of nature he painted with the most forcible colours, the lines of nature and atmosphere no pigments can give, but Turner went further than any artist of the past or present age in diffusing light and air over his pictures.'[38]

'It always seems to me that it is in his boundless prodigality of thought that Turner differs from other painters, and that the more Turneresque he was (up to his culminating point) the more full of meaning every bit of his work became,' wrote Lady Trevelyan. 'You never get to the end of a picture of his: the more you look at it the more you find out. It is not that there is a blue mist and you imagine things in it. You might fancy things in other people's blue mists, when you were in the humour, and the things would not be there next time you looked; but Turner's things are really there, and once you have seen them there they are for ever, and you know that he meant them, and meant a thousand things more that you have only to watch for and find out.'[39]

The publication of Ruskin's defence of Turner in *Modern Painters* also had some positive effect. It certainly encouraged a number of men to purchase paintings from, Ruskin was arguing, Turner's golden era – the 1830s. There was a wealth of canvases from this period which had been sitting unsold at Queen Anne Street for close to a decade.

Elhanan Bicknell was one such who, in 1844, made his way to what Trevelyan remembered as

> . . . that wonderful old house, where the old woman with her head wrapped up in dirty flannel used to open the door . . . and where on faded walls hardly weather-tight, and among bits of old furniture thick with dust like a place that had been forsaken for years, were those brilliant pictures all glowing with sunshine and colour – glittering lagunes of Venice, foaming English seas and fairy sunsets – all shining out of the dirt and neglect, and standing in rows one behind another as if they were endless, the great 'Carthage' at one end of the room and the glorious old 'Téméraire' lighting up another corner, and Turner himself careless and kind and queer to look upon, with a certain pathos under his humour, that one could hardly miss.[40]

Bicknell bought eight oils, six on one single day. Two of the works, *Calder Bridge* and *Ivy Bridge,* had been unsold for nearly thirty years, having been shown by Turner himself in his old gallery. The rest had been shown in the late 1820s and 30s at the RA.[41] Joseph Gillott also bought in this and the subsequent year *Calais Sands, Low Water, Poissards Collecting Bait* and *Grand Canal, Venice 1835* and *Mercury and Argus.* It was almost certainly Gillott who encouraged his friend Edwin Bullock, the iron foundry owner from Birmingham, to pick up

Turner's *Dogana, and Madonna della Salute, Venice* in 1843. Another friend of both Gillott and Bullock, the Midland mine owner Charles Birch, also bought Turners on show at the RA in 1844 as well as acquiring others that were in store at Queen Anne Street.

But perhaps the most significant trophy of Ruskin's labours to salvage Turner's reputation was Benjamin Godfrey Windus. Ruskin effected a reconciliation between the painter and collector which saw the pair meet at a dinner party in October 1844, with Griffith also in attendance. The evening went well and the troubles of the past were put to one side. If Windus had been suspicious that Griffith was trying to flog him 'daubs', as Leitch's comments to Barabás suggested, he finally put aside his concerns about a decline in Turner's work. Windus's patronage began to flow once more, and he committed to a new set of Swiss watercolours that Turner planned, much along the lines of those he had made after his 1841 trip.

This was a particularly piquant victory for Ruskin, who had written to Windus the very day after the reconciliatory dinner.

> I know that Griffith had something at his tongues end all the time we were at Tottenham which he never had the courage to bring out. I have several reasons both selfish – & unselfish – for being more bold . . . of the 10 drawings which Turner wishes to execute – only six are engaged – Griffith himself intends taking two – but if you – in compliment to Turner – would let your name stand to the form Griffith would be most happy to let you choose the couple you liked when executed and to take the other two remaining after your selection . . . that the selfish desire of seeing these lovely thoughts realized, weighs with me . . . I cannot deny – but from my heart – the stronger and principal motive is my desire to see those kindly relations already resumed between Turner and you – sealed by an act of condescension on the side of the injured party – and to see your noble collection completed by examples of these peculiar and vigorous conceptions.[42]

Windus was indeed good for two and took a view of *Lake Lucerne from Brunnen* as well as *A Fête Day in Zurich: Early Morning*. Not surprisingly the other watercolours were taken by Munro as well as Ruskin.

Though his late Swiss watercolours found buyers, the oil paintings that Turner executed from this point on did not. Inspired by Ruskin's advocacy, a few bold collectors commissioned work in oil in 1844 and 1845, only to return the work disappointed. This was the case with Elhanan Bicknell, who after his spending spree on earlier works commissioned a whaling subject. But when *The Whale Ship* with its great blunt-nosed sperm whale writhing in the foreground was sent to his client, Bicknell accused Turner of using watercolour on the canvas and returned it. That Turner was mixing media in an experimental manner is highly likely. But such was the abstracted nature of the image from those Bicknell had bought of the 1830s that it was as likely that he just couldn't appreciate the painting. Turner's professional pride was too wounded and what had been a very warm friendship went into decline.

Views of Venice for William Wethered, a draper from King's Lynn, also found themselves returned. Again Ruskin was behind these commissions. He had been advising Wethered since the late 1830s and in 1844 this had resulted in the latter buying *Approach to Venice*, a gorgeous depiction of a flotilla of gondolas heading across a blue lagoon dappled with gold. Urged by Ruskin to commission more, Turner duly showed *Venice, evening going to the Ball (St Martino)* and *Morning, returning from the ball, St Martha* in the RA show of 1845 with Wethered in mind and with friendly negotions on price well under way. But these differed from the *Approach*, returning to a dominant yellow palette. Wethered did not like the new Venetian works, the unkind observations in *Punch* that they revealed Venice by gaslight hardly encouraging the potential investor.

It is testimony to his complex and contradictory nature that in the midst of his great last bid for artistic freedom there was still a version of Turner keen to please a client. He went to the trouble of painting a new pair of Venetian views with a more varied palette for Wethered, which he showed in 1846. When Wethered defaulted yet again on the commission, Windus stepped in, and he would take the *Approach to Venice* off Wethered's hands three years later too. But significantly these would be the last oil paintings Turner was to sell off the walls of the Academy. The other Venetian views, his images of whalers, even his depiction of the new steam invention, the train, *Rain, Steam, and Speed – The Great Western Railway*, remained unsold. They were now considered to be paintings just too incomprehensible.

As his paintings became more obscure to his contemporaries, a veil was also drawn over his private life. Hannah Danby was still affectionately described by Turner to his friends as his 'damsel', and remained in full view as the female companion, and perhaps mistress, of the painter. Indeed, during the extended and eventually unsuccessful negotations with Wethered, a brief glimpse of their now long-established domestic life together is revealed in some correspondence between the two men.

'Allow me to thank you for the fine Norfolk Turkey and Chine,' Turner wrote to his client in 1844, 'quite equal if not superior to the olden renown of the county for sausage roles and Turkey-pie and much better (my Damsel said) in being ready for the cooking.'[43]

But the other members of his family seemed to have faded away. Sarah Danby was living in William Street with some of her daughters by her husband John. But those she had conceived with Turner had receded from sight.

His younger daughter, Georgiana, who had married a young chemist called Thomas James Thompson in Bermondsey in 1840, died three years later at the Lying-in Hospital in York Road, Lambeth. She had given birth to her first child, Thomas William, in 1842 but the baby died. A year later she died giving birth to her second child, Thomas Markham, who also died. The residual connection to her father is indicated in the name of her first son. Beyond a mention in Turner's will there seems little evidence of any particular relationship between father and daughter. Turner is not recorded on her marriage certificate. Georgiana instead offers her father as 'George Danby deceased' – and it may well be that she had considered her real father as good as such, regardless of the fact that he had made her a beneficiary of his will.

Evelina, meanwhile, had had her fair share of tragedy too when it came to children. She had gone abroad with her husband, Joseph Dupuis – despite the fact that she was seven months pregnant, the pair had boarded a store ship called the *Sarah*, heading for Kumasi,

modern-day Ghana, where Dupuis had consulate duties, and had
arrived in January 1819.

This child born on African soil would not survive. Neither would
the baby daughter Evelina bore the following year; nor her first son,
whom she named after her father. William Dupuis entered and left
the world in 1823. Four other children did, however, survive. Rosalie, Joseph, Hanmer and Evelina were all born between 1825 and 1832,
but if Turner had seen his grandchildren it would have been infre-
quently at best. Though there is indication that Evelina and Joseph
returned to England sporadically, they spent much of their time in
the 1820s and 30s at various diplomatic posts across Africa. Again the
only suggestion of any ongoing relationship is Turner's provision for
his daughter in his will.

Unknown to his colleagues and friends, however, a life with Mrs
Booth was continuing outside London. In the 1841 census Sophia is
still noted as a resident of Margate, but at some stage she moved from
the bustling business of Cold Harbour and found a house at St Margaret's at Cliffe, at 15 Beach Street, which she rented from a Richard
Chitty.[44] The tiny village, between Dover and Deal, is perched on a
cliff overlooking the sea, and 15 Beach Street would have afforded
Turner a good view.

In Margate first, and then at Cliffe, Turner painted with a sense of
abandonment, and perhaps some of the freedom he explored in the
complete privacy of his life with Mrs Booth had fed into those late
works he shared with his clients and exhibited in public. A whole body
of work associated with Thanet and Sophia Booth was left in her possession when Turner died. In the same way that he had given works to
Sarah Danby and would pay Thomas Griffith and Charles Stokes in
kind, this was perhaps, apart from a matter of affection, his accidental
way of making a financial contribution to their arrangement.

Some of the most touching of these works reveal aspects of their
domestic life together. Turner sketched girls as they sunbathed on
Margate's beaches and made delightful watercolours of the fish and
seafood that Sophia would obtain for their supper, determined to
celebrate them on paper before they were transformed by the cook.
He captures mackerel with their gleaming stripes, the odd-looking

gurnard, a collection of deep-sea fish and some prawns. In the full-ness of time Sophia passed on one watercolour to William Bartlett, who attended Turner in his final months; it is of two mackerel 'brought in for dinner at Margate of which fish Mr Turner partook of for his dinner'.[45]

Meanwhile he captured Margate and the landscape around Deal with renewed enthusiasm both in watercolour and in oil. Among these a view of the South Foreland Lighthouse from St Margaret's at Cliffe: *The Beacon Light* and also *Margate Jetty* and *Off Margate* all serve to remind of the constant stimulus Turner found in Kent's coastline.[46]

And in his relationship with Mrs Booth, Turner found not only a new lover, but also something of a son who might share his enthusi-asms. Sophia's son Daniel Pound, guided by Dr Price, trained as an engraver at Leipzig, and by 1841, at the age of twenty, he was living in Lambeth and describing himself as an artist.[47]

One senses Turner attempting to explain his extended absences from London with a degree of fabrication. In 1841 George Jones found himself writing to Benjamin Godfrey Windus to explain that Turner 'has met with an accident out of town, but where, when, and to what extent I do not know – he only desires me to apologize to you, and to assure you and Mrs Windus, with his best regards, "how much he feels the privation of the pleasure of informing you that his hand writing is quite good, or rather better than usual" – so I sin-cerely hope that he has not sustained any serious injury.'[48]

Whether this accident was genuine, there is certainly a sense that Turner's health begins to deteriorate from the beginning of the 1840s. His determination to continue to travel to Switzerland came despite the fact that in the early spring of 1842 he was recovering from a seri-ous illness. 'It has shook him a great deal. He is living by rule.'[49]

But it was in 1845 that Turner's health suffered its most marked and profound decline. In that year the then president of the Royal Acad-emy, Sir Martin Archer Shee, six years Turner's senior, became ill and retired to Brighton. It was to Turner that the Academy turned as a deputy.

The managerial responsibilities that were thrust upon the RA's most senior member took their toll. Why Turner accepted them is a mystery, though the man who had lived and breathed that institution as a boy perhaps saw this as the closest he would ever come to being President, and perhaps the hope of a knighthood, an honour extended to many of his contemporaries but visibly not to him, still lingered.

The burden of stress these official duties placed upon a Turner who was now seventy meant Margate became less a place of repose, and rather one of recovery, where Dr Price's supervision and Mrs Booth's nursing gave him just enough energy to return to duties in London. The effect that this extra burden had on Turner's outlook more generally was noticeable. A weariness set in in his dealing with people.

'Dear Sir, I have received your note via Margate,' Turner wrote to the printer and publisher Hogarth in 1845. The latter was about to publish a print of *The Temeraire*, and wanted to show the original to publicize the venture. '[I] am so ill that [?I am not] disposed to write. I differ most materially with you – and no consideration of money or favour can induce me to lend my Darling again,' Turner explained.[50]

By May the burden of his work at the Academy had reached such a level that a recuperative rest became an urgent necessity. 'I feel the sad necessity of leaving Town to morrow morning,' Turner wrote to the publisher John Murray in early May 1845, excusing himself from an agreed engagement.[51] He fled across the channel to Boulogne, at that time a fashionable health resort. Here his sketchbooks testify to the days he spent walking on the beaches and in the surrounding countryside. Even on holiday Turner's compulsion to record his surroundings could not be subdued. With the wettest wash of faint colour he seemed preoccupied with the colour spectrum, often juxtaposing washes of thin blues with pale warm oranges and then sketching the features of the French landscape in pencil over this colour base.

No wonder Turner was exhausted. He had been working on not just the new series of Swiss watercolours, but, despite persistent abuse from the press, had put on a fine display at the RA annual show: six oils in 1845. And then in 1846, seven. By the end of 1846 Turner confided to Hawksworth Fawkes, when he wrote to thank him for his annual gift of a game pie for Christmas, that he was almost broken.

'. . . in regard to my health, sorry to say the tiresome and unpleasant duties of [presiding] during the continued illness of our President for two years – viz my rotation of Council – and being senior of the lot made me Pro Pre – it distroyd my happiness and appetite [so] that what with the business and weak[ness] I was oblidged to give [up] my Summer's usual trip abroad . . .'[52]

Turner would make no more trips abroad. For the man who had once thought nothing of walking miles in a day and who could sleep on a bench in an inn comfortably, soon even the trip between Kent and London became too much. And so in 1846, when Turner felt no longer able to visit the Kent coast with such regularity, Sophia Booth moved to Chelsea, to Davis Place. They must both have known that this would mark Turner's last adventure.

24.   'The morning march that flashes to the Sun; The feast of vultures when the day is done'

The Strand must have felt like the epicentre of a brave new world in 1847. Apart from the usual farrago of shops and publishing houses, and the grand presence of Somerset House where the Royal Society's luminaries might be illustrating the latest discoveries in practical science, there were other institutions emerging that pointed to the shape of things to come. In July 1847 the Electric Telegraphy Company had opened its doors at 345 Strand. And in the same year a young man called John Jabez Edwin Mayall had set up a photographic studio at 433 West Strand where he not only produced the new technology daguerreotype portraits but where his landscape images of some of America's greatest natural wonders, such as Niagara Falls, could be viewed. It was not long after Mayall advertised his presence in the busy thoroughfare that a small white-haired man, stooping and with a tendency to look down, entered the studio and began asking questions.

'Turner's visits to my atelier were in 1847, '48, and '49,' Mayall remembered.

> I took several admirable daguerreotype portraits of him, one of which was reading, a position rather favourable for him on account of his weak eyes and their being rather bloodshot.
>
> I recollect one of these portraits was presented to a lady who accompanied him. My first interviews with him were rather mysterious; he either did state, or at least led me to believe, that he was a Master in Chancery, and his subsequent visits and conversation rather confirmed this idea. At first he was very desirous of trying curious effects of light let in on the figure from a high position, and he himself sat for the studies. He was very much pleased with a figure-study I had just completed . . . he wished to bring a lady to try something

of the kind himself. This was in 1847; and I believe he did fix a day for that purpose. However, it happened to be a November fog, and I could not work. He stayed with me some three hours, talking about light and its curious effects on films of prepared silver. He expressed a wish to see the spectral image copied, and asked me if I had ever repeated Mrs. Somerville's experiment of magnetizing a needle in the rays of the spectrum. I told him I had.

I was not then aware that the inquisitive old man was Turner, the painter . . . He came again and again, always with some new notion about light. He wished me to copy my views of Niagara then a novelty in London and inquired of me about the effect of the rainbow spanning the great falls. I was fortunate in having seized one of these fleeting shadows when I was there, and I showed it to him. He wished to buy the plate. At that time I was not very anxious to sell them . . . He told me he should like to see Niagara, as it was the greatest wonder in nature; he was never tired of my descriptions of it. In short, he had come so often, and in such an unobtrusive manner, that he had come to be regarded by all my people as 'our Mr. Turner'.

This went on through 1848, till one evening I met him at the soirée of the Royal Society; I think it was early in May, 1849. He shook me by the hand very cordially, and fell into his old topic of the spectrum. Some one came up to me and asked if I knew Mr. Turner; I answered I had had that pleasure some time. 'Yes,' said my informant, rather significantly, 'but do you know that he is *the* Turner?' I was rather surprised, I must confess; and later on in the evening I encountered him again, and fell into conversation on our old topic. I ventured to suggest to him the value of such studies for his own pursuits, and at once offered to conduct any experiments for him that he might require, and, in fact, to give up some time to work out his ideas about the treatment of light and shade. I parted with him on the understanding that he would call on me; however, he never did call again, nor did I ever see him again.[1]

In his early seventies Turner's mind was as enquiring as ever, his fascination with the science of light as intense as it always had been, and his desire for travel as keen as ever. How intriguing it must have been for the old man to see an image of a waterfall that dwarfed anything in Europe. After all, in the mid-1840s he had revisited some of the great waterfalls he had witnessed as a young man, describing anew on canvas the cascades at Schaffhausen and on the Clyde as engines generating mysterious enveloping mists.

But then, just as Mayall related, Turner vaporized. For about two years before his death he began to fade away, until one day he had just vanished from sight.

However, he did not disappear from Mayall's life before introducing Mrs Booth's son Daniel Pound to the photographer. In the 1840s Daniel Pound had been building his reputation as an engraver of portraits, and had already executed a number of works for the London Printing and Publishing Company, based on daguerreotypes by the American photographer John Fitzgibbon. But it was the larger-scale engravings of the carte-de-visite photographs that Mayall made of eminent men and women that made Pound's name in later years. There is some irony in the fact that Mayall's portraits of Turner were never engraved by Sophia Booth's son – but then Turner had always hated having his portrait taken.

Turner, meanwhile, had made sure that Davis Place, which he frequented from October 1846 onwards, was customized for his own purposes. He had a roof terrace built on which he could sit and study the sky and the views along the river. Sophia Booth would later relate that Turner described the view west as the 'English view' and that to the east as the 'Dutch'.

In Chelsea, the local boys saw something in the new resident's stance and his tendency to survey the river that reminded them of a sea captain. His ruddy features suggested another moniker. Admiral Booth, sometimes known as Puggy, was born.

And then began the routine that saw him travel no longer from London to Kent, but between Queen Anne Street and Chelsea. For the journey Turner regularly enlisted the help of two men. He used a particular cab driver, a dwarf, who became such a regular fixture in Turner's life that he joked about putting him in livery. The other man who knew more than most about Turner's second home was the boatman Charles Greaves, whom Turner also patronized regularly.

Charles Greaves was one of the few people who often witnessed Turner on his balcony as he rowed past. He would later talk of Turner on the 'look out', up on his viewing platform often before sunrise, often in terrible weather, often with a spyglass clasped tight to his eye. And Turner himself corroborated this report when he revealed to his friend the Revd William Kingsley that he would 'wake up at any hour he fixed on going to bed' and 'would swathe himself in one of the blankets on his couch . . . then ascend just before sunrise, and if there was fair promise of an effective rising he would remain to study it, making pencil notes of the form of clouds, and writing in brief their tints of colour'.[2]

For those not in the habit of rowing along the Thames, it was the appearance and the behaviour of their friend that suggested a change in his personal circumstances. Someone was clearly doing a better job than Hannah Danby had been able to, since Turner was much tidier than previously and had taken to wearing a red velvet waistcoat. That Turner was determined that no one should find out just who this was, and where she was stationed, was also obvious to his friends.

Turner's colleagues resorted to stealth and trickery to try to crack the secret of what many of them suspected was a second home. David Roberts, the painter, was no exception. Turner's studio in Queen Anne Street was just a short walk from Roberts's home in Fitzroy Street and the two painters dined and socialized together often enough. So when Roberts saw the old painter hailing a cab after dining with him one evening, he saw his chance. Roberts walked his guest to the vehicle, and asked Turner where he might instruct the cabbie to take him. But Turner was as sharp as a pin: 'Tell him to drive to Oxford Street and then I'll direct him where to go.'[3]

It was only a few months after the house at Davis Place had been secured that Turner fell dangerously ill there and for six weeks found himself under the care of a Dr Gaitskill. Sophia Booth, seeing little improvement in his condition in London, determined that Turner should be packed off to Margate, where he was put into lodgings under the assumed name of a Mr Thomas and looked after by her trusted Dr David Price. Turner may well have availed himself of the brand new railway that had opened at the very end of 1846, and this is suggested by the detail that he had some form of fit at Rochester, one of the stops on the line to the seaside resort. The new ease of communication afforded by the electric telegraph was also exploited, and this became the main point of communication between Price and his eminent patient from here on.

With poor health dominating 1847, Turner's work ground to a near halt. In that year he submitted just one painting to the Royal Academy. Meanwhile even his most vociferous supporter, John Ruskin, would later claim that he had begun to witness 'evidence of a gradual moral decline in the painter's mind from the beginning of its life to its end – at first patient, tender, self-controlling, exquisitely perceptive, hopeful, and calm, he becomes sensual, capricious – sometimes in mode of work even indolent and slovenly . . .' Only the Swiss watercolours redeemed Turner in Ruskin's eyes: 'What I call the "sunset" drawings – such as our Coblentz, Constance, Red Rigi, etc., – marks the efforts of the soul to recover itself, a peculiar calm and return of the repose or youthful spirit, preceding the approach of death.'[4]

The sensual and capricious works that even Ruskin failed to grasp were by and large Turner's mythological or biblical scenes. The young critic was dismayed at *The Angel Standing in the Sun*, for example, which Turner had shown in 1846. This depicted the archangel Michael on the day of judgement standing in another whirling vortex of light. Vultures flutter above him. 'The morning march that flashes to the sun;' Turner wrote alongside the painting, quoting from Rogers. 'The feast of vultures when the day is done.'

A few years later Ruskin would reveal his disappointment in the work, noting 'distinctive characteristics in the execution' which 'were indicative of mental disease'. Its companion piece – *Undine giving the Ring to Massaniello, Fisherman of Naples* – was another vortex painting, its strong dark blues complementing the warm pinks and golds in the *Angel*. This time the mythological water nymph Undine is at the centre of the canvas, caught in a burst of light at the moment she becomes human by marrying a fisherman. While the vengeful Old Testament angel in one painting punishes humanity for its vice and folly, Undine is a Christ-like foil who takes on the burden of humanity in the moment. Ruskin thought as little of this picture as

he did of its companion, and quietly probably agreed with the critic
who so unkindly described Undine as 'an unsmoked meerschaum
cut into the likeness of a mermaid', one of a pair of 'abortions' which
in the critics' mind at least confirmed that Turner had quite simply
gone 'mad'.[5]

Despite all this, 1847 was a landmark year for Turner. For it was in
the December of this year that the *Dogano* that Robert Vernon had
bought nearly twenty years earlier was given by him to the National
Gallery. On 27 December it became the first Turner exhibited as part
of a public collection in a special Christmas holiday show.

The enthusiasm from the public was unprecedented. Rushing to
see what had been selected from a bequest of 160 paintings by Vernon, of which four were Turners, the *Examiner* reported that 16,270
visited on the day the show opened and that 'from the numbers continually thronging into the gallery the keepers were unable to enforce
the regulation permitting 300 only to be present at one time'. And it
is this that one has to keep in sight when assessing the public perception of Turner in the late 1840s. His most recent works were
controversial, but the vast majority of his output was still loved. He
was still considered the hero of English art by his peers, despite the
apparent eccentricity of his dotage.

It may well have been a desire to view the Vernon Collection that
brought John Ruskin's mother into town in January 1848. She made
a point of calling at Queen Anne Street and leaving some eggs as a
New Year's gift. Turner was not there to thank her for this kindness.
One can imagine that the small, warm rooms in Davis Place were
now deemed far too comfortable to be exchanged for the draughty
ones at Queen Anne Street. But he wrote a note of thanks to her son
when he discovered the gift, which had been accompanied by an
invitation to John Ruskin's annual birthday party on 8 February. He
took the opportunity to update the Ruskins on issues regarding their
latest commission of Swiss watercolours from his 1844 trip – again an
important point, that Turner was continuing to work despite his
increasing infirmity. 'In regard to the mounts of the Drawings I will
carry them in on their own paper until you have finally fixed,' he
noted.[6]

By summer these drawings were ready for collection, but Turner was unable to deliver them.[7] He had returned to Kent in June, and was laid up in the cottage at St Margaret's at Cliffe that had been kept as a holiday home by Mrs Booth. Now he had 'a broken Knee-pan'.[8] It was this that almost certainly prevented him showing anything at that year's Royal Academy show.

Though his body was clearly failing, there is no evidence that Turner's mind had gone. Despite what Ruskin read on canvas, and would later put down to a corruption of his creative faculties, Mayall's descriptions of the inquisitive elderly gentleman suggest his mental faculties were as sharp as ever.

Certainly his correspondence points to a memory and sense of humour still firmly intact. In his Christmas letter to Hawksworth Fawkes, which thanked him for the PPP, 'Pie, Pheasant and Pud', he was able to summon specifics of a trip he had made to Wales back in the previous century. On hearing that Fawkes was heading to 'Aberiswith [sic]', Turner remembered 'it is well sheltered, from the East – the Town close to the sea . . . and the scenery of the natural valley, the Estwith, the Ridol and the Devil's Bridge are beautiful and Grand features. The view from the Inn near the Devil's Bridge commands the falls of the Ridol – the Devil's Bridge torrent rushes down a deep chasm, under two bridges one over the other . . . I do not think you could have hit upon a more desirable spot for your pencil and hope you may feel – just what I felt in the days of my youth when I was in search of Richard Wilson's birthplace.'[9]

The degree to which Turner was struggling now is suggested by his unprecedented decision to take on a studio assistant, a young man called Francis Sherrell. It is not without some irony that Sherrell, who came from the Home Counties, would in the year of Turner's death, when he was just twenty-three, describe himself as a hairdresser rather than an artist's assistant. But in 1848 he was just that, stretching canvases, preparing materials and cleaning some of the works in Queen Anne Street, in exchange for drawing lessons. Whether he was based primarily in Queen Anne Street or travelled with Turner to Chelsea and Deal is not known, though the fact that Sherrell ended his own days in Margate might suggest the latter.

In 1849, the last year in which Mayall saw Turner, his health continued to be generally poor. And yet both his colleagues and his public continued to crave his work. It must have been a particular disappointment to both Turner and the Society of Arts that he felt too unwell to accept their offer of a retrospective exhibition. This was an initiative the society had only begun the previous year, when their first retrospective of a living British artist had been dedicated to the genre painter William Mulready.

The retrospective shows were part of the Society's concerted attempts at this period to push the profile of art in society and British art in the world. One of its council members, Henry Cole, had successfully petitioned Prince Albert to put his support behind the idea of an international exhibition that would showcase the role of the arts in industry, an event at which Mayall's images of Niagara would be displayed along with a considerable number of other photographic works when it finally opened in 1851. Turner developed quite a fascination with the progress of this bold and ambitious initiative, as the few letters that survive from his last years reveal.

Despite his inability to mount a show for the Society of Arts, the British Institution did show Turner's *The Wreck of a Transport Ship*, painted in 1810, at an exhibition in March 1849, an event to which Turner responded with pride and for which he sent admission tickets to his closest friends, including Samuel Rogers who, himself unwell, promised to 'avail myself of the Admission whenever my Infirmities will allow me to do so'.[10]

The warm critical response that the press made to this earlier work probably encouraged Turner to persuade Munro to lend his painting *The Wreck Buoy*, painted around the same time as *The Wreck of a Transport Ship*, to the RA, which allowed paintings to be shown as long as they had not been previously exhibited. Munro dutifully sent the work from his Scottish estate but was horrified to learn that Turner then spent six days reworking the painting before admitting it. He transformed what had been an estuary painting into something with biblical resonance, thus continuing the themes of hope and destruction, salvation and punishment he had been exploring in the previous years. This was done by the addition of a huge rainbow arching over the sea, whitening the sails of a ship in the centre of the canvas so it becomes a luminescent beacon and enhancing the contrasts between sea and sky. What Munro could not have appreciated was that this would be Turner's very last seascape to be exhibited before he died.

Death was hovering over the whole of London again in 1848 and 1849. In the September of 1848 a seaman called John Harnold, just arrived on the steamer from Hamburg, disembarked and made his way to lodgings in New Lane, Gainsford Street in Lambeth. He was dead within the day – of cholera. Within weeks the whole of Lambeth was gripped by an epidemic of terrifying proportions which, by the time it was brought under control the following year, had killed over 1,600 residents living on the waterside.

Turner, upriver in Chelsea, must have thought he had had a close escape when, by 1850, he found himself, though 'much on the wain',[11] nevertheless alive and cholera-free. In fact he mustered up enough energy to show four new paintings at the RA in a burst of activity unprecedented since 1846. He had executed them all in Davis Place rather than Queen Anne Street. Sophia Booth would later recount how he painted them all together, the four canvases all laid out, with Turner loading his brush with a colour and applying it across all before changing his colour and repeating the process. The themes he chose for these final works took up again the story he had been telling all his career: that of Dido and Aeneas.

This account of betrayal and desertion continued to fascinate him, though there was a noticeably new theme in these last paintings. For in *Aeneas relating his Story to Dido*, and *The Departure of the Fleet* it is the moon rather than the sun hovering in the sky.

George Jones could not contain his delight. 'I saw your pictures this morning for the first time, and more glorious effusions of mind have never appeared – your intellect defies time to injure it, and I really believe that you never conceived more beautiful, more graceful, or more enchanting composition, than these you have sent for exhibition – God bless you & preserve you as you are for your affectionate and admiring Friends –.'[12]

Perhaps it was the sight of this series that prompted Charles Stokes to suddenly show his hand as another great collector of Turner's work. He was an unusual man, an avid antiquary and collector with wide-ranging interests who had married his enthusiasms rather than a wife. For those who knew the two men, Stokes's appeal to Turner would have been evident. A relentless thirst for knowledge and an unquenchable sense of enquiry were characteristics of both.

On 31 May 1850 Stokes bought twenty-four watercolours of the Loire through Griffith at a cost of 600 guineas. They were added to an already astonishing collection he had been quietly putting together that included samples of Turner's work in watercolour from the very earliest period of his career in the early 1790s right the way through. In what would amount to around 150 drawings, along with a complete set of the *Liber Studiorum*, Stokes also had eight of the very late Swiss watercolours.

It seems likely that Stokes normally dealt with Turner directly, and some of the collection may well have been the payment for services in kind that Turner seemed happy to make to his close associates. But in May 1850 Stokes was forced to make a purchase through Griffith because Turner himself was suddenly indisposed.

Jones's warm wishes regarding Turner's preservation meanwhile had been poorly timed. Just after his defiant last show of strength, Turner caught the cholera. It was appalling luck, given the heat of the epidemic had passed. Few could have thought the old man would survive it.

It was the electric telegraph that once again alerted Dr Price to the emergency, and Turner was dispatched to Margate to be under his personal care. From 11 May to the end of July Price battled with the terrible disease. Astonishingly Turner survived. But the episode did irreparable damage. In August he was moved to Deal to recuperate further, where Price continued to visit him until mid-September. He was left barely able to walk.

That Christmas Turner confided the state of affairs to Hawksworth Fawkes. Thanking him as ever for his Christmas pie, Turner revealed that 'Old Time has made sad work of me since I saw you in Town. I always dreaded it with horror now I feel it acutely now whatever – Gout or nervousness – it having fallen into my Pedestals – and bid adieu to the Marrow bone stage.'[13]

And yet for all his sorrow at his decrepitude Turner was still keen to talk art and progress. 'Mr Vernon's collection which he gave to the National Gallery are now moved to Marlborough House and the English Masters likewise,' he reported. 'The Crystal Palace is proceeding slowly I think considering the time, but suppose the Glass work is partially in store, for the vast Conservatory all looks confusion worse confounded.'[14]

That Christmas of 1850 was a quiet one. Though Fawkes's pie was consumed and his health drunk, Turner declined the invitation he had had from David Roberts to spend New Year's Day with the painter and his family. Equally his old friend Sir Charles Eastlake and his wife were thanked for their invitation to a party on 8 January but declined on account of 'my illness'. The same excuse was offered to the Ruskins regarding John's birthday on 8 February.

It must have been something of a surprise, then, when in May Turner suddenly appeared on one of the varnishing days at the Royal Academy's annual show, an indication of the importance he bestowed on the institution and these days which were exclusive to artists. He cut a diminutive figure in a top hat, his rather old-fashioned coat buttoned tight, and stood much as he had done over the years, hands clasped behind his back like an officer surveying his army.

For only the fourth time in sixty-one years he had failed to show a painting himself. His once stocky, robust figure was withered, and he could not sustain his typical Napoleonic stance for long. As soon as George Jones noticed this, a seat was called for. And finally another colleague, Francis Grant, offered him the support of his arm to walk the galleries.

He made some other calls that May, putting his affairs in order. He called in on Thomas Griffith in Pall Mall around 7 May, and made several visits to the Athenaeum. On 24 May the engraver Charles Turner noted in his diary that he and his namesake had met. He still continued business. Notes about sketches and prints were passed to Griffith and bills to be paid were conveyed to Charles Stokes.

All too aware of his extended absences from town and Queen Anne Street, David Roberts wrote to Turner and pleaded with him to be more forthcoming about his circumstances, swearing that if

Turner shared the details of where he was staying, he would keep that information confidential.

However, Roberts's letter remained unanswered. Until August, when, as Roberts relates in memoirs, Turner suddenly appeared at his door, full of apologies for failing to acknowledge the note but equally clear that he did not welcome further enquiry. Nevertheless, Roberts remembers that Turner was keen to conduct friendship under his own terms: 'I will never come to town without calling upon you,' Roberts recalls Turner assuring him. '*He kept his word.* I think he called once or twice after that time.'[15] Roberts left for a tour of Italy in early September and would never see Turner again. He was probably the last member of the Royal Academy to see him alive.

In the days before Christmas 1851 Turner's friends had sent their annual gifts and invitations to Queen Anne Street as usual, in the hope that either Greaves or the bandy-legged dwarf would deliver the artist to his studio to pick them up. But in fact, Christmas went unacknowledged in Queen Anne Street. The brace of hares and pheasants and the goose pie, sent by train from Yorkshire from Hawksworth Fawkes of Farnley Hall, were not skinned, plucked or tucked into. The barrel of Yarmouth herrings from Turner's namesake, the antiquary and botanist Dawson Turner, remained unopened. As did the customary invitations: the offer of Christmas lunch from the architect Philip Hardwick and his family; the requests for his company at the New Year's parties at the Ruskins, and the Eastlakes.

While Hannah Danby was wringing her hands and wondering just where her master was hiding himself, the telegraphs had been ringing with the communications between Mrs Booth and Dr Price. The latter, 'in order to save the expenses of journeys by myself to Chelsea . . . arranged . . . that Mr William Bartlett of Chelsea . . . Pharmaceutical Chemist, should see him daily and make reports to me of the daily progress.'[16]

Bartlett had been responsible for removing Turner's teeth earlier in the year, an operation which had only helped to encourage Turner's reclusiveness and probably hastened his infirmity. Turner's friend the Revd William Kingsley noted how appalled Turner had become by his own incapacity to chew properly in the last months of his life, and had consequently refused lunch invitations claiming 'he was so nasty in his eating, the only way in which he could live being by sucking meat'.[17]

Turner kept his spirits up during the last few weeks of his life, however. Bartlett would later recall how they had spoken of plans to travel abroad together once he was recovered. But perhaps both participants in this commentary knew it to be mere fiction. On 18 December, despite the three-guinea expense of making the train trip from Margate to London, David Price visited his patient for the last time. In the morning the following day, with Sophia Booth and William Bartlett at the bedside, Joseph Mallord William Turner expired.

The lack of clarity that Turner so enjoyed in his life presided over his death. The man who would tease and obscure had clearly never shared his real age with those who cared for him in his final years. On his death certificate he was recorded as being eighty-one years old. By the time he was buried in St Paul's Cathedral the age being cited for the painter was seventy-nine. He was in fact seventy-six.

At the moment of his vanishing, Turner could claim much. Despite his lifelong insistence in the fallacy of hope, in the twilight of his own life he had found a fulfilling love and companionship. He died admired by his peers, even idolized by some. And his firm belief in the power and importance of art and the profound talent of his countrymen had finally been recognized by a society that had itself been transformed and democratized. Now art was appreciated by the masses, and the work of British artists, including his own, was displayed in a National Gallery.

This commitment to art and a brotherhood of artists remained paramount to Turner until the last. He had attempted to maintain his hectic social diary and professional obligations as best he could until the point when his health prevented him. That he chose to die in private should not be mistaken for anything more than that.

That Turner played the role of Admiral Booth for the residents of Chelsea was perhaps only to be expected from a man who had always enjoyed a practical joke and found obfuscation rather amusing. Perhaps he had imagined himself as such a character while painting some of his sea canvases and readily embraced the ruddy-faced sea captain as his alter ego.

But one must not allow his final game to mislead one into thinking that he had lost that deeply intellectual mind that had defined him throughout his life. Indeed, just as Admiral Booth emerged on Chelsea's banks in 1846, Turner gave the Royal Academy a copy of Michelangelo's poetry, written in the original Italian. This book of verse had been published in 1817 and had perhaps been picked up when Turner was in Rome. It had clearly been his treasured personal copy. The touching donation seems a significant gesture on Turner's part, given he had stood and listened to Sir Joshua Reynolds uphold Michelangelo as the greatest exponent of the sublime.

Nor should his final performance as Puggy Booth overshadow the fact that in terms of a body of work, few artists have ever matched Turner in terms of their fluency and sheer quantity of output. Nor can many claim an oeuvre so potent that it has come to define experience. Today we see Turner sunsets and sunrises. Those who have looked at his canvases cannot help but regard certain phenomena of light or weather through his lens.

The sweep of his life and work was truly epic. He saw a country mired in the Napoleonic wars and then transformed by the Industrial Revolution. He witnessed kings descend into madness, tyrants deposed, and empires expand. He stood on the deck of *H.M.S. Victory*, walked on the battlefield of Waterloo, and yet also painted the banks of the rural Thames with its fishermen and cowherds. He catalogued the rise of steam, the glow of industrial furnaces, and he celebrated the science of his day. Intrepid, he walked across a largely undiscovered Britain and into a Europe waking up from endless war and political turmoil. He discovered the drama and beauty of places that his contemporaries had ignored or avoided.

But despite all that Turner could conjure with his brush, one should not doubt that the natural wonders that enthralled his eye, and the events that captured his imagination, also served to emphasize the transience of human mortality. He was as chillingly sensitive to the enduring permanence of nature as he was to the inevitability of his own demise. This painful reality was grasped by Turner early in his career and became a driving incentive behind his work. At the heart of Turner's ambition was the idea that his art might endure when the story of his own rise and fall was done.

On receiving the news of Turner's death John Ruskin managed to put aside his grief to make one of the most pertinent summaries of Turner's legacy: '. . . everything in the sunshine and the sky so talks of him,' he said. 'Their Great Witness is lost . . .'

Epilogue

Hannah Danby and Queen Anne Street

Hannah Danby, who wept so visibly at Turner's funeral, did not long survive her master. In the months after his death she continued to live in the decrepit remains of the gallery in Queen Anne Street. The one change to her previous domestic arrangements was that her friend Maria Tanner moved into the premises to keep her company. On 7 December 1853, however, just two years after Turner's death, Hannah sensed her time was nigh and drew up a will. A week later she was dead, aged sixty-seven.

Hannah's voice was never recorded by those who met her. Described warmly by Turner, and with a degree of horror and humour by Ruskin and others, she is remembered merely as a caricature.

Hannah's modest bequests provided in her will indicate the degree to which she wanted to acknowledge those who had also appreciated her master. The extent of Turner's affection for his relatives the Harpurs is suggested in Hannah's gift of her tea caddy to Henry Harpur's wife, Eleanor. The only other bequest of a personal nature was to John Ruskin, to whom she gave the self-portrait in oils that Turner had painted when he was a teenage boy. Evelina Dupuis, Turner's daughter, was left £50 with the clear instruction that this was to go to her directly, and could not be drawn on to settle any debts her husband Joseph Dupuis might have. Meanwhile Sarah Danby's other daughters, whom Hannah describes as her cousins, were left the residue of her small estate.

Hannah left Maria Tanner £60 and the responsibility for settling her affairs. This is the only clue to the strong friendship that the two women must have shared in the last years of Turner's life. Maria continued to reside at the gallery for some time after Hannah's death. The fact that Turner's glasses, a snuffbox, card case and magnifying glass were handed down through the Tanner family suggests either a further private gift from Hannah, or mementos that Tanner took herself. Lady Trevelyan remembered Tanner as the eccentric replacement to her equally eccentric predecessor when she noted that 'the old woman with her head wrapped up in dirty flannel' was replaced by 'another old woman with the same dirty flannel about her head'.[1]

Sophia Booth

Sophia Booth meanwhile became the focus of quite some interest after news of her relationship with Turner emerged. A number of friends of the painter made a point of visiting her and the house in Chelsea. David Roberts did so in the summer of 1852 and described a 'tall, lusty woman dressed in deep mourning' answering the door. 'She had more to communicate than I had to listen,' Roberts remembered. 'She showed me the bed room where he usually slept & the Room facing the water where he died.' Booth told Roberts that Turner had never contributed to the finances of their life together, but she did reveal that the painter had composed 'Verses in Honour of herself and her personal charms'.[2] She also claimed that Turner had been a jealous partner.

The artist John Wykeham Archer also made his way to Chelsea to draw the house in which Turner spent his last days, and in doing so encountered a friendly and generous woman. 'Mr Turner used to say I was the handmaid of Art,' Sophia Booth related to him.[3]

But perhaps the most surprising postscript is the unlikely friendship that developed between John Ruskin and Sophia Booth, one that proved particularly fruitful for the former's collection of material relating to Turner. Ruskin bought two of Turner's sketchbooks from her, as well as the artist's colour box and palette. Tempting though it is to see Ruskin's dealings with Mrs Booth as driven merely by self-interest, there is evidence of a genuine warmth between the two. On at least one occasion he sent her the gift of a crate of wine,[4] and he also presented her with the oval miniature of Turner as a boy which he had acquired from Ann Dart in Bristol.[5]

Ruskin was appalled at the account given of Sophia Booth in the first biography of Turner, written by Walter Thornbury and published in 1862, in which she was depicted as having purely mercenary motives. George Jones was equally disappointed in Thornbury's account, noting in his own copy of the book the fact that Sophia Booth burned all her letters from Turner rather than sell them.[6]

In fact there is much to suggest that Booth had little care for money, nor much ability to handle it. Her earlier decision to trust Dr Price to manage her financial affairs provides some evidence of this, and it may have been Price who encouraged her to claim for the years of care she provided Turner before his death, when his will was challenged in the courts. In fact, though Sophia Booth did sell some items that Turner gave her, she gave away many more. One recipient of her generosity was Dr Bartlett, who had sat with Sophia on the day Turner died. She gave him a watercolour. A decade later, in 1864, Turner's fishing rod went to the picture dealer William Vokins, who incidentally made a moving record of the admiration in which Mrs Booth held Turner. 'Illiterate as she was,' he recalled, she 'waxed so eloquent over the description of his day's work that she wound up by saying, "Well, there are times, sir, when I feel he must be a god!" '[7]

Sophia's son Daniel Pound waited until 1865 before selling some of the paintings by Turner that had remained in his mother's ownership. The timing of the sale, just two years before the lease on Davis Place ran out, is crucial. The sale raised over £4,000, and perhaps in another instance of Sophia's reluctance to handle large sums of money herself, this profit was taken by Pound himself. He duly spent about £1,000 on the purchase of Haddenham Hall in 1867. The Hall, built in the 1830s, was the largest property in the village of the same name in Buckinghamshire. Here Sophia Booth lived her remaining days with a servant called Rebecca Scott, and possibly with her niece Sophia Green.[8]

The Hall, which had high walls encompassing ample grounds, suggests that Sophia Booth sought solitude as well as comfort in her final years. Twelve miles from Lee Clump, where Turner owned a cottage, the village had only around 1,500 inhabitants in the 1860s. It was just visible from the road taken by the coach that ran between Oxford and Cambridge, and there is some suggestion that Ruskin may have recommended the location.[9]

One account of the Hall recalls an interested visitor calling on 'a Mrs. Booth, whom it was understood was Turner's widow'. The visitor related that he 'expressed a wish to look over the Hall, and was received by the old lady herself (she was a very homely body, and always wore a big cotton apron). In one of the rooms I recognised a miniature portrait of the late Dr. Price of Margate. Mrs. Booth said, "Yes! it was painted by my husband, Mr. Turner the artist; he and the Doctor were great friends."'[10]

Mrs Booth remained at Haddenham until her death in June 1878, at the age of eighty. The local newspapers recorded in her obituary that she was the widow of John Booth of Margate, and failed to mention her connection with the great painter Turner, despite the apparent openness with which she continued to talk about him. Her estate was valued at less than £300, and was left entirely to her son. That Pound himself left an estate of some £8,000 when he died suggests that Sophia Booth made sure that her sole surviving child had been the recipient of significant gifts from her long before her own demise.

Sophia Caroline Booth was buried in Margate, in the cemetery of St John's church.

Sarah Danby

While Turner's last mistress died in comfort, the same cannot be said of Sarah Danby, who had fallen on hard times by the time of Turner's death and whose naivety was exploited by those who understood the market for Turner's work better than she.

Nothing evidences this more than the note Charles Turner made in his diary on 9 September 1854, in which he recorded that he had 'Call'd on Mrs. Danby, William Street No. 29 to enquire where Mr. Turner was born. Said Hand Court, Maiden Lane. Sold me for 3 .3.0. 17 cards of his Drawings and 2 small oil sketches.'

Two months later he had returned to William Street in Marylebone for more, and picked up another 'Two Drawings of Mr. William Turner which she has had many years – nearly 50 – for which I gave her one sovereign for Both. She was delighted.'[11]

For Charles Turner, the transaction was a bargain. Less so for Sarah Danby, who had clearly failed to realize the value of the work that she had been left. However, her delight might be explained by the fact that in 1854 Mrs Danby had become grateful for small mercies.

Sarah had continued to draw a pension from the Society of Musicians after she and Turner parted company. Across the 1840s she had made special requests to the council for an uplift for 'medical advice', culminating in a particularly pathetic plea for extra relief in the summer of 1851 in which she pointed out that she was 'totally helpless and her daughter cannot assist her much as teaching is so bad'.[12]

The society struggled to meet these demands on it. When on Turner's death rumours circulated that Mrs Danby had been left an annuity by the painter, it quickly moved to establish the truth of the matter. Sarah Danby was forced to assure the institution's council that she had not been so blessed. In 1853 her daughter Marcella was yet again pleading poverty on her mother's behalf, but this time the council had been unable to offer help. No wonder the pittance from Charles Turner was so welcome.

Sarah was living with her unmarried daughter Marcella, who was a music teacher, when Charles Turner called on her. A few years later the pair moved to George Street, close to Euston Square, where Sarah Danby died in February 1861. The registrar recorded that she was 100 years old, and was sufficiently impressed to also note that she had eaten beef steak for her dinner the day before she died.

Evelina Dupuis

Evelina Dupuis's story is also one of mixed fortunes. Her husband Joseph was clearly an adventurous and in many ways admirable civil servant, but one who in the end fell foul of his employers.

Prior to his marriage with Evelina, Joseph had been an admired and efficient Vice Consul in Mogador in north Africa, working effectively to free Britons and Christians who had been kidnapped and enslaved there. But his promotion to Consul and subsequent posting to Ghana were less successful when it was deemed he had granted too many concessions to the Ashanti there, in conflict with the interests of the British empire. Joseph was nevertheless regarded as an authority on north African, Saharan and Ghanaian matters and in 1824 he published his 'Journal of a Residence in Ashantee . . . with an account of the Origin and Causes of the Present War'.

Joseph continued with various consular duties in Africa until the early 1840s, at which point it is generally believed that he moved his family to Greece and became involved in the trade in marble there. Certainly Evelina and Joseph's son Hanmer, who would also work in Africa as a diplomat, would later become established in Corfu, where the family retains connections to this day.

But by the 1850s Evelina and her husband were back in London, living in Tavistock Street in Covent Garden and facing financial difficulty, as Hannah Danby's will acknowledges. Dupuis's debts might account for his application immediately after Hannah's death to manage the gallery in Queen Anne Street, confessing as he did his state of 'absolute want'.

'I am the husband of Evelina Danby mentioned in Mr Turner's will,' he wrote to Jabez Tepper, who was the solicitor acting on behalf of members of Turner's family seeking to claim part of his estate. 'My wife is the natural daughter of Mr Turner. She was for several years recognized as his daughter, and was, till the age of womanhood brought up in the expectation of always enjoying a respectable function in Society . . .'[13]

Unsuccessful in this regard, Dupuis and Evelina did benefit from Turner's estate when his will was finally proved in 1856. The pair moved to Lambeth, where they died in the same year, 1874, Evelina surviving her husband by just a few months. Evelina's final address was 135 Upper Kennington Lane in Lambeth, the proximity of which to the Harpurs' home may not be coincidental. She left her unmarried daughter Rosalie an estate worth less than £800.

Turner's Will

After Turner's death, his will became a source of controversy that drew his mistresses and family into a complex legal battle. Turner made an initial will the day after his father's funeral, on 30 September 1829, which was replaced by one prepared by his then solicitor George Cobb in 1831. It was then revised four times until 1849. Core to the will was Turner's desire to make a charitable provision for impoverished landscape artists, while the changes reflected his changing attitudes to personal bequests and the fate of his paintings.

In the 1831 will Turner remembered his surviving uncles Price and Jonathan Turner with a gift of £50 each, and their eldest sons with a gift of £25 each. He stipulated that sufficient of his Bank of England investments should be retained to allow an annuity of £50 per annum for Hannah Danby and the same for his daughters, Evelina and Georgiana. Sarah Danby was to get £10 a year. He left two pictures to the National Gallery: *Sun Rising Through Vapour* and *Dido Building Carthage*, to be hung between *Claude's Seaport with the Embarkation of the Queen of Sheba* and *The Marriage of Isaac and Rebecca*. The residue of his estate was to be sold to provide a charitable institution for decayed artists.

In 1832 a codicil was added clarifying that his gallery was also to be retained in order that his work might be kept together. He nominated Hannah Danby as its custodian. Meanwhile he increased the annuities to his daughters to £100 per annum. He also requested that provision might be made from his estate for an annual dinner in his name at the Royal Academy and for either a professorship in Landscape or a Turner medal to be awarded for landscape painting. He expressed his wish that a monument might be erected to him and that any residue from his estate might go to 'Georgia' Danby and her heirs.

In 1846 a further codicil proposed that Sophia Booth might become a residuary legatee of his estate, replacing Georgiana Danby and her heirs (Georgiana had died in 1843).

In 1848 Turner revoked the gifts he had made to his uncles and their sons, and the bequests to Hannah, Evelina and Sarah Danby. He stated that now he wished all his finished pictures to go to the National Gallery within five years of his death, and that the gallery in Queen Anne Street should be used only until the pictures could move there. During this period Hannah Danby should be the custodian and an annuity of £150 per annum was to be provided for her.

In 1849 a final codicil extended to ten years the time which the National Gallery was given to take on board his bequest. If this time-scale was not met the pictures were to remain at Queen Anne Street, available for viewing by the public, and then sold when the leasehold on the property ran out. The sale of his paintings should then fund a pension scheme at the Royal Academy. In addition Turner made sure that Sophia Booth was given an annuity of £150 per annum and that his friend William Frederick Wells's children should all receive £100.

On his death Turner's family on his father's side immediately challenged the will on the basis that Turner had lost his mind in his final years. When this challenge proved unsuccessful, the family, represented by Turner's cousin Jabez Tepper, questioned the will on the basis that it was illegal. Turner and his advisers had indeed overlooked the fact that all charitable bequests in a will needed to be registered in the Court of Chancery.

The credibility of this second challenge opened up lengthy litigation that lasted until 1856. During this time a number of other claimants from outside the Turner family also came forward, including Turner's daughter Evelina Dupuis and Sarah Danby's daughters Marcella, Caroline and Theresa. Meanwhile Mrs Booth and Dr Price also submitted claims to the estate based on the expense of caring for Turner during the final months of his life.

In 1856 the case was finally resolved. A court decree awarded not just the finished pictures that had been previously mentioned in Turner's will, but all his artistic works, to the nation. The Turners did well, with an infant John Turner declared heir at law inheriting Turner's property at Lee Common, his land in Dagenham and the Ship and Bladebone pub in Wapping.

Another cousin, Thomas Price Turner, got a piece of land at Twickenham that Turner had foreseen would be used to build his almshouses for decayed artists.

Meanwhile the townhouses on the junction of Harley and Queen Anne Streets, which Turner had made into his gallery and living accommodation, and their contents (including his engraved work), were divided between a number of Turner cousins.

Sarah Danby's daughters had made a claim based on Turner's provision for Hannah Danby, who had subsequently died. They were awarded £200. Evelina was also awarded annuities based on £3,333 worth of Turner's 3 per cent consols, while Sophia Booth was awarded yearly payments based on £5,000 of the same. The remainder of Turner's investments were awarded to his cousins. The desire for a charitable bequest to impoverished artists was never fulfilled.

John Ruskin

Although John Ruskin was named one of Turner's executors, he stood down from this role and took on instead the responsibility for cataloguing the vast quantities of Turner's work. In 1857 Ruskin found Turner's erotica. It was a moment that marked a changing point in his attitude to an artist whom he had worshipped.

The discovery of sketches of sexual acts was unfortunate in its timing. In 1857 the Obscene Publications Act had been introduced, making it illegal to sell or possess pornography. Ruskin bundled up the material and marked it as an example of Turner's failure of mind. Five years later, however, he wrote to the Keeper of the National Gallery, Ralph Wornum, and made a written statement about the fate of the work.

'As the authorities have not thought proper to register the reserved parcel of Turner's sketchbooks,' he wrote, 'and have given no directions about them, and as the grossly obscene drawings contained in them could not be lawfully in anyone's possession, I am satisfied that you had no other course than to burn them, both for the sake of Turner's reputation, (they have assuredly been drawn under a certain condition of insanity) and for your own peace. And I am glad to be able to bear witness to their destruction; and hereby declare that the parcel of them was undone by me, and all the obscene drawings in it burnt in my prescence in the month of December 1858.'[14]

This strange retrospective letter was the source of the belief held for many years that these sketches had in fact been destroyed, until a new examination of the original inventories of Turner's sketchbooks suggested that the incineration never did in fact occur. The small but significant number of erotic sketches and drawings that remain in the Turner Bequest supports this.[15] Ruskin, it seems, was protecting the gallery from damage to its reputation. Unable to actually burn the work of an artist, he said he had for the record.

Nevertheless, the images of sexual activity Ruskin witnessed played on his mind. Their emergence in the same year that his own sexual life – or lack of it – became the focus of a humiliating national scandal, when his wife sued him for divorce on the basis of the non-consummation of their marriage, contributed to bouts of anxiety and mental illness that characterized the rest of his life.

Gradually Ruskin revised his views on Turner. As the fragility of his own mental health increased, so too did his view that Turner had succumbed to mental decay. Nevertheless, his extensive writing on Turner in the years both before and after the painter's death, and his exhaustive work on the Bequest, have left his and Turner's names inextricably linked, and his scholarship remains the foundation for the study of the artist.

Acknowledgements

I am extremely indebted to Ian Warrell and Cecilia Powell, both of whom took considerable time to go through this book at its manuscript stage with a fine-tooth comb, alerting me to passages that needed correction or qualification. The generosity Ian and Cecilia showed with their scholarship is typical of many of the scholars and curators with whom I have come into contact and whose work continues to add to our knowledge of J. M. W. Turner. Selby Whittingham shared his extensive genealogical research into Turner and his circle. Dr Tim Marshall sent me his study of historic Brentford and Turner's family there. Mora Abell invited me into her home and shared the transcriptions she had in her possession of the diary of E. T. Monro. Catherine Parry-Wingfield, chair of the Trustees of Turner's House in Twickenham, walked me around Sandycombe Lodge, and also allowed me to purchase an extensive library of books about Turner that was in her possession. Marty Krause showed me the wonderful Kurt Pantzer Collection of works by Turner in the Indianapolis Museum of Art. Rosalind Turner allowed me to view Turner's library, what remains of his own collection of art and other personal items that have been passed down through his family. Nick Tapley, a descendant of Turner's daughter Evelina Dupuis, was kind enough to bring two miniatures in his possession, and Evelina's ring, to London for me to see. I would also like to thank Professor Stephen Wildman at the Ruskin Library at the University of Lancaster, Andrew Loukes, Curator of Collections and Exhibitions at Petworth House, the Royal Academy of Art's archivist Mark Pomeroy, and Professor Sam Smiles for their kind attentions to my enquiries. I am grateful to the staff in the Prints and Drawings Room at Tate Britain, who made Turner's sketchbooks and other items in the Tate's Turner Bequest available to me. The Fitzwilliam Museum in Cambridge and Balliol College, Oxford kindly allowed me to access their material pertaining to

Turner. The staff at the archive of the Bank of England made available their ledgers revealing Turner's investments. I have greatly enjoyed events organized or promoted by the Turner Society, not least a trip led by Andrew Wilton to Farnley Hall in Yorkshire to see the magnificent collection of Turner works there and to wander around the countryside that so inspired the painter.

On a more personal note, I am most grateful to Professor Christopher Dobson at St John's College, Cambridge, for inviting me to spend a term as a Fellow Commoner at the college. I used this precious fellowship to write much of this book, to immerse myself once again in the wonderful life at St John's and to benefit from the eighteenth- and nineteenth-century collections in the Cambridge University Library. I was only able to take up this fellowship with the blessing of my long-suffering family, who have put up with my being absent for much of the last three years. My husband Richard, daughter Rosa, and sons Tommy and Vincent have seen many evenings and weekends, as well as the working week, lost to Turner. I must also acknowledge the continuing support of my literary agent Georgina Capel. Meanwhile Eleo Gordon at Viking deserves special mention – I am deeply grateful to her for commissioning this book. Eleo and Annie Lee also deserve much applause for wading through my terribly messy manuscript – my ability to spot my numerous typing errors has not, alas, improved with age.

Notes on Turner holdings, and a very select bibliography

Turner's letters and works are held by many institutions in the UK, including the British Library, the British Museum, the Royal Academy of Arts, the National Gallery, the Victoria and Albert Museum, the Fitzwilliam Museum, the Ashmolean Museum, and of course Tate Britain, which houses the considerable Turner Bequest. One annual event for the Turner enthusiast is the January exhibition of the extensive Vaughan Bequest of Turner watercolours, which goes on show for just that month in the National Galleries of Scotland, in Edinburgh, and at the National Gallery of Ireland in Dublin. Turner's work remains in situ at Petworth House in Sussex and at Farnley Hall in Yorkshire, both of which can be visited, the latter by appointment. One of the most exciting ways to experience Turner's work in an intimate manner is to view his sketchbooks and works on paper in Tate Britain's Prints and Drawings Rooms, a service available to anyone who makes an appointment. Finally, the house that Turner designed and built, Sandycombe Lodge, is still extant in Twickenham.

In the USA Turner is well represented in major galleries, but the Indianapolis Museum of Art is particularly noted for holding one of the largest collections of watercolours, drawings and prints outside the UK, largely thanks to a bequest from the collector Kurt Pantzer.

In terms of further reading, Turner scholarship is vast and provides a wonderful onward journey for anyone enthused by this necessarily limited biography. Journals such as *Turner Studies* (Tate) and the *Turner Society News* (available via subscription) provide a range of fascinating essays. These, along with the publications below, are the ones I have found myself reaching for *most often* during the course of my research, but this is by no means the definitive list. More publications and mss to which I have referred are indicated in my notes.

Bailey, Anthony, *Standing in the Sun – A Biography of J. M. W. Turner*, London, Sinclair-Stevenson, 1997.

Brown, David Blayney, *Turner and Byron*, London, Tate, 1992.

Butlin, Martin, and Joll, Evelyn, *The Paintings of J. M. W. Turner*, 2 vols, New Haven, Yale University Press, 1984.

Butlin, Martin, Luther, Mollie, and Warrell, Ian, *Turner at Petworth: painter & patron*, London, Tate, 1989.

Davies, Maurice, *Turner as Professor: the Artist and Linear Perspective,* London, Tate, 1992.

Falk, Bernard, *Turner the Painter: His Hidden Life. A frank and revealing biography*, London, Hutchinson, 1938.

Finberg, A. J., *The Life of J. M. W. Turner R.A.*, second edition revised, with a supplement by Hilda F. Finberg, Oxford, Clarendon Press, 1961.

Gage, John, *The Collected Correspondence of J. M. W. Turner, with an early diary and a memoir by George Jones*, Oxford, Clarendon Press, 1980.

Hamilton, James, *Turner, A Life*, London, Hodder & Stoughton, 1997.

Hamilton, James, *Turner and the Scientists*, London, Tate, 1998.

Hill, David, *Turner in the Alps*, London, George Philip, 1992.

Hill, David, *Turner in the North*, New Haven, Yale University Press, 1996.

Joll, Evelyn, Butlin, Martin, and Herrmann, Luke, *The Oxford Companion to J. M. W. Turner*, Oxford University Press, 2001.

Krause, Martin F., *Turner in Indianapolis*, Indianapolis, Indiana University Press, 1997.

Piggott, Jan, *Turner's Vignettes*, London, Tate, 1993.

Powell, Cecilia, *Turner's Rivers of Europe*, London, Tate, 1991.

Powell, Cecilia, *Turner in Germany*, London, Tate, 1995.

Powell, Cecilia, *Italy in the Age of Turner: 'The Garden of the World'*, London, Merrell Holberton, 1998.

Riding, Christine, and Johns, Richard, *Turner and the Sea*, London, Thames & Hudson, 2013.

Rowell, Christopher, Warrell, Ian, and Brown, David Blayney, *Turner at Petworth*, London, Tate, 2002.

Shanes, Eric, *Turner's Picturesque Views in England and Wales 1825–1838*, London, Chatto & Windus, 1979.

Shanes, Eric, *J. M. W. Turner, A Life in Art, Vol. 1, Young Mr. Turner, The First Forty Years, 1775–1815*, London and New Haven, Yale University Press, 2016.

Thornbury, Walter, *The Life of J. M. W. Turner R.A.: Founded on Letters and Papers Furnished by his Friends and Fellow Academicians*, London, Hurst & Blackett, 1862.

Warrell, Ian, *Through Switzerland with Turner*, London, Tate, 1995.

Warrell, Ian, *Turner's Secret Sketches*, London, Tate, 2012.

Warrell, Ian, *Turner's Wessex: Architecture and Ambition*, London, Scala Arts & Heritage Publishers, 2015.

Whittingham, Selby, *Of Geese, Mallards and Drakes: Some Notes on Turner's Family*, 4 vols, London, J. M. W. Turner, R.A. Publications, 1993–9.

Whittingham, Selby, *Brentford to Oxford: J. M. W. Turner's Early Career under the Guardianship of his Uncle, J. M. W. Marshall*, London, J. M. W. Turner, R.A. Publications, 2009.

Wilton, Andrew, with transcriptions by Rosalind Mallord Turner, *Painting and Poetry: Turner's 'Verse Book' and his Work of 1804–1812*, London, Tate, 1990.

Wilton, Andrew, *The Life and Work of J. M. W. Turner*, London, Academy Editions, 1979.

Wilton, Andrew, *Turner in His Time*, London, Thames & Hudson, 1987.

Notes

Chapter 1: *Admiral Booth*

1. Edward Walford, *Old and New London: a narrative of its history, its people and its places*, London, 1878, Vol. 4, pp. 441–67.
2. John James Ruskin to John Ruskin, 26/27 December 1851. MSL 2/3/170, Ruskin Library, Lancaster University.
3. After Turner's death Maria Tanner lived at 47 Queen Anne Street with Hannah Danby.
4. William Cosmo Monkhouse, *Turner*, London, 1879, p. 131.
5. *London Daily News*, 6 May 1846.
6. John Gage, *The Collected Correspondence of J. M. W. Turner, with an early diary and a memoir by George Jones*, Oxford, Clarendon Press, 1980, p. 230.
7. This is now in the collection of the castle itself.
8. Now part of the Felton Bequest in the National Gallery of Victoria, Melbourne.
9. RFMSL 2/3/167, John James Ruskin to John Ruskin, London, 21 December 1851, Ruskin Foundation, Ruskin Library, University of Lancaster.
10. RFMSL 2/3/169, John James Ruskin to John Ruskin, 25 December 1851, Ruskin Foundation.
11. Unbeknown to Ruskin, another old family friend of Turner's, the Revd Henry Trimmer, had also been appointed and would go on to prove the will alongside Charles Turner, Jones, Harpur and Hardwick.
12. RFMSL 2/3/168, John James Ruskin to John Ruskin, 23 December 1851, Ruskin Foundation.
13. RFMSL 2/3/169, John James Ruskin to John Ruskin, London, 25 December 1851, Ruskin Foundation.
14. ibid.
15. ibid.
16. RFMSL 2/3/170, John James Ruskin to John Ruskin, 26/27 December 1851, Ruskin Foundation.

17. There is some speculation that Mrs Danby's daughters may have been fathered by Turner's father rather than by Turner himself, though the descendants of Evelina Danby are quite clear that the family tradition is that J. M. W. Turner was their ancestor, and contemporaries of Turner refer quite easily to his natural children (see Eastlake to Rogers, Peter William Clayden, *Samuel Rogers and His Contemporaries*, Vol. 2, London, 1889, p. 406).

18. *London Daily News*, 31 December 1851.

19. RFMSL 2/3/171, John James Ruskin to John Ruskin, 30 December 1851, Ruskin Foundation.

20. Clayden, *Samuel Rogers and His Contemporaries*, Vol. 2, p. 406.

21. *Hampshire Telegraph*, Saturday 3 January 1852.

22. *Westmorland Gazette*, Saturday 10 January 1852.

23. Ian Warrell has written extensively on Turner's erotica: 'A checklist of erotic sketches in the Turner Bequest', *British Art Journal*, Vol. 4, No. 1, Spring 2003, pp. 15–46; *Turner's Secret Sketches*, London, Tate, 2012.

24. Letter from George Jones to Lord Henry Lennox MP, 8 Park Square, 18 July 1861, Kurt F. Pantzer Collecting Papers, 1832–1983, Indianapolis Museum of Art Archives.

25. Sessional Papers, House of Lords, in the session 1861, Vol. xxii, Accounts and Papers, p. 401.

26. E. T. Cook and Alexander Wedderburn (eds.), *The Works of John Ruskin*, Cambridge University Press, 2010, Vol. 7, *Modern Painters V*, Chapter IX, pp. 374–88.

Chapter 2: The beginning

1. Turner's baptism was registered in mid-May. There is no actual evidence of the date of his birth. Turner's own claim that it was 23 April, which also happens to be St George's day and Shakespeare's birthday, may have been wishful thinking.

2. Hardwicke Lewis, *An Excursion to Margate: In the Month of June, 1786: Interspersed with a Variety of Anecdotes of Well-known Characters*, London, Ritchie & Sammells, 1787, p. 3.

3. Add MS 45982, British Library.

4. ibid.

5. Margaret Mare and W. Quarrell (eds.), *Lichtenberg's Visits to England, as Described in his Letters and Diaries*, Oxford, Clarendon Press, 1938.

6. I am indebted to Dr Tim Marshall, reader in Planning, Oxford Brookes University, who has shared his meticulous research into the Marshalls at Islington, J. M. W. Marshall at Brentford and Sunningwell, and the young J. M. W. Turner in these locations.

7. These are the grandparents of Henry Harpur IV, Turner's solicitor, mentioned in Chapter 1.

8. Glynne had been a long-time legal associate of Wilkes and had pleaded against his outlawry.

9. *Reminiscences of Henry Angelo with Memoirs of his Late Father and Friends*, Vol. 1, London, 1830, p. 139.

10. The earliest mention of Mr Burghall is in James Boswell's *Attic Miscellany*, No. XVI, of 1791. Edward Dayes advertises his selling exhibitions of drawings at Mr Burghall's Great Room, Maiden Lane, in May 1801, in the *Morning Post*, where he demands a shilling entrance fee.

11. Charles Saumarez Smith, *The Company of Artists, The Origins of the Royal Academy of Arts in London*, London, Modern Art Press, 2012, p. 24. This book details the various societies of artists in eighteenth-century London more generally, and the formation of the RA.

12. Kenneth Garlick and Angus Macintyre (eds.), *The Diary of Joseph Farington*, Vol. IV, January 1799–July 1801, New Haven and London, Yale University Press, 1979, p. 1425.

13. SA/35/5, Memorandum of agreement between Moreing and Society, Royal Academy of Arts Archive.

Chapter 3: 'A pleasant good tempered youth, not fond of society'

1. Tomkinson would go on to be a significant client of Turner's, as would his son.

2. Sir Walter Armstrong, *Turner*, London, Thos Agnew and Sons, 1902, p. 21.

3. RFMS 54/A, Ann Dart to John Ruskin, 30 May 1860 (transcript), Ruskin Foundation.

4. *The Works of the Late Edward Dayes: Containing an Excursion through the Principal Parts of Derbyshire and Yorkshire, Essays on Painting and Professional Sketches of Modern Artists*, London, 1805, p. 352.

5. Most recent biographers have taken the child who died in 1783 to be Turner's only sister, and have dismissed the child who passed away in 1786 because the William and Mary Turner cited as parents were from St Martin's in the Fields rather than Maiden Lane. But the fact that William Turner disappears from records associated with Maiden Lane between 1776 and 1790 suggests that the Turners may have moved to a different address at the point a second daughter was born, and that like so many eighteenth-century parents, William and Mary lost one child called Mary Anne only to call a second, equally doomed daughter by the same name.

6. Walter Thornbury, *The Life of J. M. W. Turner R.A.: Founded on Letters and Papers Furnished by his Friends and Fellow Academicians*, London, Hurst & Blackett, 1862, p. 5.

7. RFMS 54/A, Ann Dart to John Ruskin, 30 May 1860 (transcript), Ruskin Foundation.

8. Now in the National Portrait Gallery, London, NPG 1421.

9. Thornbury, *Life of J. M. W. Turner*, p. 7, p. 20.

10. *The Return from Margate* [1782].

11. Mrs Pilkington, *Margate!!! Or Sketches Amply Descriptive of that Celebrated Place of Resort with its Environs*, London, 1813, p. 2.

12. ibid., p. 10.

13. ibid., p. 211.

14. Selby Whittingham, 'New Light on J. M. W. Turner in Kent', *British Art Journal*, Spring 2015. The watercolours remain in private hands today.

15. Thornbury, *Life of J. M. W. Turner*, p. 24.

16. Dr William Barrow, *An Essay on Education*, Vol. II, London, 1804, p. 223.

17. *Works of the Late Edward Dayes*, p. 352.

18. Some scholars have Joseph Marshall moving to Sunningwell in 1789 but Brentford trade directories suggest he continued to trade in Brentford until 1797.

19. *Turner Society News*, No. 84, March 2000, p. 5 notes that an early view of Oxford came up for sale at Phillips in November 1999, and had been given by Turner to the Narraway family, as he was in the habit of doing.

20. Ellen G. D'Oench, 'Prints, Drawings, and a Turner in John Raphael Smith's Will', *Print Quarterly*, Vol. 17, No. 4 (December 2000), pp. 381–3. D'Oench reiterates Turner's work in Raphael's studio circa 1788.

21. This is the Princeton Sketchbook, so called because it is in the Princeton University Art Museum.

22. Henry Boswell, *Historical descriptions of new and elegant picturesque views of the antiquities of England and Wales*, printed for Alex Hogg, 1786, Chiswick Library.

23. Carlyle to *The Times*, 28 January 1856, Carlyle Letters Online, http://carlyleletters.dukejournals.org/cgi/content/long/31/1/lt-18560128-TC-EOT-01.

24. *Works of the Late Edward Dayes*, p. 352.

25. D'Oench, 'Prints, Drawings, and a Turner in John Raphael Smith's Will'.

Chapter 4: A bee of the same hive

1. This depiction of King Lear in the storm is now in the Museum of Fine Arts, Boston.

2. This explanation of the title was included in a later edition of the publication: *The Bee, or a Companion to the Shakespeare Gallery*, London 1789.

3. Elizabeth was born in 1776 and Stephen in 1777.

4. In 1790 Rigaud also secured admission for his children's writing master George Chinnery, who went on to have a career as a painter of portraits and Asian subjects.

5. John Jolliffe (ed.), *Neglected Genius: The Diaries of Benjamin Robert Haydon*, London, Hutchinson, 1990, p. 101.

6. Stephen Rigaud, *The Facts and Recollections of the XIIIth Century in a Memoir of J. F. Rigaud Esq. R.A.*, reprinted in *Volumes of the Walpole Society*, 1984, Vol. 50, p. 86.

7. RAA/KEE/2/1/1/, Attendance in the plaister academy, Royal Academy of Arts Archive.

8. Now in the Indianapolis Museum of Art.

9. Rigaud, *A Memoir of J. F. Rigaud*, p. 90.

10. Eric Shanes pointed out the similarities in Malton's and Turner's views of Henry VII's chapel in Westminster Abbey in his Kurt Pantzer lecture

at the Paul Mellon Centre on 23 April 2014, and noted that one view by
Malton of Melbourne House, Whitehall includes a depiction of the
young Turner at work nearby. See also Eric Shanes, *J. M. W. Turner, A
Life in Art, Vol. 1, Young Mr Turner, The First Forty Years 1775–1815*,
London and New Haven, 2016, pp. 21–4.

11. G,2,128, British Museum.

12. Thornbury, *Life of J. M. W. Turner*, p. 55.

13. RFMS 54/A, Ann Dart to John Ruskin, 30 May 1860 (transcript), Ruskin
Foundation.

14. ibid. Some scholars doubt Dart's account that Turner stayed in Bristol
before 1791. However, in local documentation Narraway's occupation
of 'fellmonger' is often wrongly transcribed as 'fishmonger' – notably
in 1824 bankruptcy papers. Turner's early biographers who gathered
anecdotal information about his childhood suggested Turner visited a
relative in Margate who was a fishmonger. Perhaps they conflated Turner's visits to Margate and those to Bristol. He visited a family friend in
Bristol who was a fellmonger, not a fishmonger, and later visited Margate. The fact that correspondence in the Turner family today suggests
that John Narraway was someone who intervened in settling a dispute
over the will of Turner's paternal grandmother also strengthens the idea
that if not actual family, he was certainly considered as good as.

15. ibid.

16. ibid.

17. ibid.

18. RFMS 54/A, Ann Dart to John Ruskin, 16 April 1860, Ruskin Foundation.

19. Letters from Hermann Ludwig Heinrich von Pückler-Muskau, 1828,
quoted in Gerry Brooke, 'A Prince in search of love who fell for the
charms of Bristol', *Bristol Evening Post*, 13 April 2012.

20. *A View Looking up the Avon from Cook's Folly*, Bristol and Malmesbury
Sketchbook, Tate, Turner Bequest V 124, D00107.

21. RFMS 54/A, Ann Dart to John Ruskin, 30 May 1860 (transcript), Ruskin
Foundation.

22. I am grateful to Ian Warrell for pointing me to this.

23. *Reminiscences of Henry Angelo*, Vol. 1, p. 93.

24. Sir Joshua Reynolds, *Discourses on Art*, ed. Robert R. Wark, New Haven
and London, Yale University Press, 1981, Discourse XV, p. 276.

25. *Reminiscences of Henry Angelo*, Vol. 1, p. 94.
26. TB IX-A, British Museum.
27. RFMS 54/A, Ann Dart to John Ruskin, 30 May 1860 (transcript), Ruskin Foundation.

Chapter 5: The most liberal encouragers of watercolour art

1. *Reminiscences of Henry Angelo*, vol. 1, p. 226.
2. *Dr Monro*, by the very Revd W. Foxley Norris, DD Dean of York, Old Water-colour Society's Club 1924–25, London, 1925, p. 3.
3. Martin Archer Shee, *The Life of Sir Martin Archer Shee, President of the Royal Academy, by his Son*, London, Longman, 1860, p. 210.
4. *Diary of Joseph Farington*, Vol. II, January 1795–August 1796, p. 489.
5. Most scholars have suggested that Turner's attendance at Monro's informal academy began in 1794 when Monro had moved to Adelphi Terrace. However, John Lewis Roget points out that engraver John Pye, who had seen Monro's journal, dated the relationship to 1793. This would be consistent with Turner's depiction of the church at Monken Hadley, a village where the Monro family had a country home. Turner himself dated this watercolour 1793. John Lewis Roget, *A History of the Old Watercolour Society*, Vol. 1, London, Longman, 1891, pp. 81–2.
6. ibid.
7. Other students to attend later than Girtin and Turner included Peter de Wint, John Sell Cotman and Cornelius Varley.
8. These annotations were made in the Cooper Notebooks, which list 150 drawings that Charles Stokes gave to his niece Hannah Cooper in 1853. Kurt F. Pantzer Collecting Papers, 1832–1983, Indianapolis Museum of Art Archives.
9. Shanes, *J. M. W. Turner*, pp. 49–53.
10. WD74A, Victoria & Albert Museum, Prints and Drawings.
11. *Diary of Joseph Farington*, vol. III, September 1796–December 1798, p. 1091.
12. Mora Abell, *Doctor Thomas Monro: Physician, Patron and Painter*, Bloomington, Indiana, Trafford Publishing, 2009, p. 182.
13. Inscription by Turner: A List of Names and Figures in the Smaller South Wales Sketchbook, Tate, Turner Bequest, XXVI, D000462.

14. Rigaud, *A Memoir of J. F. Rigaud,* pp. 86–7.

15. *Diary of Joseph Farington*, Vol. I, July 1793–December 1794, p. 94.

16. Most of these 'Monro School' sketches are in the Kurt F. Pantzer Collecting Papers in the Indianapolis Museum of Art. That institution has photographs of associated sketches given back to the Monro family in the 1950s, one a pencil portrait of Monro that may well have been by Turner.

17. Andrew Wilton suggests that Turner's views of Dover may have been copied by the senior members of the club. 'The Monro School Questions: Some Answers', *Turner Studies*, Winter 1984, Vol. 4, No. 2, pp. 8–24.

18. Conal Shields (as reported in exh. cat., Tate Gallery 1973–4, p. 88) tentatively suggests that the peculiar character of two paintings of Walton Bridges that Turner made later derives from the use of the camera lucida patented by W.H. Wollaston in 1807.

19. Andrew Wilton, *Turner as Draughtsman*, Aldershot, Ashgate Publishing, 2006, p. 51.

20. Martin Krause notices that when one compares Turner and Girtin's copy of *South Gate of Sargans* by Cozens with the original, the ink washes added by Turner reverse Cozens's original. *Turner in Indianapolis*, Indianapolis Museum of Art, 1997, p. 80.

21. This self-portrait is now in the collection of the Indianapolis Museum of Art (72.206). Ruskin would write rhapsodically about it and his letter is also held there, where he describes it as 'the loveliest boys face I ever saw . . . A singular piercing in the grey eyes however contrasting with the softness of long flowing dark hair on shoulders . . . They say 16 but the painting is impossibly firm & fine for that age – and yet this boy can't be more than 19 – his old servant bequeathed it to me – He gave it her himself !!!!!!!!!!!'

22. Thornbury, *Life of J. M. W. Turner*, p. 67.

23. *Some Account of the Life and Writings of Mrs. Trimmer with original letters, and meditations and prayers, selected from her journal*, London, C&J.

24. Bell may well have been the source of the story about Turner's love life, originally recounted to Turner's first biographer, Walter Thornbury.

25. Inscription by Turner: A Midlands Itinerary 1794, Tate, Turner Bequest, XIX2, D00208.

26. ibid.

Chapter 6: M'lord Turner

1. A transcript of the diary of Edward Monro is in the possession of Mora Abell. It is evident from the entries in this that Turner was continuing to draw as well as socialize with the Monros well into the nineteenth century.
2. Diary of Edward Monro, as above.
3. *Diary of Joseph Farington*, Vol. II, p. 296.
4. Thornbury, *Life of J. M. W. Turner*, p. 23. However, other accounts suggest that Turner also had a separate set of rooms in Hand Court which he used as a studio, next to his father's property. Roget, *A History of the Old Watercolour Society*, p. 82.
5. Jane Zaring, 'The Romantic Face of Wales', *Annals of the Association of American Geographers*, Vol. 67, No. 3, September 1977, p. 403.
6. According to Ann Dart's letters to Ruskin, this happened on at least one other occasion.
7. Turner to William Delamotte, postmark 1800, Gage, *Collected Correspondence*, p. 22.
8. Distant View of Penllyn Castle with Cowbridge in Foreground: Two Figures with a Horse, Smaller South Wales Sketchbook, Tate, Turner Bequest, XXV 7, D00468.
9. ibid., D00491.
10. Sir Richard Joseph Sulivan, *Observations Made During a Tour through parts of England, Scotland and Wales in a series of Letters*, London, 1780, p. 199.
11. P. J. Marshall and John A. Wood (eds.), *The Correspondence of Edmund Burke*, Vol. VII, p. 75.
12. William Sandby, *The History of the Royal Academy From its Foundation in 1768 to the Present Time*, Vol. 1, London, Longman, 1862, p. 171.
13. Christine Riding and Richard Johns, *Turner and the Sea*, London, Thames & Hudson, 2013, p. 31.
14. Thornbury, *Life of J. M. W. Turner*, p. 18.
15. Ian Warrell's catalogue for Salisbury Museum's *Turner's Wessex: Architecture and Ambition* carefully argues this timeline, which establishes Turner's trip to Stourhead in 1795 and charts the subsequent relationship between patron and artist.

16. *Gateway to the Close, Salisbury,* 1802–5, Fitzwilliam Museum, Cambridge (W208).
17. Charles Tomkins, *A Tour to the Isle of Wight,* Vol. 1, London, 1796, p. 43.
18. Some have suggested these are rocks off Freshwater Bay, since disappeared.
19. Possibly Lieutenant General Sir William Stewart (1774–1827).

Chapter 7: 'W Turner called'

1. Shee, *The Life of Sir Martin Archer Shee,* p. 210.
2. *Diary of Joseph Farington,* Vol. III, p. 1060.
3. ibid., p. 1075
4. ibid.
5. Rigaud, *A Memoir of J. F. Rigaud,* p. 106.
6. Selby Whittingham has written about the Whites in both 'New Light on J. M. W. Turner in Kent', and 'J. M. W. Turner, marriage and morals', *British Art Journal,* Spring 2015.
7. Studies near Brighton Sketchbook, Tate Turner Bequest, XXX 1–96a.
8. Clara Wheeler (née Wells)'s full description of her relationship with the young Turner is in Thornbury, *Life of J. M. W. Turner,* Vol. 2, pp. 53–7.
9. *Diaries of Benjamin Robert Haydon,* p. 100.
10. *Recollections of J. M. W. Turner by George Jones,* in Gage, *Collected Correspondence,* p. 2.
11. *Diary of Joseph Farington,* Vol. III, p. 1075.
12. Thomas Shepherd Munden, *The Memoirs of Joseph Shepherd Munden,* London, Richard Bentley, 1844, p. 55.
13. ibid., p. 68.
14. ibid., p. 56.
15. Thornbury suggests Turner acquired rooms further into Hand Court that afforded him more space.
16. CLC/B/192/F001/MS/11936/431, London Metropolitan Archive.
17. Though the recommendation could have equally come via Dr Monro or Viscount Malden, both of whom were also on friendly terms with the Lascelles family.
18. Shee, *The Life of Sir Martin Archer Shee,* Vol. 1, p. 243.

19. *Moonlight, A Study at Millbank* (featuring the moon over the Thames) and *Fishermen Coming Ashore at Sun Set, previous to a Gale.*

20. Munden's and the other clients' names are noted against a list of views inside the front cover of the North of England Sketchbook, Tate, Turner Bequest, XXXIV, D41412. The view of Holy Island for Mr Munden may have been either *Holy Island Cathedral, Northumberland*, which Turner exhibited at the RA in 1798 and is now untraced, or perhaps *Off Holy Island*, sold as part of the Sara Austen collection at Christie's in 1889.

21. David Hill has covered this tour extensively, in *Turner in the North: a tour through Derbyshire, Yorkshire, Durham, Northumberland, the Scottish Borders, the Lake District, Lancashire and Lincolnshire in the year 1797*, New Haven and London, Yale University Press, *c.* 1996.

22. ibid., p. 88.

23. This is now in the Victoria and Albert Museum.

24. The diaries of E. T. Monro mention this spectacle on more than one occasion.

25. *Diary of Joseph Farington*, Vol. IV, p. 1154.

26. Turner also painted a second version around the same time. *Norham Castle Sunrise* was bought by Edward Lasalles, as David Hill points out in 'A Taste for the Arts', *Turner Studies*, Vol. 5, No. 1, p. 38.

27. John Callcott Horsley R.A., *Recollections of a Royal Academician*, New York, 1903, p. 245.

28. Hill, *Turner in the North*, p. 88.

29. *Whitehall Evening Post*, 2 June 1798, quoted by David Hill in 'A Taste for the Arts', *Turner Studies*, Vol. 5, No. 1.

30. *St James's Chronicle*, 1–3 May, quoted by David Hill in ibid.

31. Roget, *A History of the Old Watercolour Society*, quoted by David Hill in ibid.

32. Edmund Burke, *On Taste, On the Sublime and Beautiful, Reflections on the French Revolution, A Letter to a Noble Lord*, New York, Cosimo Classics, 2009, p. 51.

33. Minutes of Royal Academy Council meeting 20 January 1798, cited by Jerrald Ziff in *Turner Studies*, Vol. 2, No. 1, p. 2.

34. *Diary of Joseph Farington*, Vol. III, p. 1081.

Chapter 8: Gothick

1. *The Times*, 25 May 1798.
2. I am indebted to Selby Whittingham for alerting me to these connections.
3. The baby, a daughter, survived, as did the daughter born in 1784.
4. *Diary of Joseph Farington*, Vol. III, p. 1117.
5. Ian Warrell charts Turner's watercolours of Fonthill and the different stages of the build in his catalogue for *Turner's Wessex: Architecture and Ambition*, Salisbury Museum, 2015, pp. 82–5.
6. Ian Warrell points out that these watercolours exhibited at the RA bore Wyatt's name despite being executed by Turner, ibid., p. 83.
7. At this time the Pope had a legal right to first refusal to buy any works of art before they were removed from the country.
8. *Diary of Joseph Farington*, Vol. IV, p. 1218.
9. ibid.
10. *The Recollections of J. M. W. Turner by George Jones*, in Gage, *Collected Correspondence*, p. 4. The chronology is a little unclear here. Angerstein had bought Claude's *St Ursula* by 1802, though it is possible he acquired it earlier, which makes it the most likely candidate for the anecdote.
11. William Beckford, *Italy with Sketches of Spain and Portugal, by the author of 'Vathek'*, 2 vols, 3rd edition, London, Richard Bentley, 1835, p. 159.
12. ibid., p. 184.
13. *Diary of Joseph Farington*, Vol. III, p. 1084.
14. Hubert Rigg, *Turner and Dr Whitaker*, Towneley Hall and Art Gallery & Museums, 1982, p. 7.
15. Turner made a watercolour of Browsholme for him that September.
16. W. G. Rawlinson, *The Engraved Works of J. M. W. Turner R.A.*, Macmillan, London, 1908, p. 188. The compromise alluded to seems to have been the handing over to the engraver of the responsibility of reproducing the objectionable picture.

Chapter 9: Charitable relief

1. *Reasons for the Establishment and Further Encouragement of St Luke's Hospital for Lunatics, 1786*, London Metropolitan Archive.

2. *Diary of Joseph Farington*, Vol. III, p. 887.

3. *The Diary of William Godwin*, eds. Victoria Myers, David O'Shaughnessy and Mark Philp, Oxford Digital Library, 2010. http://godwindiary.bodleian.ox.ac.uk, 17 May 1800.

4. H64/B/04/002/02 and H64/B/0/004, London Metropolitan Archive. Only the summaries of paperwork exist in the hospital records, the original petitions and bonds do not.

5. The Bills of Mortality refer to the number of parishes in London where, during plague years, notices about the rise of the plague were posted. The Bills of Mortality became fixed in 1636 and excluded major parts of London such as, for example, Chelsea, Kensington, Marylebone, Paddington and St Pancras.

6. Jean Golt, 'Sarah Danby: Out of the Shadows', *Turner Studies*, Vol. 9, No. 2, Winter 1989, pp. 3–9.

7. ibid.

8. Now in the Indianapolis Museum of Art.

9. The title of this work is a puzzle. The fifth plague of Egypt attacked livestock, while the seventh plague was a great hailstorm. The clear emphasis on storm in the canvas and the dim figure of Moses suggest Turner was really depicting the seventh plague, and as if there was any doubt he included a quotation from Exodus alongside the work. So was it a typo made by the printsetters who prepared the RA catalogue that year?

10. H. A. N. Brockman, *The Caliph of Fonthill*, London, Werner Laurie, 1956, p. 124.

11. *Life and Correspondence of Major Cartwright*, Vol. 1, London, Henry Colburn, 1826, p. 287.

12. Tate, Turner Bequest, LXIX.

13. They are not in the catalogue.

14. *Life and Correspondence of Major Cartwright*, Vol. 2, appendix, pp. 350–57.

15. *The Tate Gallery 1984-86: Illustrated Catalogue of Acquisitions Including Supplement to Catalogue of Acquisitions 1982–84*, Tate Gallery, London, 1988, pp. 82–3.

16. From an original commission of seven watercolours.

17. *St James's Chronicle*, 6 May 1800.

18. Warrell, *Turner's Wessex*, p. 88.

19. The tower was completed but Beckford sold the abbey in 1822. The tower, however, fell down again in 1825.
20. BL 10857 a 55, *Recollections of the Late William Beckford*, privately published by Charlotte Lansdown, 1893, British Library, p. 15.
21. Tate, N00458.

Chapter 10: Politics

1. Faramerz Dabhoiwala, *The Origins of Sex*, London, Allen Lane, 2012, p. 204.
2. Stolen from the Isabella Stewart Gardner Museum in Boston in 1990.
3. *Diary of Joseph Farington*, Vol. IV, p. 1541.
4. Martin Archer Shee, *Rhymes on Art or The Remonstrance of a Painter*, London, 1805, p. xv.
5. This is revealed in the inventory of his household effects in Queen Anne Street made after his death.
6. Dorothy Wordsworth, *Recollections of a Tour in Scotland A.D.1803*, ed. J. C. Shairp, p. 68.
7. ibid., p. 26.
8. ibid., p. 52.
9. *Diary of Joseph Farington*, Vol. V, August 1801–March 1803, p. 1742.
10. *Morning Chronicle*, 14 October 1801.
11. John Goldworth Alger, *Napoleon's British Visitors and Captives 1801–1815*, New York, 1904, p. 18.
12. *Diary of Joseph Farington*, Vol. V, p. 1746.

Chapter 11: Adventure

1. *Diary of Joseph Farington*, Vol. V, p. 1746.
2. Mark Philp, *Resisting Napoleon: The British Response to the Threat and Invasion*, Aldershot, Ashgate, 2006, p. 221.
3. 'Sketch of a journey to Paris in Autumn 1802 during the Peace of Amiens, in a series of Original Letters, written from memory by A Lady in 1810', *American Monthly Magazine and Critical Review*, Vol. 3, New York, 1818.

4. *Les Anglais en France après la Paix d'Amiens. Impressions de voyage de Sir John Carr. Etude, traduction et notes*, Paris, 1898, Albert Babeau.

5. Early sources describe the sponsors as three noblemen, a description that would not fit Fawkes. The notion that it may have been Boyd who was the third sponsor was raised in *J. M. W. Turner*, ed. Ian Warrell with an essay by Franklin Kelly, London, Tate Publishing, 2007.

6. Cecilia Powell has provided an account of Newbey Lowson in *Turner Society News*, No. 54, February 1990, p. 12.

7. A travellers' album in an inn has Lord Darlington and Newbey Lowson's signatures following those of Percy Shelley and his party in 1816. The note about Newbey was made in pencil by an anonymous observer. H. D. Traill, *Among My Books: Papers on Literary Subjects Reported From Literature*, London, Elliot Stock, 1898, p. 73.

8. 'Sketch of a journey to Paris in Autumn 1802 during the Peace of Amiens'.

9. Calais Pier Sketchbook, Tate, Turner Bequest, LXXXI 58, D04960.

10. 'Sketch of a journey to Paris in Autumn 1802 during the peace of Amiens'.

11. *Diary of Joseph Farington*, Vol. V, p. 1810.

12. 'Sketch of a journey to Paris in Autumn 1802 during the Peace of Amiens'.

13. *Diary of Joseph Farington*, Vol. V, p. 1890.

14. Turner, quoted by Barry Venning, 'Turner's Annotated Books: Opie's "Lectures on painting" and Shee's "Elements of Art"' (II), *Turner Studies*, Vol. 2, No. 2, '1983' for 1982, p. 45.

15. Shee, *The Life of Sir Martin Archer Shee*, p. 243.

16. Studies in Louvre Sketchbook, Tate D04314.

17. Beckford's Letters from Italy, *Gentleman's Magazine and Chronicle*, Vol. 38, 1834, p. 238.

18. The Sir John Soane's Museum collection.

19. Warrell, *Turner's Wessex*, p. 114.

20. *Diary of Joseph Farington*, Vol. V, p. 1890.

21. ibid.

22. ibid., p. 1936.

23. *Before and after Waterloo: Letters from Edward Stanley, sometime Bishop of Norwich (1802; 1814; 1816)*, ed. Jane H. Adeane and Maud Grenfell, London, T. Fisher Unwin, 1907, p. 43.

24. *Diary of Joseph Farington*, Vol. V, p. 1890.

25. Grenoble Sketchbook, Tate, Turner Bequest, LXXIV.

26. *Diary of Joseph Farington*, Vol. V, p. 1890.

27. David Hill has charted Turner's tour of 1802 in *Turner in the Alps: The Artist's Journey through France and Switzerland in 1802*, George Philip, 1992.

28. ibid., p. 67.

29. *The handbook for travellers in Switzerland and the Alps of Savoy*, London, John Murray, 1811.

30. *Diary of Joseph Farington*, Vol. V, p. 1890.

31. Hill, *Turner in the Alps*, p. 68.

Chapter 12: A little reptile

1. After Berne, Turner and Lowson visited Lake Thun, the Grindelwald and the Eiger, the Reichenbach Falls, Brienz, and then went through the Brünig Pass to Lucerne. After this the St Gotthard Pass presented some of the most dramatic scenery that captivated Turner's imagination, from where they proceeded to Zurich, saw the Falls of the Rhine and visited Basle before returning to Paris.

2. *Diary of Joseph Farington*, Vol. V, p. 1900.

3. Studies in the Louvre Sketchbook, Tate, Turner Bequest, LXXII 41a, D04327.

4. *Diary of Joseph Farington*, Vol. V, p. 1944.

5. ibid., Vol. VI, April 1803–December 1804, p. 2203.

6. ibid., p. 2031. By far not the only mention of Turner's arrogance, which peppers the diaries in the spring of 1803.

7. ibid., p. 2235. Turner had provided Smirke with a similar message just days before, too, saying he never promised a vote, p. 2227.

8. ibid., p. 2320, 11 May 1804.

9. David Irwin, 'Fuseli's Milton Gallery: Unpublished Letters', *Burlington Magazine*, Vol. 101, No. 681 (December 1959), pp. 436–7 and 439–40.

10. *Diary of Joseph Farington*, Vol. VI, p. 2287.

11. Revd Richard Hale, quoted in *Turner Society News*, No. 96, March 2004, Karen Lynch and David Hill, p. 11.

12. *Diary of Joseph Farington*, Vol. VI, p. 2299.

13. Lord Auckland to Turner, 13 May 1804, Gage, *Collected Correspondence*, p. 22.

14. An entirely fanciful painting since Turner showed little interest in Macon when he was actually there, according to evidence in his sketchbooks. This painting is now in the collection of Sheffield Galleries and Trust.
15. Now part of the Paul Mellon Collection at the Yale Center for British Art.
16. Now in Southampton Art Gallery.
17. Gage, *Collected Correspondence*, p. 23.
18. ibid.
19. Both watercolours are now in the Sir John Soane's Museum.
20. Turner to John Soane, 4 July 1804, Gage, *Collected Correspondence*, p. 24.
21. *Diary of Joseph Farington*, Vol. VI, p. 2306.
22. Holger Hoock, *The King's Artists: The Royal Academy and the Politics of British Culture 1760–1840*, Oxford, Clarendon Press, 2003, p. 197.

Chapter 13: Reimagined pasts

1. Selby Whittingham, '"A Most liberal Patron": Sir John Fleming Leicester, Bart', *Turner Studies*, Vol. 6, no. 2, p. 24.
2. Much of the documentation for the sale is held in the London Metropolitan Archive, ACC/1525/016, and Professor Sam Smiles has written about the tontine in 'Turner and the Slave Trade: speculation and representation 1804–40', *British Art Journal*, Vol. VIII, No. 3.
3. Stephen Drew, *Principles of Self Knowledge or An Attempt to Demonstrate the Truth of Christianity and the Efficacy of Experimental Religion Against the Cavils of the Infidel and the Objections of the Formalist*, London, Longman, 1828.
4. *Diary of Joseph Farington*, Vol. VIII, July 1806–December 1807, p. 2892.
5. Turner to the Earl of Elgin, 7 August 1806, Gage, *Collected Correspondence*, p. 31.
6. Diagram of Ship Positions and Notes on the Battle of Trafalgar, Nelson Sketchbook, Tate, Turner Bequest, LXXXIX, D05456.
7. ibid., D05462.
8. *Diary of Joseph Farington*, Vol. VII, January 1805–June 1806, p. 2777.
9. *Notes and Memoranda Respecting the Liber Studiorum of J. M. W. Turner R. A. written and collected by the late John Pye*, John Lewis Roget (ed.), London, John van Voorst, 1879, p. 37.

10. *Diary of Joseph Farington*, Vol. VIII, p. 2683.

11. George Jones suggested the engraver was a distant relative of Turner's, though most suppose they were not related.

12. Note written on the reverse of a letter from Mr Gilly to Turner, May 1805, Gage, *Collected Correspondence*, p. 27.

13. Thornbury, *Life of J. M. W. Turner*, Vol. 2, p. 55.

14. Turner to F. C. Lewis, early 1807, Gage, *Collected Correspondence*, p. 34.

Chapter 14: The eye and the intellect

1. Elizabeth Inglis-Jones, 'The Knights of Downton Castle', *National Library of Wales Journal*, 15, 3, p. 260.

2. By 1809 Turner had let his rooms in Harley Street to a dentist called Benjamin Young. Turner also knew a famous dentist from Bath, Dr Joseph Sigmond, and his son the eminent physician George Gabriel Sigmond of Dover Street. Turner bought a manuscript of correspondence between Samuel Richardson and Dr Cheyne on medical matters from the sale of the library. Sigmond's librarian, John Dillon, became a collector of Turner's work.

3. *Examiner*, 15 May 1808.

4. Finance Sketchbook, Tate, Turner Bequest, CXXII 42, D08350. Matthew Imms, 'Inscription by Turner: Notes, Probably from Richard Payne Knight's "Account of the Remains of the Worship of Priapus", c. 1807–14 by Joseph Mallord William Turner', catalogue entry, September 2013, in David Blayney Brown (ed.), *J. M. W. Turner Sketchbooks, Drawings and Watercolours*, Tate Research Publication, September 2014.

5. Richard Payne Knight, *An Analytical Inquiry into the Principles of Taste*, London, 1805, p. 148.

6. Andrew Wilton, *Painting and Poetry: Turner's 'Verse Book' and his work of 1804–1812*, Tate, 1990, with transcriptions by Rosalind Mallord Turner, p. 34.

7. Inscription by Turner: Draft of Poetry circa 1809, Perspective Sketchbook, Tate, Turner Bequest, CVIII 31, D07403.

8. Jean Golt researched Sarah Danby and her daughters in 'Sarah Danby: Out of the Shadows', pp. 3–10.

9. Wilton, *Painting and Poetry*, p. 31.

10. Maurice Davies, *Turner as Professor: The Artist and Linear Perspective*, Tate, 1992, p. 21.

Chapter 15: *The overturner*

1. Transcription of the diary of E. T. Monro, in the possession of Mora Abell.
2. *Diary of Joseph Farington*, Vol. X, July 1809–December 1810, pp. 3505–9.
3. ibid.
4. Elizabeth Rigby, who would marry Turner's colleague Charles Eastlake.
5. *Harvest Home* and *Cassiobury Park Reaping* were unfinished in Turner's studio at his death, and are now in the Tate Collection.
6. *Diary of Joseph Farington*, Vol. IV, p. 1303.
7. Allan Cunningham, *The Life of Sir David Wilkie*, Vol. 1, London, John Murray, 1843, p. 143.
8. *The Oxford Companion to J. M. W. Turner*, eds. Evelyn Joll, Martin Butlin and Luke Herrmann, Oxford University Press, 2001, p. 355.
9. J. Greig (ed.), *The Farington Diary*, Vol. 2, 1802–1804, London, 1923, p. 97. This quote is provided in a footnote in this version of Farington's diaries, and is an extract from the diary of J. C. Wardrop.
10. *Diary of Joseph Farington*, Vol. VII, p. 2735.
11. Turner to John Taylor, 9 January 1811, Gage, *Collected Correspondence*, p. 45.
12. Thornbury, *Life of J. M. W. Turner*, Vol. 1, p. 173.
13. ibid., Vol. 2, pp. 87–8.
14. *The Parallel between England and Carthage and between France and Rome, by a citizen of Dublin*, London, John Murray, 1803.
15. AND 25/3, Royal Academy of Arts Archive.
16. Now in the Fitzwilliam Museum, Cambridge.
17. *Hulks on the Tamar* and *Teignmouth*, both still in situ at Petworth House.
18. Turner to John Young, 14 January 1814, Gage, *Collected Correspondence*, p. 56.
19. Patricia Morales, *Mere Good Taste Is Nothing Else but Genius Without the Power of Execution: Artists as Arbiters of Taste 1792–1836*, PhD thesis, University of Warwick, 2003. Morales gives a great account of Beaumont and the white painters and cites the Preface to the Exhibition of 1815 on p. 162.
20. *Diary of Joseph Farington*, Vol. XIII, January 1814–December 1815, p. 4626.

21. *Catalogue Raisonée of the pictures now exhibiting at the British Institution*, 1815, cited in Morales, *Mere Good Taste*, p. 166.

22. *Diary of Joseph Farington*, Vol. XIII, p. 4650.

23. Warrell, *Turner's Wessex*, p. 37.

Chapter 16: Summertimes

1. Mary Shelley, 'The English in Italy', *Westminster Review*, October 1826, cited in Benjamin Colbert (ed.), 'Bibliography of British Travel Writing, 1780–1840: The European Tour, 1814–1818 (excluding Britain and Ireland)', *Cardiff Corvey: Reading the Romantic Text* 13 (Winter 2004). http://www.cf.ac.uk/encap/corvey/articles/cc13_no1.html>.

2. Review of J. Jorgenson, *Travels through France and Germany* (1817), in *Edinburgh Review* 28 (August 1817), 371, cited in Colbert as above.

3. Colbert (ed.), 'Bibliography of British Travel Writing, 1780–1840'.

4. Turner to James Wyatt, Saturday 6 March 1812, Gage, *Collected Correspondence*, p. 51.

5. Turner to W. B. Cooke, Saturday 4 December 1813, Gage, *Collected Correspondence*, p. 55.

6. The *Salvador del Mundo* was a guardship at Hamoaze with all the connotations that would have delighted Turner. Once a Spanish ship of the line, she had been captured in the Battle of St Vincent in 1797, having been raked by the *Victory*.

7. Lady Eastlake, 'Memoir of Sir Charles Lock Eastlake', in Sir Charles Lock Eastlake, *Contributions to the Literature of the Fine Arts: Second Series*, London, 1870, p. 23.

8. Turner pointed out his Barnstaple heritage to the journalist Cyrus Redding. Thornbury, *Life of J. M. W. Turner*, Vol. 1, p. 218.

9. ibid., p. 219.

10. Cyrus Redding, *Past Celebrities Whom I Have Known*, Vol. 1, London, Charles Skeet, 1866, p. 47.

11. ibid., pp. 48–50. The island Redding is referring to is now known as Burgh Island.

12. ibid., pp. 52–3.

13. ibid., p. 58.

14. Thornbury, *Life of J. M. W. Turner*, Vol. 1, p. 220.

15. Turner to Ambrose Johns, October 1814, Gage, *Collected Correspondence*, p. 59.

16. Turner to James Wyatt, May/June 1811, ibid., p. 49.

17. Transcription of the diary of E. T. Monro, in the possession of Mora Abell.

18. Probably the sculptor Samuel Joseph.

19. Horsley, *Recollections of a Royal Academician*, p. 247.

20. Turner to George Cooke, Tuesday 23 May 1815, Gage, *Collected Correspondence*, p. 59.

21. Turner to Henry Scott Trimmer, 1 August 1815, Gage, *Collected Correspondence*, p. 60.

22. ibid., p. 61.

23. Patrick Youngblood, 'The painter as architect: Turner and Sandycombe Lodge', *Turner Studies*, Vol. 2, No. 1, p. 23.

24. Thornbury, *Life of J. M. W. Turner*, Vol. 1, p. 167.

25. ibid.

26. ibid., p. 168. Hollands was a brand of gin.

27. Turner to Abraham Cooper, 7 August 1821, Gage, *Collected Correspondence*, p. 86.

28. An Itinerary &c, Hastings Sketchbook, Tate, Turner Bequest, CX 199, D07751.

29. William Cosmo Monkhouse, *Turner*, London, 1879, Sampson Low, p. 77.

30. Thornbury, *Life of J. M. W. Turner*, Vol. 1, p. 170.

31. I am indebted to Nick Tapley, Evelina's direct descendant, for allowing me to see this miniature and to reproduce it.

32. *Diary of Joseph Farington*, Vol. XIV, January 1816–December 1817, p. 4835.

33. Transcripts of Maria Fawkes's diary in A. J. Finberg, *Turner's watercolours at Farnley Hall*, London, The Studio, 1912.

34. Turner to James Holworthy, 31 July 1816, Gage, *Collected Correspondence*, p. 67.

35. Turner to James Holworthy, 11 September 1816, ibid., p. 70.

Chapter 17: Waterloo

1. Steamers had been introduced into the Thames in 1815 and Turner just missed the Scottish-built *Caledonia*, which undertook a virgin voyage

on the Rhine in October and November 1817. Another steamer, the *Defiance* or *Defiant*, had reached as far as Cologne in June 1816.

2. Lord Byron, *Childe Harold's Pilgrimage*, Canto III.

3. *Diary, Reminiscences and Correspondence of Henry Crabb Robinson*, London, Macmillan, 1869, p. 497.

4. Cecilia Powell covers this tour in *Turner's Rivers of Europe: the Rhine, Meuse and Mosel*, Tate, 1991, p. 21.

5. Lord Byron, *Childe Harold's Pilgrimage*, Canto III.

6. Inscriptions by Turner, Itinerary Rhine Tour Sketchbook, Tate, Turner Bequest, CLIX 101, D12698.

7. Clara Wells to Robert Finch, 10 August 1829, in footnotes of Gage, *Collected Correspondence*, p. 132.

8. Itinerary Rhine Tour Sketchbook, Tate D12545

9. *Howell Wood, or The Raby Hunt in Yorkshire, A New Hunting Song*, Pontefract, John Fox, 1806.

10. Turner to James Holworthy, 21 November 1817, Gage, *Collected Correspondence*, p. 71.

11. ibid.

12. Transcript of Maria Fawkes's diary, in Finberg, *Turner's Water-colours*.

13. The number of drawings is debated, with Cecilia Powell (*Turner in Germany*, 1995, p. 26) suggesting 50. The Farnley Hall Catalogue lists the Rhine drawings as a group of 51.

14. Horsley, *Recollections of a Royal Academician*, p. 283.

15. *Annals of the Fine Arts*, Vol. 3, 1819.

16. *Diary of Joseph Farington*, Vol. XV, January 1818–December 1819, p. 5191.

17. *Diary, Reminiscences and Correspondence of Henry Crabb Robinson*, Vol. 1, p. 387.

18. Turner charged interest on the loan – though whether this was a Fawkes insistence is unknown.

19. Turner to Artists/General Benevolent Institution, 4 June 1816, Gage, *Collected Correspondence*, p. 65.

20. Maria Fawkes's diary, in Finberg, *Turner's Water-colours*.

21. *Diary, Reminiscences and Correspondence of Henry Crabb Robinson*, p. 125.

22. June 1819.

23. *The Literary Gazette and Journal of Belles Lettres, Arts, Sciences*, Part 1, 1819, p. 234.

24. This quotation and that above were reprinted in Walter Fawkes's catalogue for his second exhibition, which I have viewed as part of the Kurt F. Pantzer Collecting Papers, Indianapolis Museum of Art Archives.

25. W. Carey, *Some Memoirs of the Patronage and Progress of the Fine Arts*, London, Saunders & Ottley, 1826, p. 147.

Chapter 18: Earth and Heaven

1. D. E. Williams, *The Life and Correspondence of Sir Thomas Lawrence, Kt*, Vol. 2, London, 1831, Thomas Lawrence to Samuel Lysons, 27 June 1819, p. 161.

2. LAW 3/52, Thomas Lawrence to Joseph Farington, 2 July 1819, Royal Academy of Arts Archive.

3. Notes by James Hakewill on Travelling in Italy, Route to Rome Sketchbook, Tate, Turner Bequest, CLXXI 38a, D13933. Cecilia Powell identified Hakewill as the author of the notes in 'Topography, Imagination and Travel, Turner's Relationship with James Hakewill', *Art History*, Vol. V, No. 4, and has covered this trip to Rome in *Turner in the South: Rome, Naples, Florence*, London, Yale University Press, 1987.

4. William Berrian, *Travels in France and Italy in 1817 and 1818*, New York, 1821, p. 305.

5. *Encyclopaedia Britannica*, Vol. 21, 1860, p. 387.

6. LAW 3/210, Thomas Lawrence to Joseph Farington, 5 October 1820, Royal Academy of Arts Archive.

7. LAW 3/73, Royal Academy of Arts Archive.

8. LAW 5/375, William A'Court to Thomas Lawrence, 12 October 1819, Royal Academy of Arts Archive.

9. LAW 3/73, Thomas Lawrence to Joseph Farington, 6 October 1819, Royal Academy of Arts Archive.

10. Cecilia Powell, *Italy in the Age of Turner*, London, Merrell Holberton, 1998.

11. LAW 3/63, Duchess of Devonshire to Thomas Lawrence, Royal Academy of Arts Archive.

12. Thomas Ashby, 'Turner in Rome', *Burlington Magazine*, Vol. 24, January 1914, p. 223.

13. Gillian Darley, *John Soane, An Accidental Romantic*, London and New Haven, Yale University Press, 1999, p. 261.

14. Turner to Antonio Canova, 27 November 1819, Gage, *Collected Correspondence*, p. 80.

15. Turner to James Holworthy, 7 January 1826, ibid., p. 97.

16. Lord Byron, *Beppo – A Venetian Story*, Stanza XLVI.

17. *Annals of the Fine Arts*, Vol. 5, London, 1820.

18. *Diaries of Benjamin Robert Haydon*, p. 74.

19. John Gage, *Colour in Turner, Poetry and Truth*, London, Studio Vista, 1969, p. 162.

20. The sideboard and hall chairs are today in Hastings Town Hall, while the Wedgwood vases remain in the possession of Turner's family.

21. Turner to W. F. Wells, 13 November 1820, Gage, *Collected Correspondence*, p. 82.

22. ibid.

23. Turner to James Holworthy, 23 December 1820, ibid., p. 83.

24. Harpur's share of the properties, Nos. 9 and 10, were then further divided between Harpur and his business partner the solicitor William Evans, which presumably was a reflection of a private financial matter between the two.

25. Professor Sam Smiles covers the story of Turner's interests in New Gravel Lane extensively in 'On the Waterfront: The Darker Side of the Ship and Bladebone', *Turner Society News*, No. 107, December 2007.

26. ADDMS 50118 f 67, British Library.

27. For example 'Heir At Law!', 1808, by Charles Williams.

28. RFMS 54A, Ann Dart to John Ruskin, 16 April 1860 (transcript), Ruskin Foundation.

29. Turner to Clara Wells, 4 May 1820, Gage, *Collected Correspondence*, p. 81.

30. Maria Fawkes's diary, in Finberg, *Turner's Water-colours*.

31. ibid.

32. Turner to James Holworthy, 7 January 1826, Gage, *Collected Correspondence*, p. 96.

33. Turner to Henry Howard, April 1826, ibid., p. 98.

34. Transcript of the diary of E. T. Monro, in the possession of Mora Abell.

Chapter 19: In search of the King

1. *The Houghton Club Commonplace Book*, MS 127/2, British Library.
2. ibid.
3. Turner to James Holworthy, 7 January 1826, Gage, *Collected Correspond-ence*, p. 96.
4. Ian Warrell suggested to the author that this may have been part of a perspectival effect that Turner was attempting to achieve.
5. LAW/5/31, Sir Charles Long to Sir Thomas Lawrence, 25 April (1826?), Royal Academy of Arts Archive.
6. Nicholas Tracy, *Britannia's Palette, The Arts of Naval Victory*, Montreal and Kingston, McGill-Queens University Press, 2007, p. 140.
7. LAW/4/348, J. M. W. Turner to Sir Thomas Lawrence, 1 July 1825, Royal Academy of Arts Archive.
8. LAW/5/130, Farnborough to Sir Thomas Lawrence, 19 May (c. 1827?), Royal Academy of Arts Archive.
9. Turner to William Turner senior, August 1827, Gage, *Collected Correspondence*, p. 108.
10. 15 November 1826, *Diaries of Benjamin Robert Haydon*, p. 109.
11. *The Times*, 9 December 1959.
12. George Jones on Chantrey, reprinted in A. J. Finberg, *The Life of J. M. W. Turner R.A.*, Oxford, Clarendon Press, 1961, p. 325.
13. Though this was in fact a copy.
14. John Soane, Richard Payne Knight and James Holworthy.
15. Martin Butlin, Mollie Luther, Ian Warrell, *Turner at Petworth, Painter and Patron*, Tate, 1989, p. 144.
16. Gerard Finley, 'A new route in 1822 Turner's colour and optics', *Journal of the Warburg and Courtauld Institutes*, Vol. 36, 1973.
17. This painting is still in situ at Petworth today.

Chapter 20: Brilliance

1. Turner to James Holworthy, 4 December 1826, Gage, *Collected Correspondence*, p. 103.

2. Turner to C. L. Eastlake, Paris, August 1828, ibid., p. 118.

3. *An American Lady in Paris 1828–29: The Diary of Mrs John Mayo*, ed. Mary Mayo Crenshaw, New York, Houghton Mifflin, 1927, p. 7.

4. Mariana Starke, *Travels in Europe Between the Years 1824 and 1828*, London, John Murray, 1828.

5. Turner to George Jones, 13 October 1828, Gage, *Collected Correspondence*, p. 119.

6. Starke, *Travels in Europe*.

7. Turner to George Jones, 13 October 1828, Gage, *Collected Correspondence*, p. 119.

8. Turner was in fact miles away in northern France.

9. Turner to James Holworthy, December 1826, Gage, *Collected Correspondence*, p. 102.

10. Turner to George Jones, 13 October 1828, ibid., p. 119, written once Turner had arrived in Rome.

11. ibid.

12. Turner to C. L. Eastlake, Paris, August 1828, ibid., p. 118.

13. Lady Eastlake, 'Memoir of Sir Charles Lock Eastlake', p. 134.

14. LAW/5/287, C. Eastlake to Sir Thomas Lawrence, 9 December 1828, Royal Academy of Arts Archive.

15. The *Regulus* was repainted for later exhibition in 1837 and so the exact nature of the 1828 work has been lost.

16. Powell, *Turner in the South*, page 142.

17. LAW/5/293, Thomas Lawrence to Charles Eastlake, 29 December 1828.

18. Eastlake, 'Memoir of Sir Charles Lock Eastlake', p. 135.

19. Turner to C. L. Eastlake, 16 February 1829, Gage, *Collected Correspondence*, p. 124. Turner committed the journey to posterity on his immediate return to London, in the form of a watercolour which showed at the 1829 RA exhibition.

20. Turner to Clara Wells, 19 March 1829, Gage, *Collected Correspondence*, p. 126.

21. *Diary of Benjamin Robert Haydon*, p. 118.

22. Turner to C. L. Eastlake, 11 August 1829, Gage, *Collected Correspondence*, p. 131.

23. Turner to Francis Leggatt Chantrey, 9 September 1829.

24. Turner to Clara Wells, Gage, *Collected Correspondence*, p. 135.

25. The Academician George Dawe.
26. Turner to George Jones, 22 February 1830, Gage, *Collected Correspondence*, p. 137.

Chapter 21: Industry

1. Turner to Charles Turner, 15 December 1828, Gage, *Collected Correspondence*, p. 121.
2. James Nasmyth, *Engineer: An Autobiography*, London, 1883, p. 163.
3. ibid.
4. Andrew Lambert made this observation in his lecture at the conference 'Maritime Culture and Britain in the Age of J. M. W. Turner', Royal Museums, Greenwich, 2014, identifiying the steamboat in Turner's *Between Quilleboeuf and Villequier* in his Rivers of France series as the *Aaron Manby*.
5. Whittingham, 'New Light on J. M. W. Turner in Kent'.
6. Turner to Robert Cadell, 25 February 1832, Gage, *Collected Correspondence*, p. 147.
7. Cholera Remedy; and Buildings on a Hill, 1831, Berwick Sketchbook, Tate, Turner Bequest, TB CCLXV 42, D25718.
8. Recipe for a Cure; Grouped Figures and Coastal Architecture, Guernsey Sketchbook, Tate D41076. Ian Warrell, *Turner on the Seine*, 1999, p. 47.
9. Will of John Booth, PRO National Archives Prob 11/1814.
10. Alfred Whitman, *Charles Turner A.R.A.*, London, George Bell, 1907, p. 20, CT's diary entry of 6 September 1852.
11. In his article on the pub, Sam Smiles has also pointed out that the landlady, Mrs Crosset, ran an illegal closed-shop racket that deprived men of working unless they lodged at the establishment.
12. Thornbury, *Life of J. M. W. Turner*, Vol. 2, p. 168.

Chapter 22: Indistinct, unintelligible, unstoppable

1. *Literary Gazette*, 31 May 1834.
2. *Vernon Heath's Recollections*, London, Cassell & Co., 1892, p. 5–6.
3. Jan Piggott, *Turner's Vignettes*, Tate, 1993.

4. Turner to Sir Walter Scott, 20 April 1831, Gage, *Collected Correspondence*, p. 143.

5. Turner to Robert Cadell, Tuesday 24 October 1832, Gage, *Collected Correspondence*, p. 148.

6. Piggott, *Turner's Vignettes*, p. 44.

7. John Gage, 'Further Correspondence of J. M. W. Turner', *Turner Studies*, Vol. 6, No. 1, 1986, p. 4, Turner to King Louis Philippe, 26 April 1836, in which Turner thanks the King for the medal which the King has sent in receipt of the engravings.

8. *The Recollections of J. M. W. Turner by George Jones*, in Gage, *Collected Correspondence*, p. 4.

9. Charles Robert Leslie R.A., *Autobiographical Recollections*, ed. Tom Taylor, London, John Murray, 1860, Vol. 1, p. 202.

10. Turner to James Lenox, 16 August 1845, Gage, *Collected Correspondence*, p. 209.

11. Judy Egerton, *Making and Meaning: Turner, The Fighting Temeraire*, London, National Gallery, 1995.

12. *Morning Chronicle*, 7 May 1839.

13. Thackeray, William Makepeace, 'May Gambols; or, Titmarsh on the Picture Galleries', *Ballads and Miscellanies* (Vol. 13 in the 'Biographical Edition' of *Works*), London, Smith Elder, 1899, pp. 419–45.

Chapter 23: To please himself

1. The book, *Modern Painters*, was published in early May 1843 when Ruskin was twenty-four. For the Preface, see Cook and Wedderburn (eds.), *The Works of John Ruskin*, Vol. 1, p. 3.

2. John Ruskin, *Praeterita I, Works*, Vol. 35, p. 79.

3. *Blackwood's Magazine*, October 1836.

4. Turner to John Ruskin, 6 October 1836, Gage, *Collected Correspondence*, p. 161.

5. Ruskin, *Works*, Vol. 3, p. 638.

6. Edward Coleridge to Thomas Griffith, 5 October 1836, Thomas Griffith Papers 11021-Z, Rare Book Literary and Historical Papers, Wilson Library, University of North Carolina at Chapel Hill.

7. Ruskin, *Works*, Vol. 35, p. 305.

8. Ruskin, *Praeterita I, Works*, Vol. 35, p. 116.

9. Joan Evans and John Howard Whitehouse, *The Diaries of John Ruskin*, Oxford, Clarendon Press, 1956, 23 June 1840, p. 83.

10. This painting is now in the Museum of Fine Arts, Boston.

11. John Ruskin to Thomas Griffith, 18 February 1841, Thomas Griffith Papers.

12. Martin Royalton-Kisch, 'An archive of letters to John Sheepshanks', Volumes of the Walpole Society, Vol. 66 (2004), p. 240.

13. This painting is now in the collection of the Victoria and Albert Museum.

14. Cecilia Powell, *Turner in Germany*, London, Tate, 1995, p. 65.

15. E. H. to Turner, 24 August 1840, Gage, *Collected Correspondence*, p. 178.

16. Turner to Dawson Turner, 29 November 1842, Gage, *Collected Correspondence*, p. 190.

17. Contemporary accounts suggest between fifty and seventy watercolours were shown, though the collection was vaster still. Selby Whittingham, 'The Turner Collector B. G. Windus', *Turner Studies*, Vol. 7, No. 2, Winter 1987, p. 29.

18. Ruskin, *Praeterita, II, Works*, Vol. 35, p. 253.

19. Selby Whittingham, 'Windus, Turner and Ruskin, New Documents', *J. M. W. Turner RA*, No. 2, December 1993.

20. Ruskin said that all the Swiss sketches were 'direct impressions from nature' (Epilogue, *Works*, Vol. 13, p. 478), and mss in the Indianapolis Museum of Art substantiate this. Hannah Cooper's catalogue of nine views from Charles Stokes notes that they were 'coloured on the spot'.

21. 'Epilogue' to Notes by Mr Ruskin on his Drawings by the Late J. M. W. Turner, RA, 1878, *Works*, Vol. 13, pp. 476–9.

22. Turner to B. G. Windus, 29 July 1840, in Whittingham, 'Windus, Turner and Ruskin', p. 95.

23. Turner to B. G. Windus, 14 March 1842, ibid., p. 96.

24. Turner to B. G. Windus, 18 March 1842, ibid., p. 97.

25. Van Akin Burd (ed.), *The Ruskin Family Letters*, Ithaca and London, Cornell University Press, 1973, p. 734.

26. The appendix of Ian Warrell's *Through Switzerland with Turner, Ruskin's First Selection from the Turner Bequest*, London, Tate, 1995, lays out the whole genesis of the project and the subsequent sales.

27. Lady Trevelyan to Dr John Brown, *Letters of Dr John Brown with Letters from Ruskin, Thackeray and others*, London, Adam and Charles Black, 1907, p. 334.

28. Gage, *Collected Correspondence*, p. 3.

29. Works initially acquired by the Chantrey Bequest were exhibited at the Victoria & Albert Museum, but in 1898 the collection was transferred to the National Gallery of British Art – now known as Tate Britain.

30. *Journals and Correspondence of Lady Eastlake*, Vol. 1, ed. Charles Eastlake Smith, London, John Murray, 1895, p. 189.

31. Silvanus Thompson (ed.), *Michael Faraday: His Life and Work*, London, Cassell, 1898, p. 246.

32. *Personal Recollections from Early Life to Old Age of Mary Somerville*, London, John Murray, 1874, p. 268.

33. This thesis is James Hamilton's and is part of a wider study of Turner's relationship with science in *Turner and the Scientists*, Tate, 1998, p. 128.

34. Dr Melanie Vandenbrouck, 'Vernet, Turner and near-death experience', paper delivered at 'Maritime Culture and Britain in the Age of J. M. W. Turner', Royal Museums, Greenwich, 2014.

35. *The Times*, 11 May 1843.

36. *A Piece of Canvas Smeared with Colours: The Hungarian Painter Miklós Barabás on J. M. W. Turner*. Hungarianarthist.wordpress.com, 16 December 2012.

37. September to December 1844. Conversations with Beckford, *Memoirs of William Beckford from the New Monthly Magazine*, 1844. Cook and Wedderburn (eds.), *Works of John Ruskin*, Vol. 13, 1904, p. 161. Ian Warrell, *Turner's Wessex*, p. 117, and Jan Piggott, *Turner Society News*, 124, 2002, p. 17.

38. Gage, *Collected Correspondence*, p. 4.

39. *Letters of Dr John Brown*, p. 334.

40. ibid.

41. *Port Ruysdale*, exhibited RA 1827, now in the Yale Center for British Art; *Palestrina*, exhibited RA 1830, for which he paid £1,050, a very high sum for Turner; *Wreckers – Coast of Northumberland,* exhibited RA 1834, Yale; *Bright Stone of Honour (Ehrenbreitstein)*, exhibited RA 1835; *Helvoetsluys*, exhibited RA 1832; *Antwerp*, exhibited RA 1833, Frick Collection, New York.

42. John Ruskin to B. G. Windus, Monday 21 October 1844, in Whittingham, 'Windus, Turner and Ruskin', p. 103.

43. Turner to William Wethered, December 1844, Gage, *Collected Correspondence*, p. 203.

44. Whittingham, 'New Light on J. M. W. Turner in Kent'.

45. Andrew Wilton, *The Life and Work of J. M. W. Turner*, London, Academy Editions, 1979, p. 468.

46. The attribution to Turner of these works, now in the collection of the National Museum of Wales, was doubted. They derived from a sale of Turner's work held by Mrs Booth's son at Christie's in March 1865 and have now been confirmed as being by the artist.

47. 1841 census.

48. George Jones to B. G. Windus, 17 January 1842, Whittingham, 'Windus, Turner and Ruskin', p. 96.

49. Thornbury, *Life of J. M. W. Turner*, Vol. 2, p. 97.

50. Turner to J. Hogarth, 1845, Gage, *Collected Correspondence*, p. 211.

51. Turner to John Murray III, 4 May 1845, ibid., p. 206.

52. Turner to F. H. Fawkes, 26 December 1846, Gage, ibid., p. 216.

Chapter 24: 'The morning march that flashes to the Sun; The feast of Vultures when the day is done'

1. Thornbury, *Life of J. M. W. Turner*, Vol. 2, p. 259.

2. Horsley, *Recollections of a Royal Academician*, p. 284.

3. Helen Guiterman, '"The Great Painter": Roberts on Turner', *Turner Studies*, Vol. 9, No. 1, p. 2.

4. Ruskin, *Works*, Vol. 13, p. 555.

5. *London Daily News*, 6 May 1846.

6. Turner to John Ruskin, 13 January 1848, Gage, *Collected Correspondence*, p. 219.

7. *The Brunig Pass from Meiringen*, now in a private collection, and *The Descent of the St Gothard*, now in the collection of the Koriyama Municipal Art Museum.

8. Turner to John James Ruskin, Midsummer day, 1848, Gage, *Collected Correspondence*, p. 220.

9. Turner to F. H. Fawkes, 27 December 1847, Gage, *Collected Correspondence*, p. 218.

10. Samuel Rogers to Turner, 17 March 1849, Gage, 'Further Correspondence of J. M. W. Turner', p. 8.

11. Turner to F. H. Fawkes, 24 December 1849, Gage, *Collected Correspondence*, p. 222.
12. George Jones to Turner, 14 April 1850, ibid., p. 223.
13. Turner to F. H. Fawkes, 27 December 1850, ibid., p. 224.
14. ibid.
15. Guiterman, '"The Great Painter"', p. 6.
16. James Hamilton, *Turner: a Life*, London, Hodder & Stoughton, 1997, appendix 3, p. 343.
17. J. R. Piggott, 'Turner's Chelsea Cottage: The Controversy of 1895', *Turner Society News*, 116, Autumn 2011, p. 8.

Epilogue

1. *Letters of Dr John Brown*, p. 333.
2. Guiterman, '"The Great Painter"'.
3. J. W. Archer, 'Reminiscences', *Turner Studies*, Vol. 1, p. 1.
4. Tim Hilton, *John Ruskin*, New Haven and London, Yale University Press, 2002, p. 291.
5. National Portrait Gallery NPG 1314.
6. Anthony Bailey, *Standing in the Sun*, London, Sinclair-Stevenson, 1997, p. 410.
7. Horsley, *Recollections of a Royal Academician*, p. 285.
8. Or at least, Sophia Green was at the property on the day of the 1871 census.
9. John Davis, 'J. M. W. Turner and Haddenham Hall', *Haddenham Chronicles*, No. 1, Spring 2006.
10. C. Lewis Hind, *Turner's Golden Visions*, London, T. C. and E. C. Jack, 1910, p. 238.
11. Whitman, *Charles Turner*, p. 20.
12. Golt, 'Sarah Danby: Out of the Shadows', p. 5.
13. Bailey, *Standing in the Sun*, p. 412.
14. ibid., p. 406; the original letter is in the archives of the National Gallery.
15. A checklist of erotic sketches in the Turner Bequest, *British Art Journal*, Vol. 4, No. 1, Spring 2003, pp. 15–46; Warrell, *Turner's Secret Sketches*.

Index